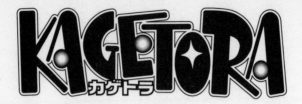

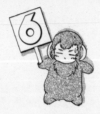

Akira Segami

TRANSLATED BY
Satsuki Yamashita

ADAPTED BY
Nunzio DeFilippis & Christina Weir

LETTERED BY
North Market Street Graphics

BALLANTINE BOOKS · NEW YORK

Kagetora, volume 6 copyright © 2003 by Akira Segami
English translation copyright © 2007 by Satsuki Yamashita

All rights reserved.

Published in the United States by Del Rey Books, an imprint of The Random House Publishing Group, a division of Random House, Inc., New York.

DEL REY is a registered trademark and the Del Rey colophon is a trademark of Random House, Inc.

Publication rights arranged through Kodansha Ltd.

First published in Japan in 2003 by Kodansha Ltd., Tokyo.

ISBN 978-0-345-49146-6

Printed in the United States of America

www.delreymanga.com

9 8 7 6 5 4 3 2

Translator—Satsuki Yamashita
Adaptor—Nunzio DeFilippis & Christina Weir
Lettering—North Market Street Graphics

CONTENTS

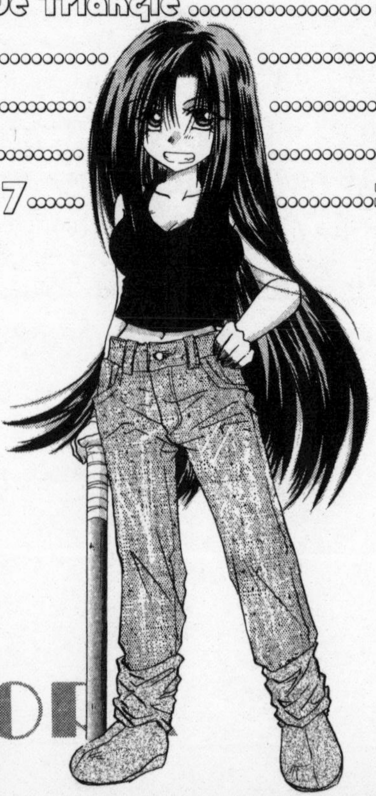

KAGETOR

A Note from the Author

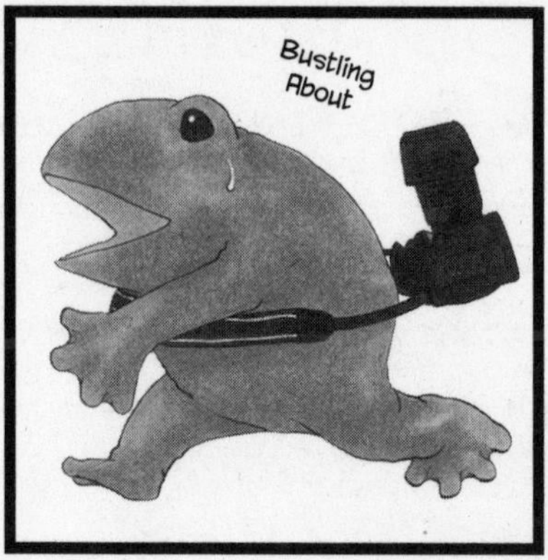
Bustling About

I bought an SLR to use when I go out for research. I haven't learned anything, I'm just trying to get used to it first. But I'm having a really hard time. So if you see a person (or a frog) in the city holding a camera awkwardly, that might be me . . . (laugh)

Segami

Honorifics Explained

Throughout the Del Rey Manga books, you will find Japanese honorifics left intact in the translations. For those not familiar with how the Japanese use honorifics and, more important, how they differ from American honorifics, we present this brief overview.

Politeness has always been a critical facet of Japanese culture. Ever since the feudal era, when Japan was a highly stratified society, use of honorifics—which can be defined as polite speech that indicates relationship or status—has played an essential role in the Japanese language. When addressing someone in Japanese, an honorific usually takes the form of a suffix attached to one's name (example: "Asuna-san"), is used as a title at the end of one's name, or appears in place of the name itself (example: "Negi-sensei," or simply "Sensei!").

Honorifics can be expressions of respect or endearment. In the context of manga and anime, honorifics give insight into the nature of the relationship between characters. Many translations into English leave out these important honorifics and therefore distort the feel of the original Japanese. Because Japanese honorifics contain nuances that English honorifics lack, it is our policy at Del Rey not to translate them. Here, instead, is a guide to some of the honorifics you may encounter in Del Rey Manga.

-san: This is the most common honorific and is equivalent to Mr., Miss, Ms., or Mrs. It is the all-purpose honorific and can be used in any situation where politeness is required.

-sama: This is one level higher than "-san," and it is used to confer great respect.

-dono: This comes from the word "tono," which means "lord." It is an even higher level than "-sama" and confers utmost respect.

-kun: This suffix is used at the end of boys' names to express familiarity or endearment. It is also sometimes used by men among friends, or when addressing someone younger or of a lower station.

-chan: This is used to express endearment, mostly toward girls. It is also used for little boys, pets, and even among lovers. It gives a sense of childish cuteness.

Bozu: This is an informal way to refer to a boy, similar to the English terms "kid" and "squirt."

Sempai/
Senpai: This title suggests that the addressee is one's senior in a group or organization. It is most often used in a school setting, where underclassmen refer to their upperclassmen as "sempai." It can also be used in the workplace, such as when a newer employee addresses an employee who has seniority in the company.

Kohai: This is the opposite of "sempai" and is used toward underclassmen in school or newcomers in the workplace. It connotes that the addressee is of a lower station.

Sensei: Literally meaning "one who has come before," this title is used for teachers, doctors, or masters of any profession or art.

[blank]: This is usually forgotten in these lists, but it is perhaps the most significant difference between Japanese and English. The lack of honorific means that the speaker has permission to address the person in a very intimate way. Usually, only family, spouses, or very close friends have this kind of permission. Known as yobisute, it can be gratifying when someone who has earned the intimacy starts to call one by one's name without an honorific. But when that intimacy hasn't been earned, it can be very insulting.

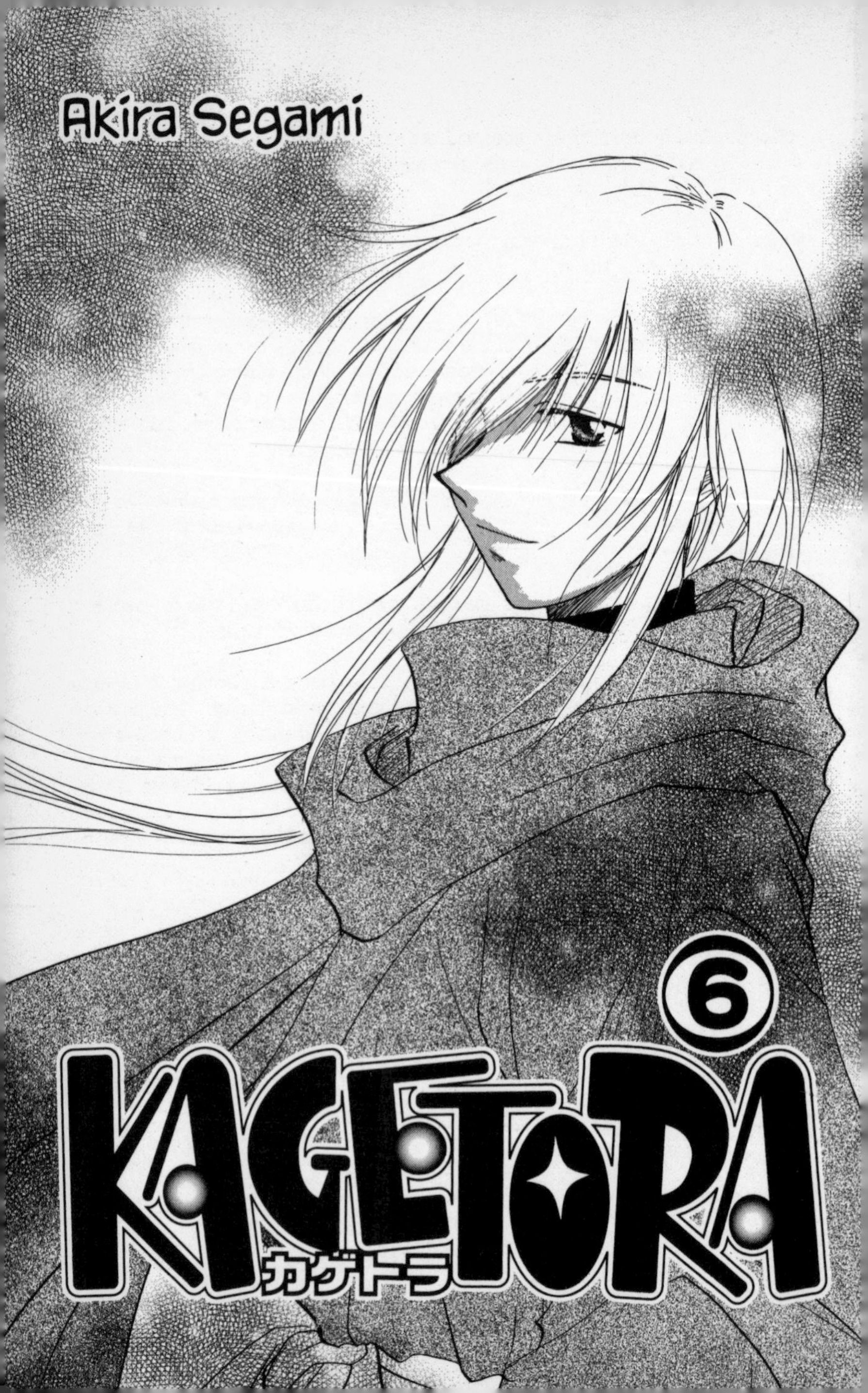
Akira Segami
6
KAGETORA
カゲトラ

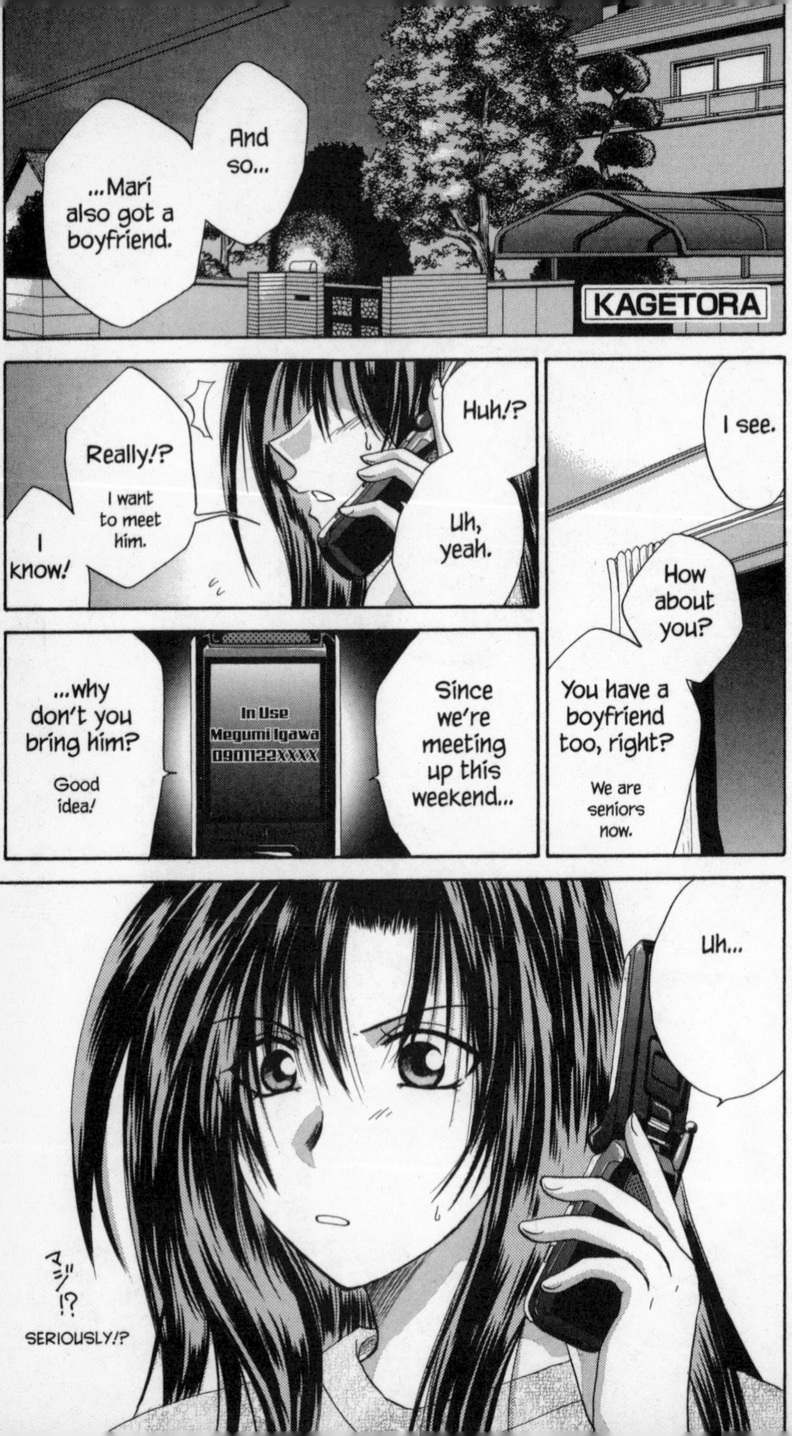
And so...
...Mari also got a boyfriend.
KAGETORA
I see.
How about you?
You have a boyfriend too, right?
We are seniors now.
Huh!?
Uh, yeah.
Really!?
I want to meet him.
I know!
Since we're meeting up this weekend...
In Use
Megumi Igawa
0901122XXXX
...why don't you bring him?
Good idea!
Uh...
マジ!?
SERIOUSLY!?

26 Kagetora and Aki on a Date?

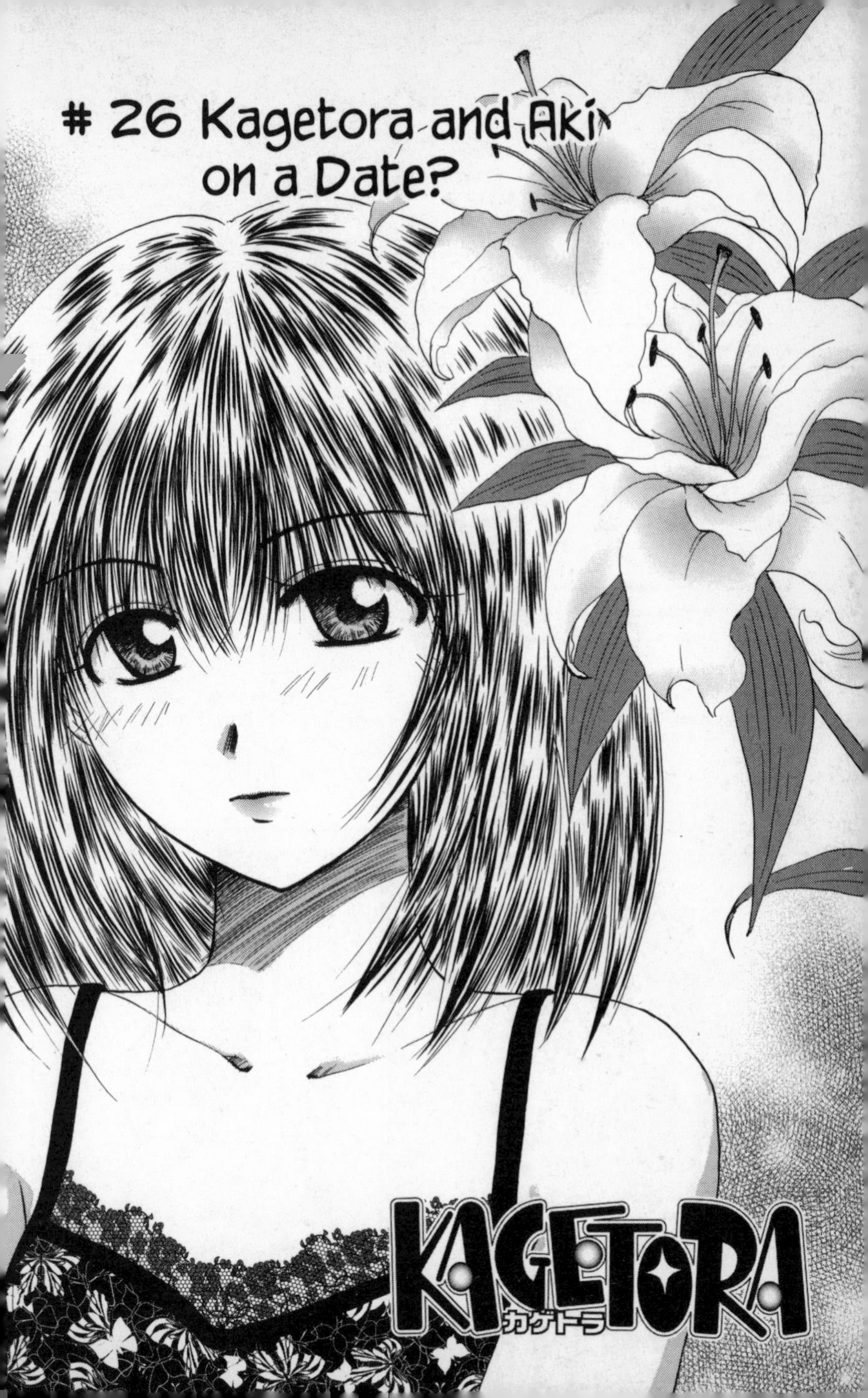
KAGETORA
カゲトラ

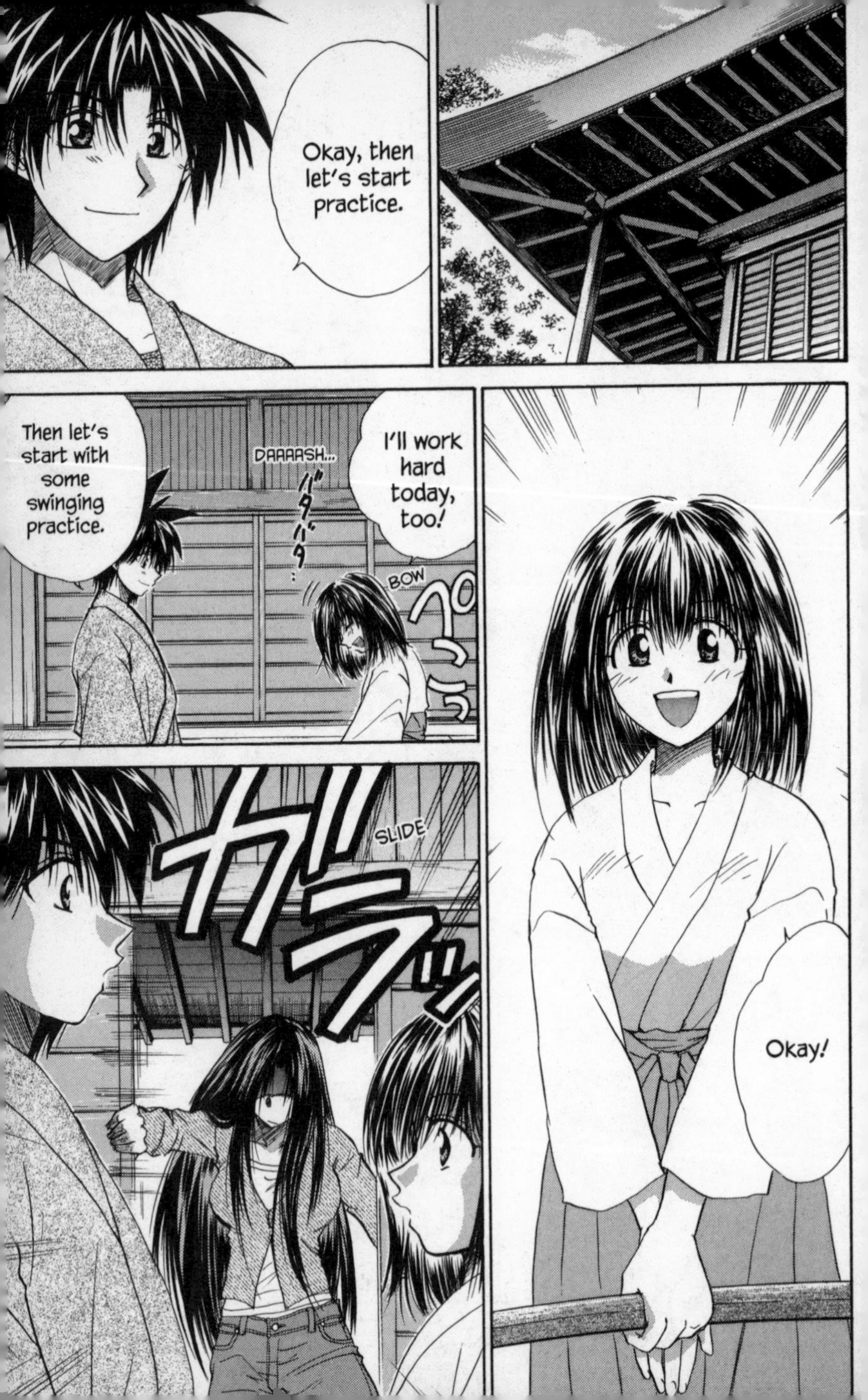
Okay, then let's start practice.
Okay!
I'll work hard today, too!
BOW
DAAAASH...
Then let's start with some swinging practice.
SLIDE

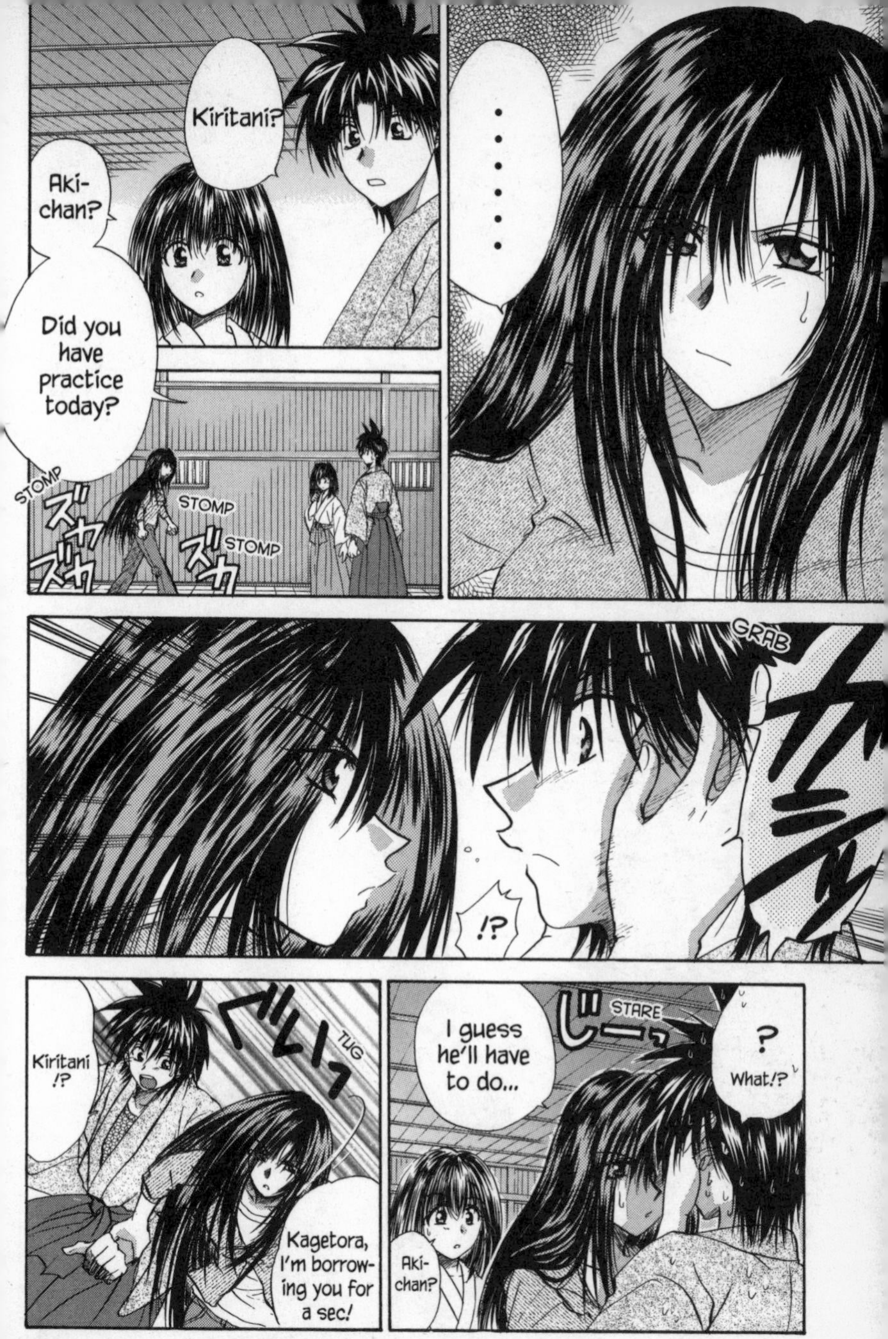
......
Kiritani?
Aki-chan?
Did you have practice today?
STOMP
STOMP
STOMP
GRAB
!?
STARE
?
What!?
I guess he'll have to do...
Aki-chan?
TUG
Kiritani !?
Kagetora, I'm borrowing you for a sec!

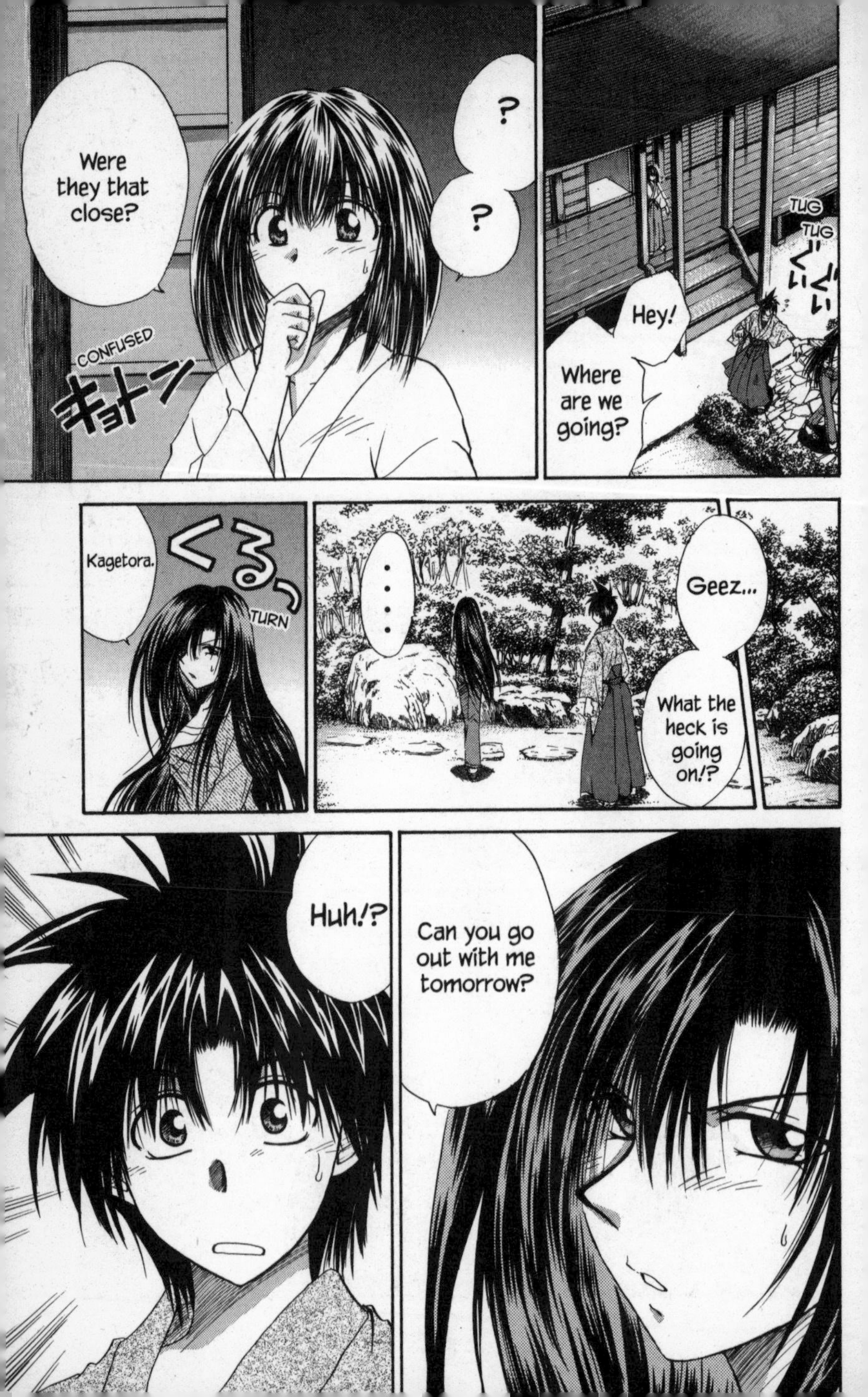

TUG
TUG
ぐいぐい
Hey!
Where are we going?
?
?
Were they that close?
CONFUSED
キョトン
Geez...
What the heck is going on!?
....
Kagetora.
くるっ
TURN
Can you go out with me tomorrow?
Huh!?

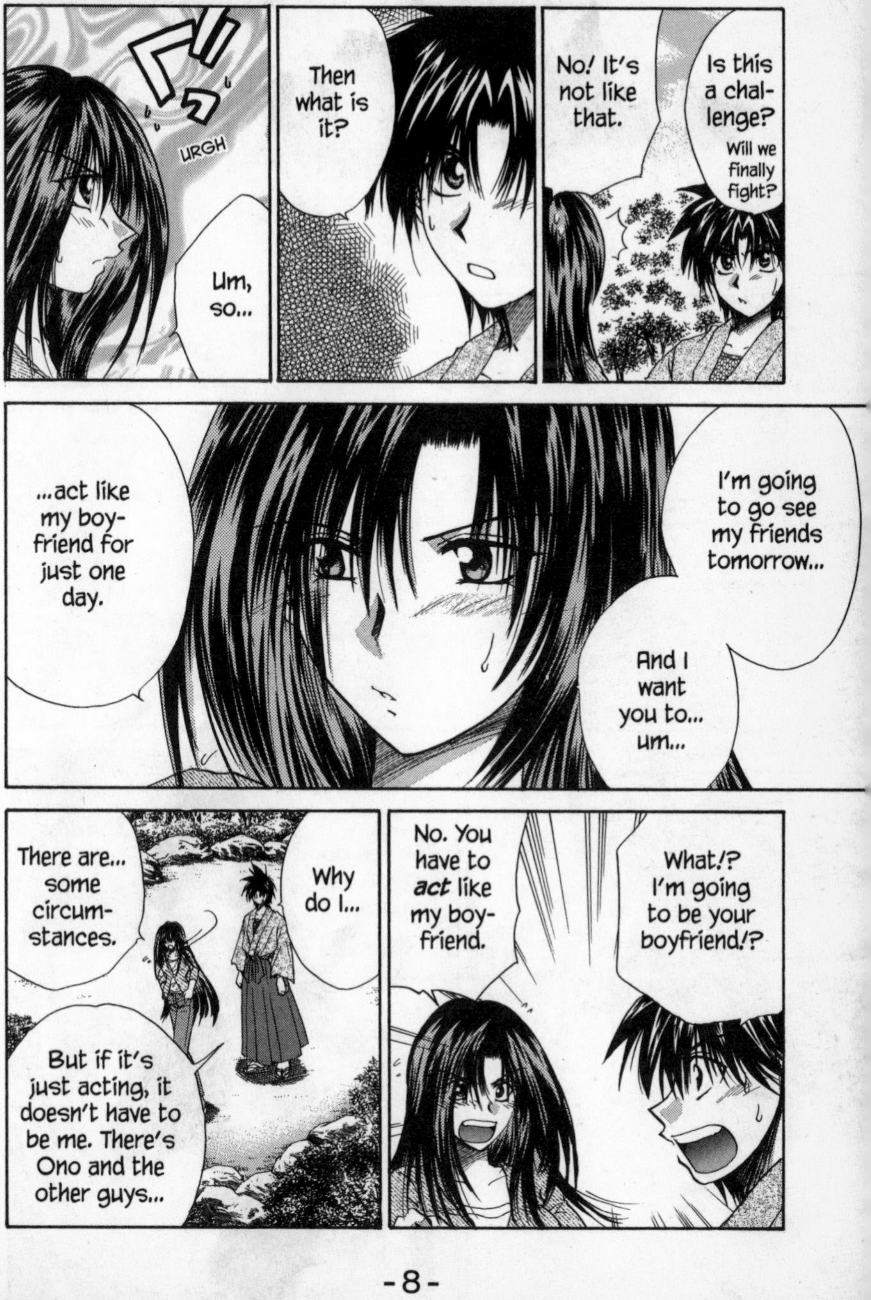
Is this a chal-lenge?
Will we finally fight?
No! It's not like that.
Then what is it?
URGH
Um, so...
I'm going to go see my friends tomorrow...
And I want you to... um...
...act like my boy-friend for just one day.
What!? I'm going to be your boyfriend!?
No. You have to act like my boy-friend.
Why do I...
There are... some circum-stances.
But if it's just acting, it doesn't have to be me. There's Ono and the other guys...

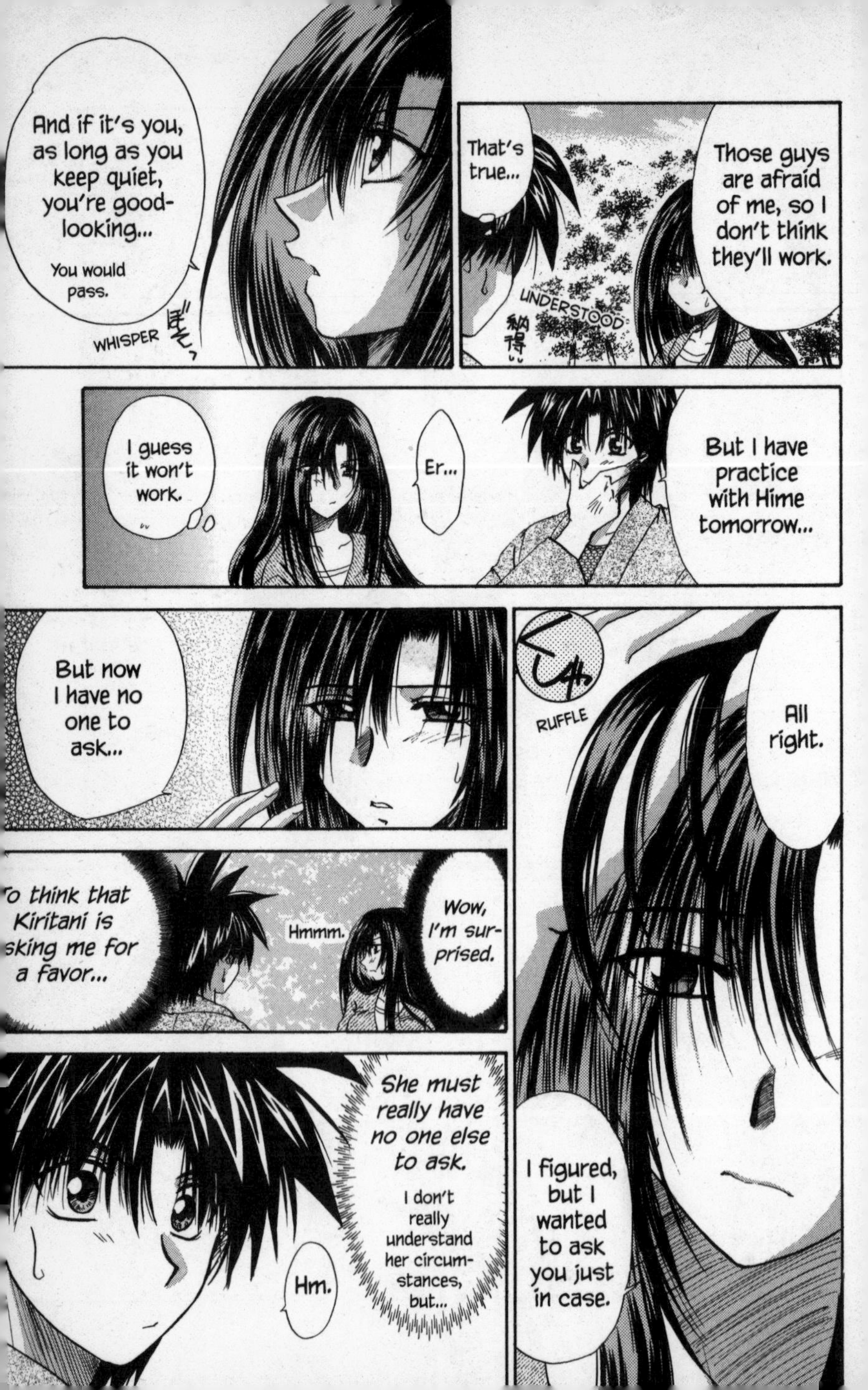
Those guys are afraid of me, so I don't think they'll work.
That's true...
UNDERSTOOD
納得
And if it's you, as long as you keep quiet, you're good-looking...
You would pass.
WHISPER
But I have practice with Hime tomorrow...
Er...
I guess it won't work.
RUFFLE
All right.
I figured, but I wanted to ask you just in case.
But now I have no one to ask...
Wow, I'm surprised.
Hmmm.
o think that Kiritani is sking me for a favor...
She must really have no one else to ask.
I don't really understand her circumstances, but...
Hm.

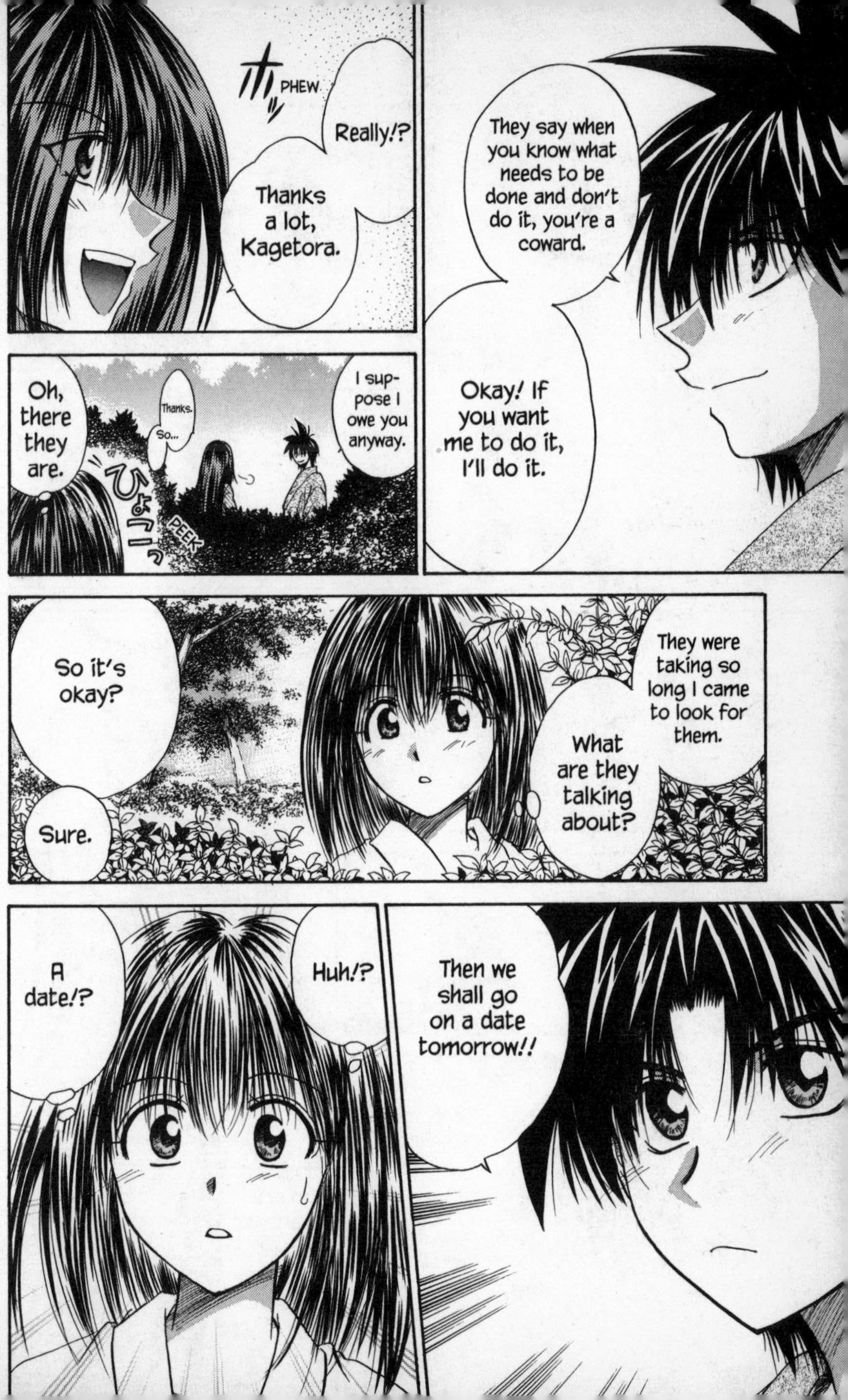

They say when you know what needs to be done and don't do it, you're a coward.
Okay! If you want me to do it, I'll do it.
PHEW
Really!?
Thanks a lot, Kagetora.
I suppose I owe you anyway.
Thanks.
So...
Oh, there they are.
PEEK
They were taking so long I came to look for them.
What are they talking about?
So it's okay?
Sure.
Then we shall go on a date tomorrow!!
Huh!?
A date!?

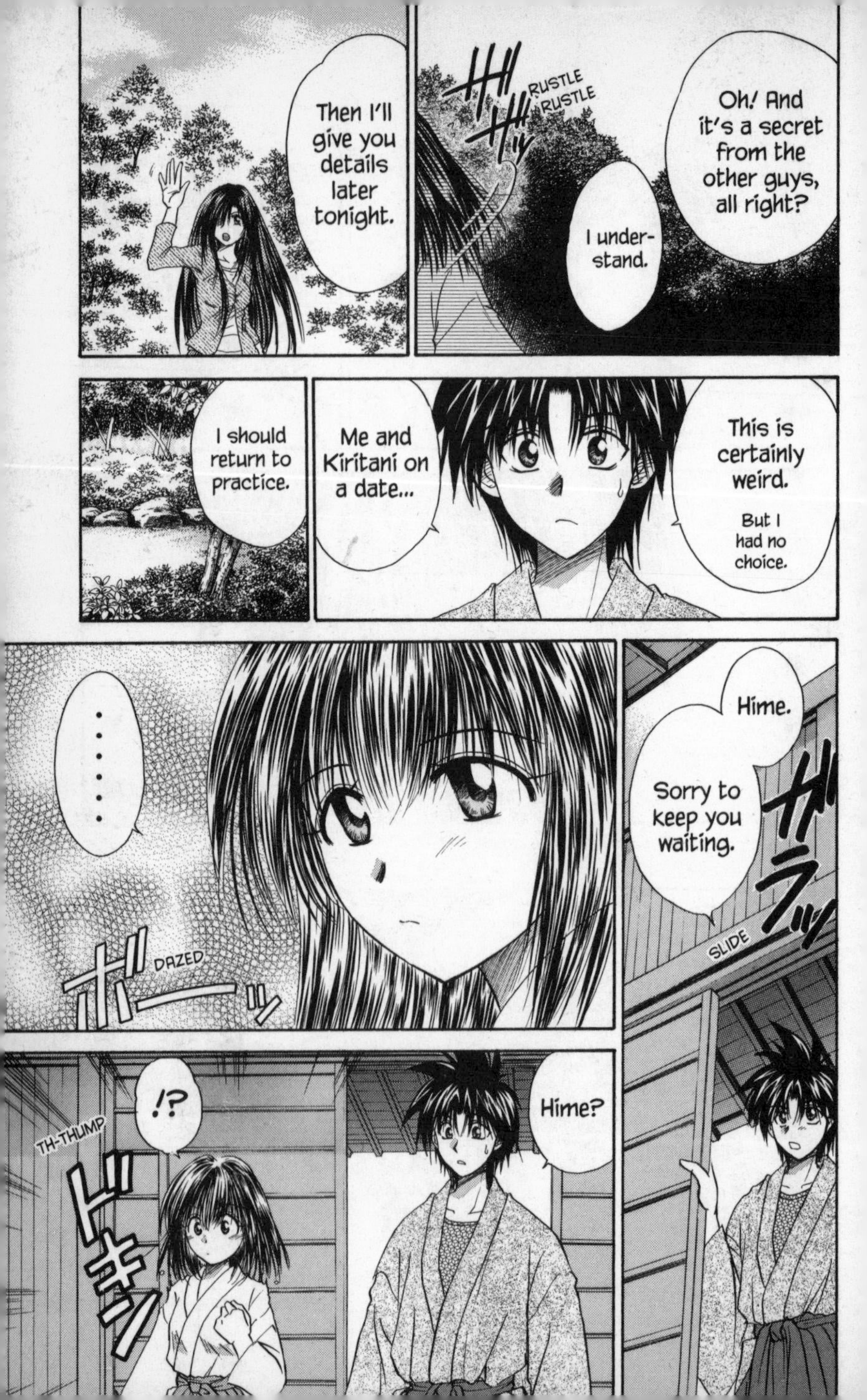
Oh! And it's a secret from the other guys, all right?
RUSTLE RUSTLE
I under-stand.
Then I'll give you details later tonight.
This is certainly weird.
But I had no choice.
Me and Kiritani on a date...
I should return to practice.
Hime.
Sorry to keep you waiting.
SLIDE
......
DAZED
Hime?
!?
TH-THUMP

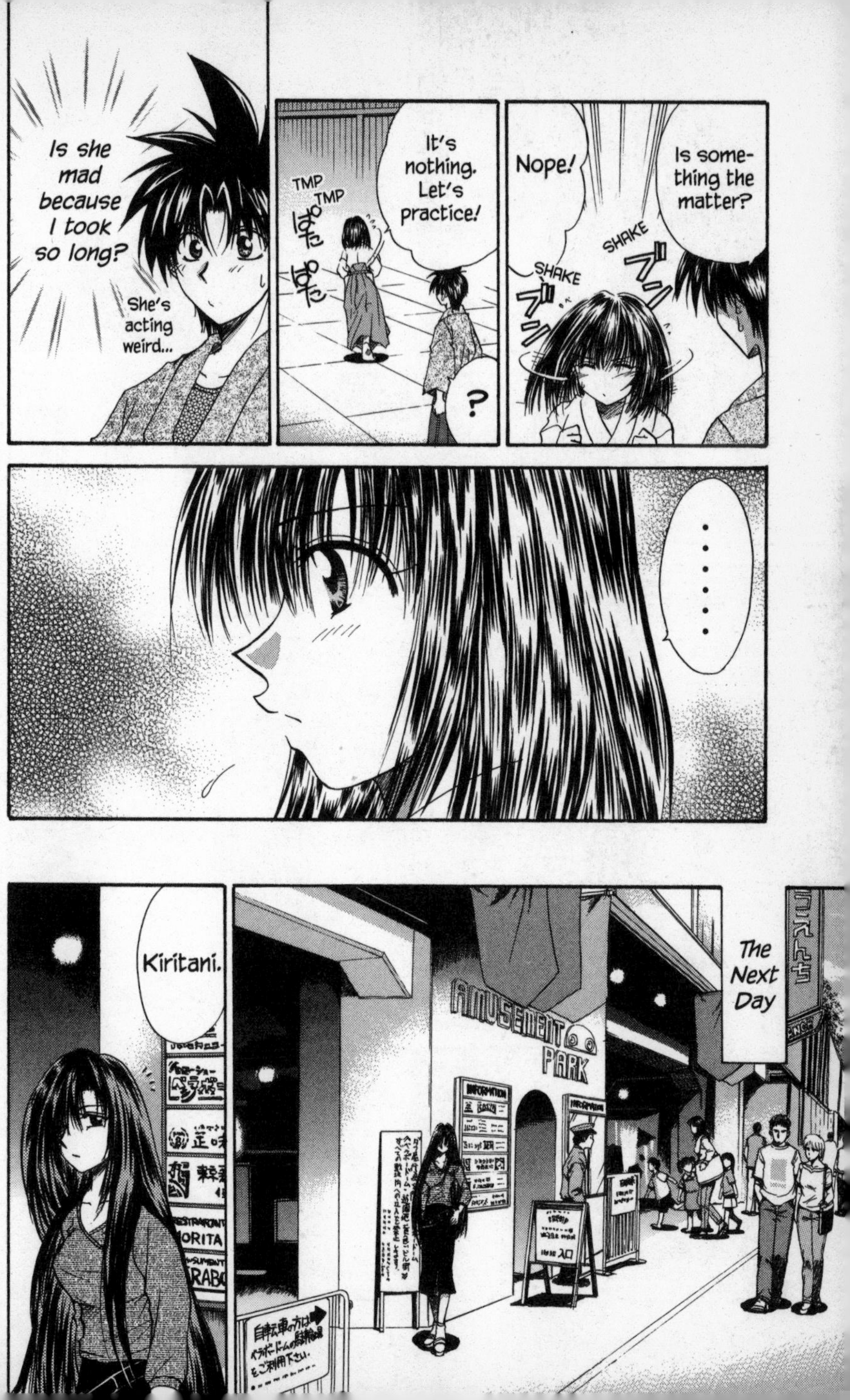

Is some-thing the matter?
SHAKE
SHAKE
Nope!
It's nothing. Let's practice!
TMP TMP
?
Is she mad because I took so long?
She's acting weird...
......
The Next Day
AMUSEMENT PARK
Kiritani.

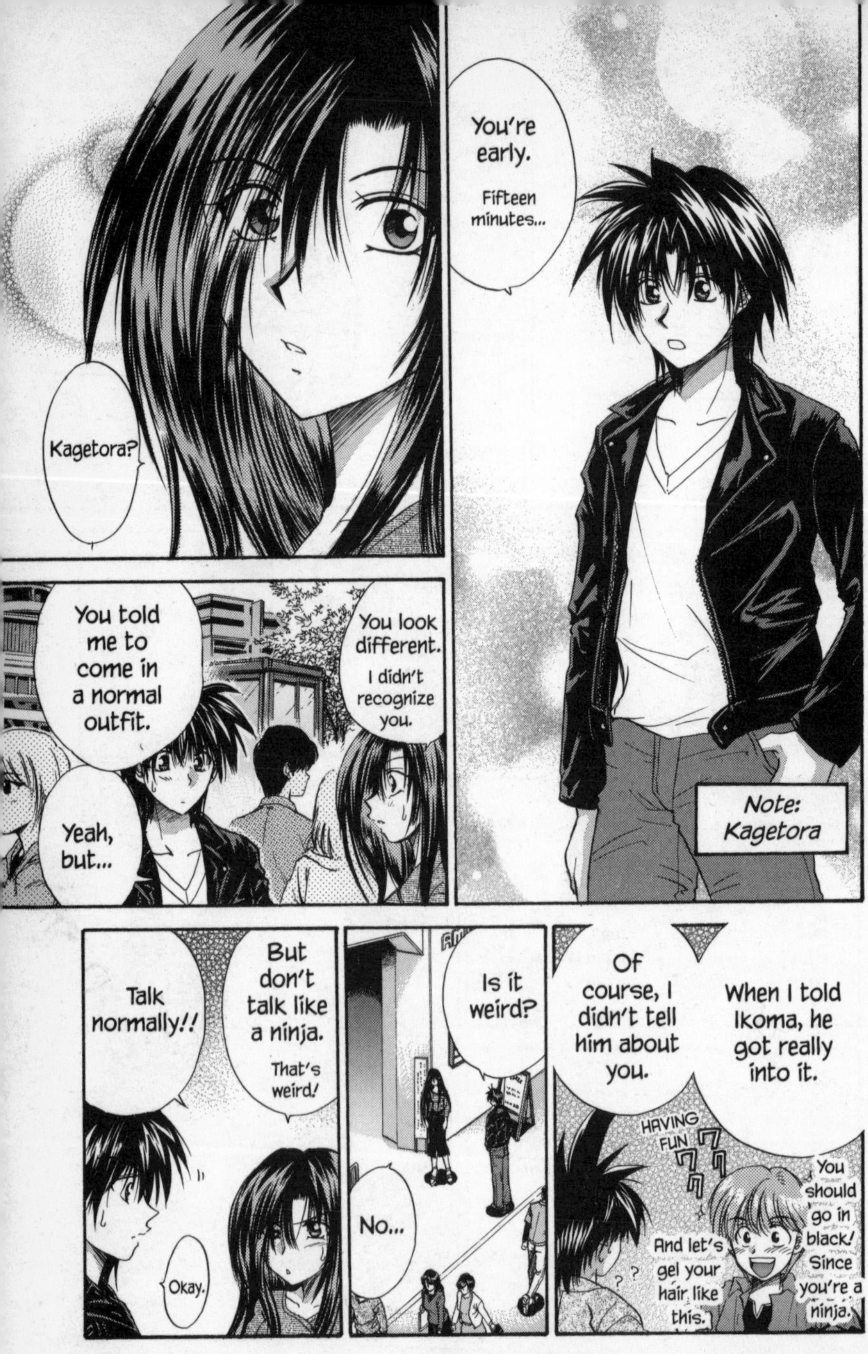

You're early.
Fifteen minutes...
Note: Kagetora
Kagetora?
You look different.
I didn't recognize you.
You told me to come in a normal outfit.
Yeah, but...
When I told Ikoma, he got really into it.
Of course, I didn't tell him about you.
You should go in black! Since you're a ninja.
HAVING FUN
And let's gel your hair like this.
Is it weird?
No...
But don't talk like a ninja.
That's weird!
Talk normally!!
Okay.

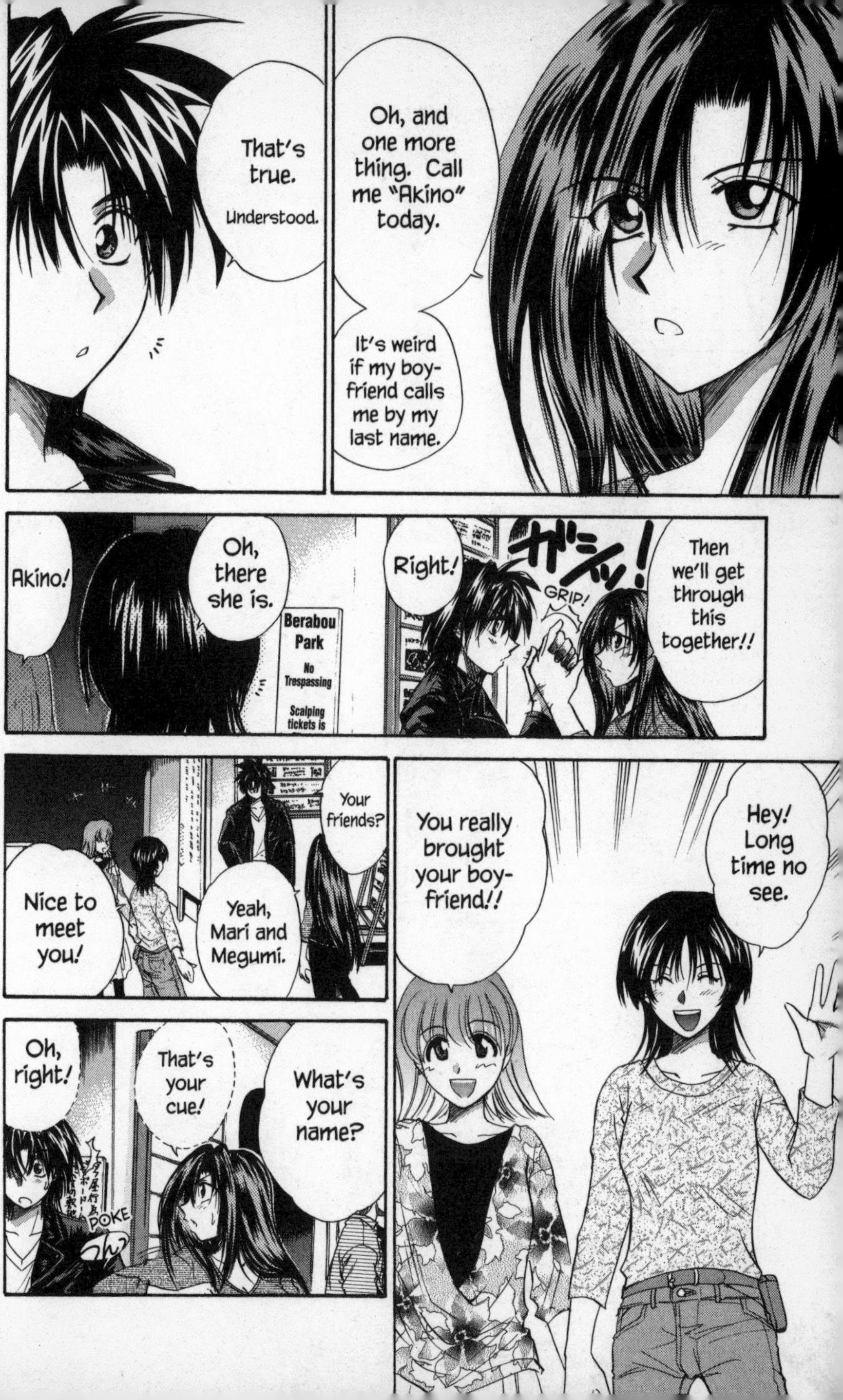
Oh, and one more thing. Call me "Akino" today.
It's weird if my boy-friend calls me by my last name.
That's true.
Understood.
Then we'll get through this together!!
GRIP!
Right!
Oh, there she is.
Akino!
Berabou Park
No Trespassing
Scalping tickets is
Hey! Long time no see.
You really brought your boy-friend!!
Your friends?
Yeah, Mari and Megumi.
Nice to meet you!
What's your name?
That's your cue!
Oh, right!
POKE

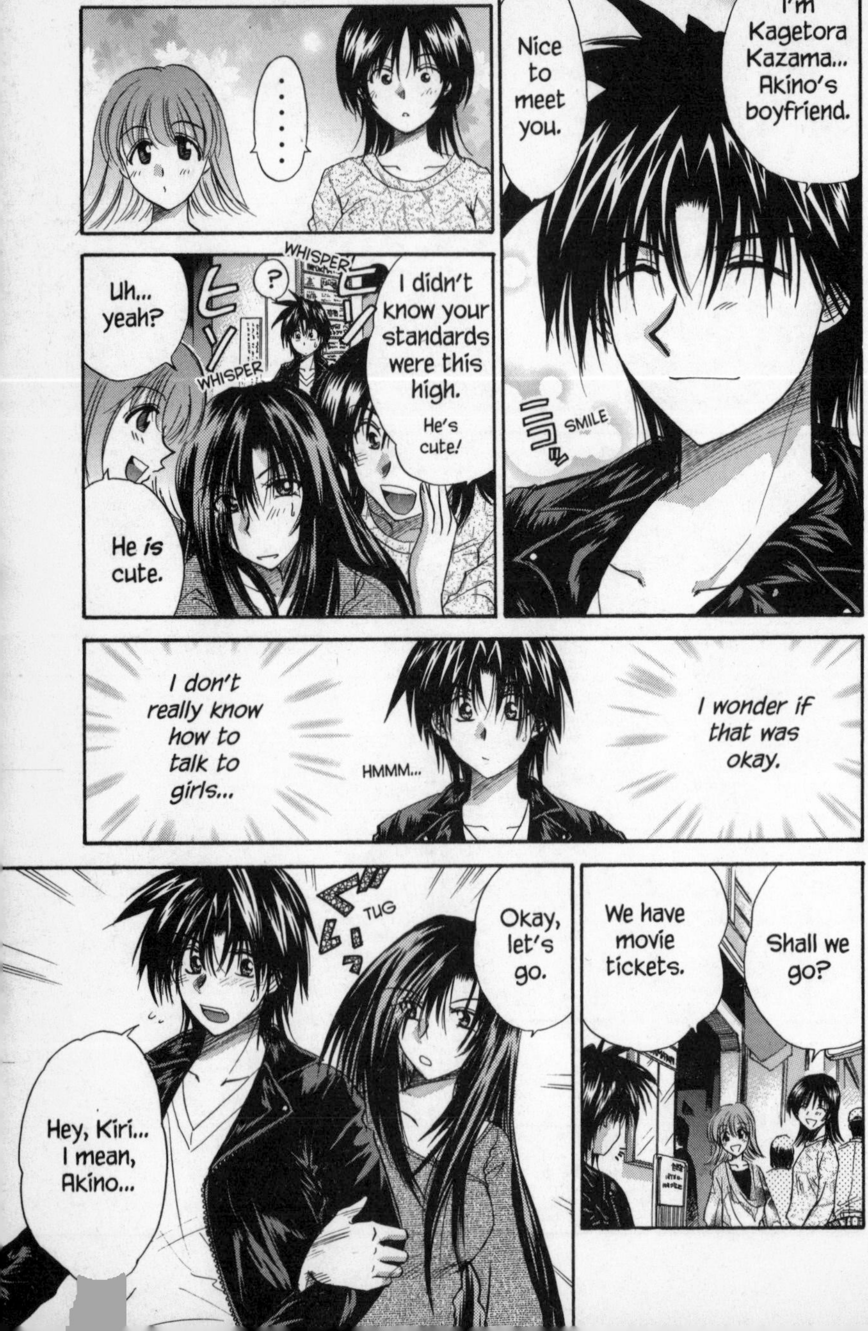
I'm Kagetora Kazama... Akino's boyfriend.
Nice to meet you.
SMILE
......
I didn't know your standards were this high.
He's cute!
WHISPER
?
Uh... yeah?
WHISPER
He *is* cute.
I wonder if that was okay.
HMMM...
I don't really know how to talk to girls...
Shall we go?
We have movie tickets.
Okay, let's go.
TUG
Hey, Kiri... I mean, Akino...

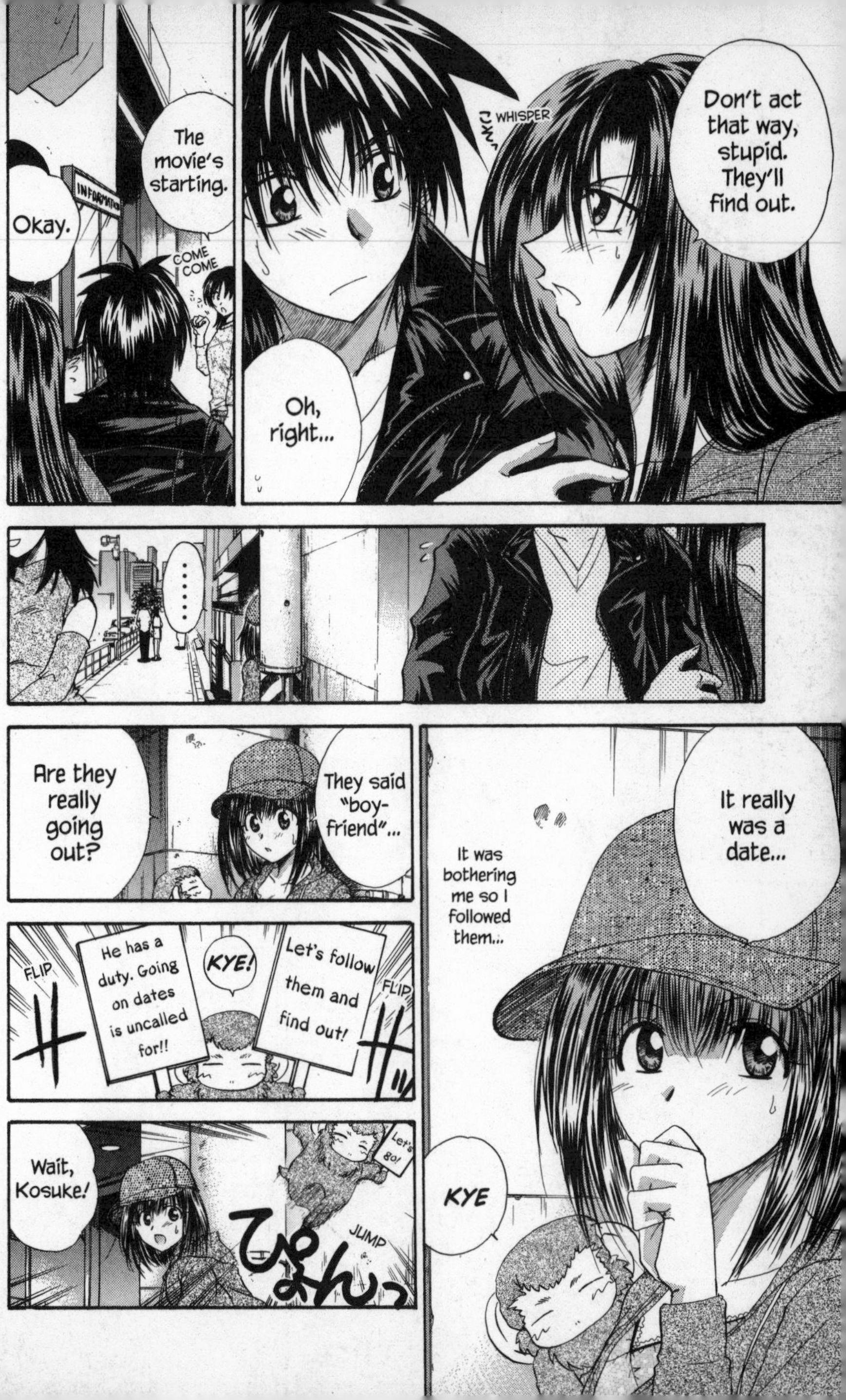

Don't act that way, stupid. They'll find out.
WHISPER
Oh, right...
The movie's starting.
Okay.
COME COME
INFORMATION
......
It really was a date...
It was bothering me so I followed them...
KYE
They said "boy-friend"...
Are they really going out?
FLIP
Let's follow them and find out!
KYE!
He has a duty. Going on dates is uncalled for!!
FLIP
Let's go!
JUMP
ぴょんっ
Wait, Kosuke!

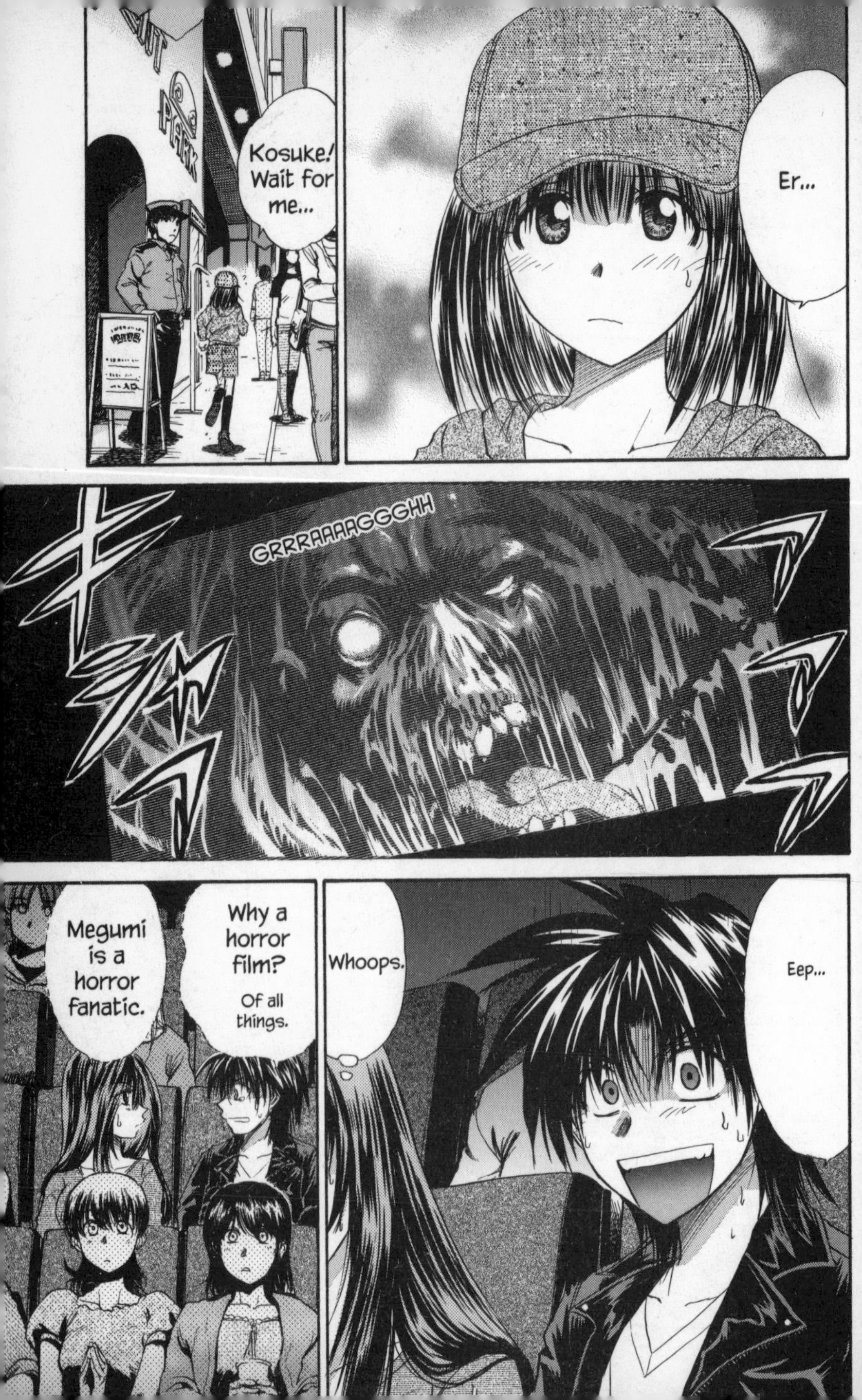
Er...
Kosuke! Wait for me...
GRRRAAAAGGGHH
Eep...
Whoops.
Why a horror film? Of all things.
Megumi is a horror fanatic.

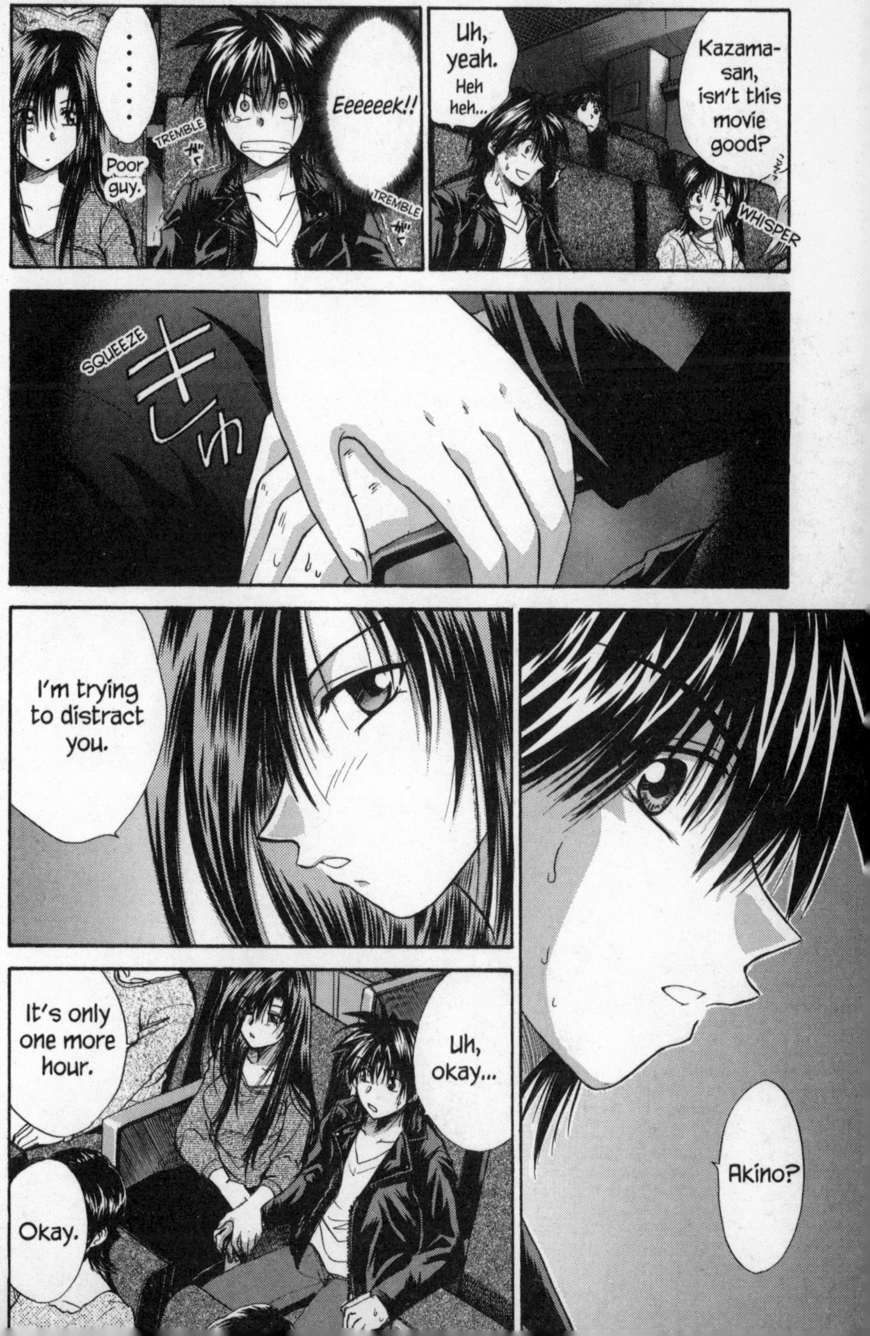
Kazama-san, isn't this movie good?
WHISPER
Uh, yeah.
Heh heh...
Eeeeeek!!
TREMBLE
TREMBLE
......
Poor guy.
SQUEEZE
きゅ
Akino?
I'm trying to distract you.
Uh, okay...
It's only one more hour.
Okay.

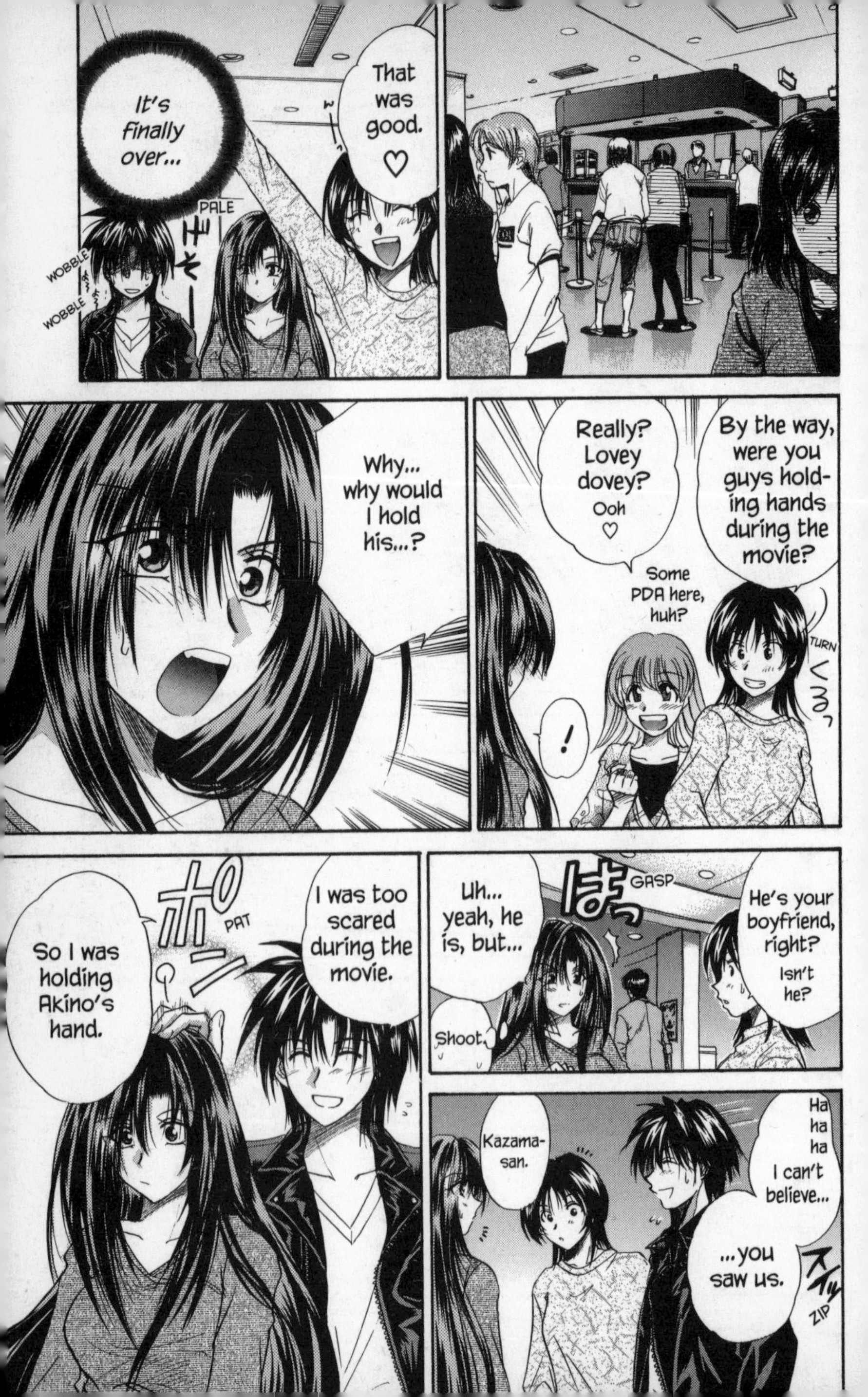
That was good. ♡
It's finally over...
PALE
WOBBLE
WOBBLE
By the way, were you guys holding hands during the movie?
TURN
Really? Lovey dovey? Ooh ♡
Some PDA here, huh?
!
Why... why would I hold his...?
He's your boyfriend, right? Isn't he?
GASP
Uh... yeah, he is, but...
Shoot.
Ha ha ha I can't believe...
...you saw us.
ZIP
Kazama-san.
I was too scared during the movie.
PAT
So I was holding Akino's hand.

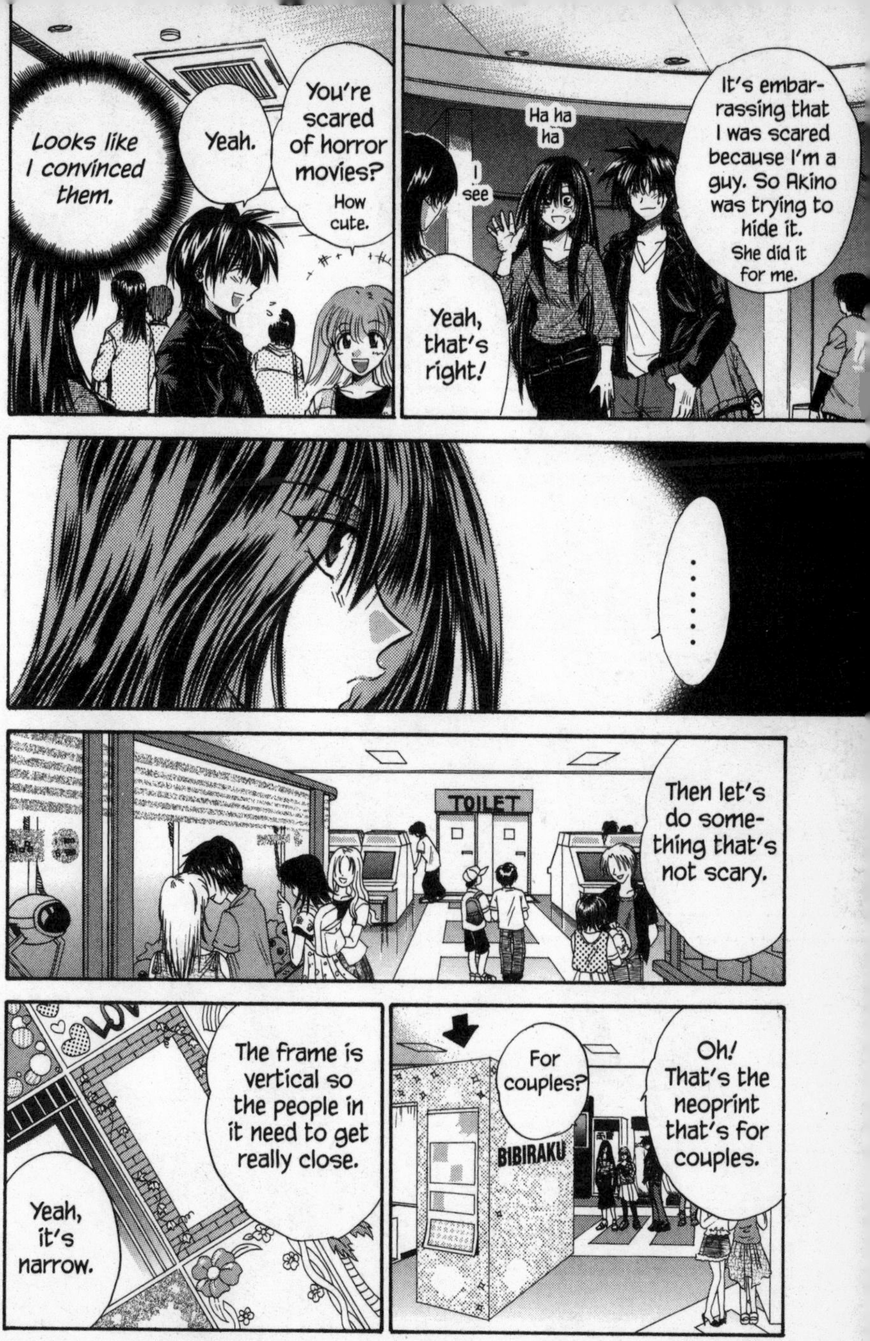
It's embarrassing that I was scared because I'm a guy. So Akino was trying to hide it.
She did it for me.
Ha ha ha
I see
Yeah, that's right!
You're scared of horror movies?
How cute.
Yeah.
Looks like I convinced them.
......
TOILET
Then let's do something that's not scary.
Oh! That's the neoprint that's for couples.
For couples?
BIBIRAKU
The frame is vertical so the people in it need to get really close.
Yeah, it's narrow.

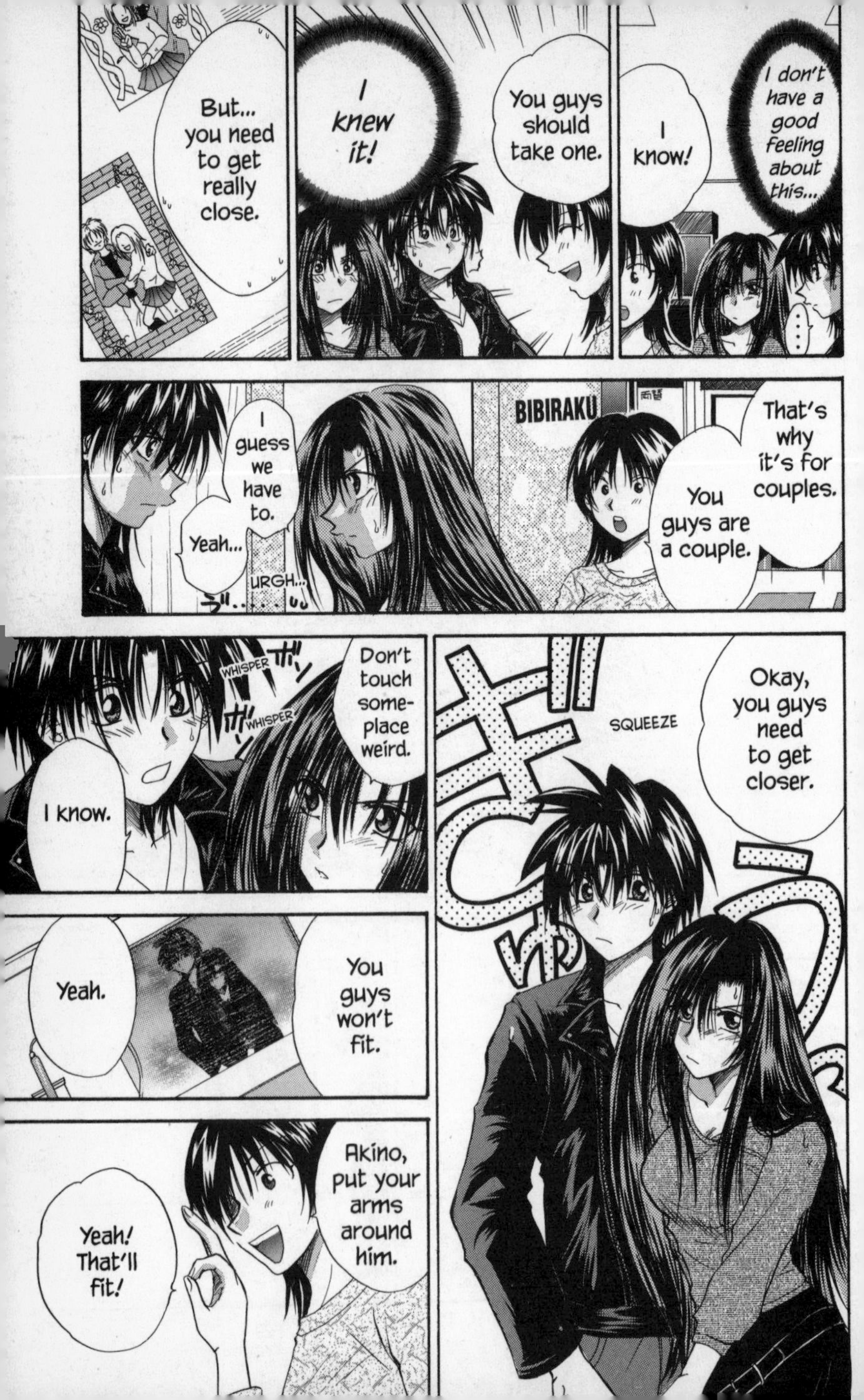
I don't have a good feeling about this...
I know!
You guys should take one.
I knew it!
But... you need to get really close.
That's why it's for couples.
You guys are a couple.
BIBIRAKU
I guess we have to.
Yeah...
URGH...
Okay, you guys need to get closer.
SQUEEZE
Don't touch some-place weird.
WHISPER
WHISPER
I know.
You guys won't fit.
Yeah.
Akino, put your arms around him.
Yeah! That'll fit!

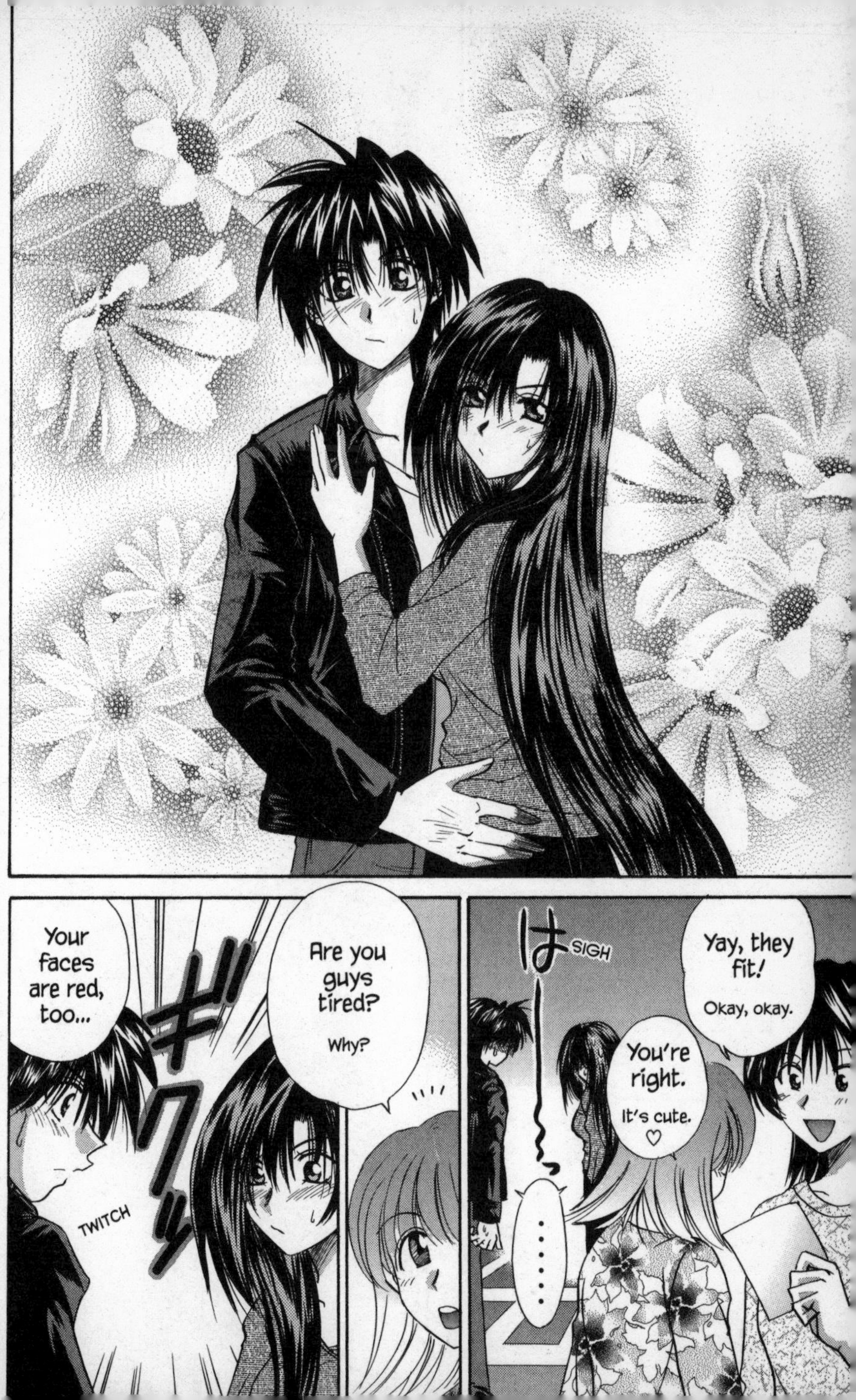

Yay, they fit!
Okay, okay.
You're right.
It's cute. ♡
SIGH
......
Are you guys tired?
Why?
Your faces are red, too...
TWITCH

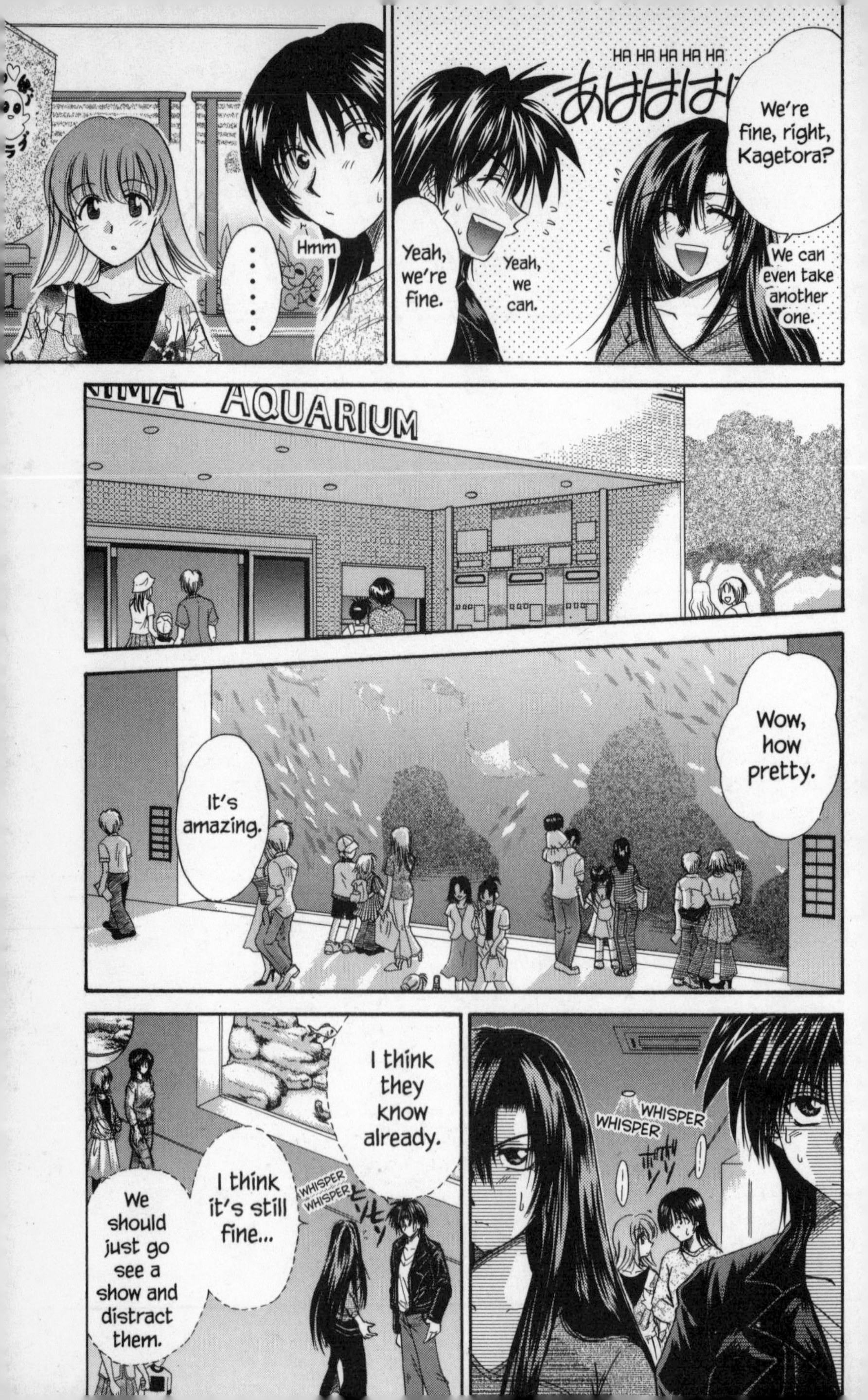
HA HA HA HA HA
あははは
We're fine, right, Kagetora?
We can even take another one.
Yeah, we can.
Yeah, we're fine.
Hmm
......
AQUARIUM
Wow, how pretty.
It's amazing.
WHISPER
WHISPER
!
!
I think they know already.
I think it's still fine...
WHISPER
WHISPER
We should just go see a show and distract them.

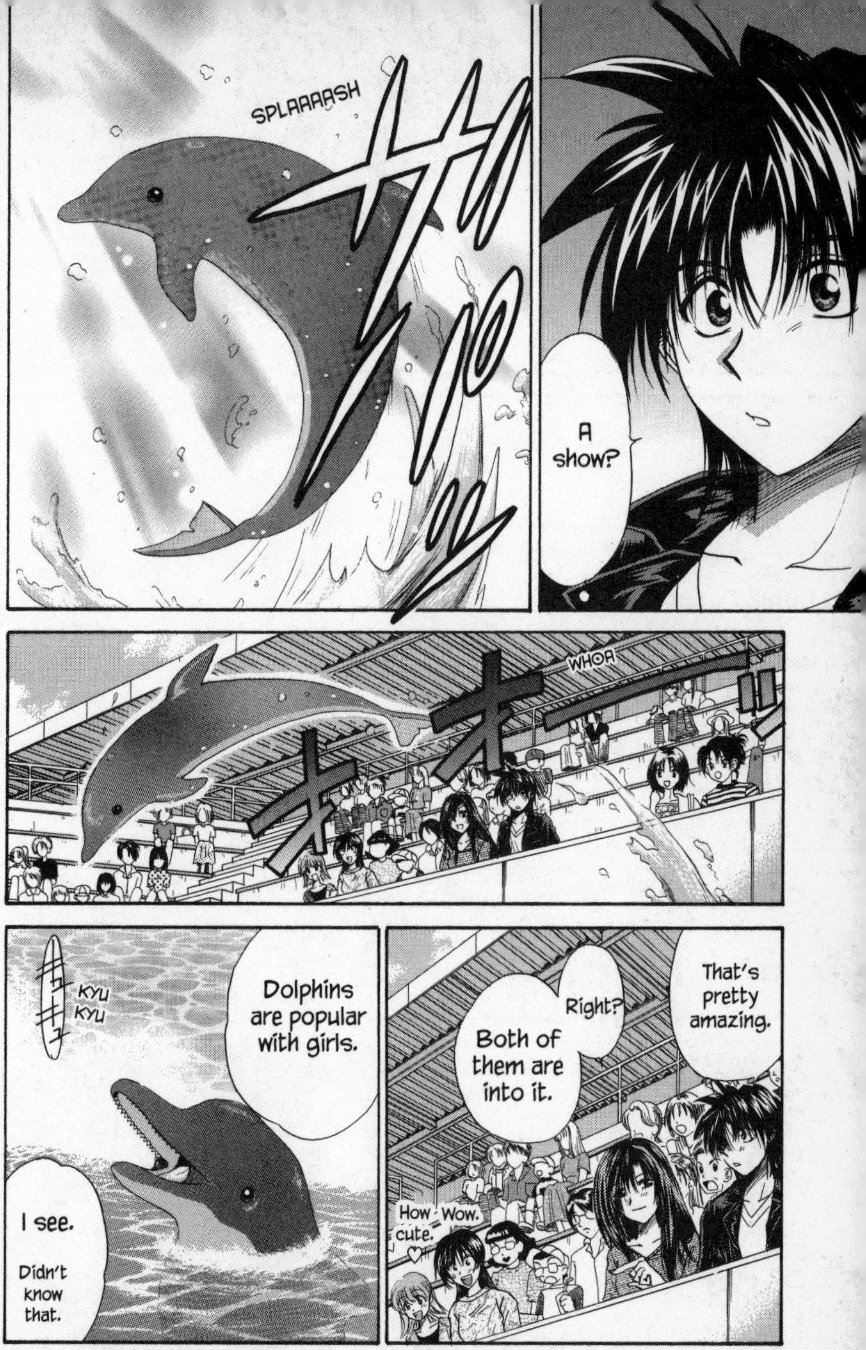
A show?
SPLAAAASH
WHOA
That's pretty amazing.
Right?
Both of them are into it.
Wow.
How cute.
Dolphins are popular with girls.
KYU KYU
I see.
Didn't know that.

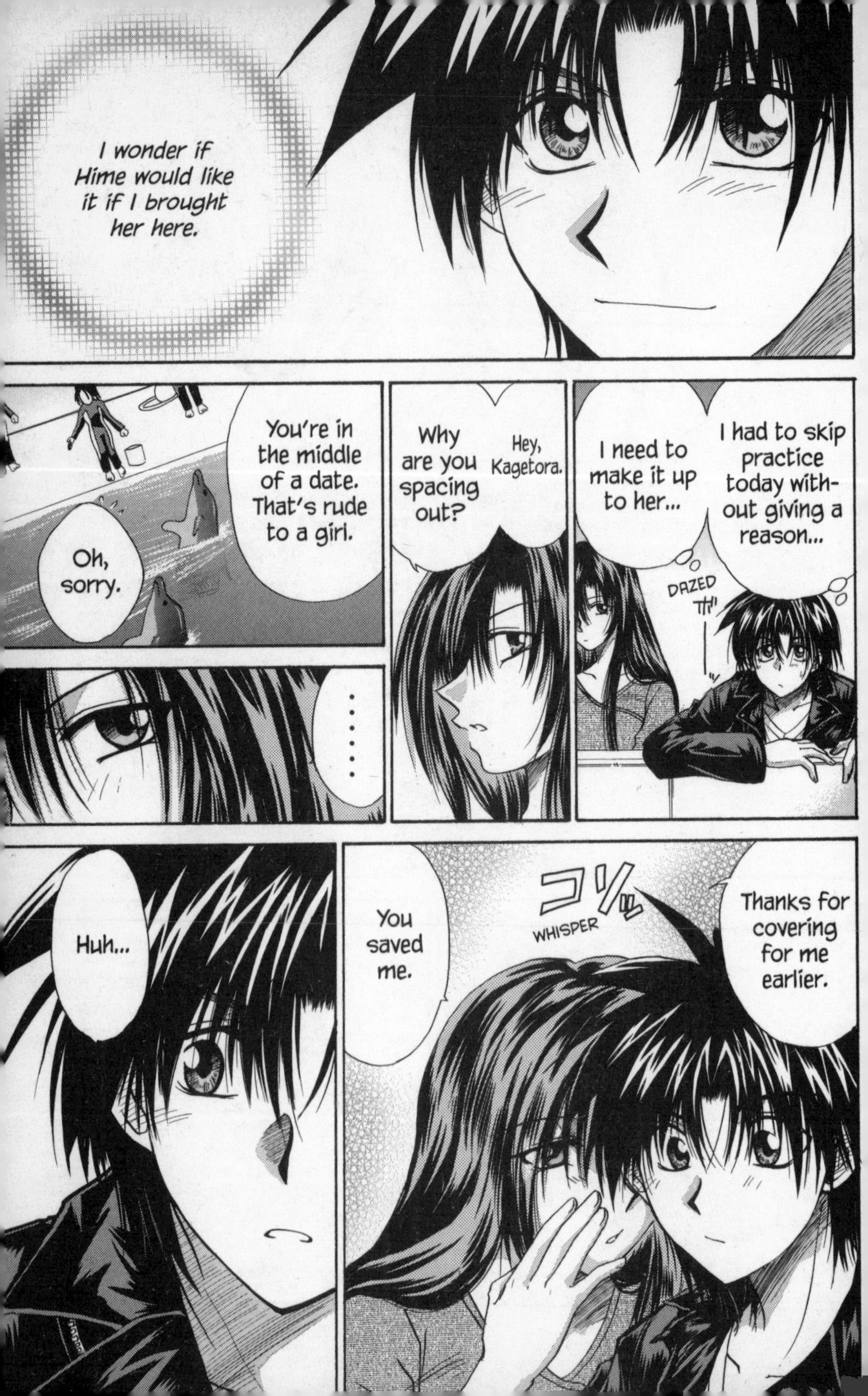
I wonder if Hime would like it if I brought her here.
I had to skip practice today with-out giving a reason...
I need to make it up to her...
DAZED
Hey, Kagetora.
Why are you spacing out?
You're in the middle of a date. That's rude to a girl.
Oh, sorry.
......
Thanks for covering for me earlier.
WHISPER
You saved me.
Huh...

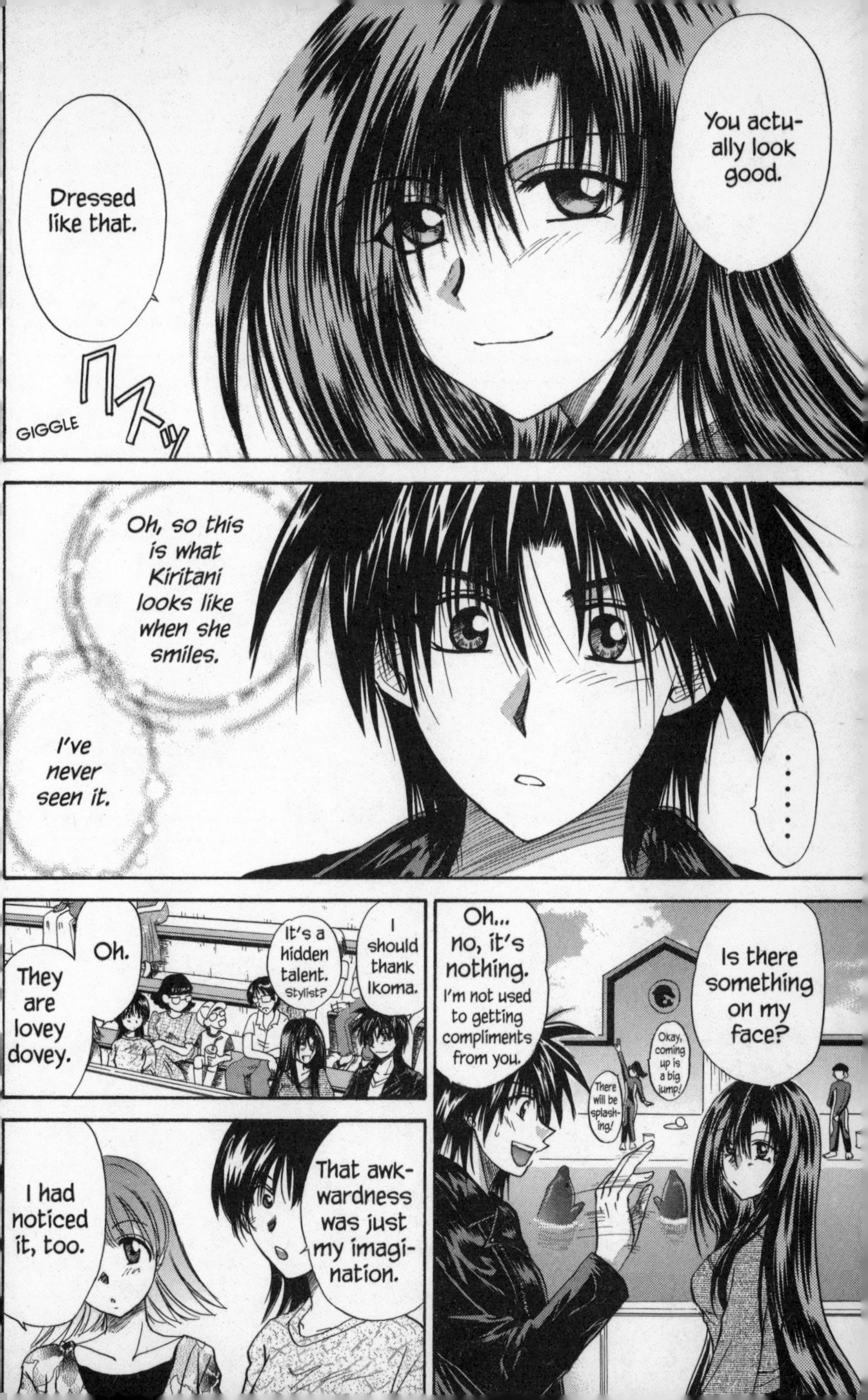

You actually look good.
Dressed like that.
GIGGLE
......
Oh, so this is what Kiritani looks like when she smiles.
I've never seen it.
Is there something on my face?
Oh... no, it's nothing.
I'm not used to getting compliments from you.
Okay, coming up is a big jump!
There will be splashing!
I should thank Ikoma.
It's a hidden talent.
Stylist?
Oh.
They are lovey dovey.
That awkwardness was just my imagination.
I had noticed it, too.

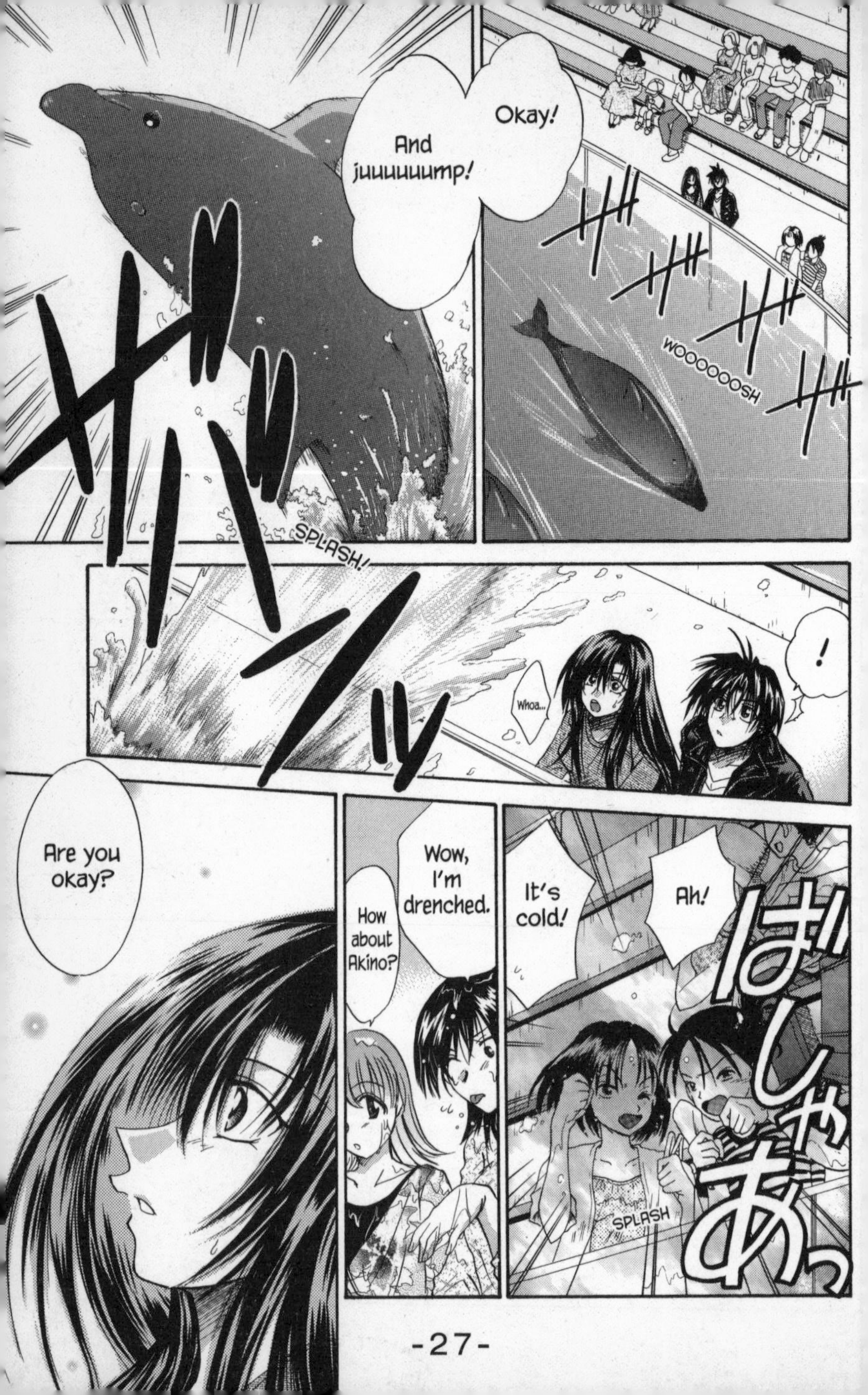
Okay!
And juuuuuump!
WOOOOOOSH
SPLASH!
!
Whoa...
Ah!
It's cold!
ばしゃあっ
SPLASH
Wow, I'm drenched.
How about Akino?
Are you okay?

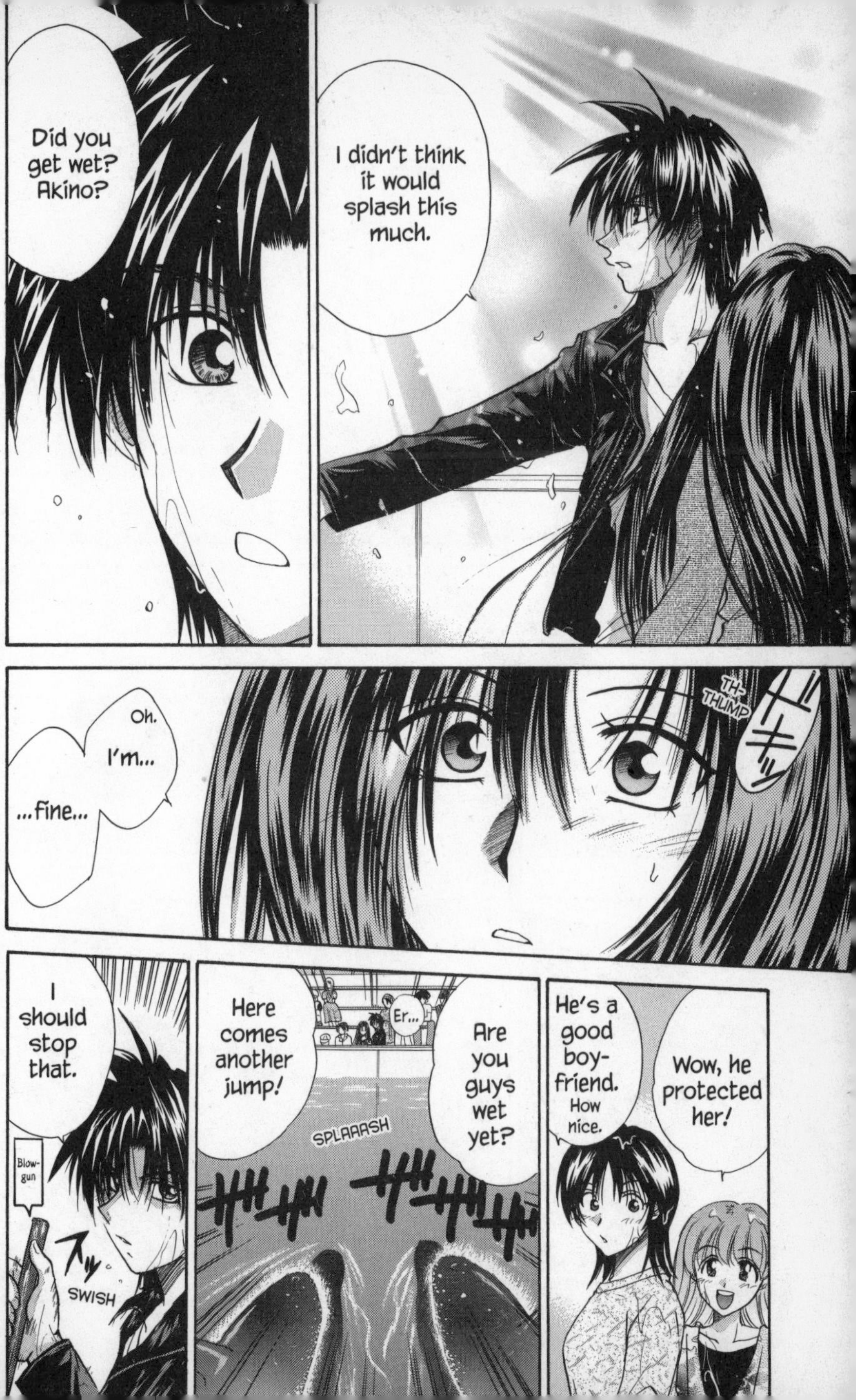
I didn't think it would splash this much.
Did you get wet? Akino?
TH-THUMP
Oh.
I'm...
...fine...
Wow, he protected her!
He's a good boy-friend.
How nice.
Are you guys wet yet?
Er...
Here comes another jump!
SPLAAASH
I should stop that.
Blow-gun
SWISH

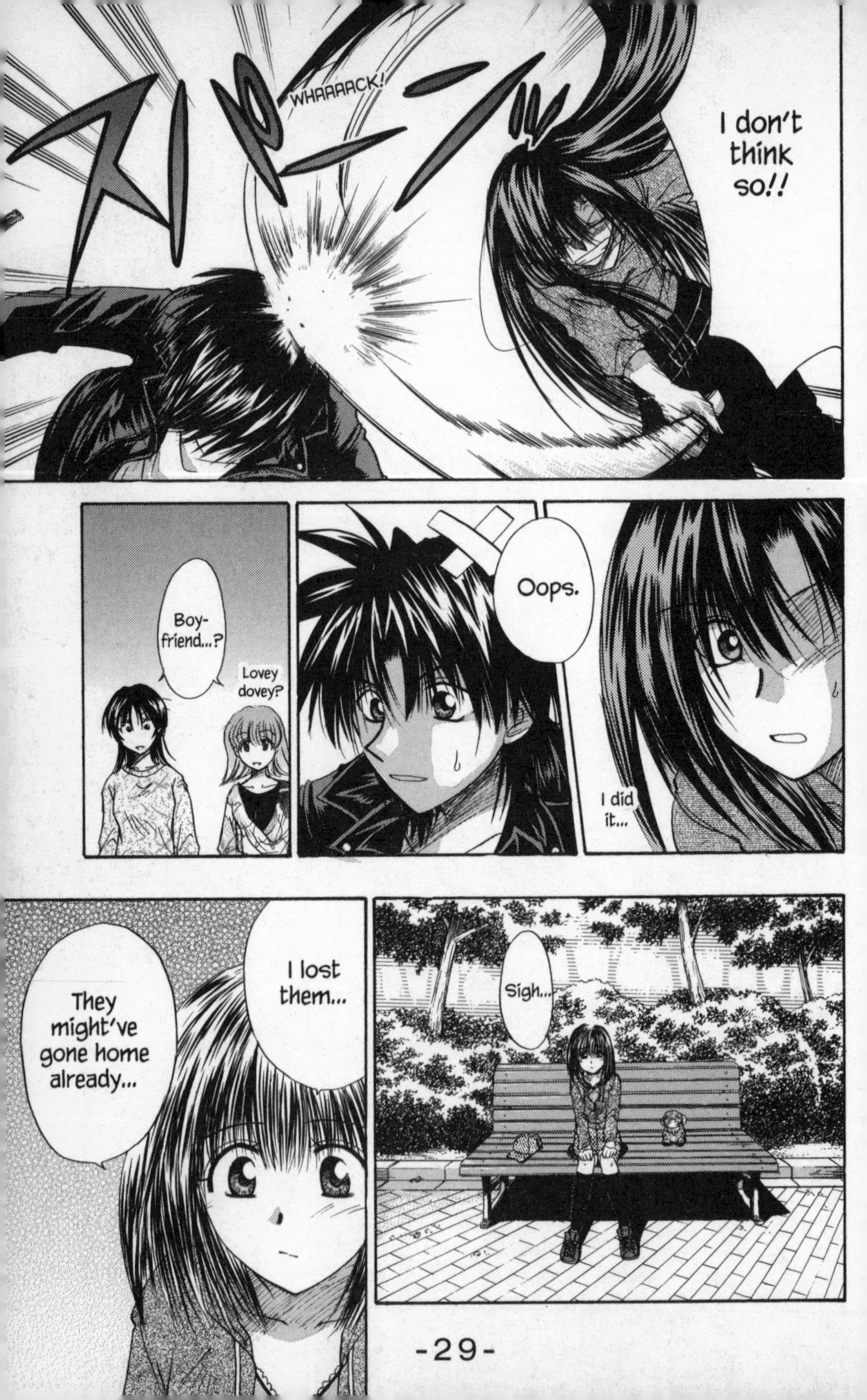
WHAAAACK!
I don't think so!!
I did it...
Oops.
Boy-friend...?
Lovey dovey?
Sigh...
I lost them...
They might've gone home already...

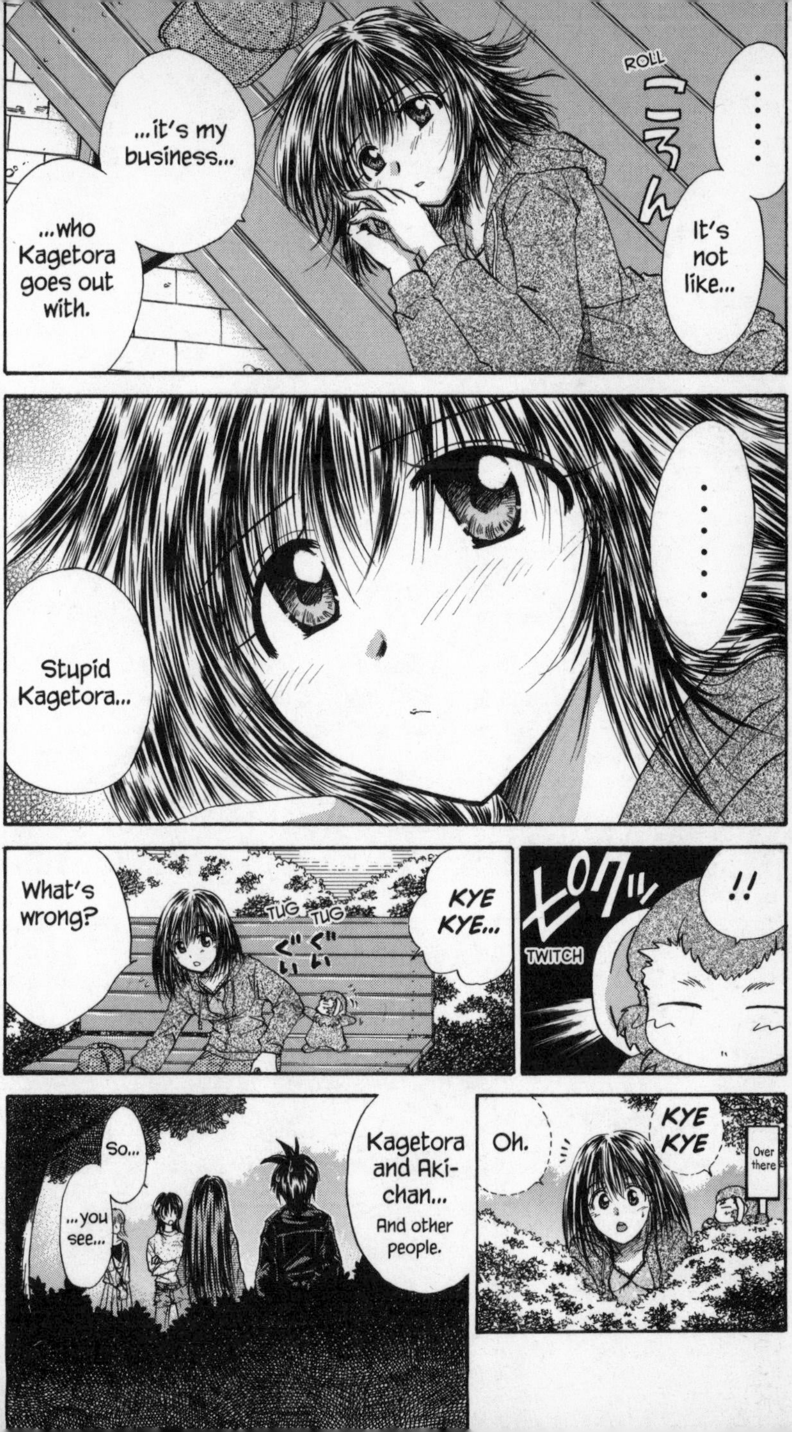
......
It's not like...
ROLL
ころん
...it's my business...
...who Kagetora goes out with.
......
Stupid Kagetora...
!!
ピクッ
TWITCH
KYE KYE...
TUG TUG
ぐい ぐい
What's wrong?
Over there
KYE KYE
Oh.
Kagetora and Aki-chan...
And other people.
So...
...you see...

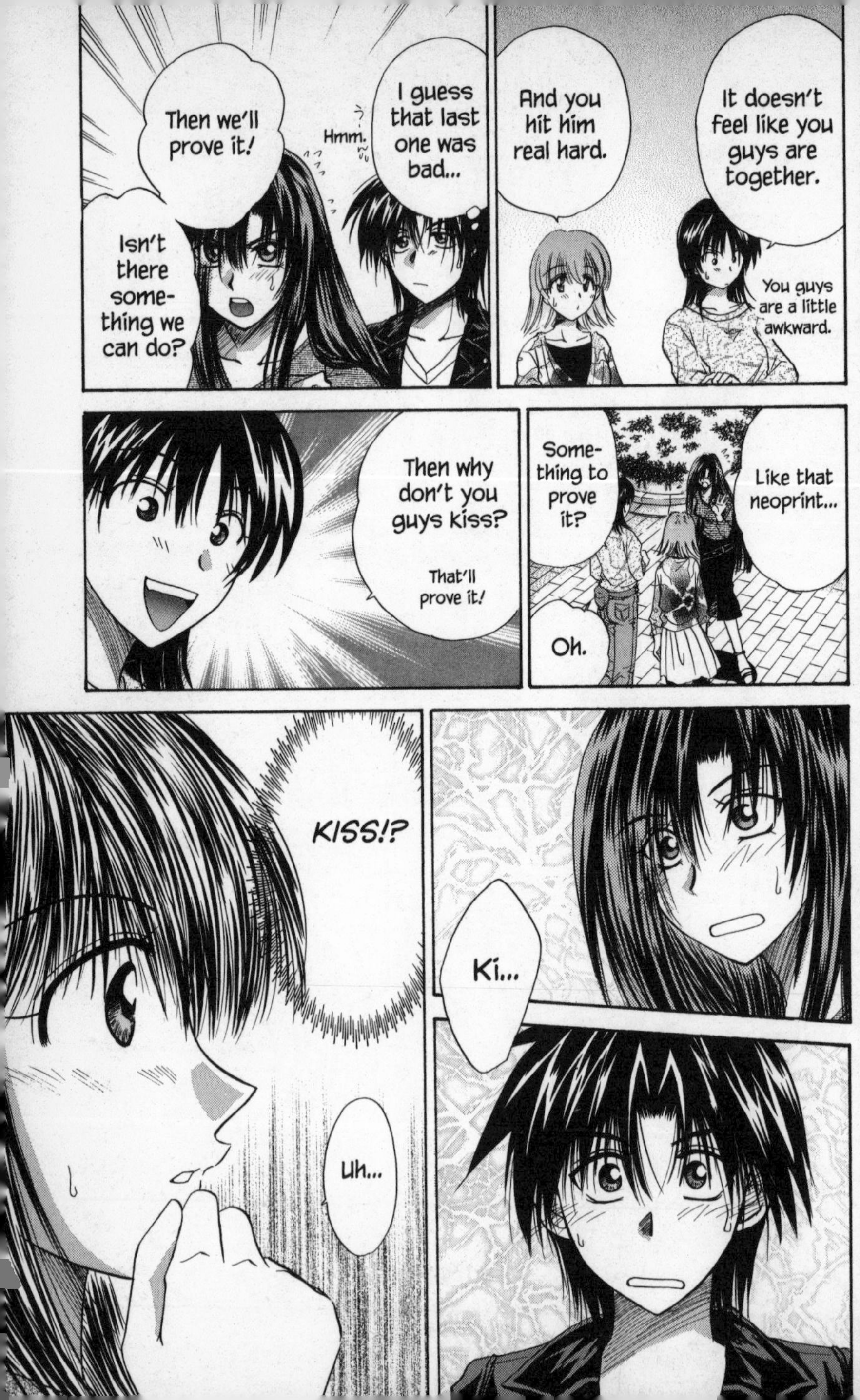
It doesn't feel like you guys are together.
You guys are a little awkward.
And you hit him real hard.
I guess that last one was bad...
Hmm.
Then we'll prove it!
Isn't there something we can do?
Like that neoprint...
Something to prove it?
Oh.
Then why don't you guys kiss?
That'll prove it!
Ki...
KISS!?
Uh...

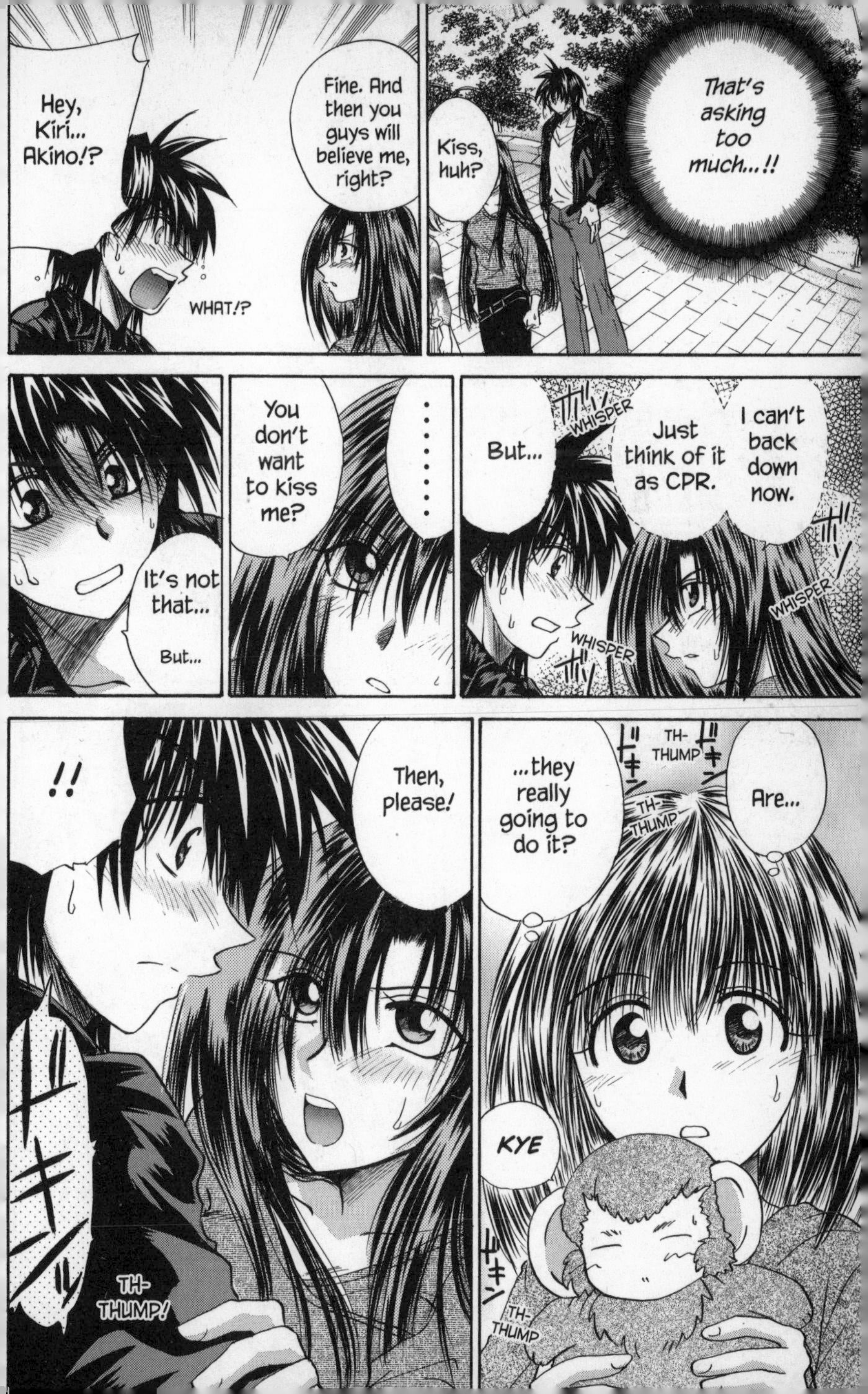
That's asking too much...!!
Kiss, huh?
Fine. And then you guys will believe me, right?
Hey, Kiri... Akino!?
WHAT!?
I can't back down now.
WHISPER
Just think of it as CPR.
WHISPER
But...
WHISPER
......
You don't want to kiss me?
It's not that...
But...
Are...
TH-THUMP
TH-THUMP
...they really going to do it?
KYE
TH-THUMP
Then, please!
!!
TH-THUMP!

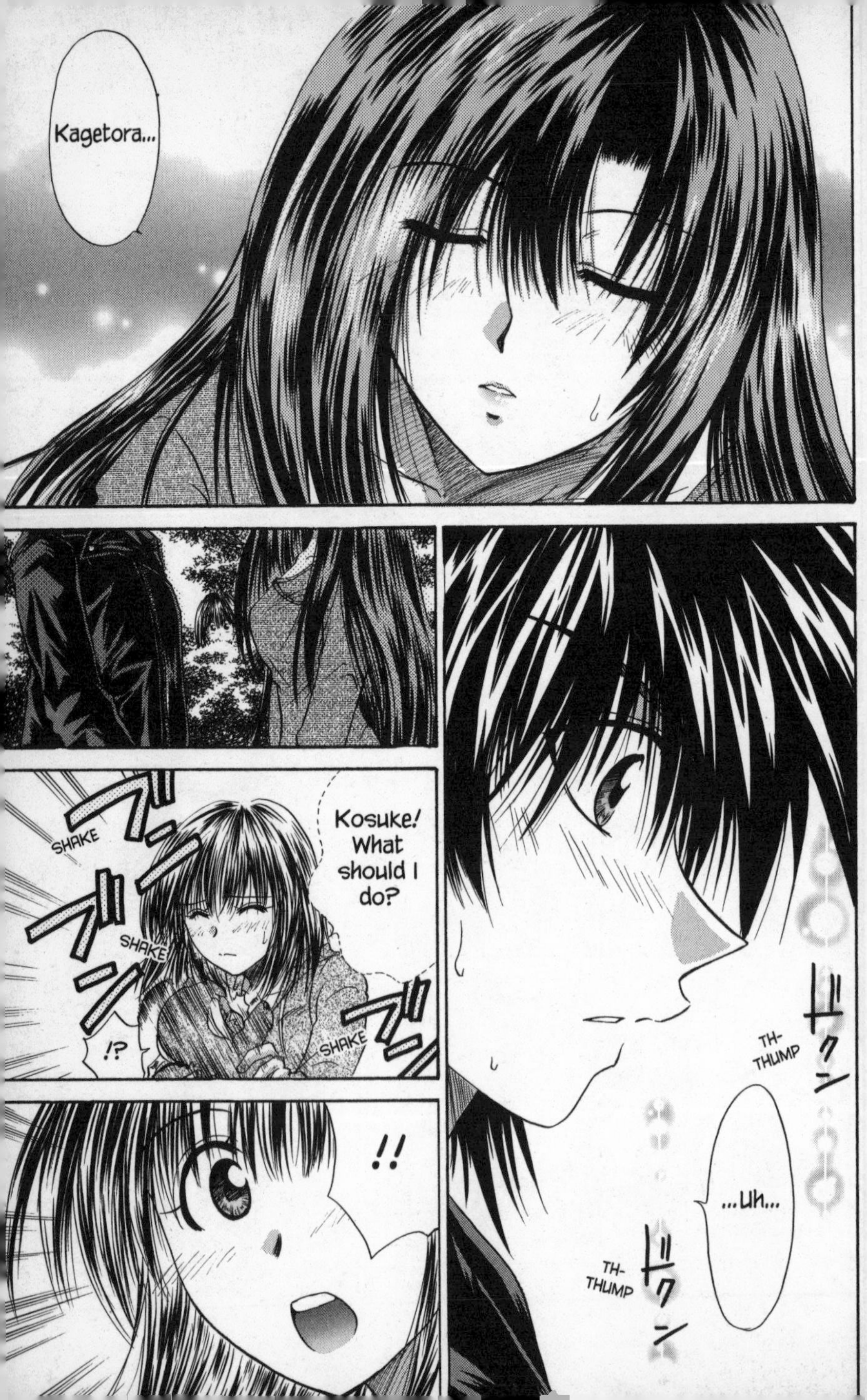
Kagetora...
TH-THUMP
...uh...
TH-THUMP
Kosuke! What should I do?
SHAKE
SHAKE
SHAKE
!?
!!

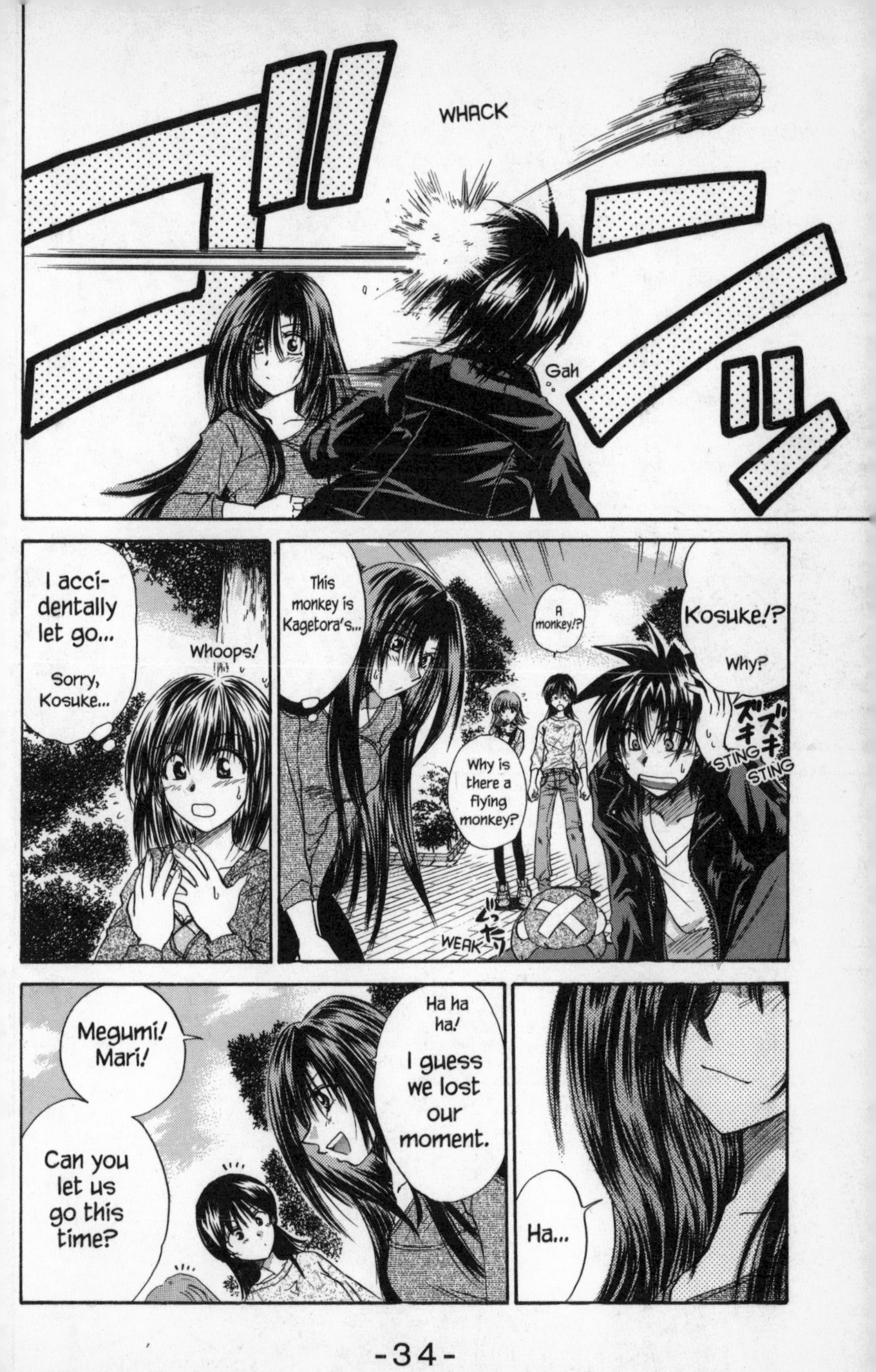
WHACK
Gah
Kosuke!?
Why?
STING
STING
A monkey!?
This monkey is Kagetora's...
Why is there a flying monkey?
WEAK
I acci-dentally let go...
Whoops!
Sorry, Kosuke...
Ha...
Ha ha ha!
I guess we lost our moment.
Megumi! Mari!
Can you let us go this time?

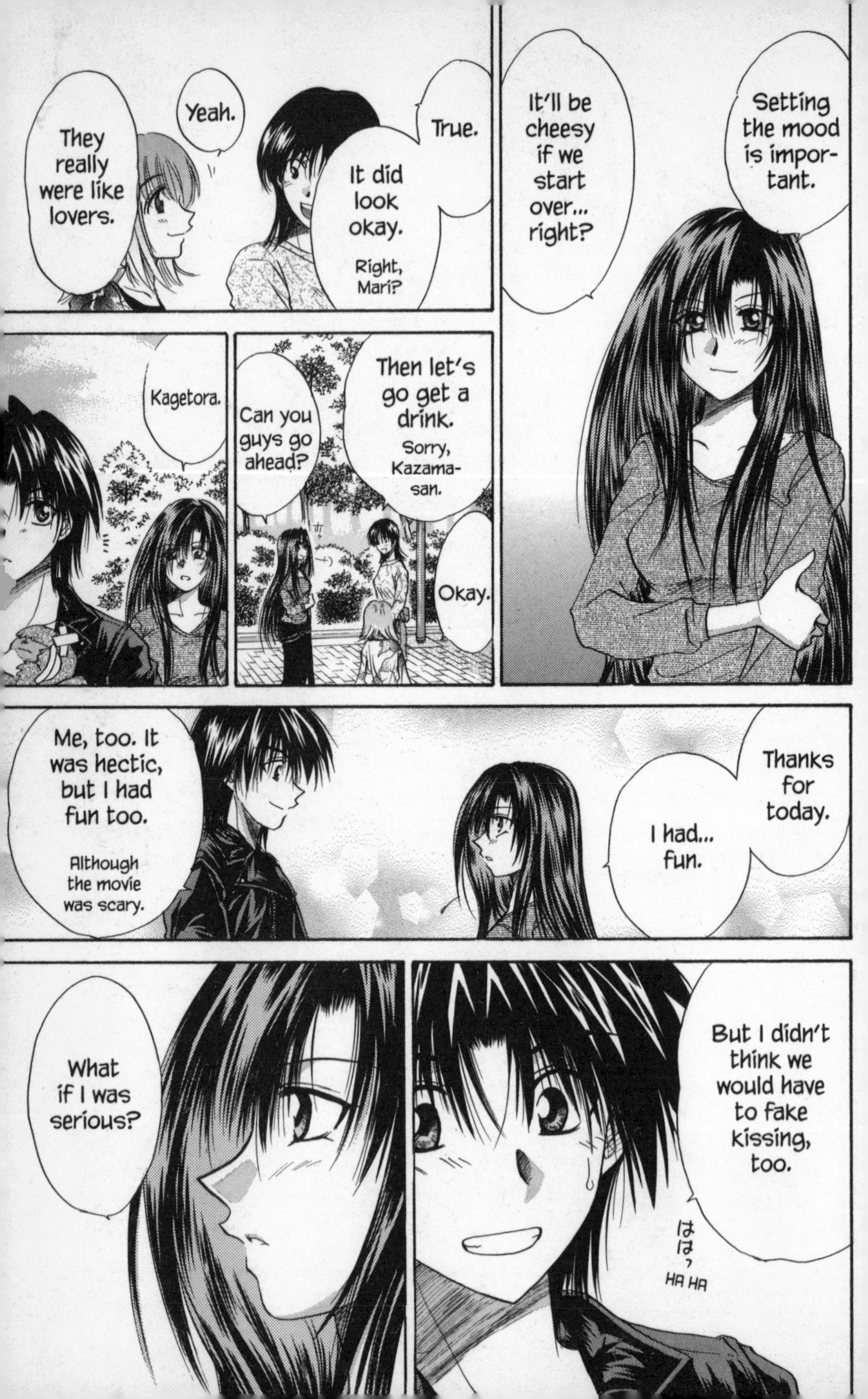
Setting the mood is important.
It'll be cheesy if we start over... right?
True.
It did look okay.
Right, Mari?
Yeah.
They really were like lovers.
Then let's go get a drink.
Sorry, Kazama-san.
Okay.
Can you guys go ahead?
Kagetora.
Thanks for today.
I had... fun.
Me, too. It was hectic, but I had fun too.
Although the movie was scary.
But I didn't think we would have to fake kissing, too.
はは,
HA HA
What if I was serious?

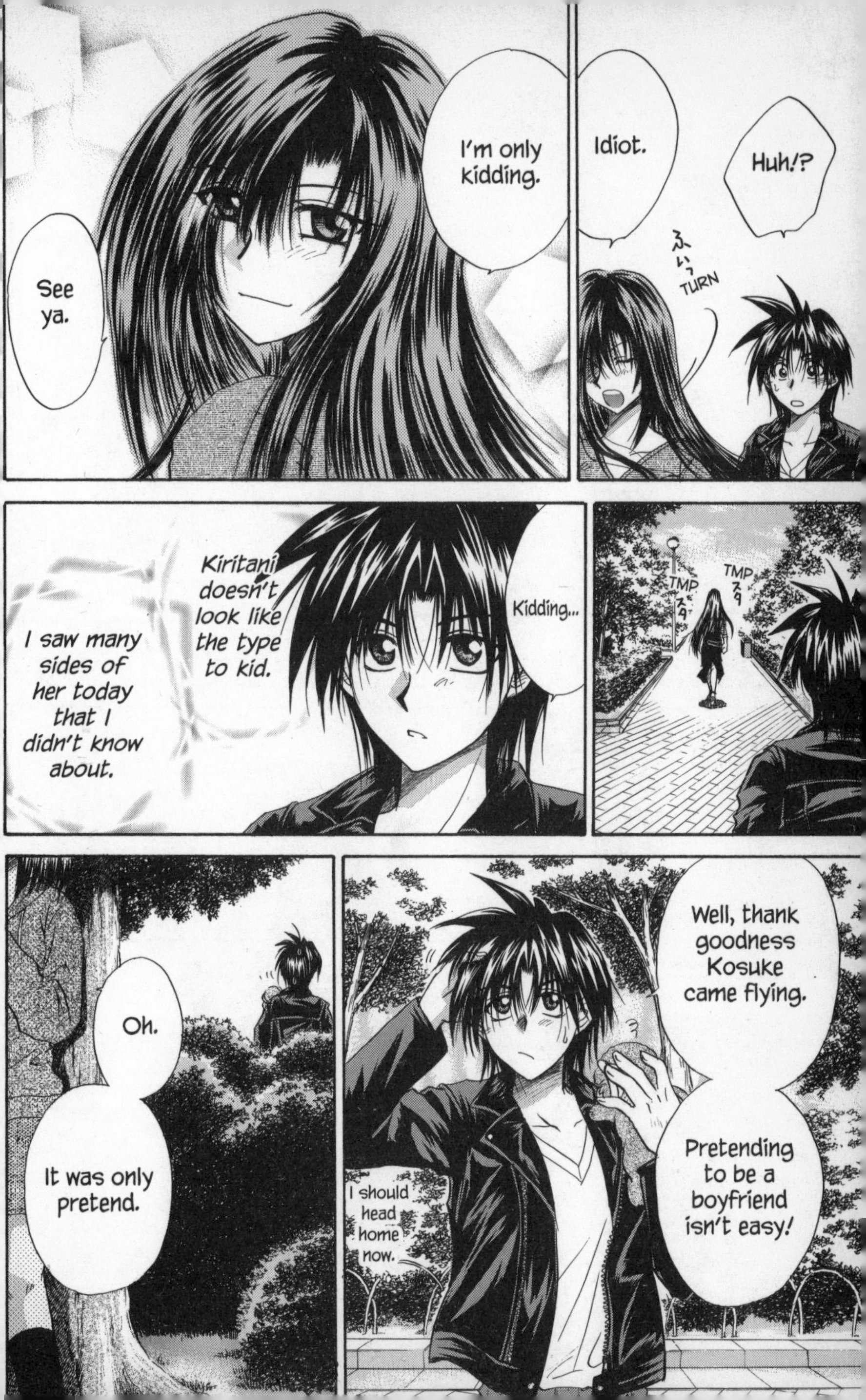
Huh!?
ふいっ TURN
Idiot.
I'm only kidding.
See ya.
TMP スタ
TMP スタ
Kidding...
Kiritani doesn't look like the type to kid.
I saw many sides of her today that I didn't know about.
Well, thank goodness Kosuke came flying.
Pretending to be a boyfriend isn't easy!
I should head home now.
Oh.
It was only pretend.

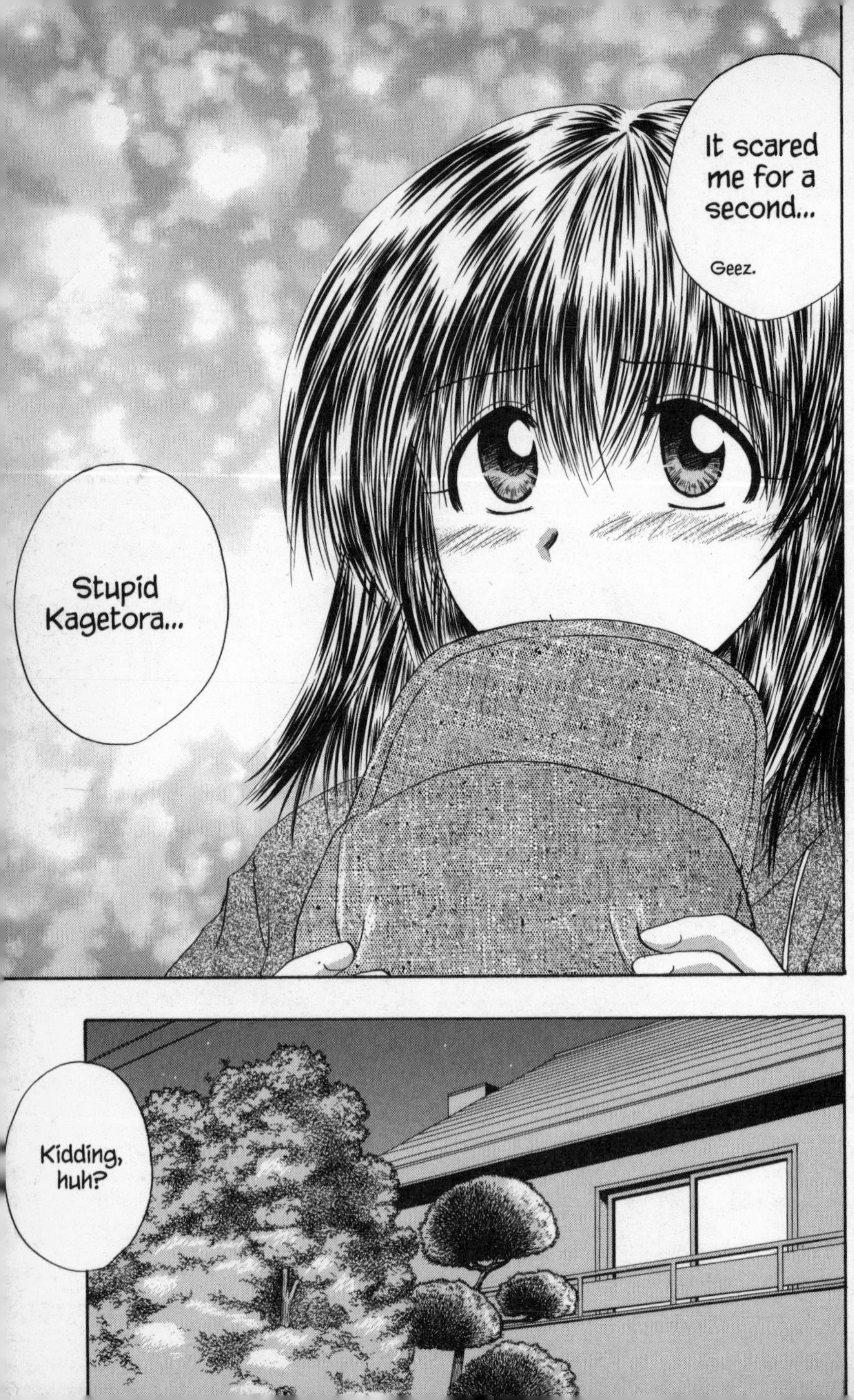
It scared me for a second...
Geez.
Stupid Kagetora...
Kidding, huh?

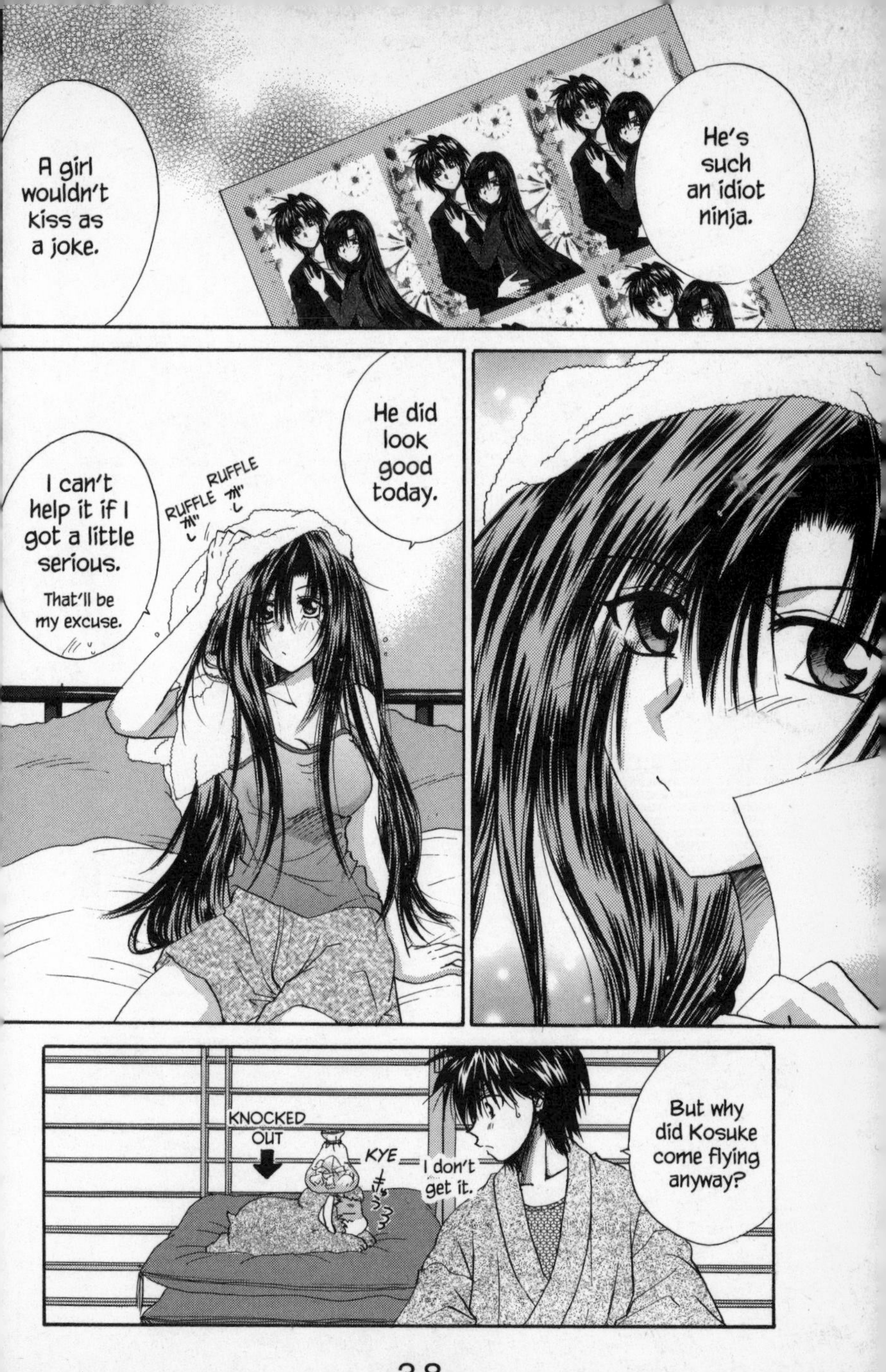
He's such an idiot ninja.
A girl wouldn't kiss as a joke.
He did look good today.
RUFFLE
RUFFLE
I can't help it if I got a little serious.
That'll be my excuse.
But why did Kosuke come flying anyway?
I don't get it.
KYE
KNOCKED OUT

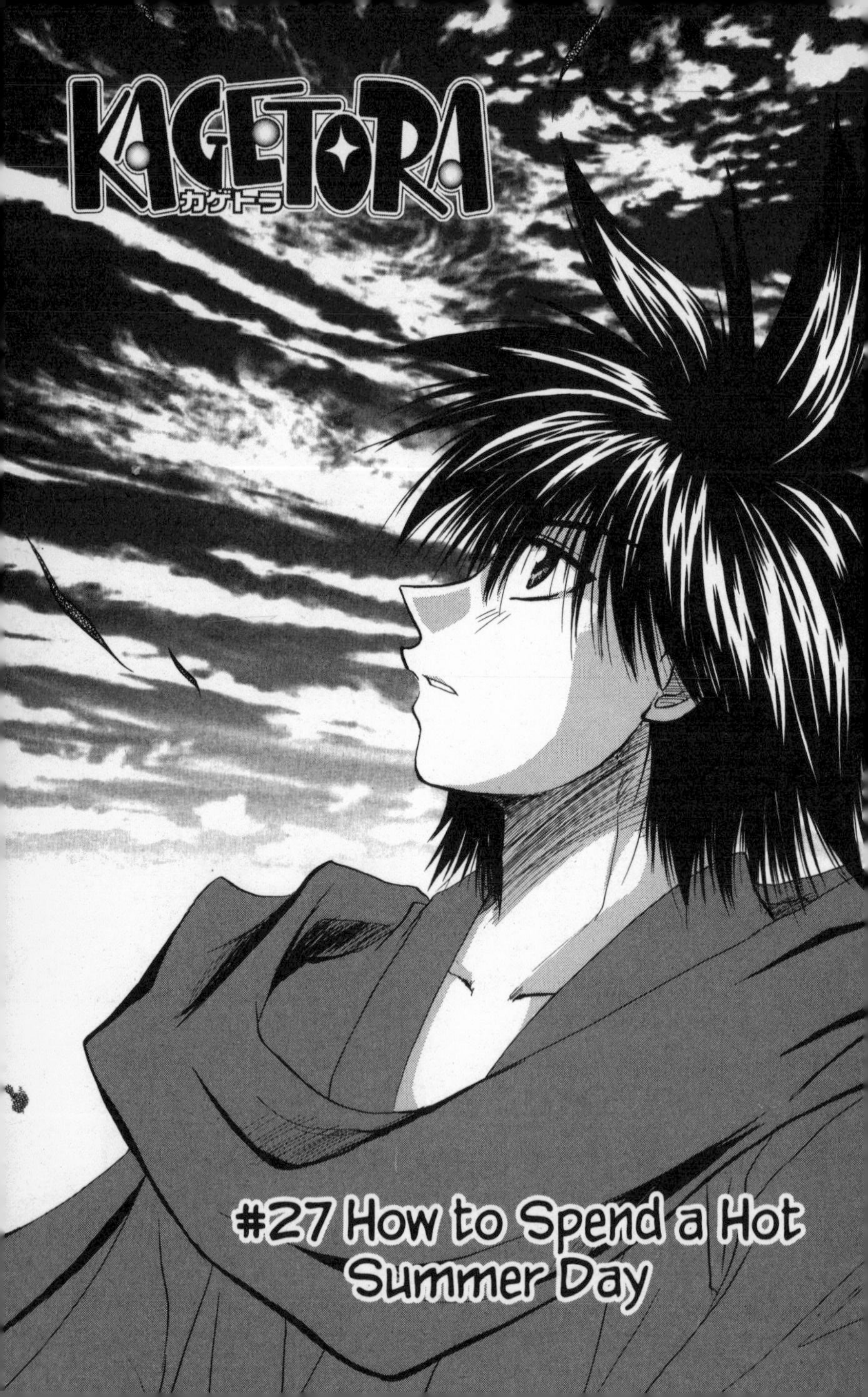
KAGETORA
カゲトラ
#27 How to Spend a Hot Summer Day

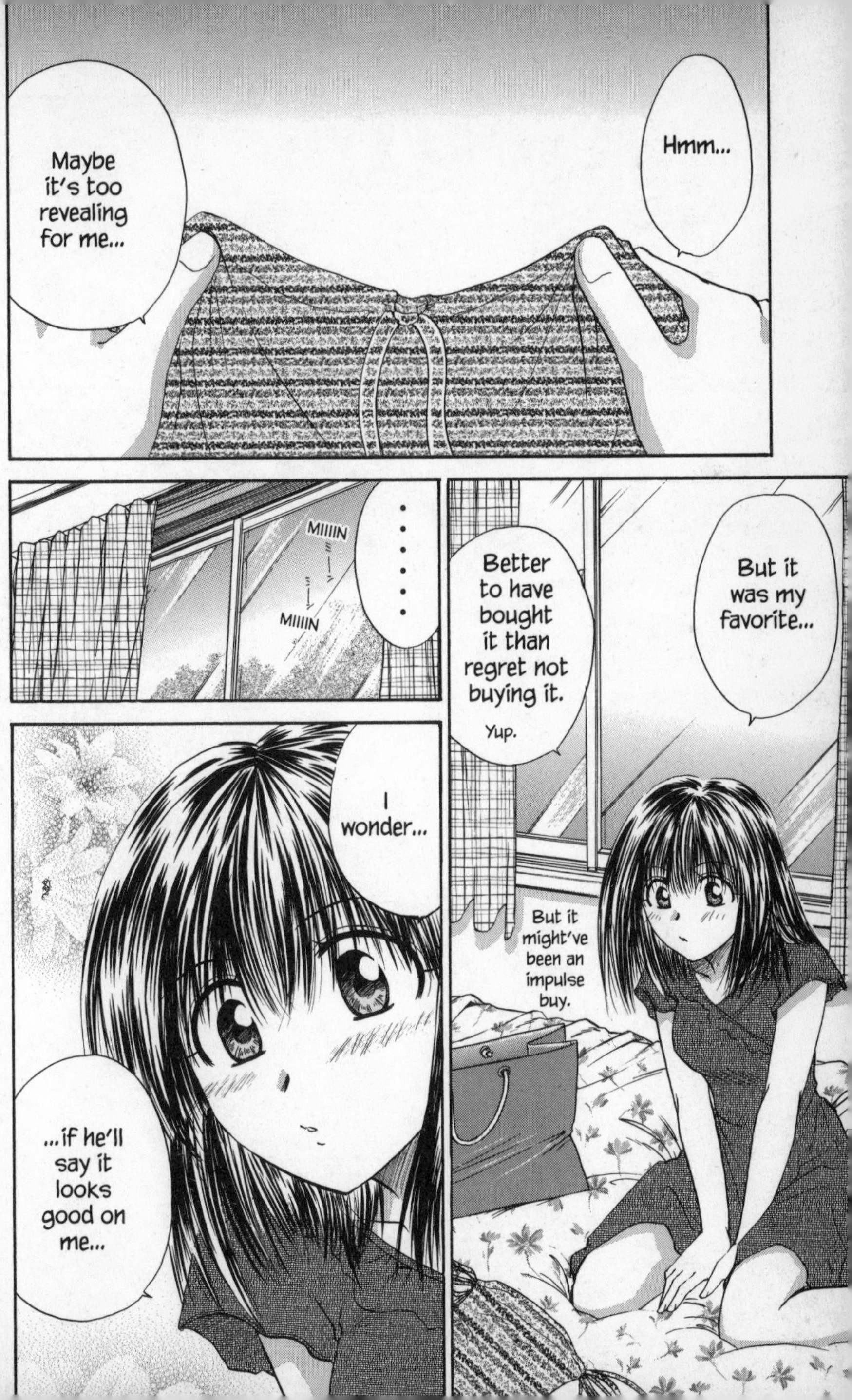
Hmm...
Maybe it's too revealing for me...
But it was my favorite...
Better to have bought it than regret not buying it.
Yup.
But it might've been an impulse buy.
MIIIN MIIIN
......
I wonder...
...if he'll say it looks good on me...

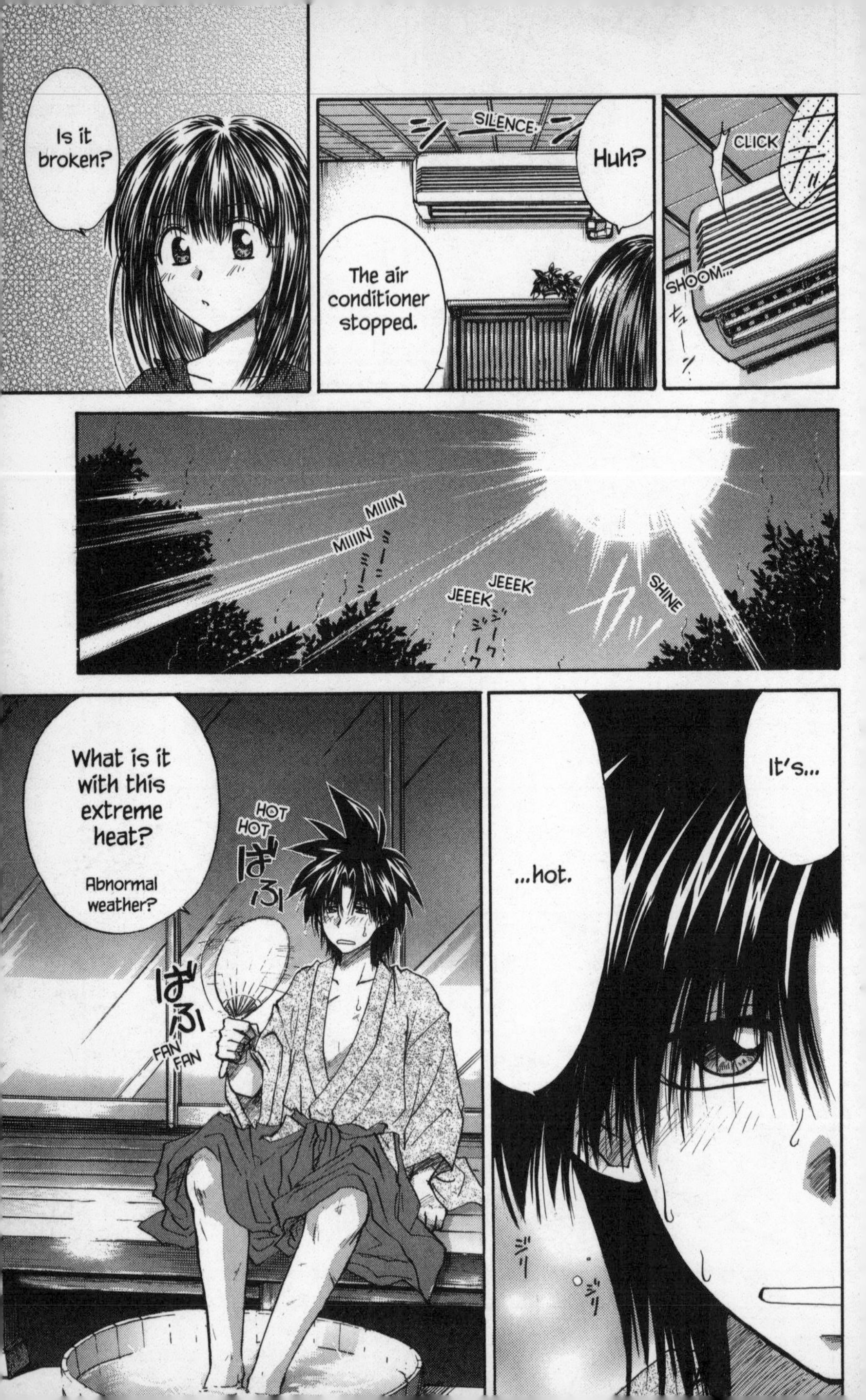
CLICK
SHOOM...
SILENCE
Huh?
The air conditioner stopped.
Is it broken?
MIIIN
MIIIN
SHINE
JEEEK
JEEEK
It's...
...hot.
What is it with this extreme heat?
Abnormal weather?
HOT
HOT
FAN
FAN

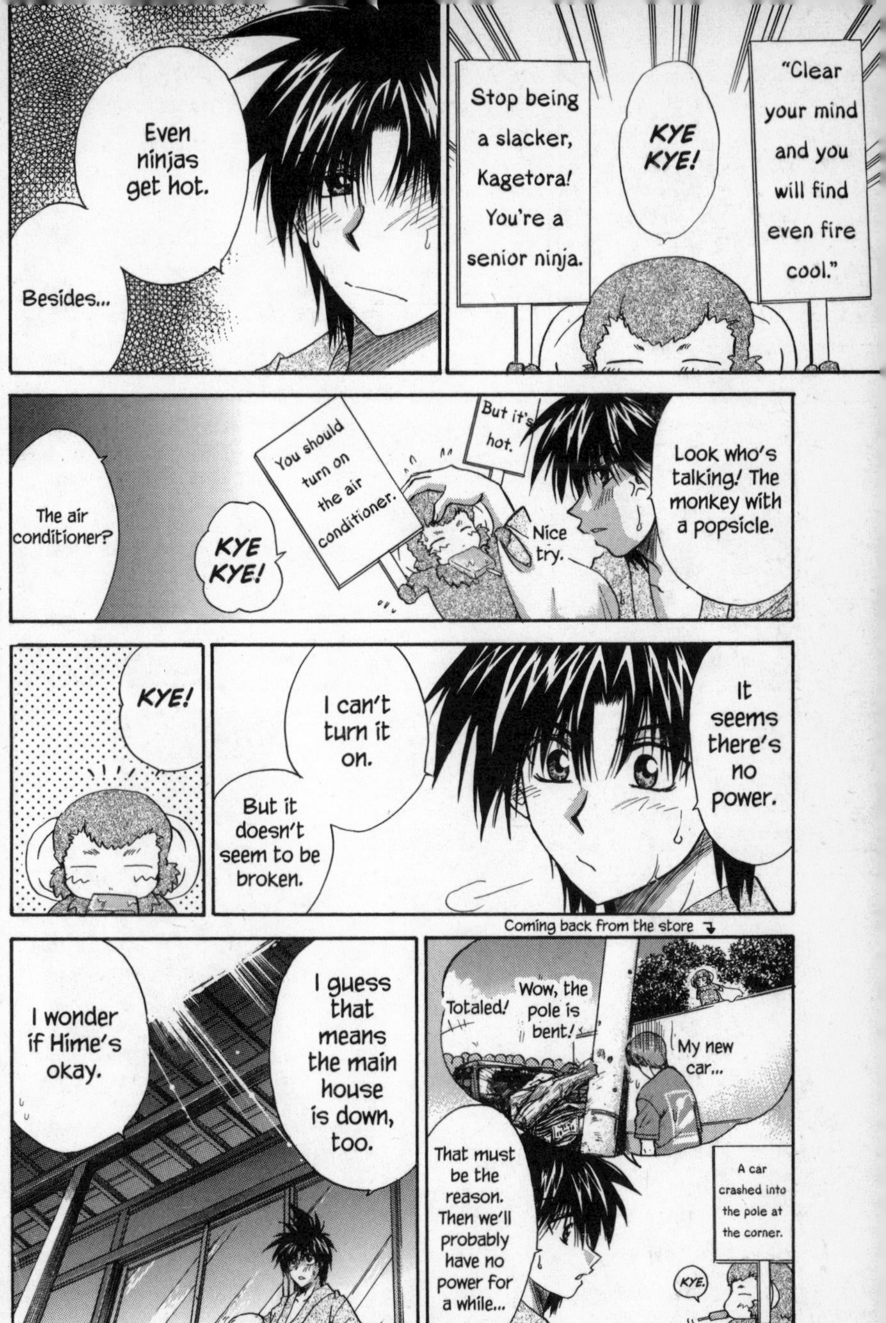
"Clear your mind and you will find even fire cool."
KYE KYE!
Stop being a slacker, Kagetora! You're a senior ninja.
Even ninjas get hot.
Besides...
Look who's talking! The monkey with a popsicle.
But it's hot.
Nice try.
You should turn on the air conditioner.
KYE KYE!
The air conditioner?
It seems there's no power.
I can't turn it on.
But it doesn't seem to be broken.
KYE!
Coming back from the store
A car crashed into the pole at the corner.
My new car...
Wow, the pole is bent!
Totaled!
That must be the reason. Then we'll probably have no power for a while...
KYE.
I guess that means the main house is down, too.
I wonder if Hime's okay.

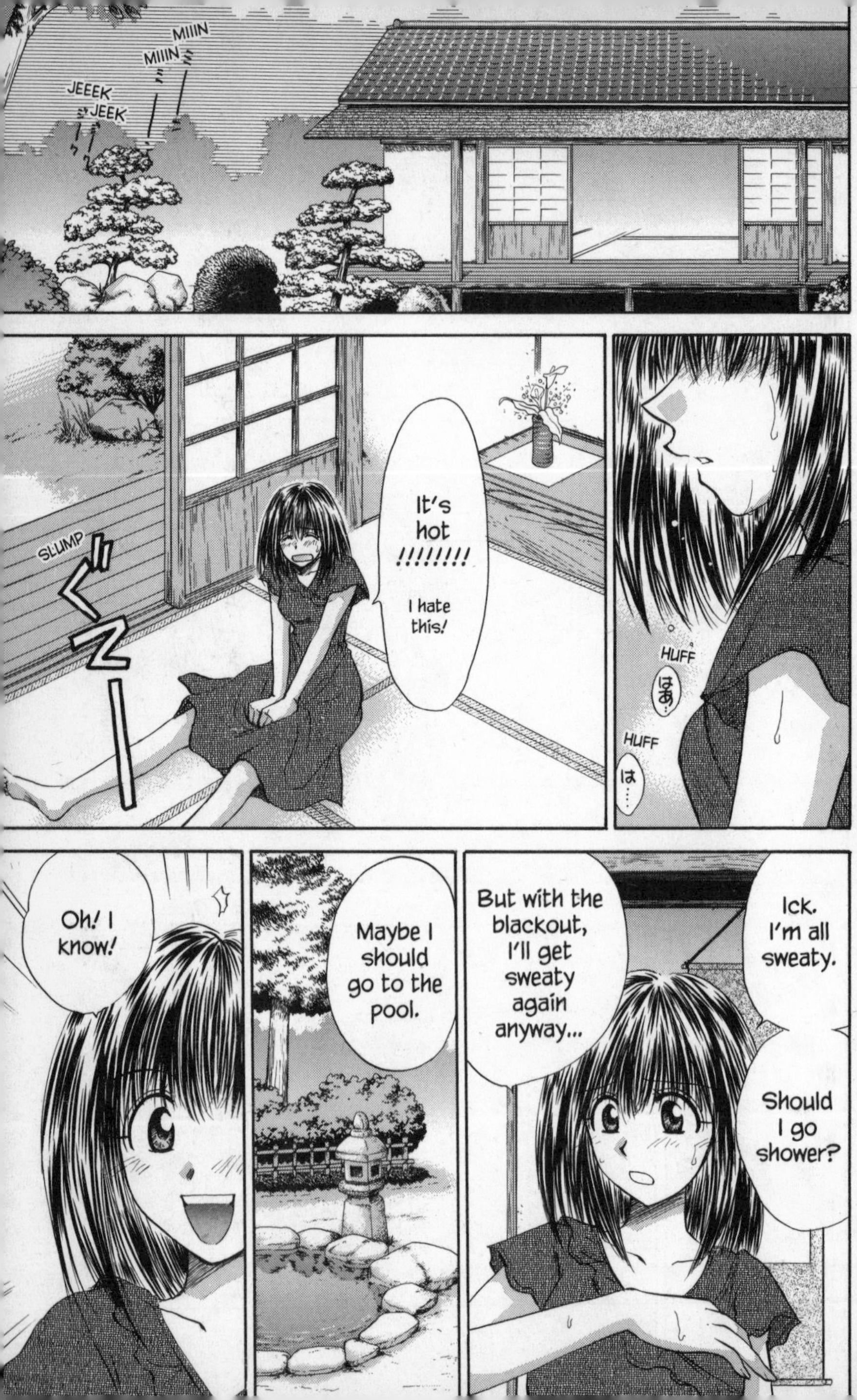
MIIIN
MIIIN
JEEEK
JEEK
HUFF
はあ…
HUFF
は…
It's hot !!!!!!!!!
I hate this!
SLUMP
Ick. I'm all sweaty.
Should I go shower?
But with the blackout, I'll get sweaty again anyway...
Maybe I should go to the pool.
Oh! I know!

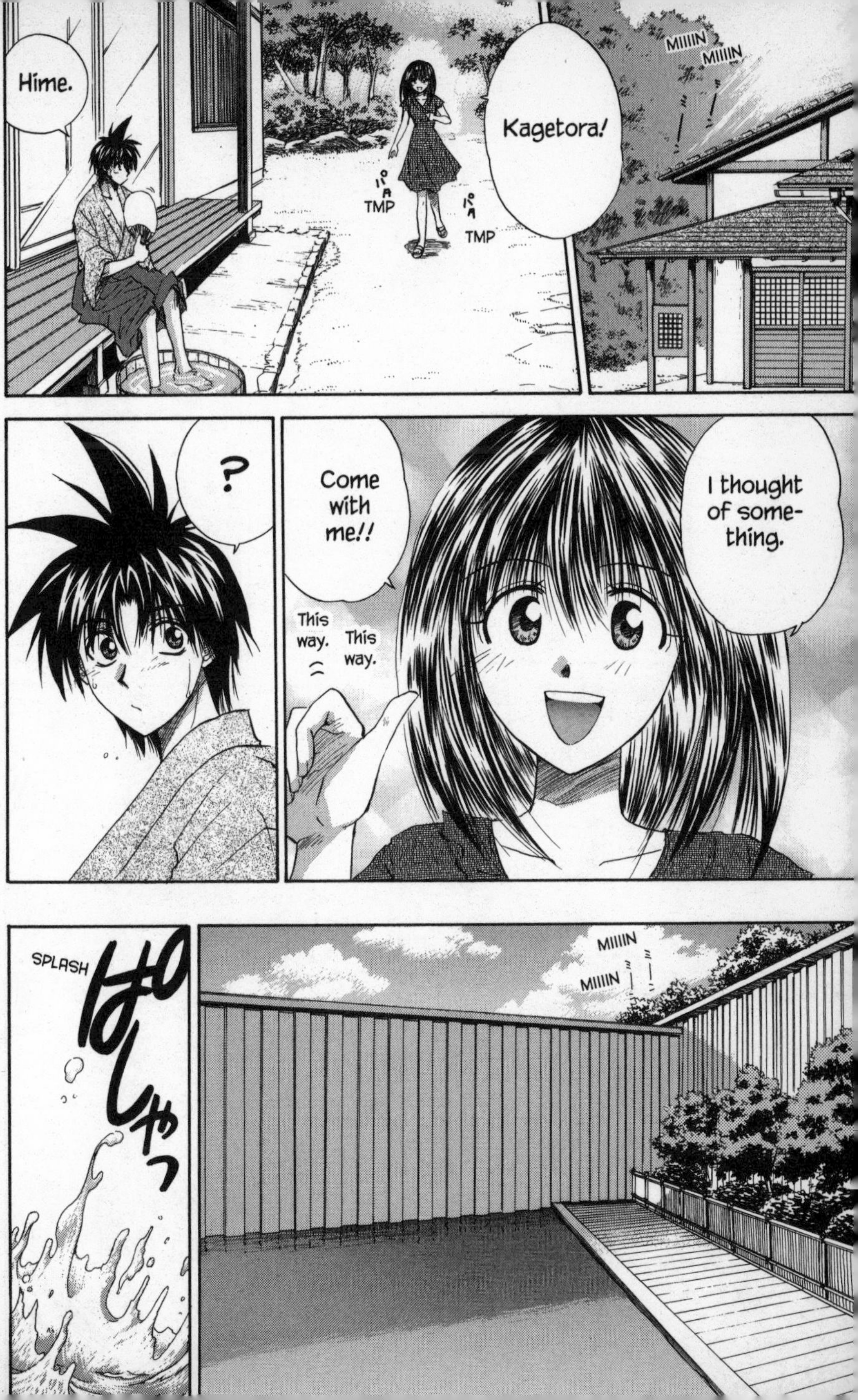
MIIIN
MIIIN
Kagetora!
TMP
TMP
Hime.
I thought of some-thing.
Come with me!!
This way.
This way.
?
MIIIN
MIIIN
SPLASH

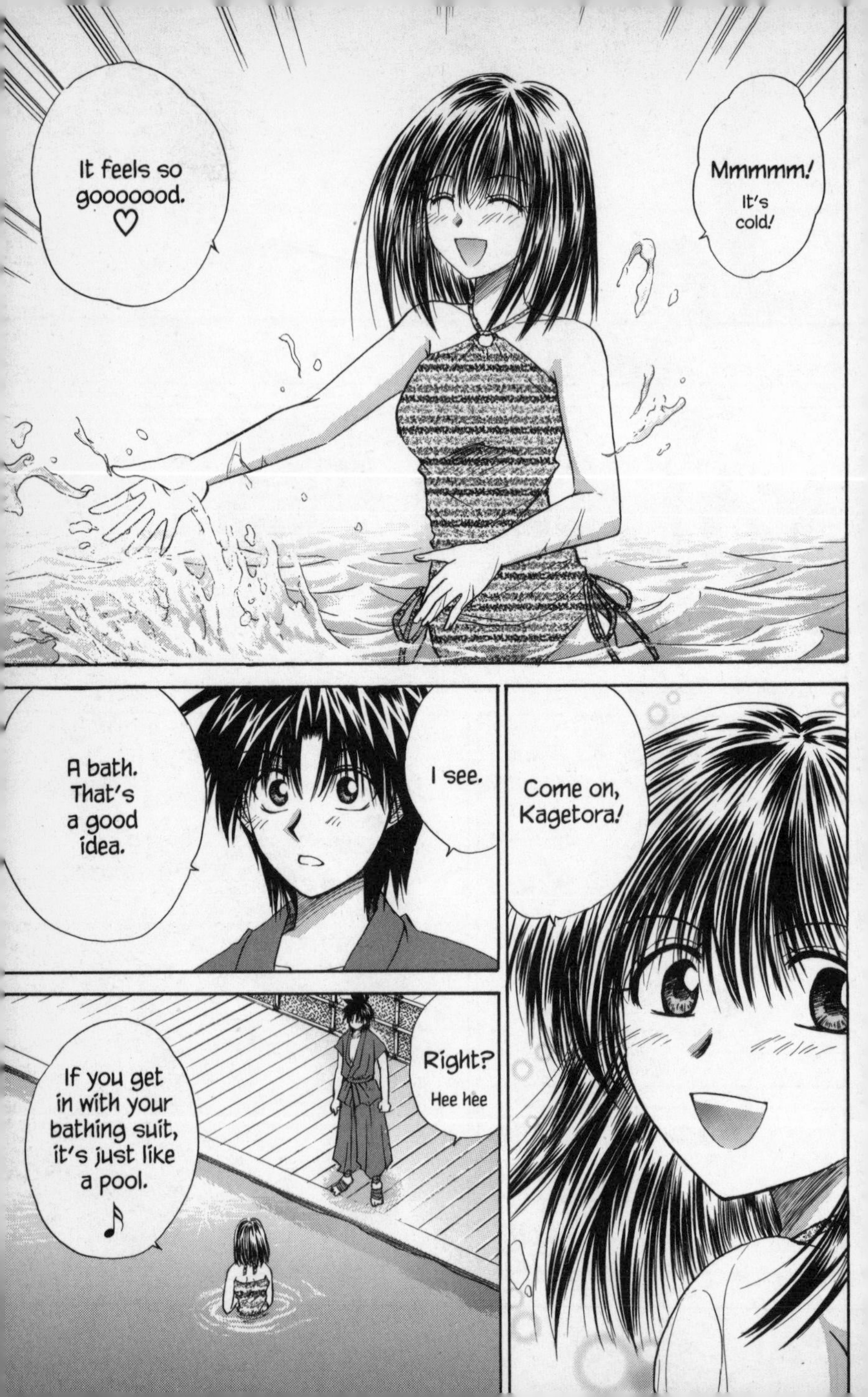
Mmmmm! It's cold!
It feels so goooood. ♡
Come on, Kagetora!
I see.
A bath. That's a good idea.
Right? Hee hee
If you get in with your bathing suit, it's just like a pool. ♪

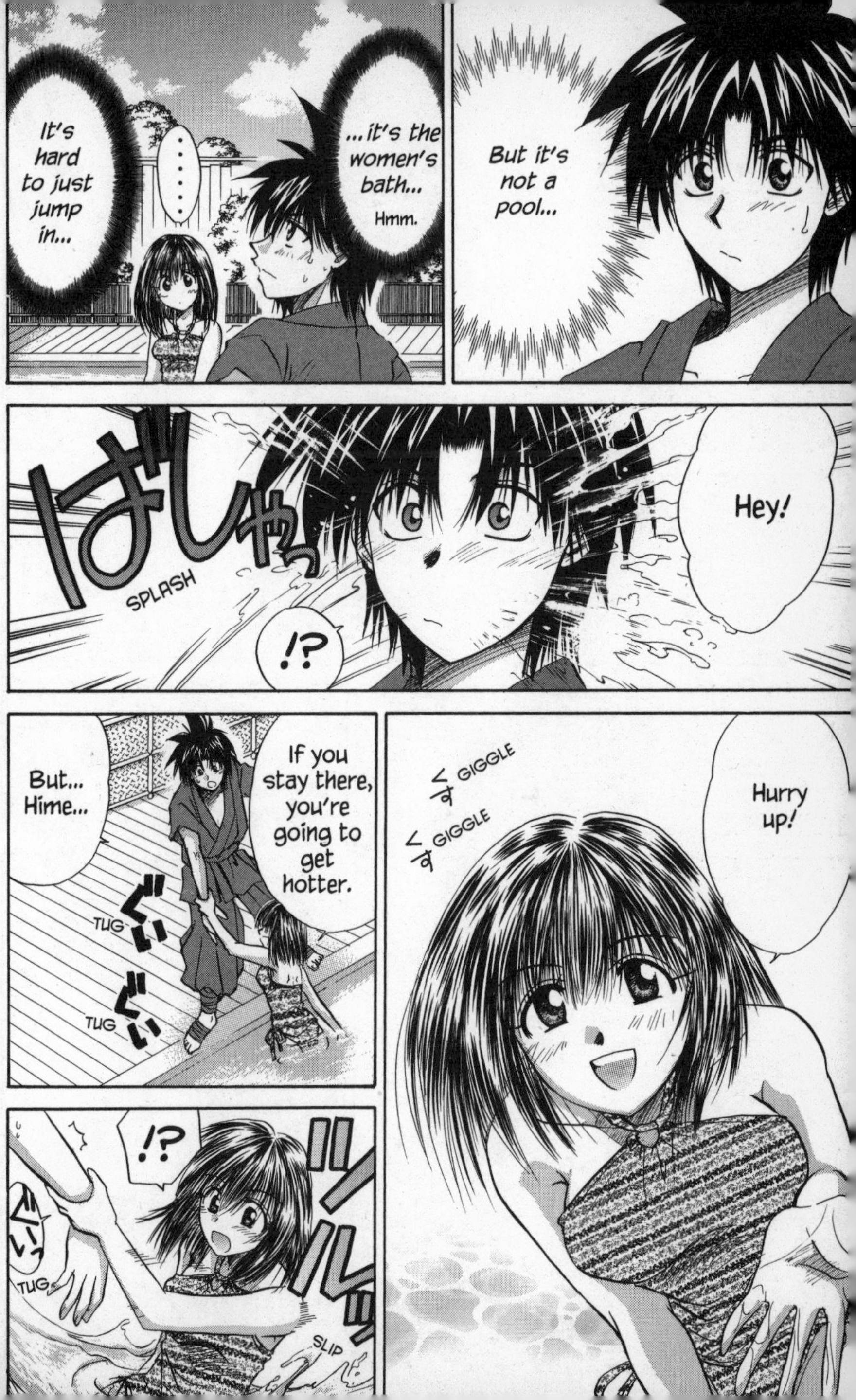
But it's not a pool...
...it's the women's bath...
Hmm.
......
It's hard to just jump in...
Hey!
ばしゃっ
SPLASH
!?
Hurry up!
くす GIGGLE
くす GIGGLE
If you stay there, you're going to get hotter.
But... Hime...
ぐい
TUG
ぐい
TUG
!?
SLIP
ぐいっ
TUG

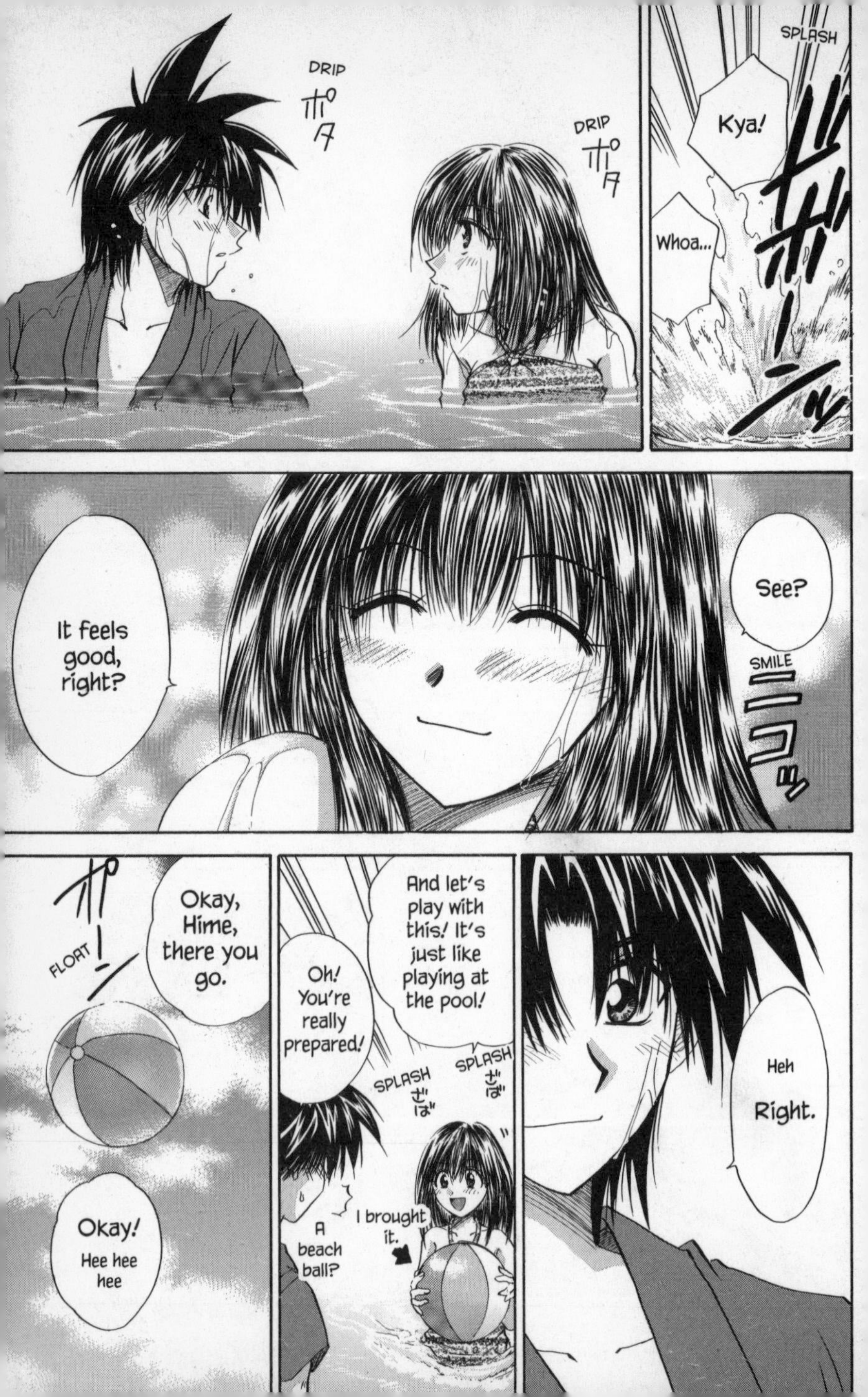
SPLASH
ザボーンッ
Kya!
Whoa...
DRIP
ポタ
DRIP
ポタ
See?
SMILE
ニコッ
It feels good, right?
Heh
Right.
And let's play with this! It's just like playing at the pool!
Oh! You're really prepared!
SPLASH
ざば
SPLASH
ざば
I brought it.
A beach ball?
Okay, Hime, there you go.
FLOAT
ポーン
Okay!
Hee hee hee

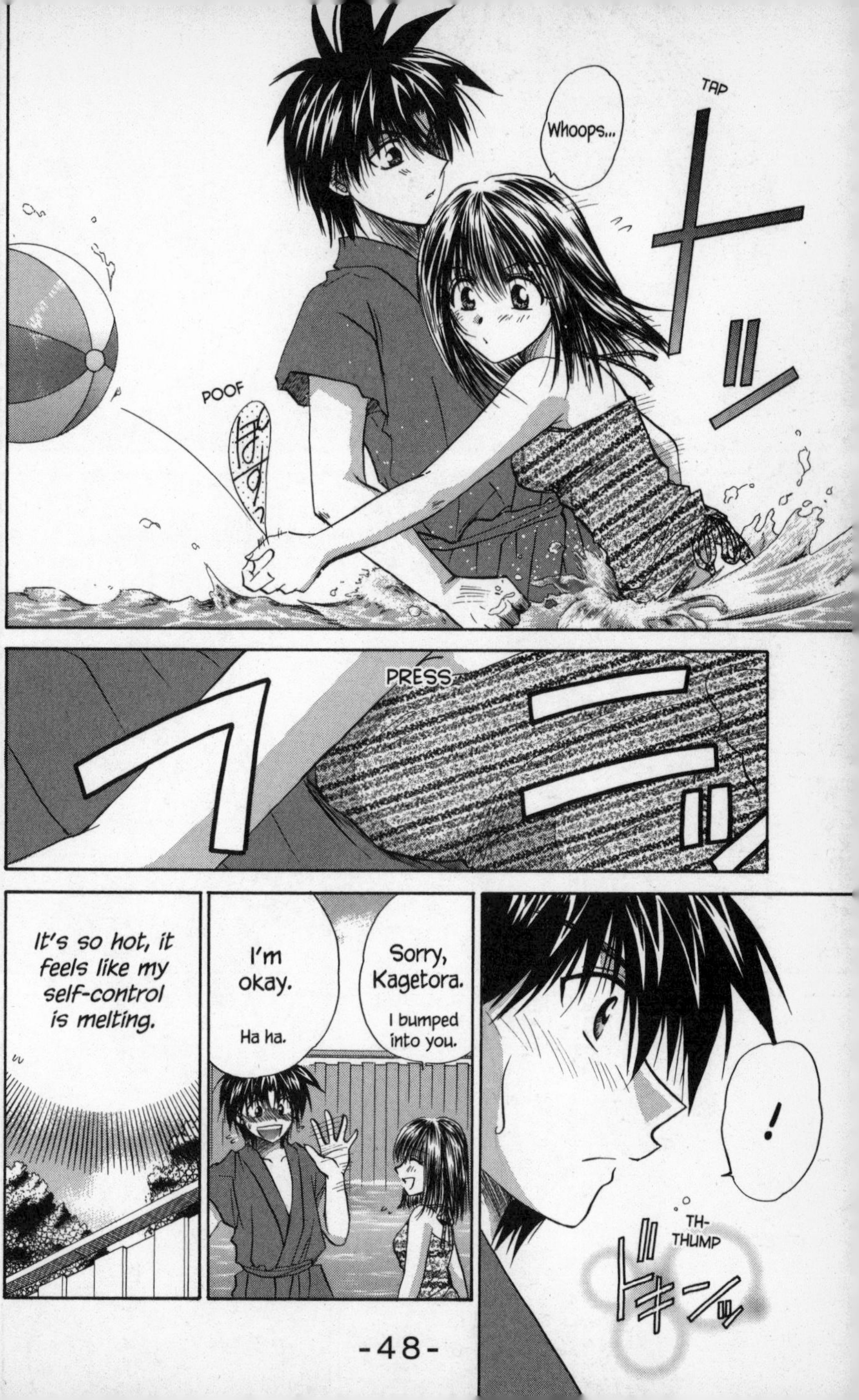
TAP
Whoops...
POOF
PRESS
!
TH-THUMP
Sorry, Kagetora.
I bumped into you.
I'm okay.
Ha ha.
It's so hot, it feels like my self-control is melting.

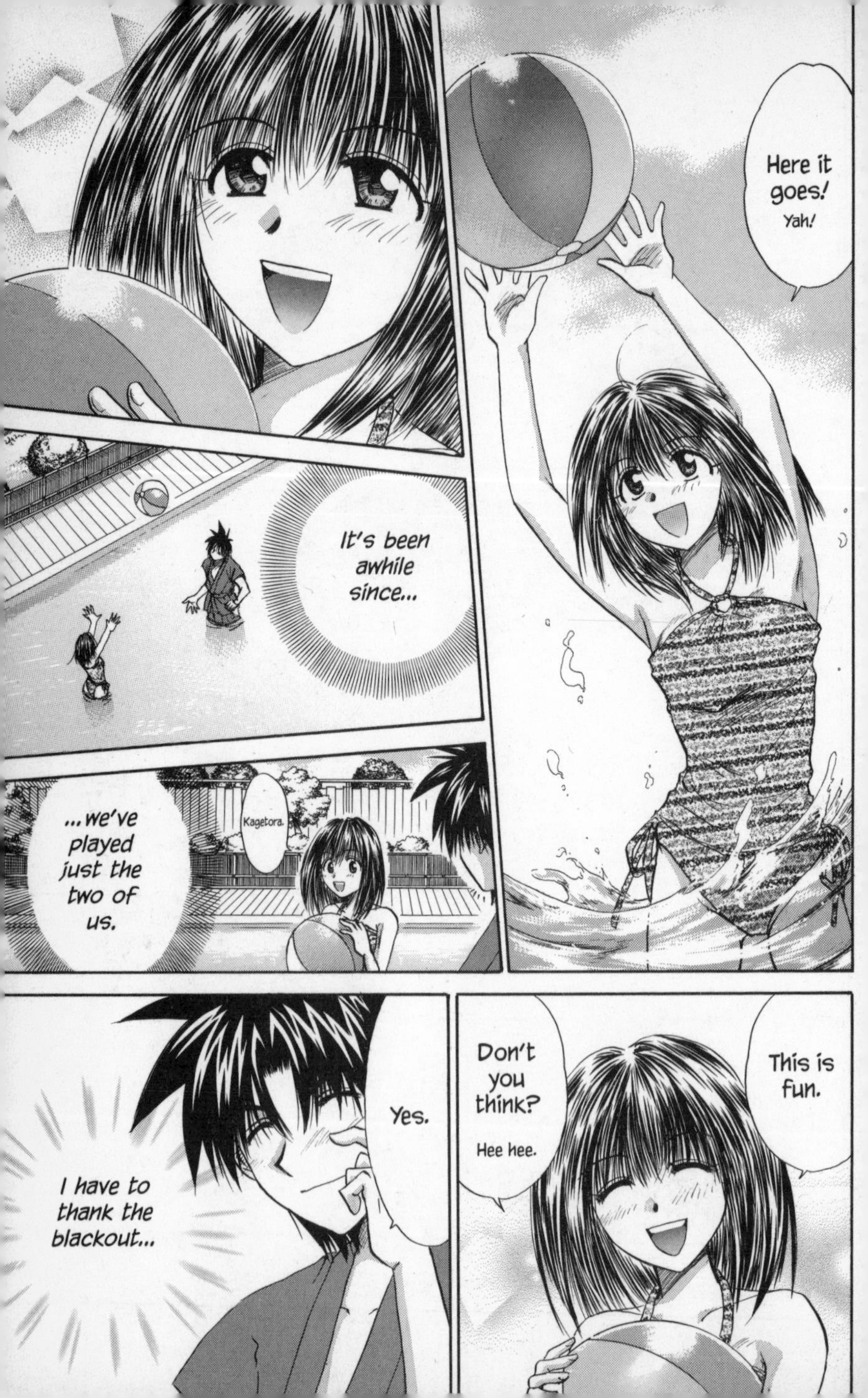
Here it goes!
Yah!
It's been awhile since...
Kagetora.
...we've played just the two of us.
This is fun.
Don't you think?
Hee hee.
Yes.
I have to thank the blackout...

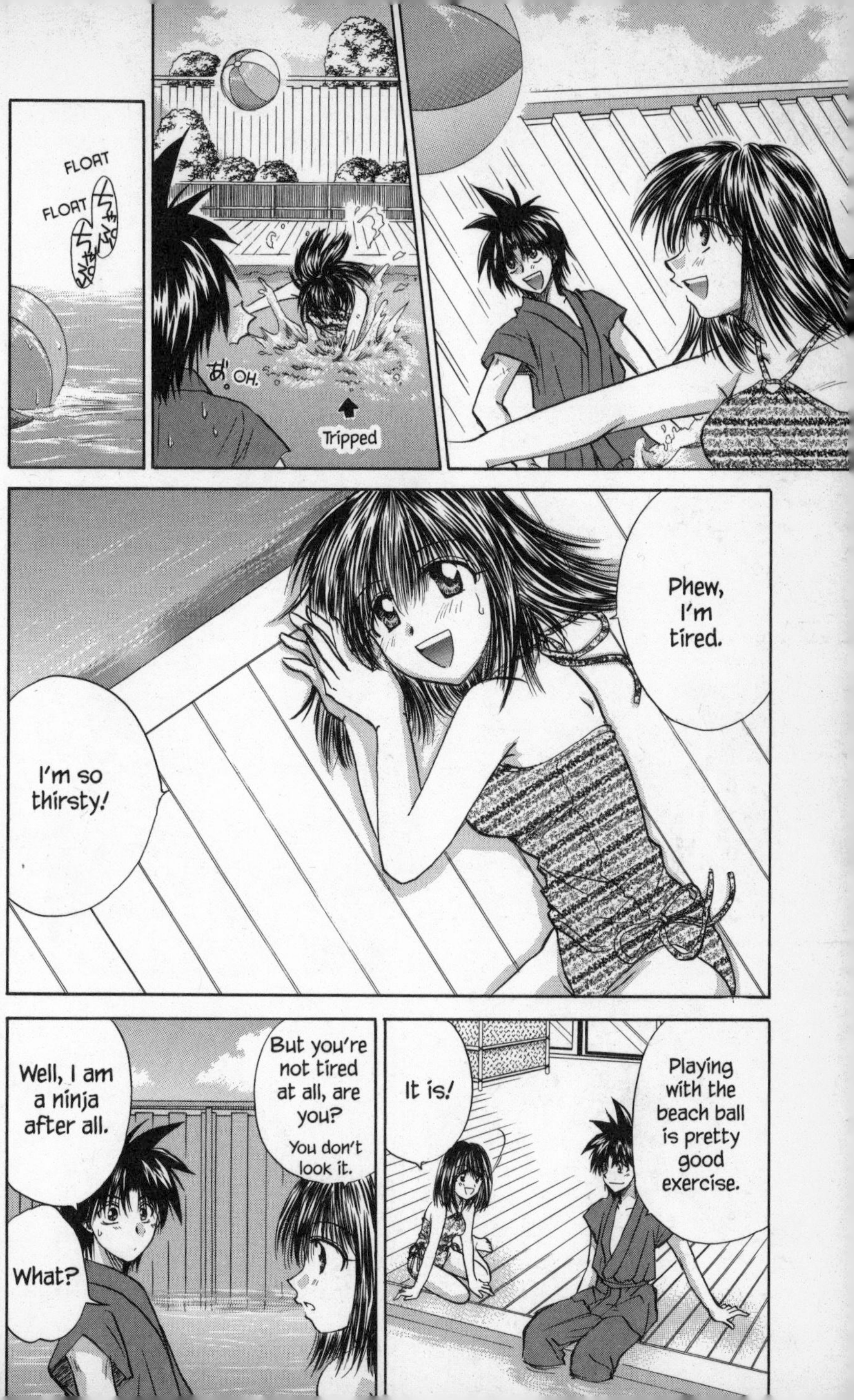

OH.
Tripped
FLOAT
FLOAT
Phew, I'm tired.
I'm so thirsty!
Playing with the beach ball is pretty good exercise.
It is!
But you're not tired at all, are you?
You don't look it.
Well, I am a ninja after all.
What?

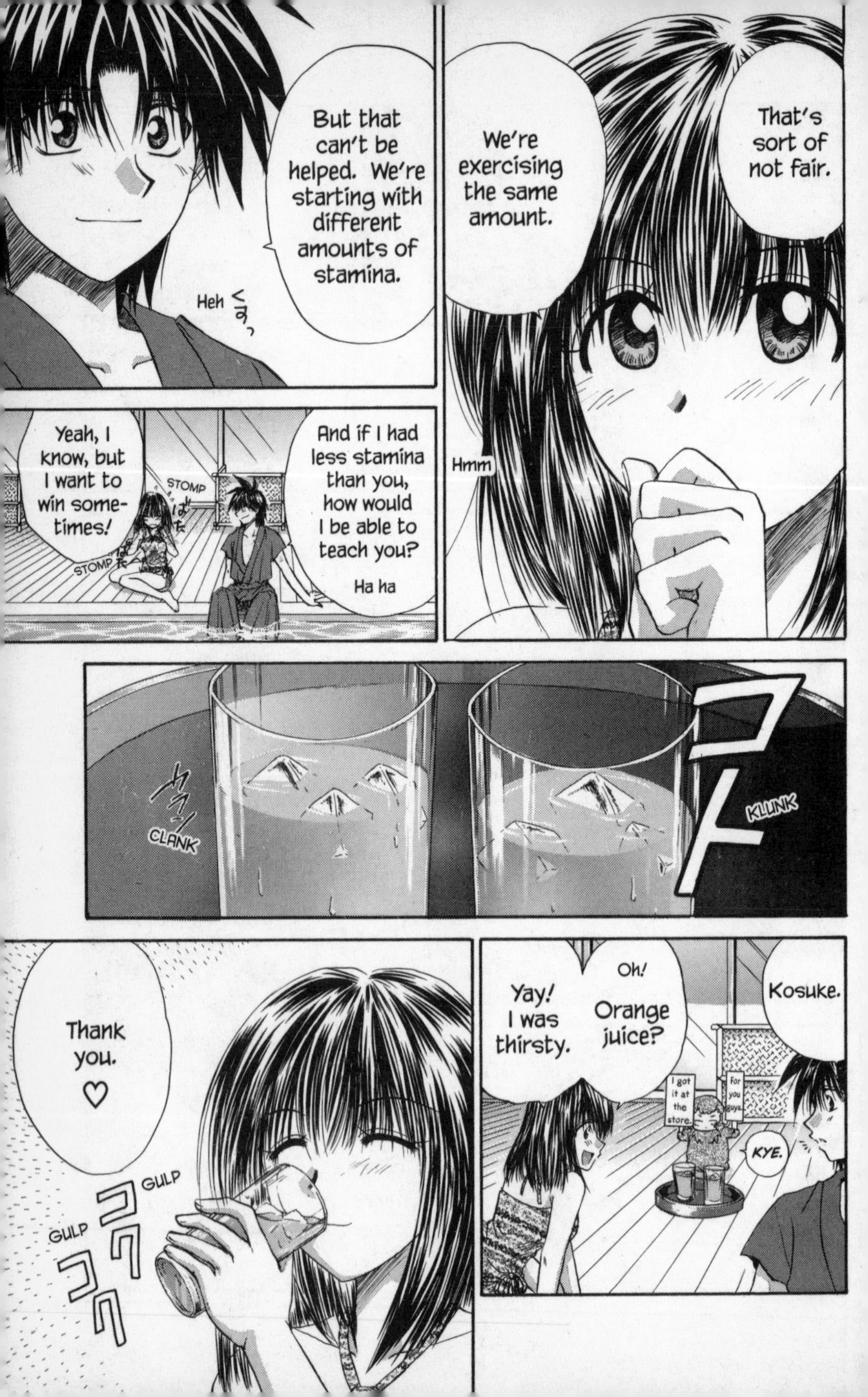
That's sort of not fair.
We're exercising the same amount.
Hmm
But that can't be helped. We're starting with different amounts of stamina.
Heh
And if I had less stamina than you, how would I be able to teach you?
Ha ha
Yeah, I know, but I want to win some-times!
STOMP
STOMP
KLUNK
CLANK
Kosuke.
For you guys.
I got it at the store.
KYE.
Oh! Orange juice?
Yay! I was thirsty.
Thank you. ♡
GULP
GULP

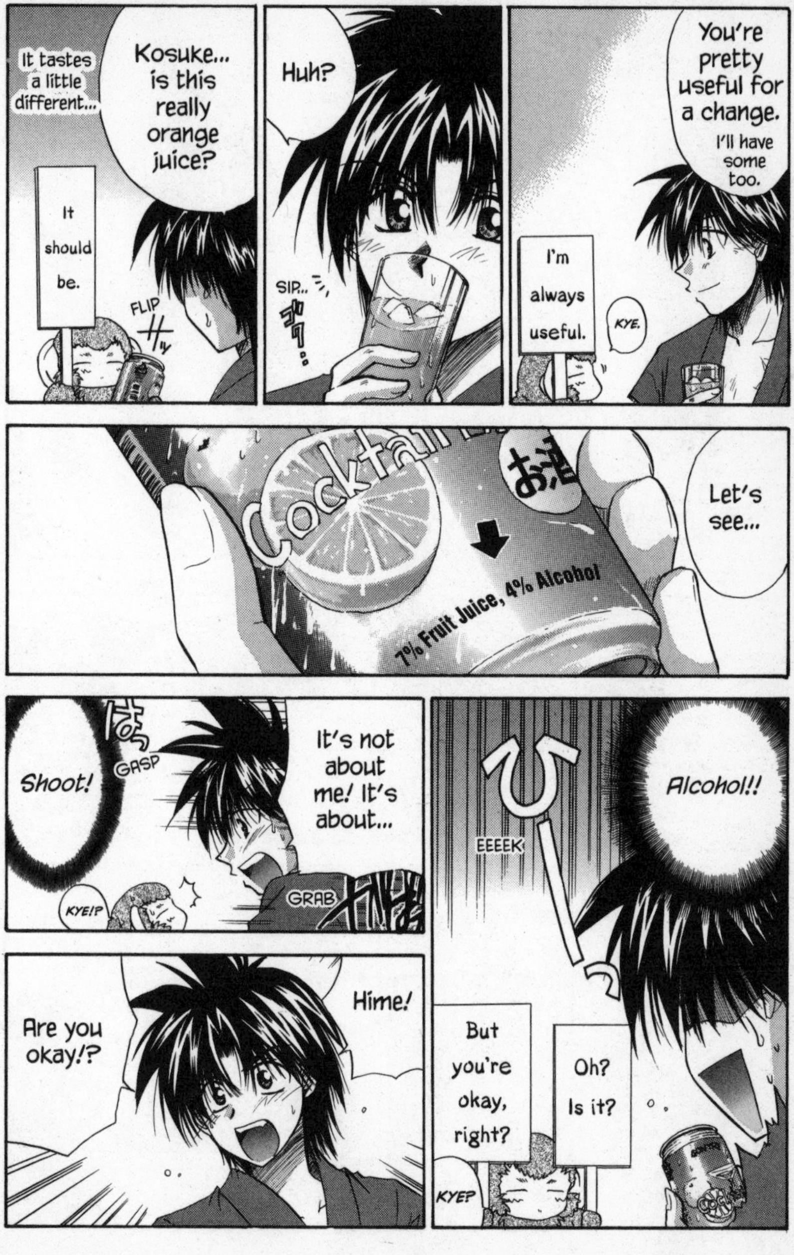
You're pretty useful for a change.
I'll have some too.
I'm always useful.
KYE.
Huh?
SIP...
Kosuke... is this really orange juice?
It tastes a little different...
It should be.
FLIP
Let's see...
Cocktail
7% Fruit Juice, 4% Alcohol
Alcohol!!
EEEK
Oh? Is it?
But you're okay, right?
KYE?
It's not about me! It's about...
Shoot!
GASP
GRAB
KYE!?
Hime!
Are you okay!?

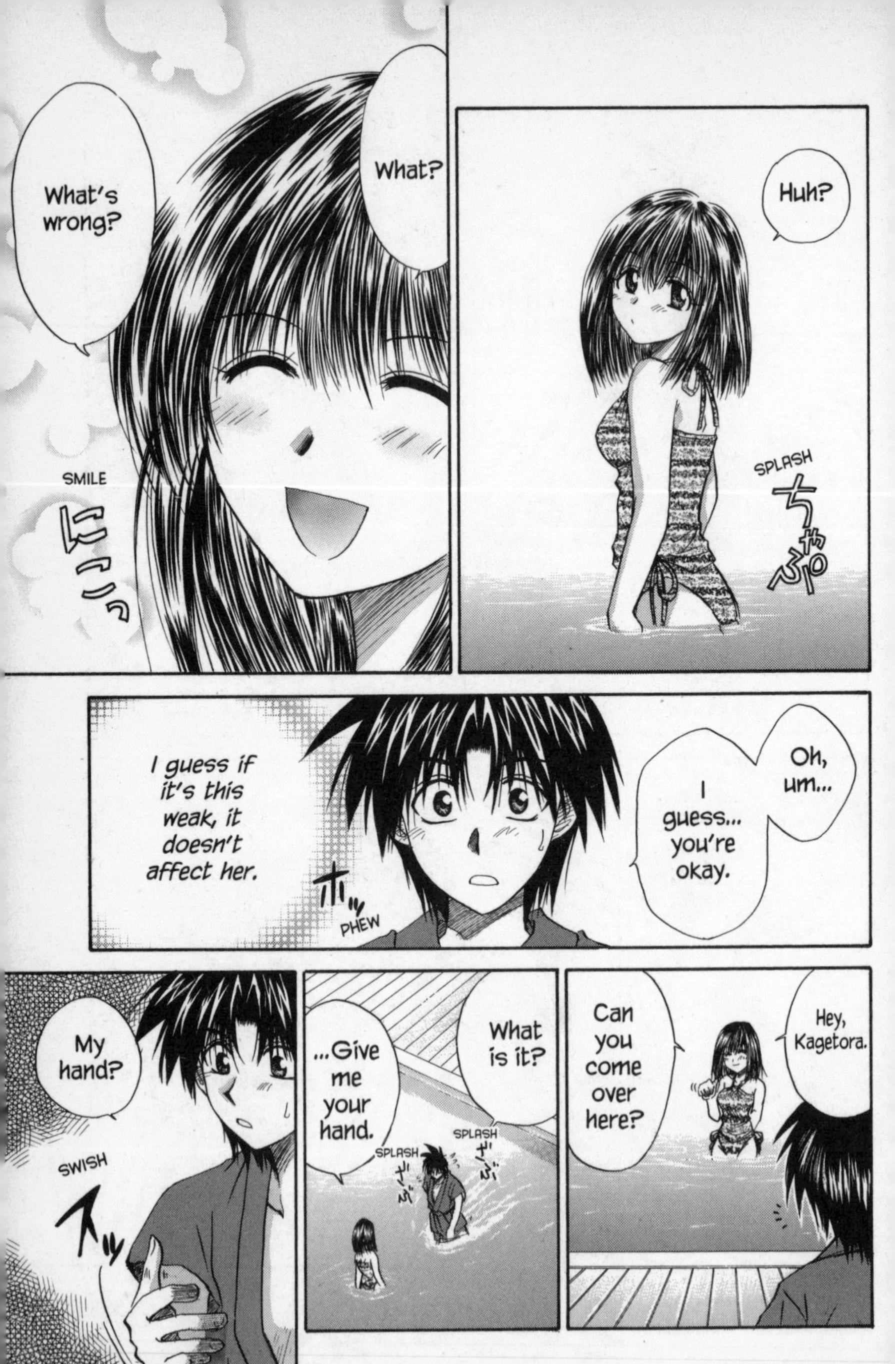
Huh?
SPLASH
ちゃぷ
What?
What's wrong?
SMILE
にこっ
Oh, um...
I guess... you're okay.
I guess if it's this weak, it doesn't affect her.
ホッ
PHEW
Hey, Kagetora.
Can you come over here?
What is it?
...Give me your hand.
SPLASH
ざぶ
SPLASH
ざぶ
My hand?
SWISH
スッ

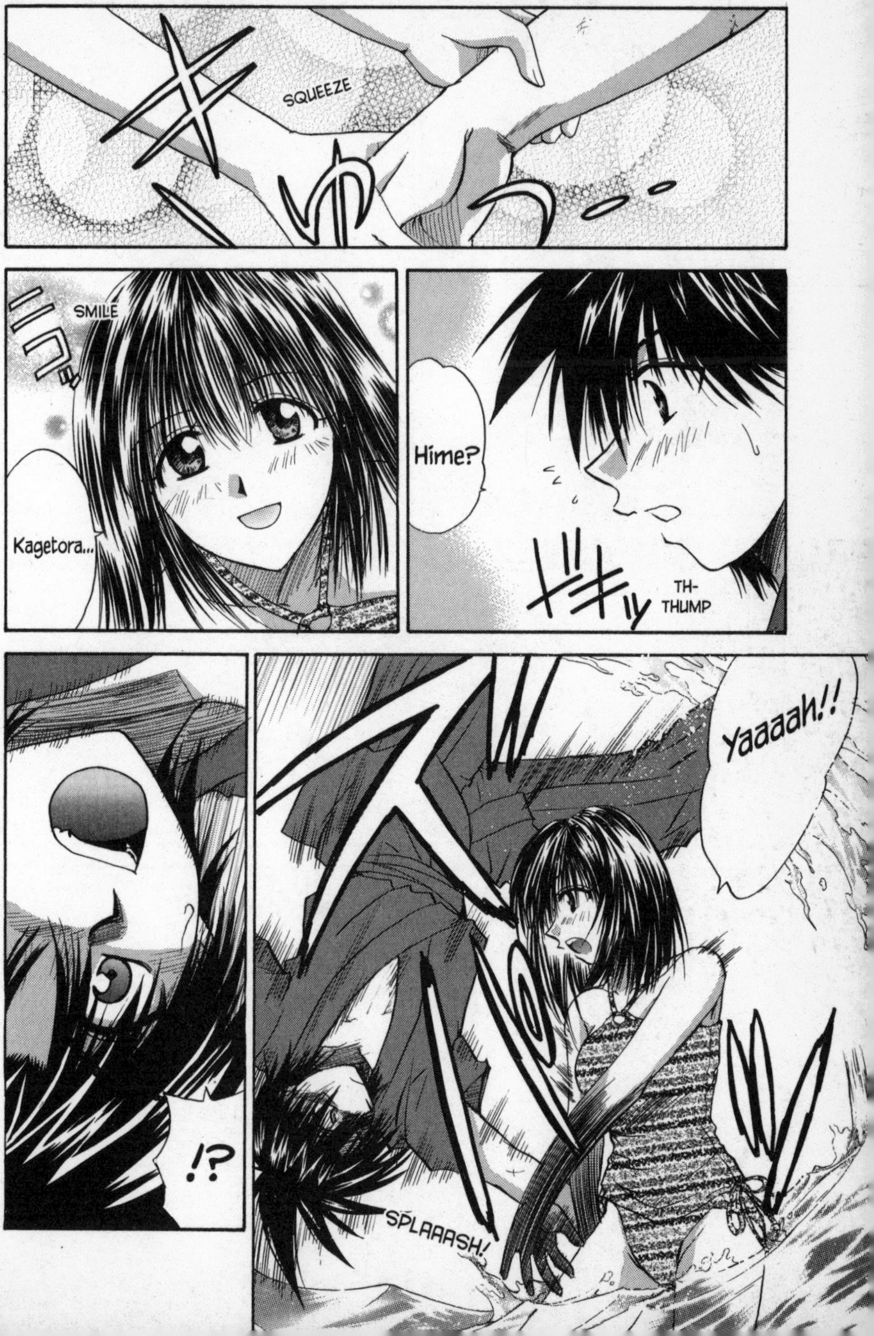
SQUEEZE
Hime?
TH-THUMP
SMILE
Kagetora...
Yaaaah!!
SPLAAASH!
!?

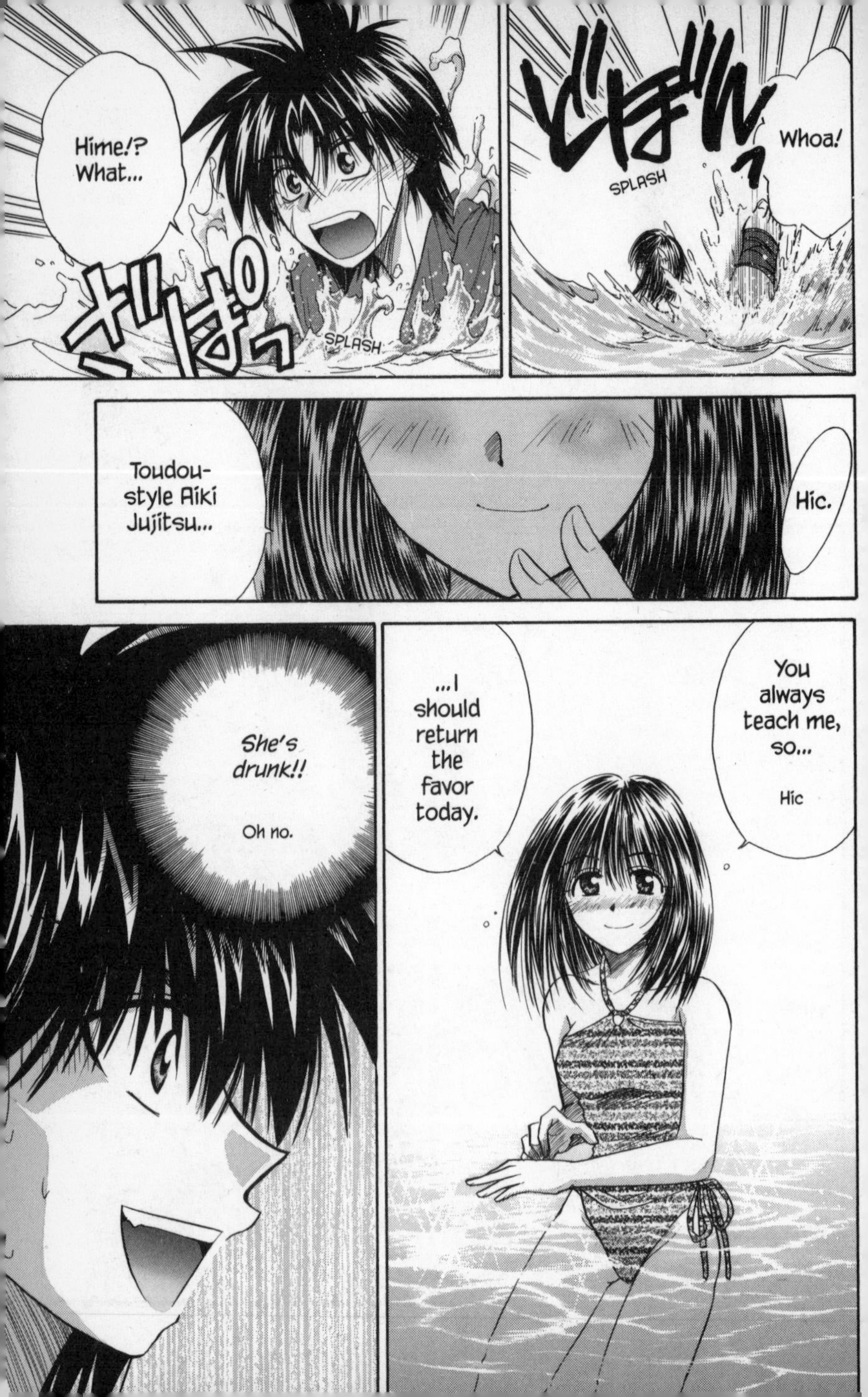

どぼんっ
SPLASH
Whoa!
ざぱっ
SPLASH
Hime!? What...
Hic.
Toudou-style Aiki Jujitsu...
You always teach me, so... Hic
...I should return the favor today.
She's drunk!! Oh no.

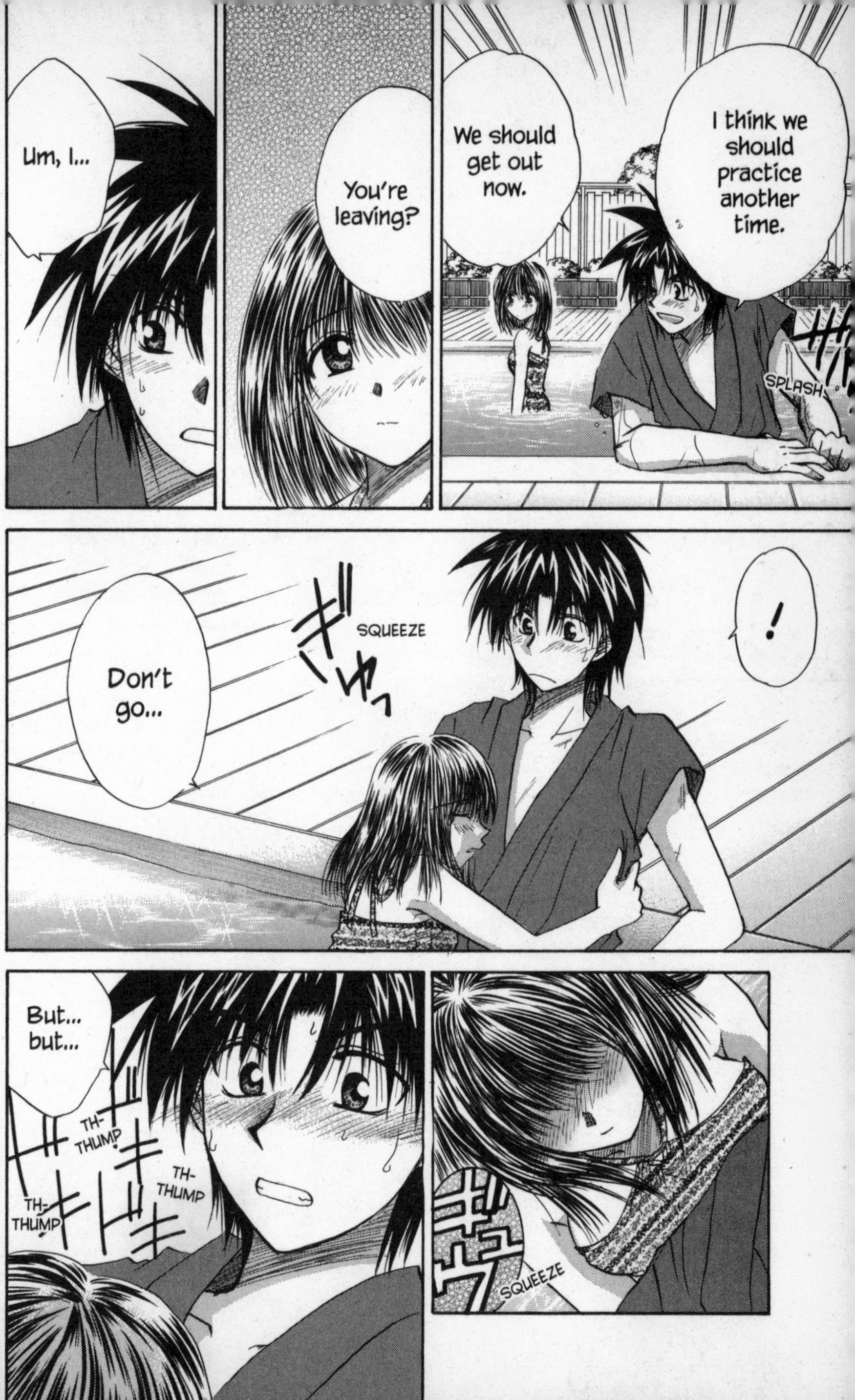
I think we should practice another time.
We should get out now.
SPLASH
You're leaving?
Um, I...
!
ぎゅっ
SQUEEZE
Don't go...
SQUEEZE
But... but...
TH-THUMP
TH-THUMP
TH-THUMP

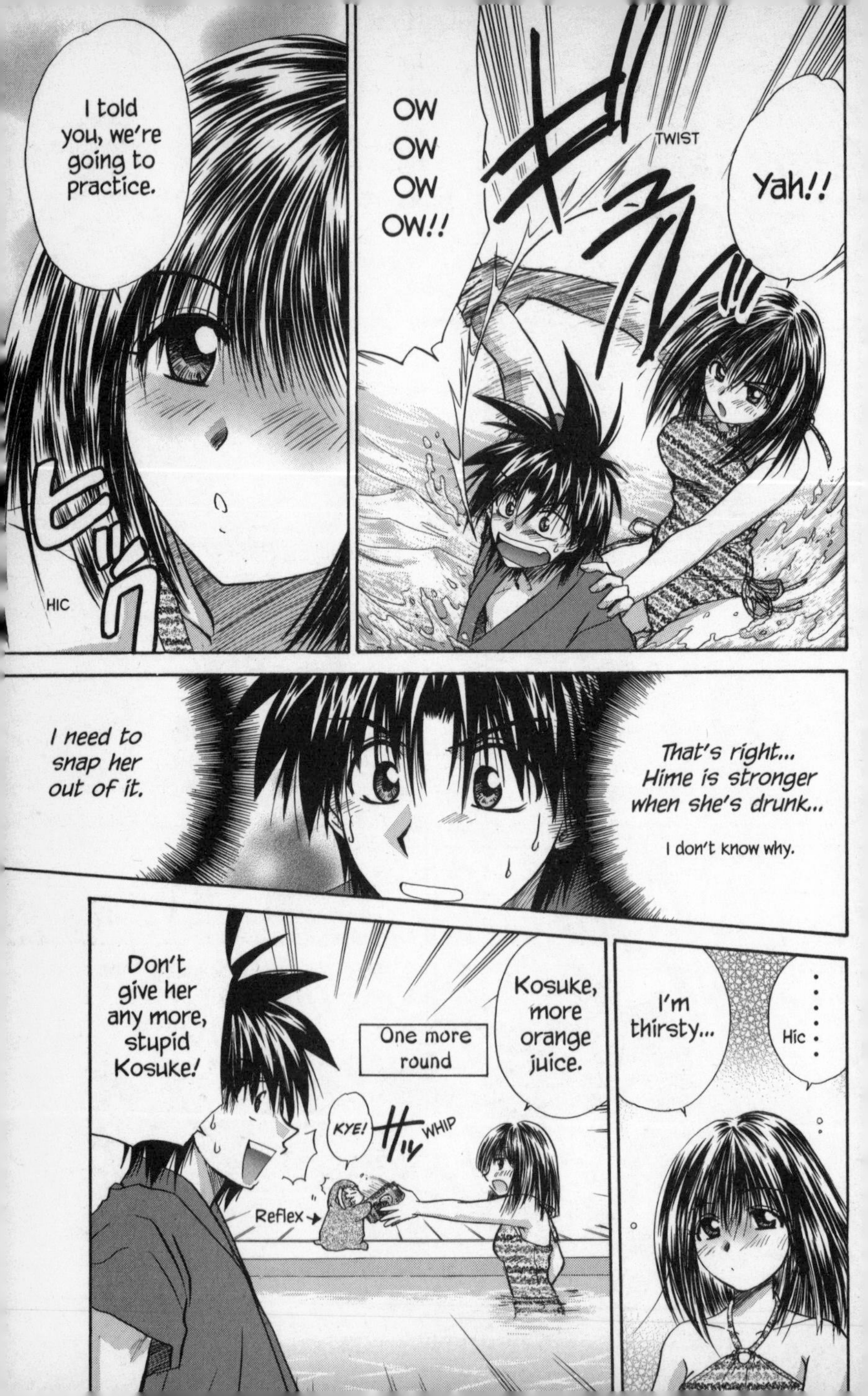
Yah!!
TWIST
OW OW OW OW!!
I told you, we're going to practice.
HIC
That's right... Hime is stronger when she's drunk...
I don't know why.
I need to snap her out of it.
...Hic...
I'm thirsty...
Kosuke, more orange juice.
One more round
Don't give her any more, stupid Kosuke!
WHIP
KYE!
Reflex

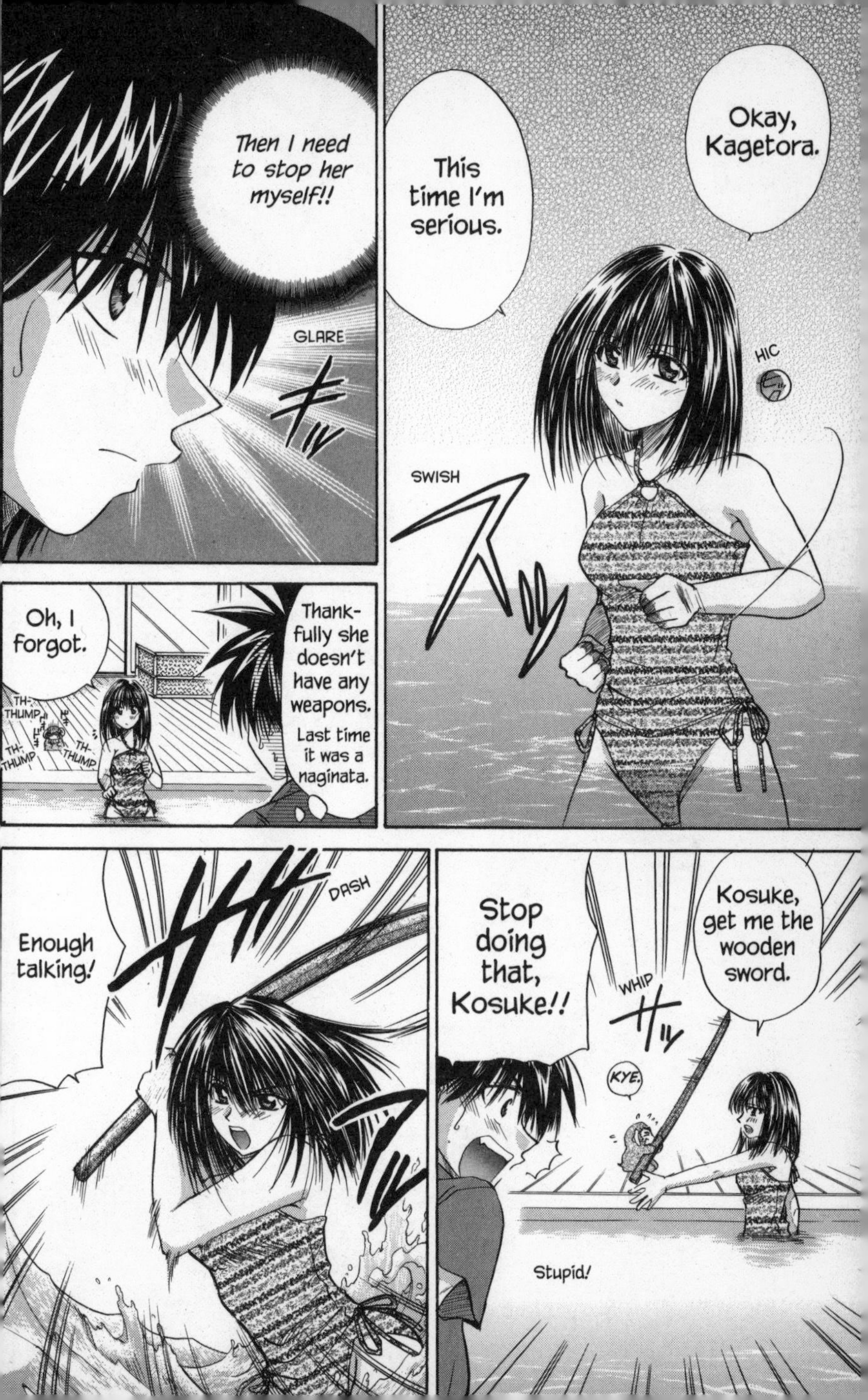

Okay, Kagetora.
This time I'm serious.
HIC
SWISH
Then I need to stop her myself!!
GLARE
Thankfully she doesn't have any weapons.
Last time it was a naginata.
Oh, I forgot.
TH-THUMP
TH-THUMP
TH-THUMP
Kosuke, get me the wooden sword.
Stop doing that, Kosuke!!
WHIP
KYE.
Stupid!
DASH
Enough talking!

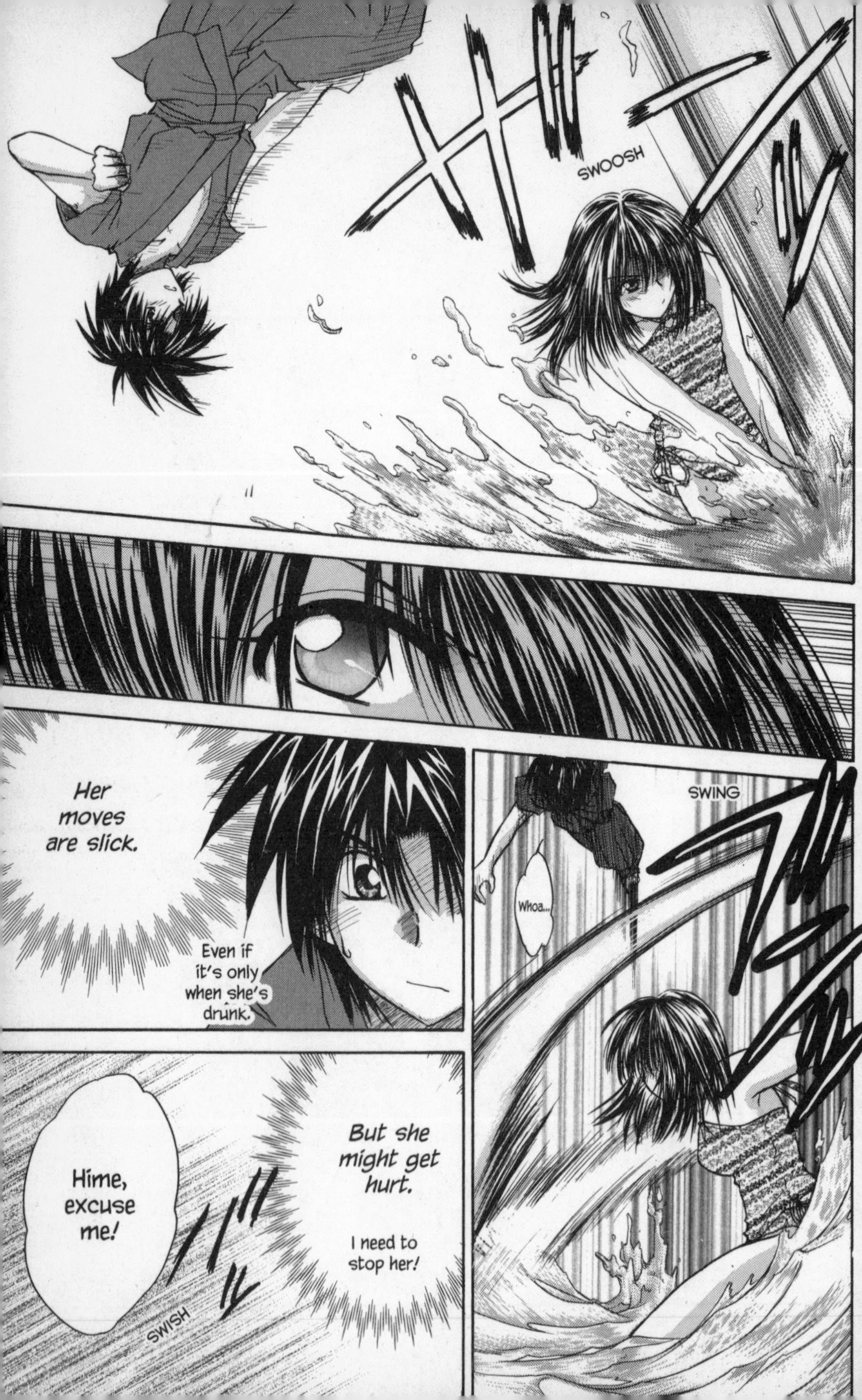
SWOOSH
SWING
Whoa...
Her moves are slick.
Even if it's only when she's drunk.
But she might get hurt.
I need to stop her!
Hime, excuse me!
SWISH

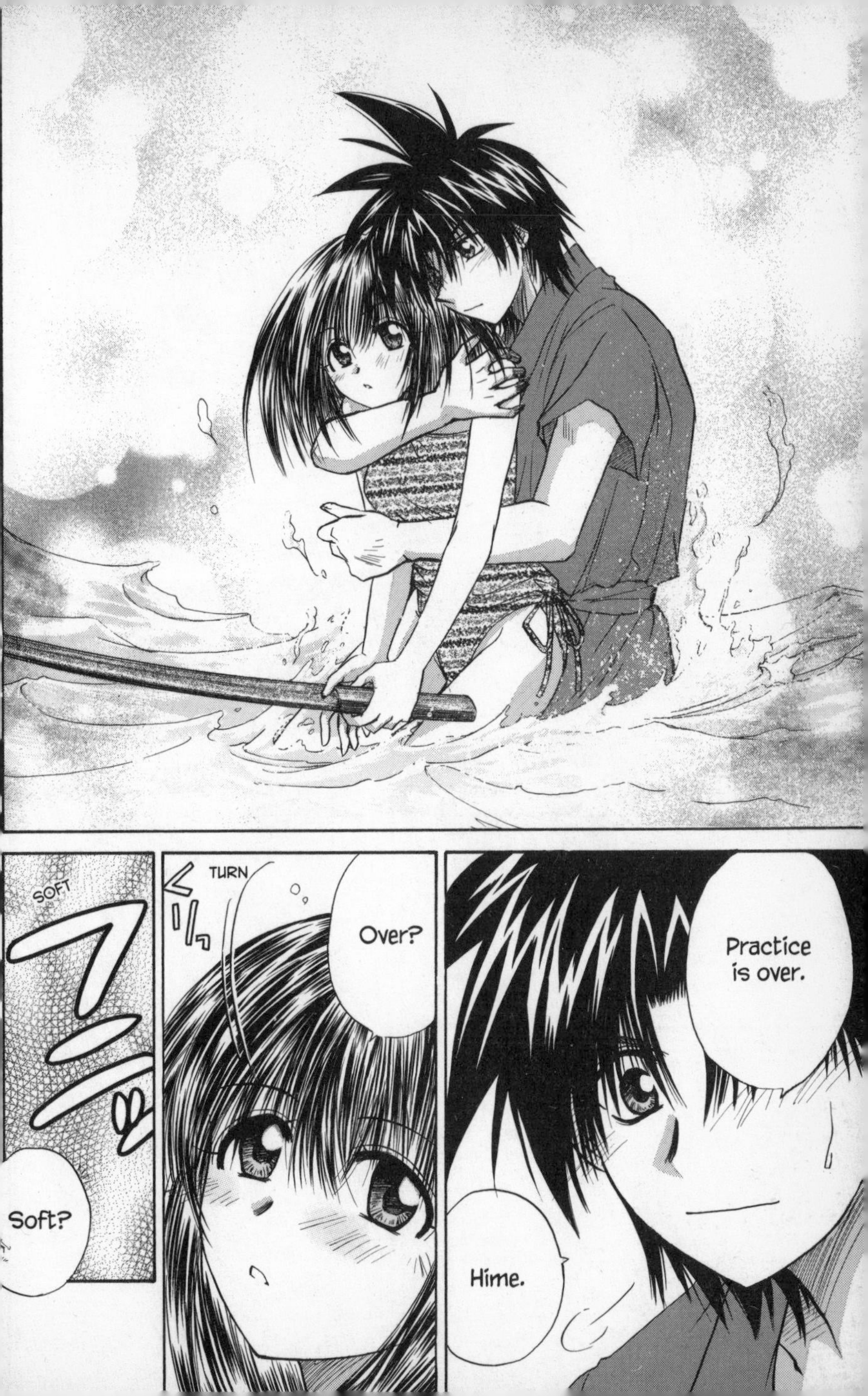
Practice is over.
Hime.
Over?
TURN
SOFT
Soft?

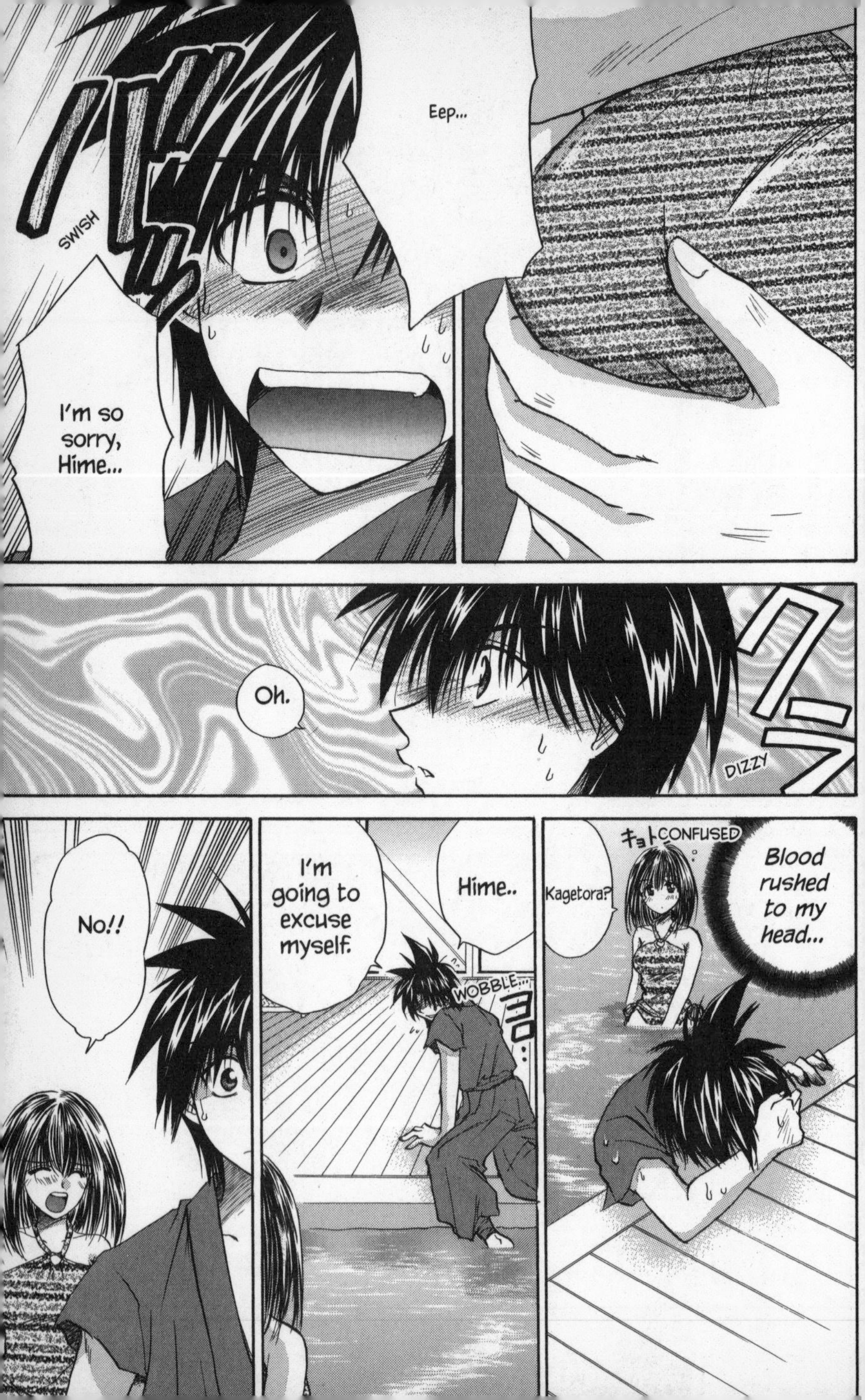
Eep...
SWISH
I'm so sorry, Hime...
DIZZY
Oh.
キョト CONFUSED
Blood rushed to my head...
Kagetora?
Hime..
I'm going to excuse myself.
WOBBLE...
ヨロ...
No!!

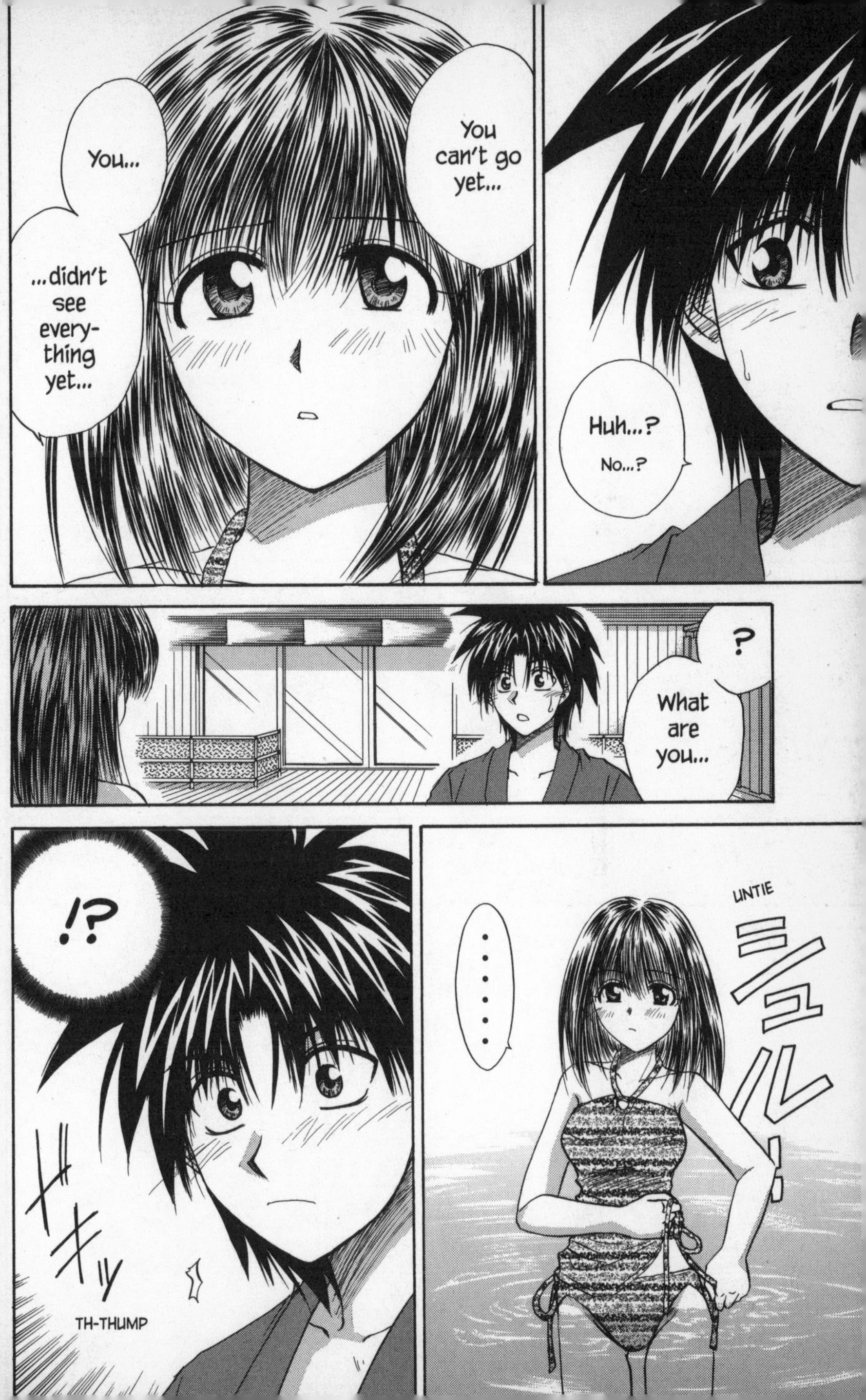
Huh...?
No...?
You can't go yet...
You...
...didn't see every-thing yet...
?
What are you...
UNTIE
......
!?
TH-THUMP

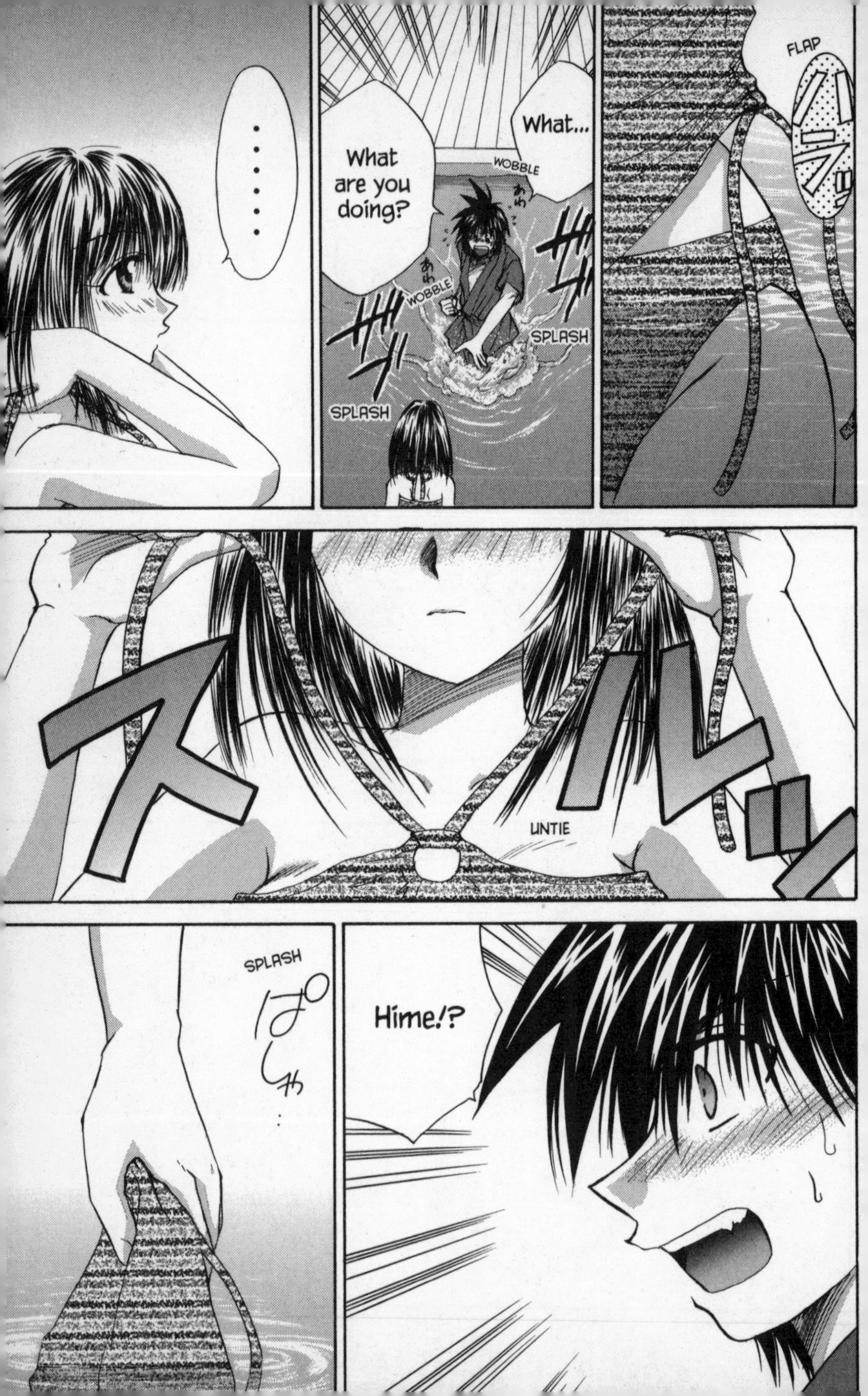
FLAP
What...
What are you doing?
WOBBLE
WOBBLE
SPLASH
SPLASH
. . . . . .
UNTIE
Hime!?
SPLASH

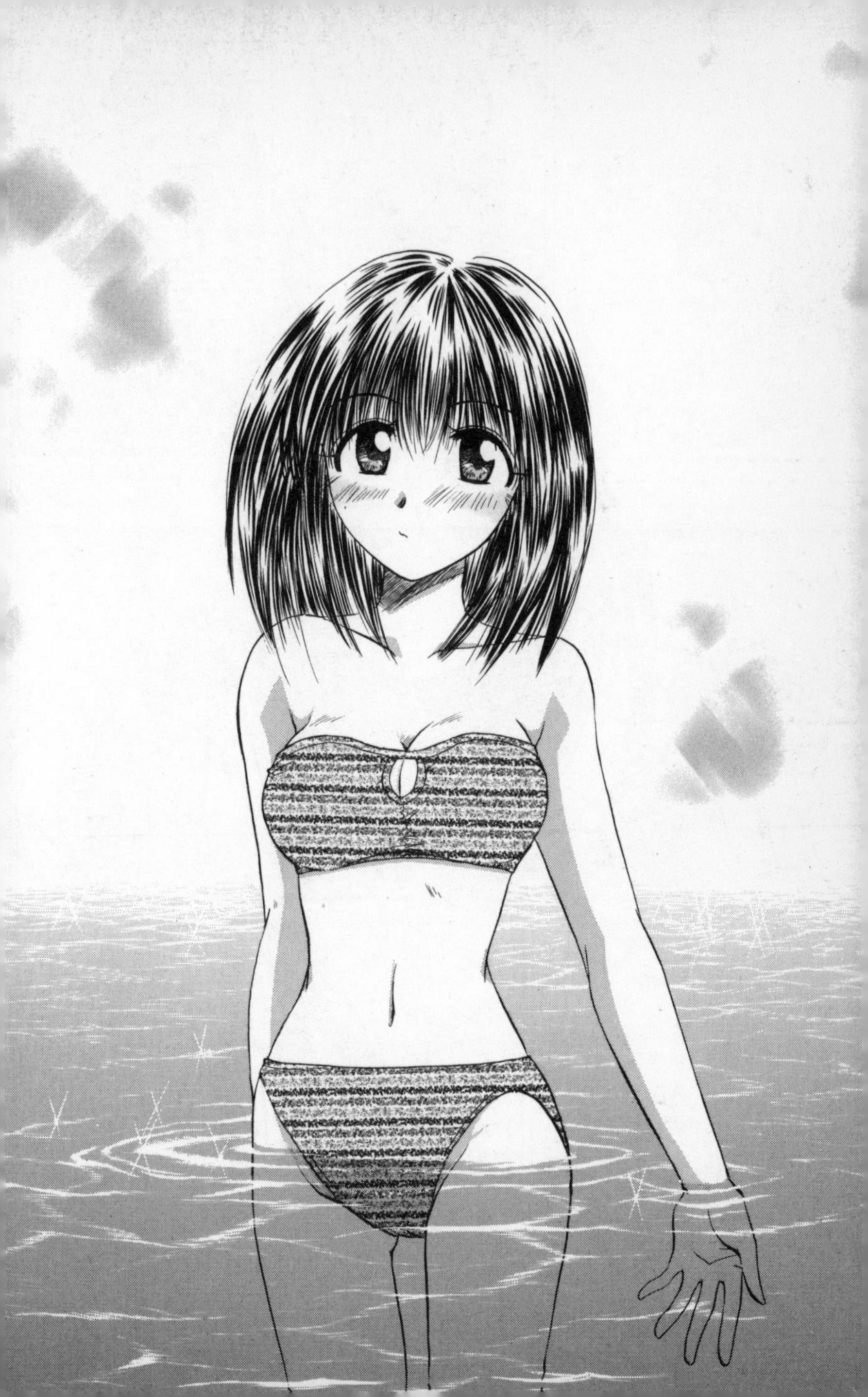

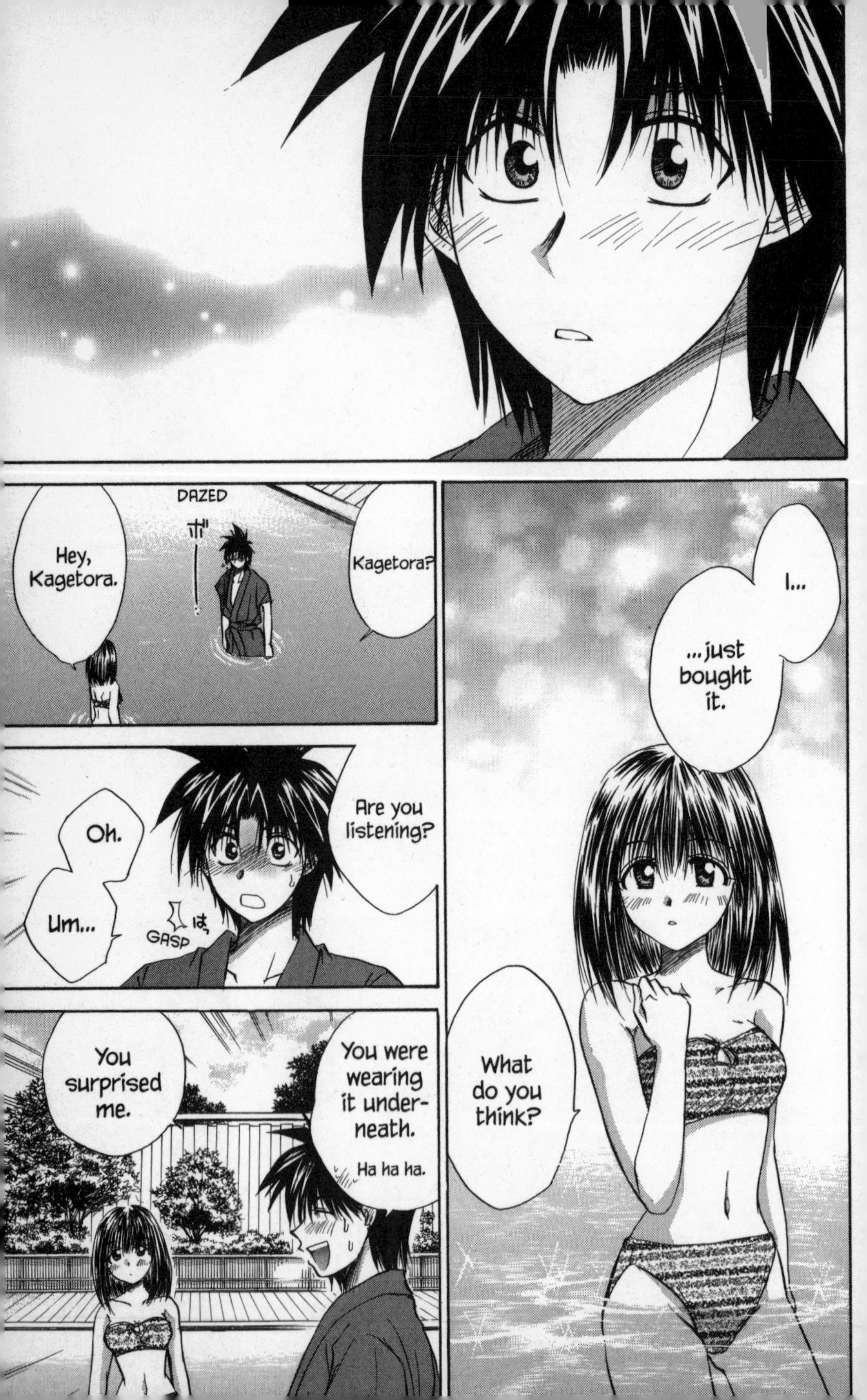

I...
...just bought it.
What do you think?
Kagetora?
DAZED
ボー
Hey, Kagetora.
Are you listening?
Oh.
は、
GASP
Um...
You were wearing it underneath.
Ha ha ha.
You surprised me.

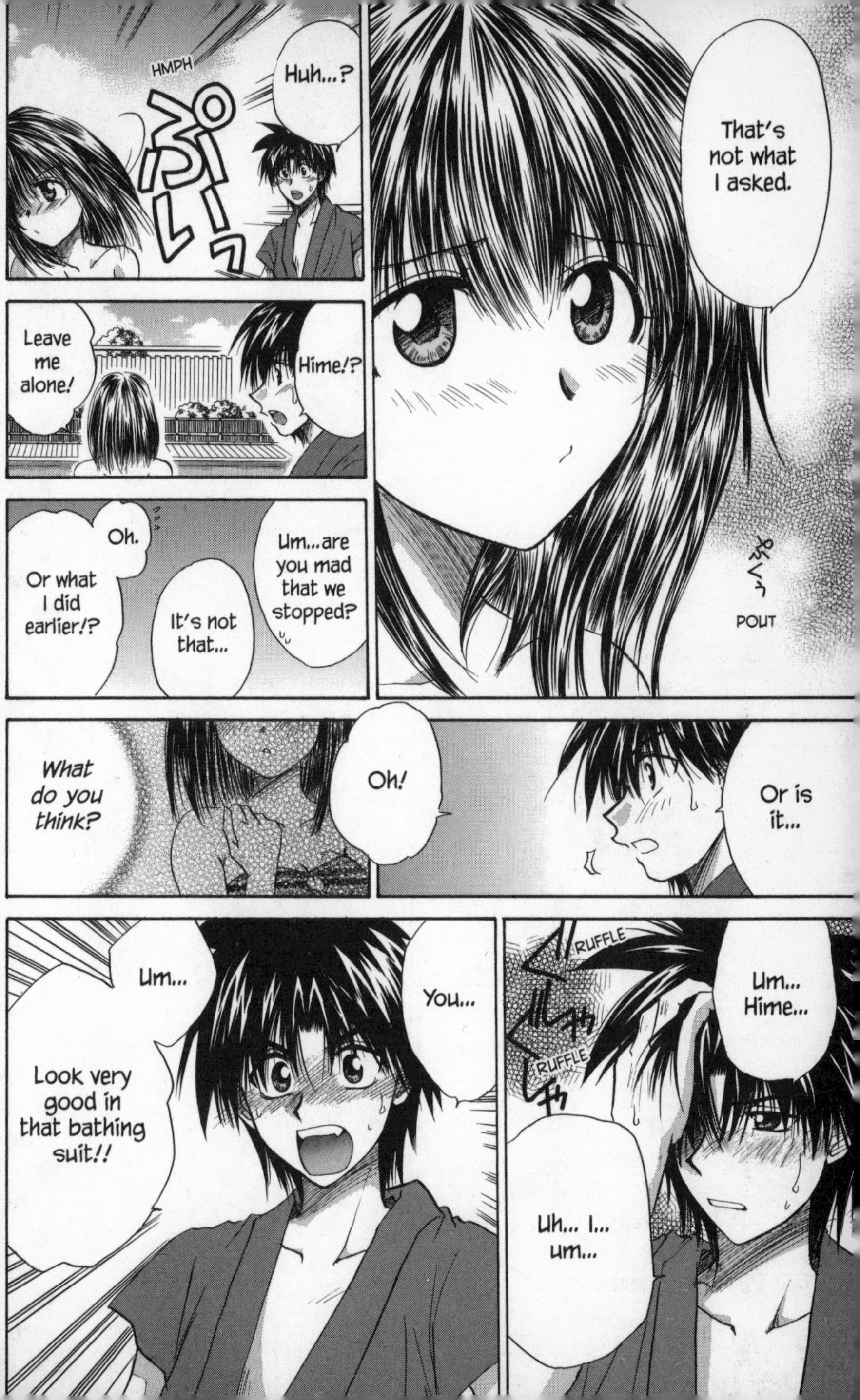
That's not what I asked.
POUT
HMPH
Huh...?
Hime!?
Leave me alone!
Um...are you mad that we stopped?
It's not that...
Oh.
Or what I did earlier!?
Or is it...
Oh!
What do you think?
Um... Hime...
RUFFLE
RUFFLE
Uh... I... um...
You...
Um...
Look very good in that bathing suit!!

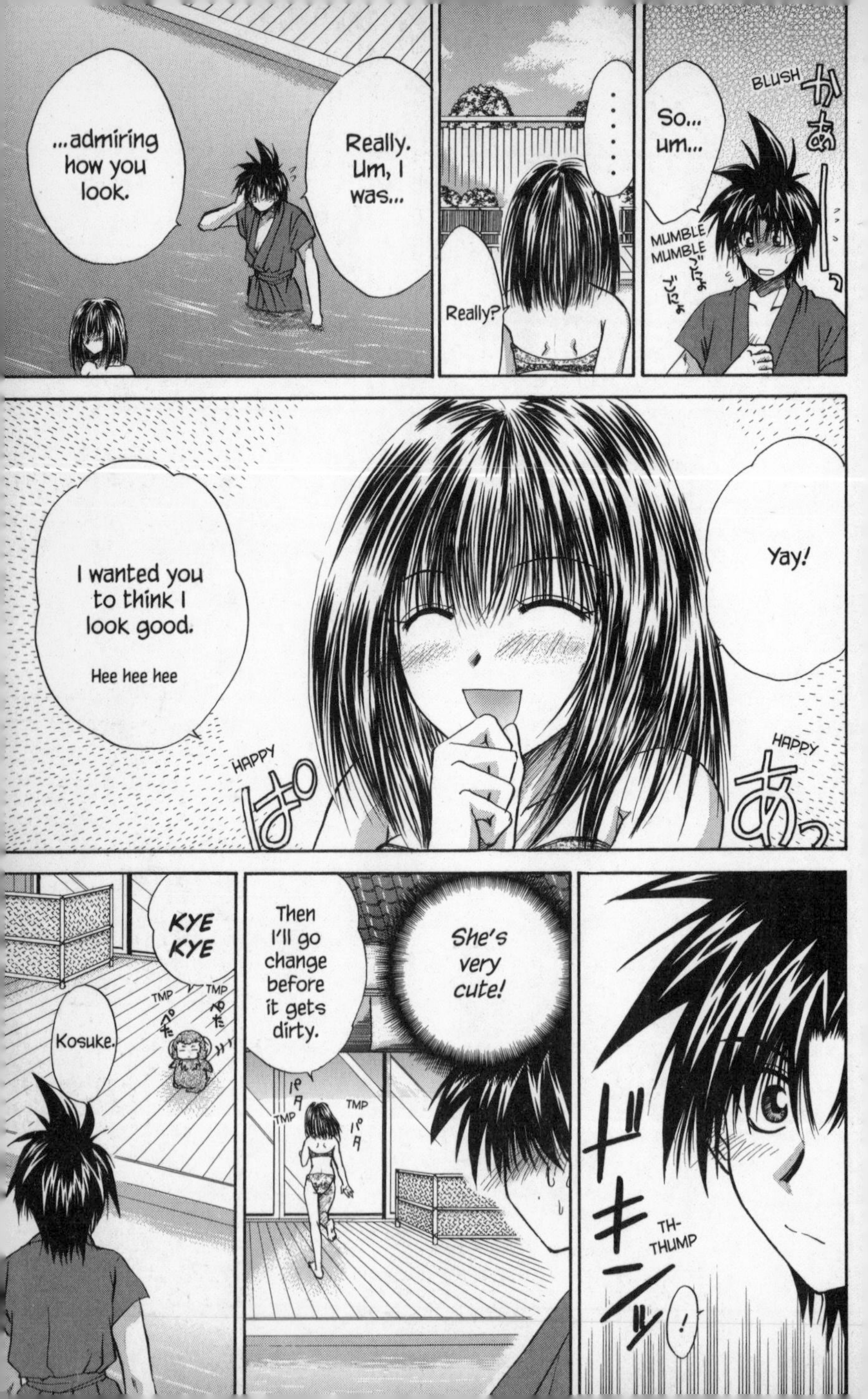
BLUSH
So... um...
MUMBLE MUMBLE
......
Really?
Really. Um, I was...
...admiring how you look.
Yay!
HAPPY
I wanted you to think I look good.
Hee hee hee
HAPPY
TH-THUMP
!
She's very cute!
Then I'll go change before it gets dirty.
TMP
TMP
KYE KYE
TMP
TMP
Kosuke.

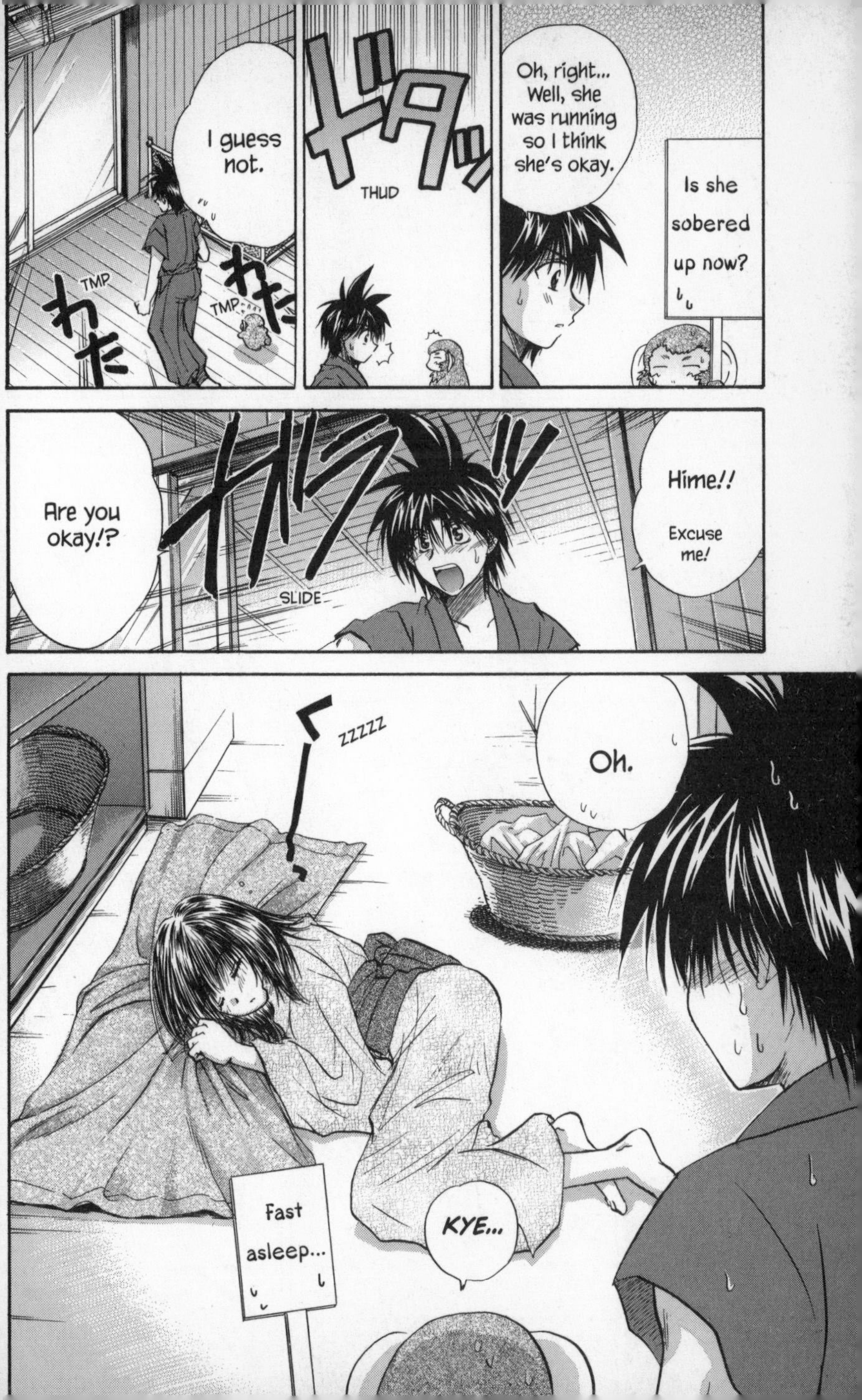
Is she sobered up now?
Oh, right... Well, she was running so I think she's okay.
ドタッ
THUD
I guess not.
わたわた
TMP
TMP
Hime!!
Excuse me!
ガラッ
SLIDE
Are you okay!?
Oh.
ZZZZZ
KYE...
Fast asleep...

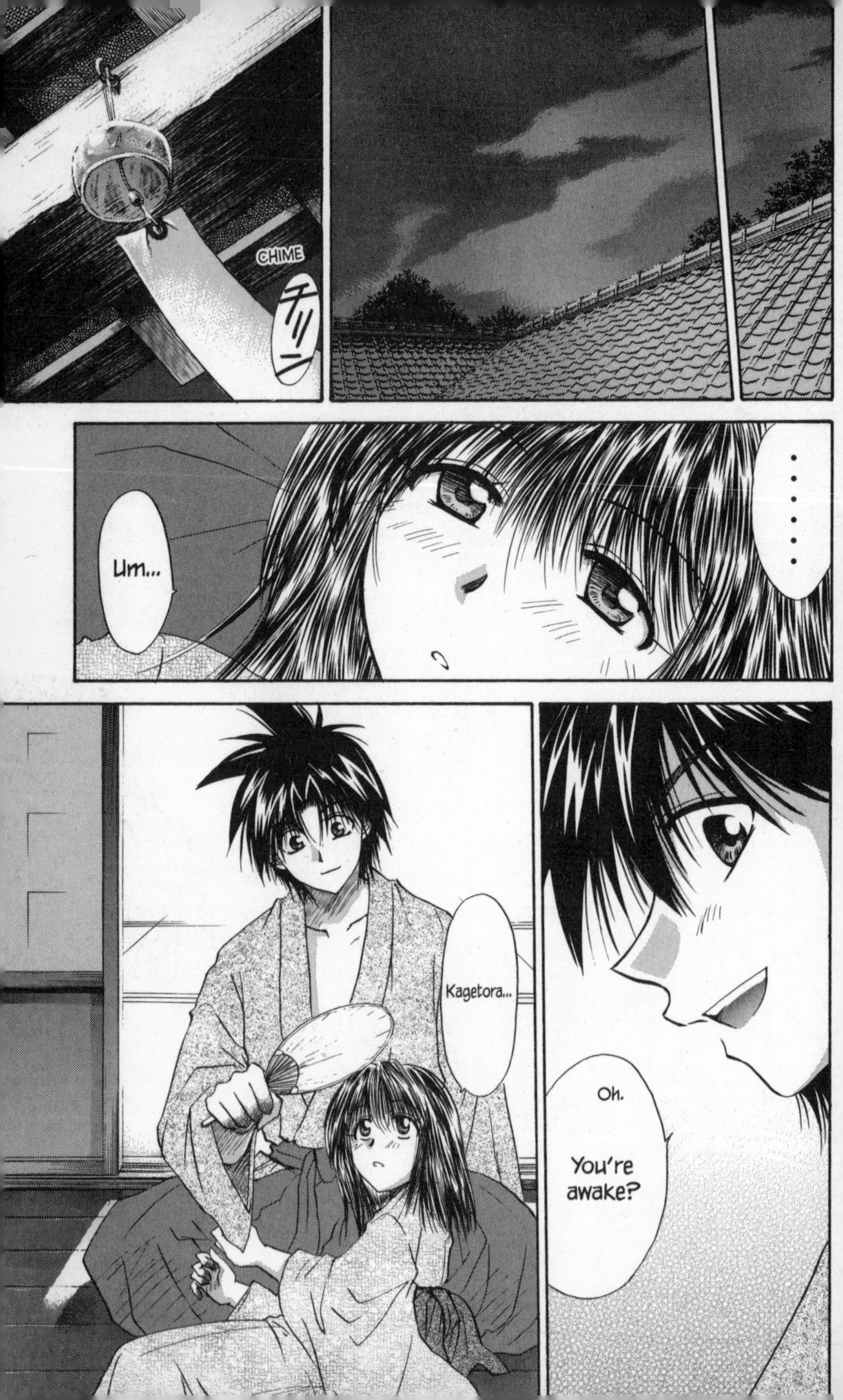
CHIME
チリーン
......
Um...
Oh. You're awake?
Kagetora...

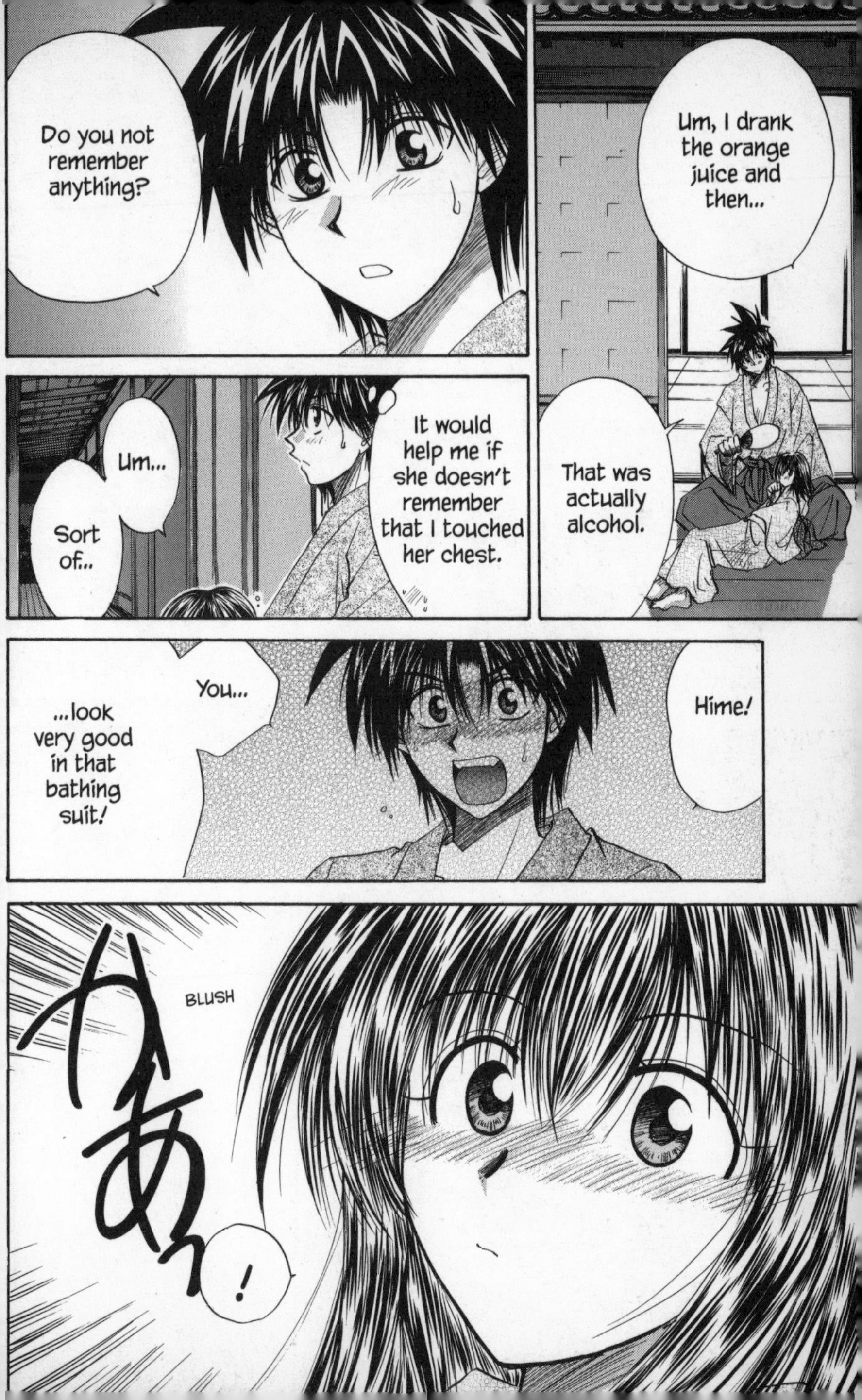

Um, I drank the orange juice and then...
That was actually alcohol.
Do you not remember anything?
It would help me if she doesn't remember that I touched her chest.
Um...
Sort of...
Hime!
You...
...look very good in that bathing suit!
BLUSH
!

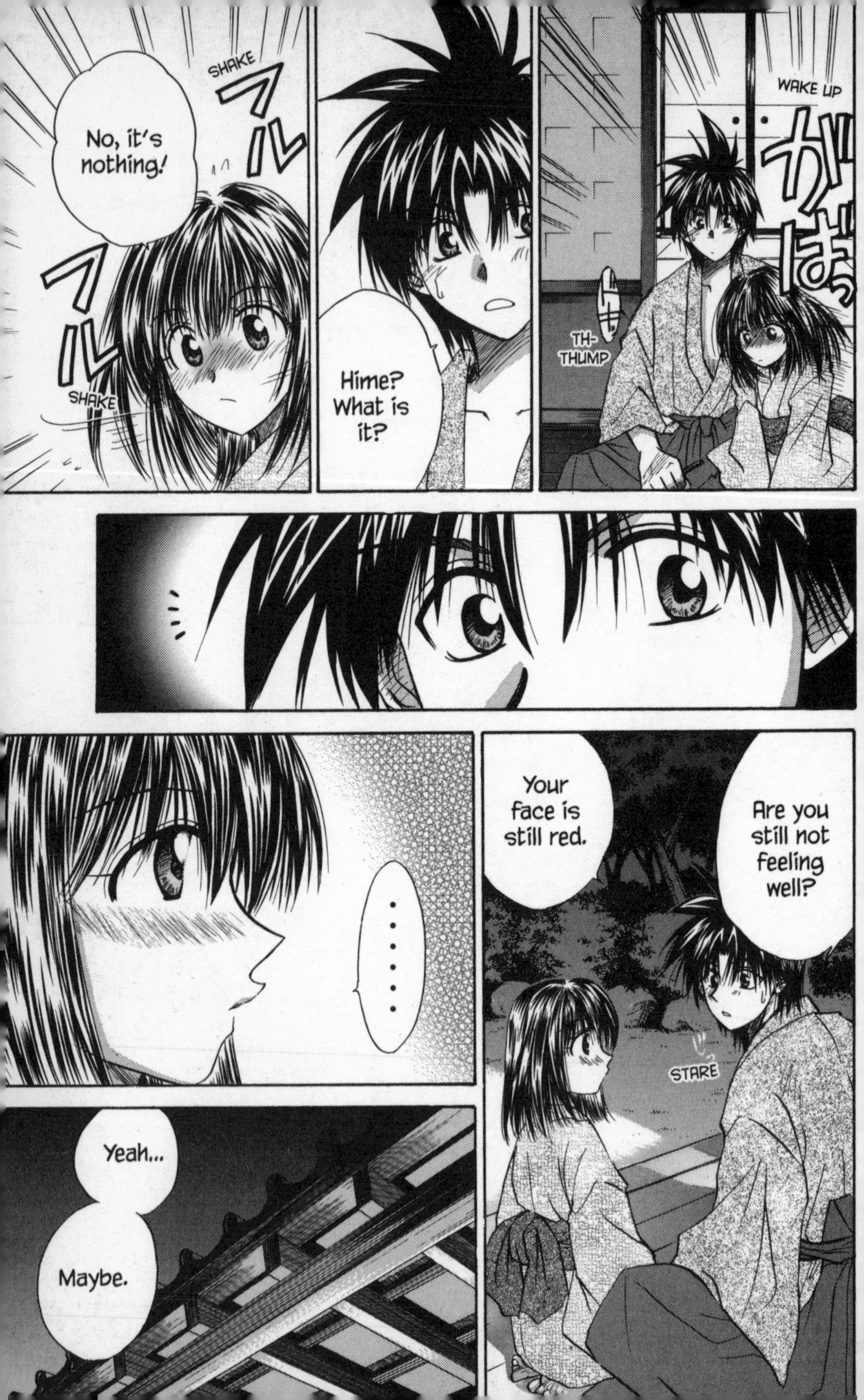
WAKE UP
TH-THUMP
Hime? What is it?
SHAKE
No, it's nothing!
SHAKE
Are you still not feeling well?
Your face is still red.
STARE
......
Yeah...
Maybe.

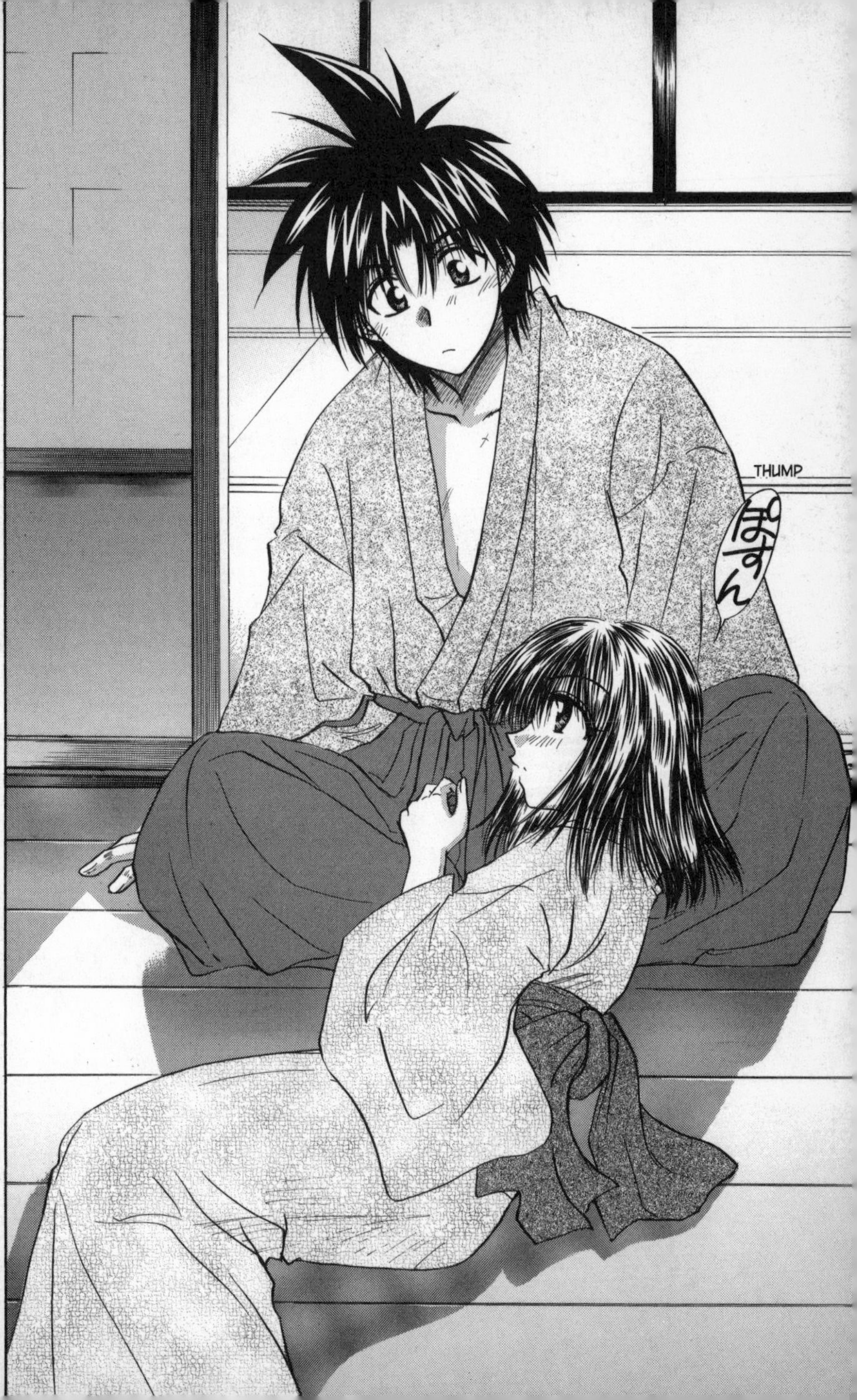
THUMP
ぽすん

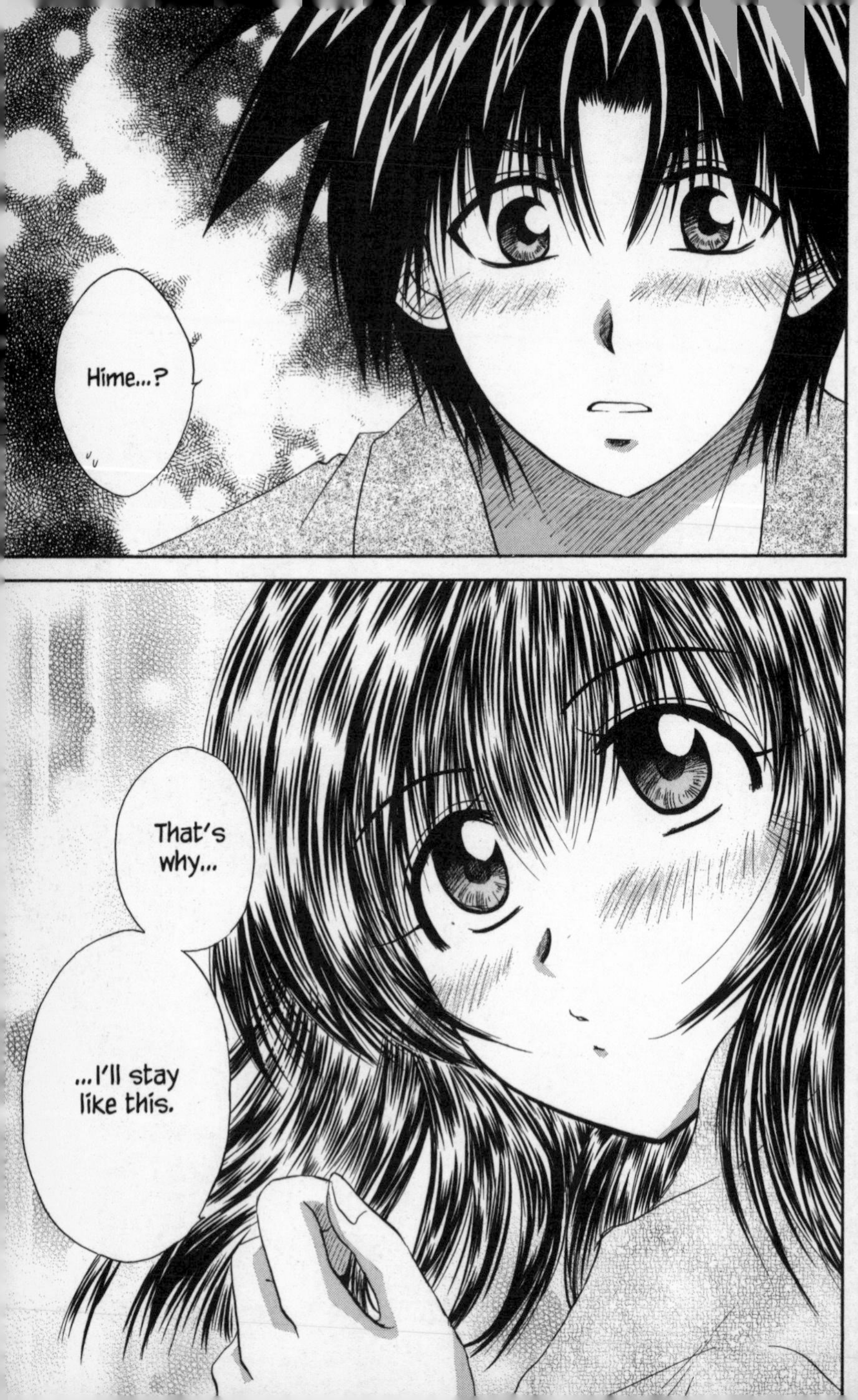
Hime...?
That's why...
...I'll stay like this.

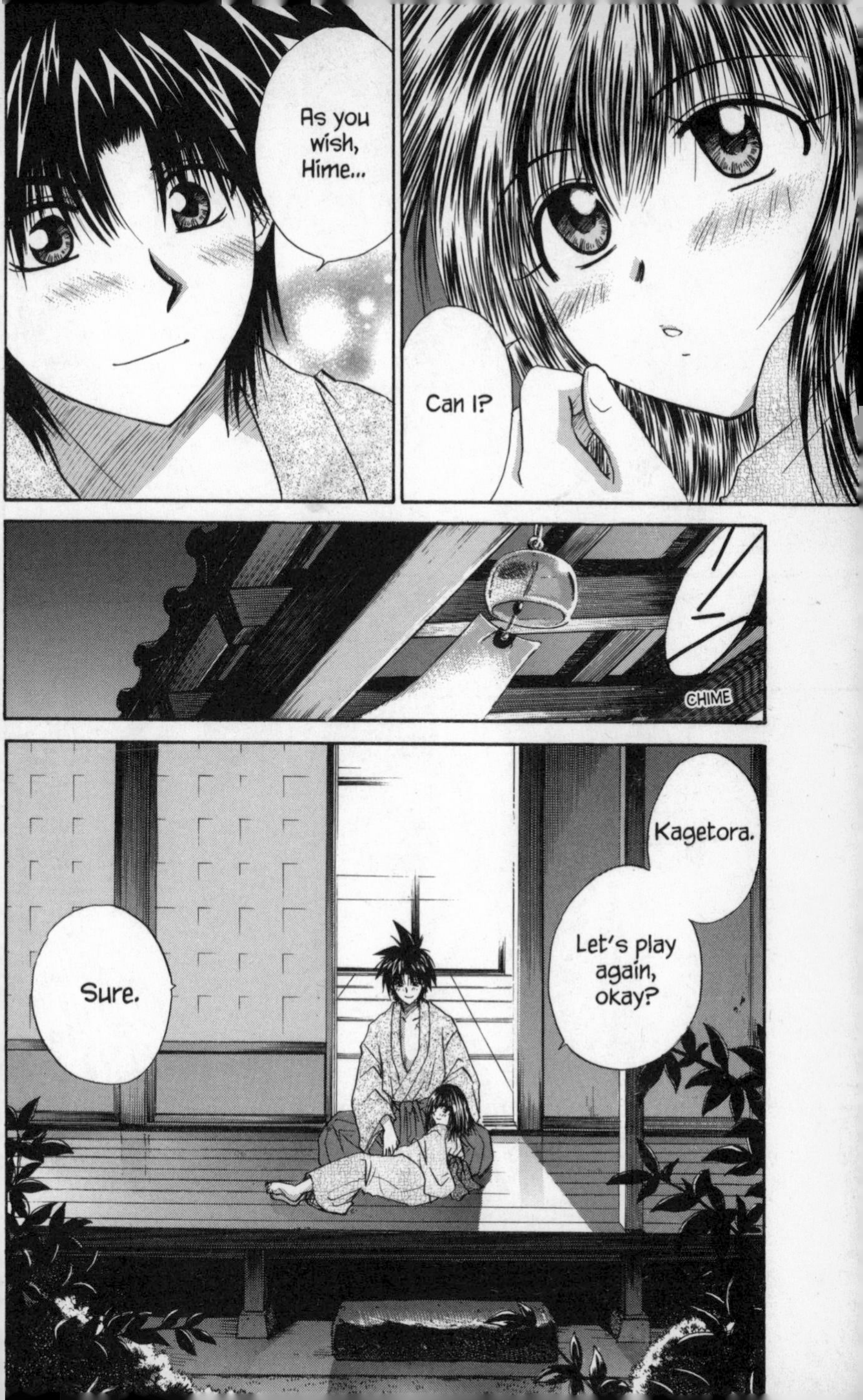
Can I?
As you wish, Hime...
CHIME
Kagetora.
Let's play again, okay?
Sure.

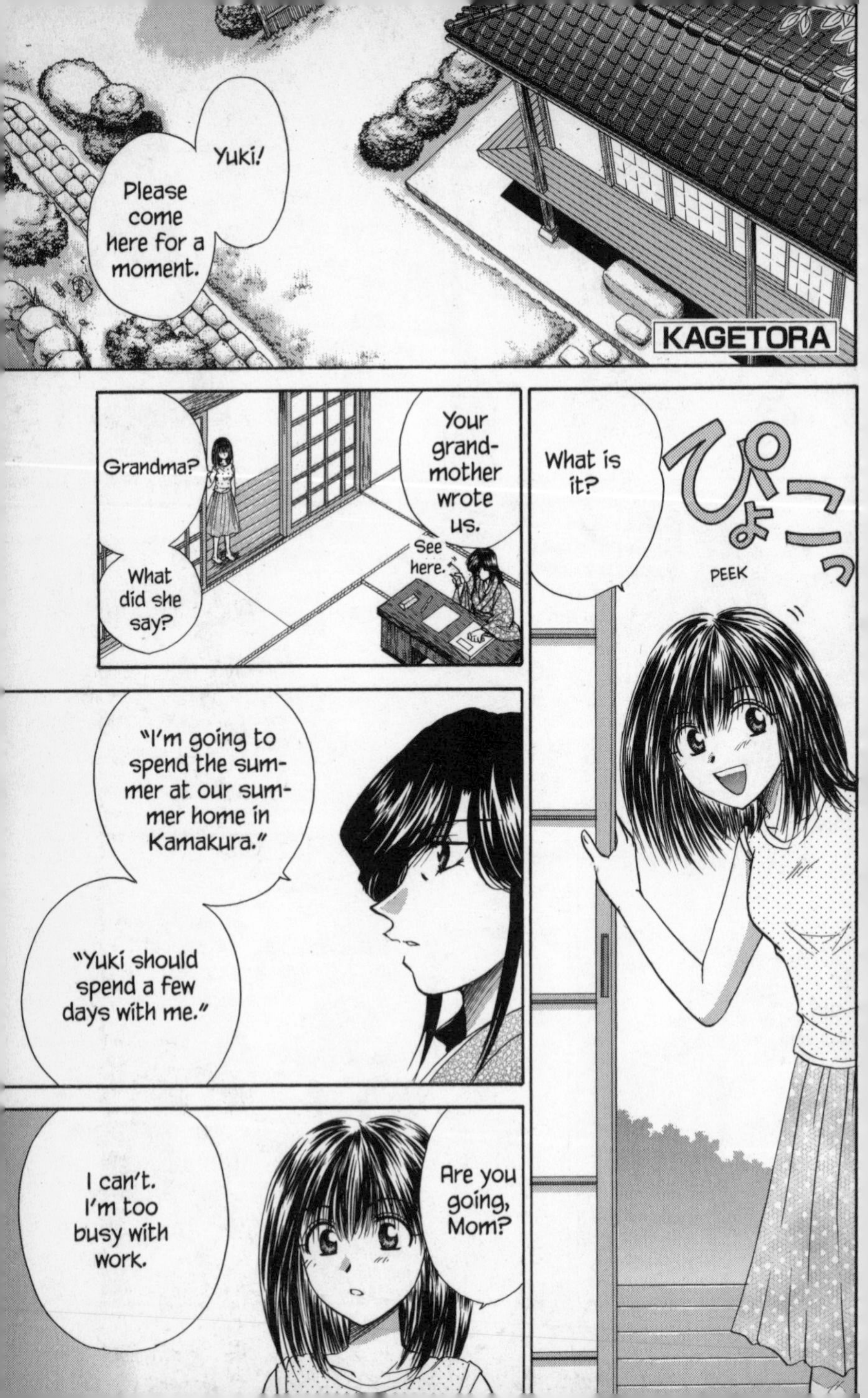
Yuki!
Please come here for a moment.
KAGETORA
What is it?
ぴょこっ
PEEK
Your grandmother wrote us.
See here.
Grandma?
What did she say?
"I'm going to spend the summer at our summer home in Kamakura."
"Yuki should spend a few days with me."
Are you going, Mom?
I can't. I'm too busy with work.

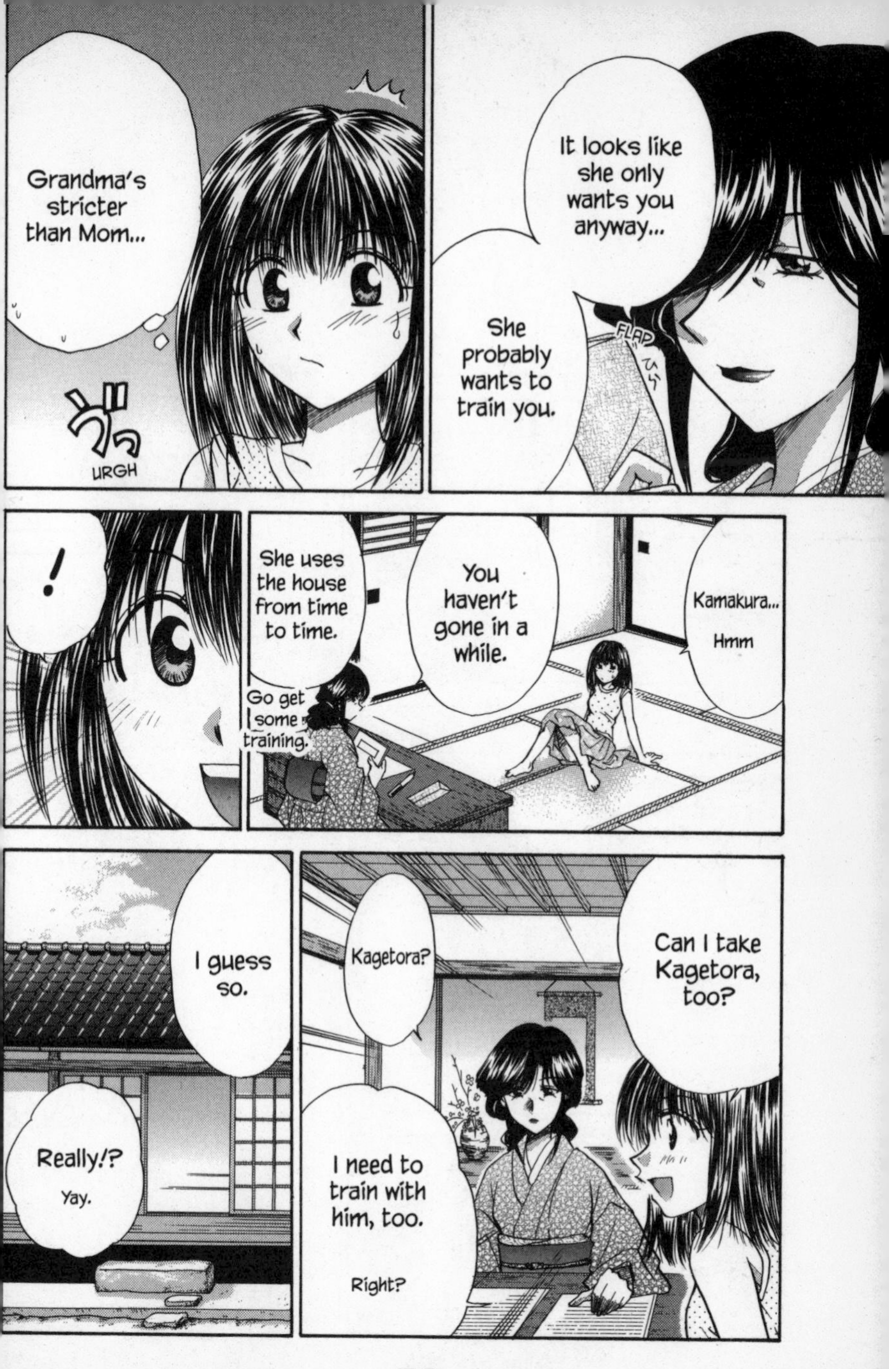
It looks like she only wants you anyway...
She probably wants to train you.
FLAP
Grandma's stricter than Mom...
URGH
Kamakura... Hmm
You haven't gone in a while.
She uses the house from time to time.
Go get some training.
!
Can I take Kagetora, too?
Kagetora?
I need to train with him, too.
Right?
I guess so.
Really!?
Yay.

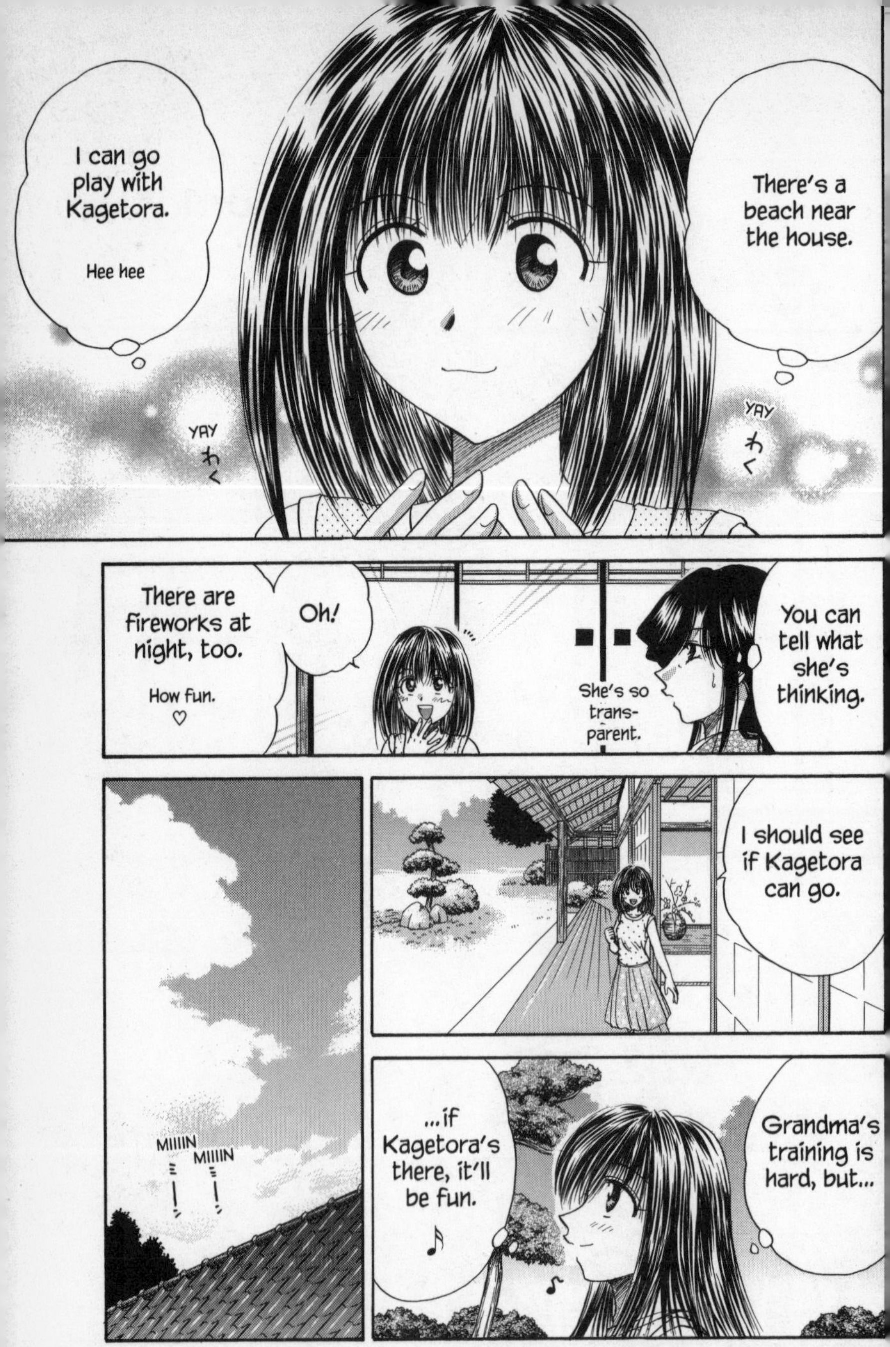
There's a beach near the house.
YAY
わく
I can go play with Kagetora.
Hee hee
YAY
わく
You can tell what she's thinking.
She's so trans-parent.
Oh!
There are fireworks at night, too.
How fun. ♡
I should see if Kagetora can go.
Grandma's training is hard, but...
...if Kagetora's there, it'll be fun. ♪
MIIIN
MIIIN

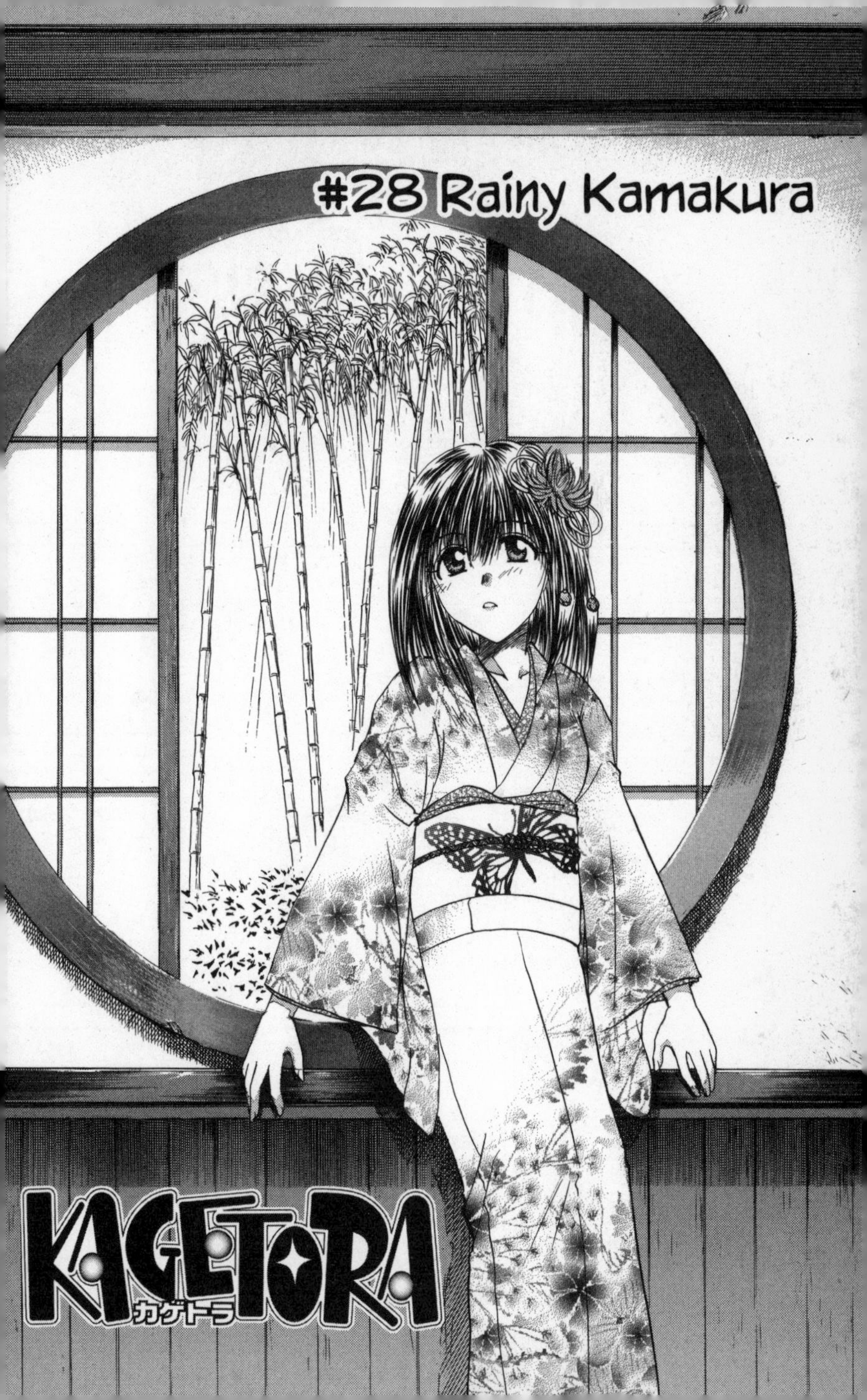
#28 Rainy Kamakura
KAGETORA
カゲトラ

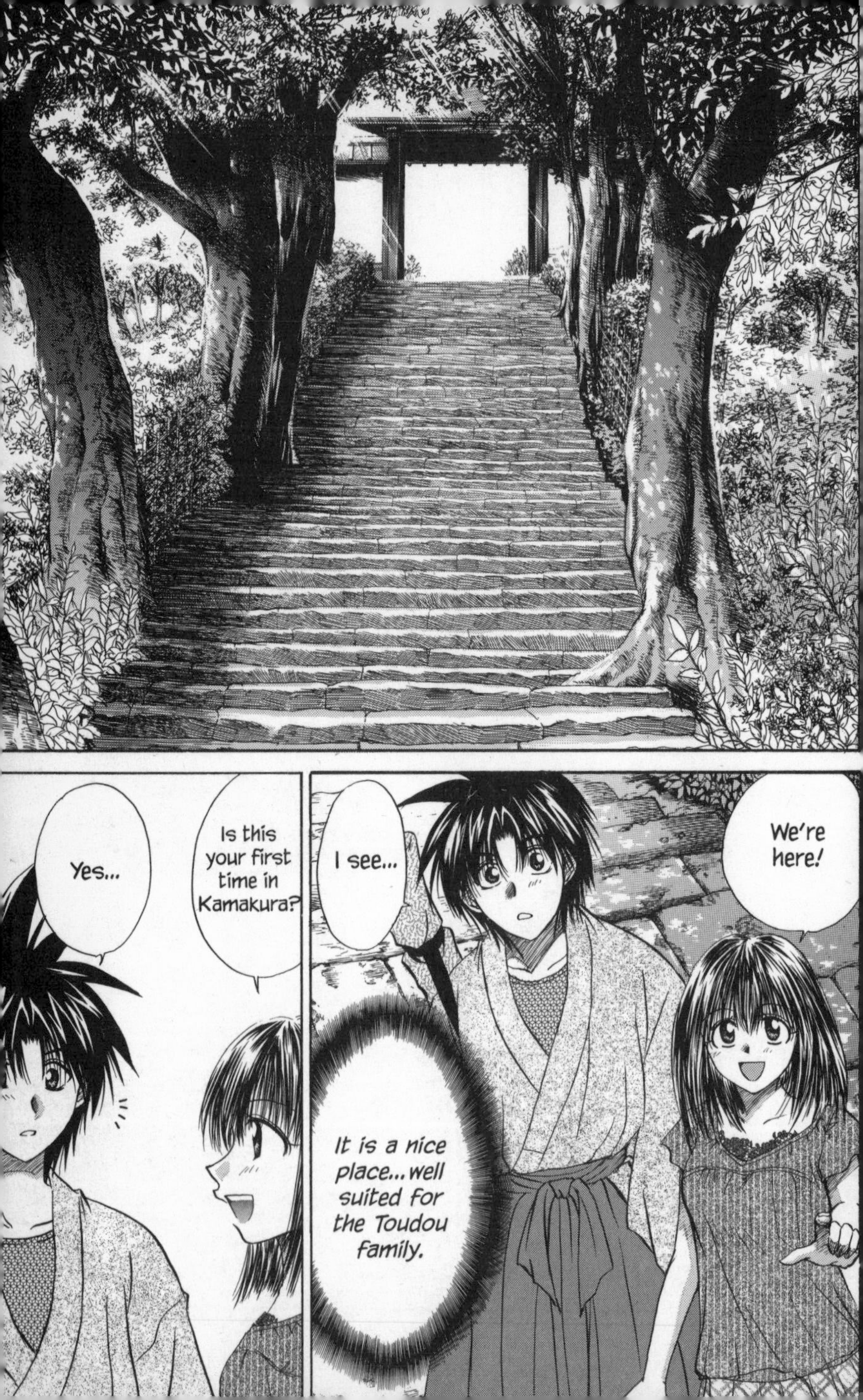
We're here!
I see...
It is a nice place...well suited for the Toudou family.
Is this your first time in Kamakura?
Yes...

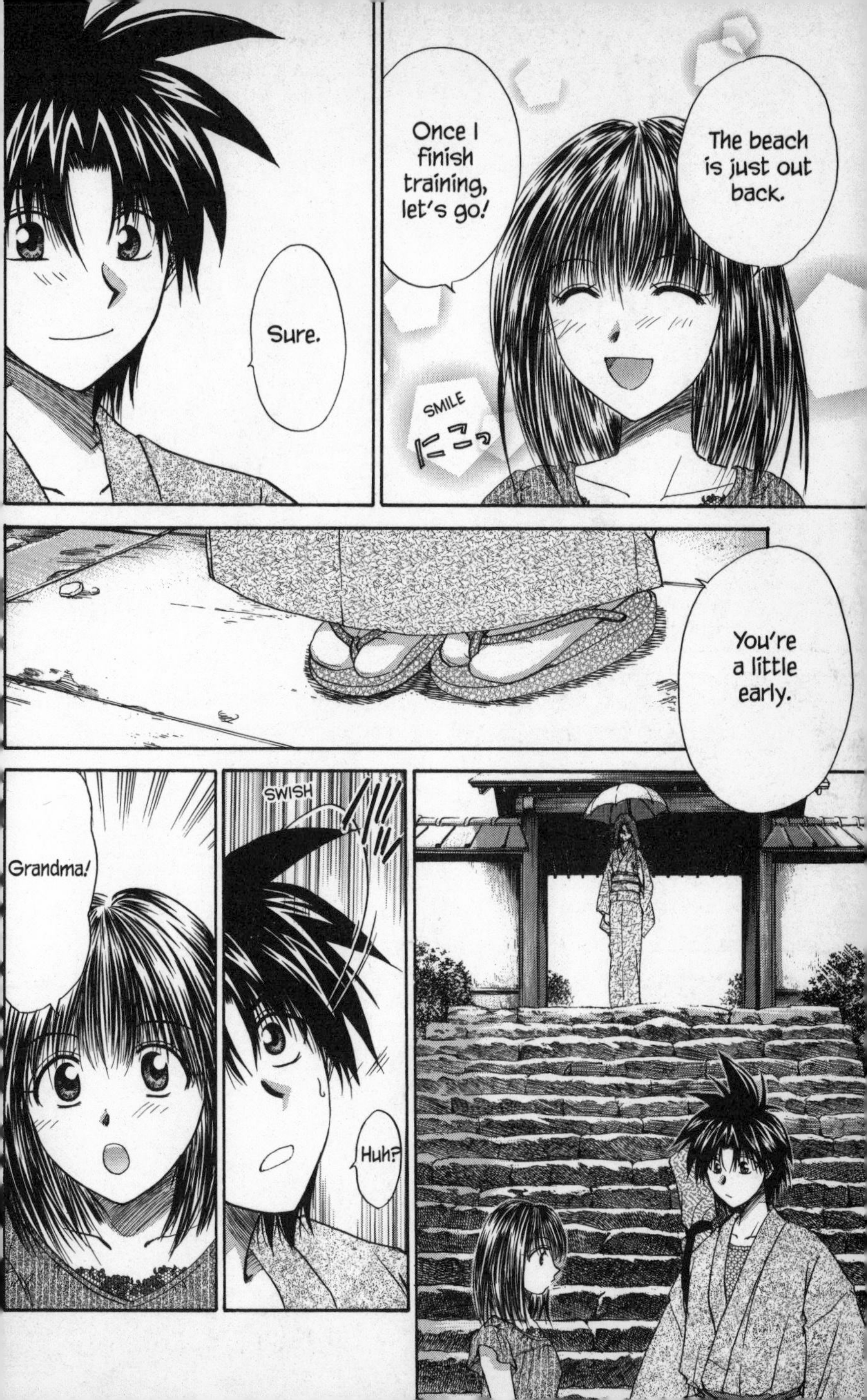
The beach is just out back.
Once I finish training, let's go!
SMILE
にこっ
Sure.
You're a little early.
SWISH
Huh?
Grandma!

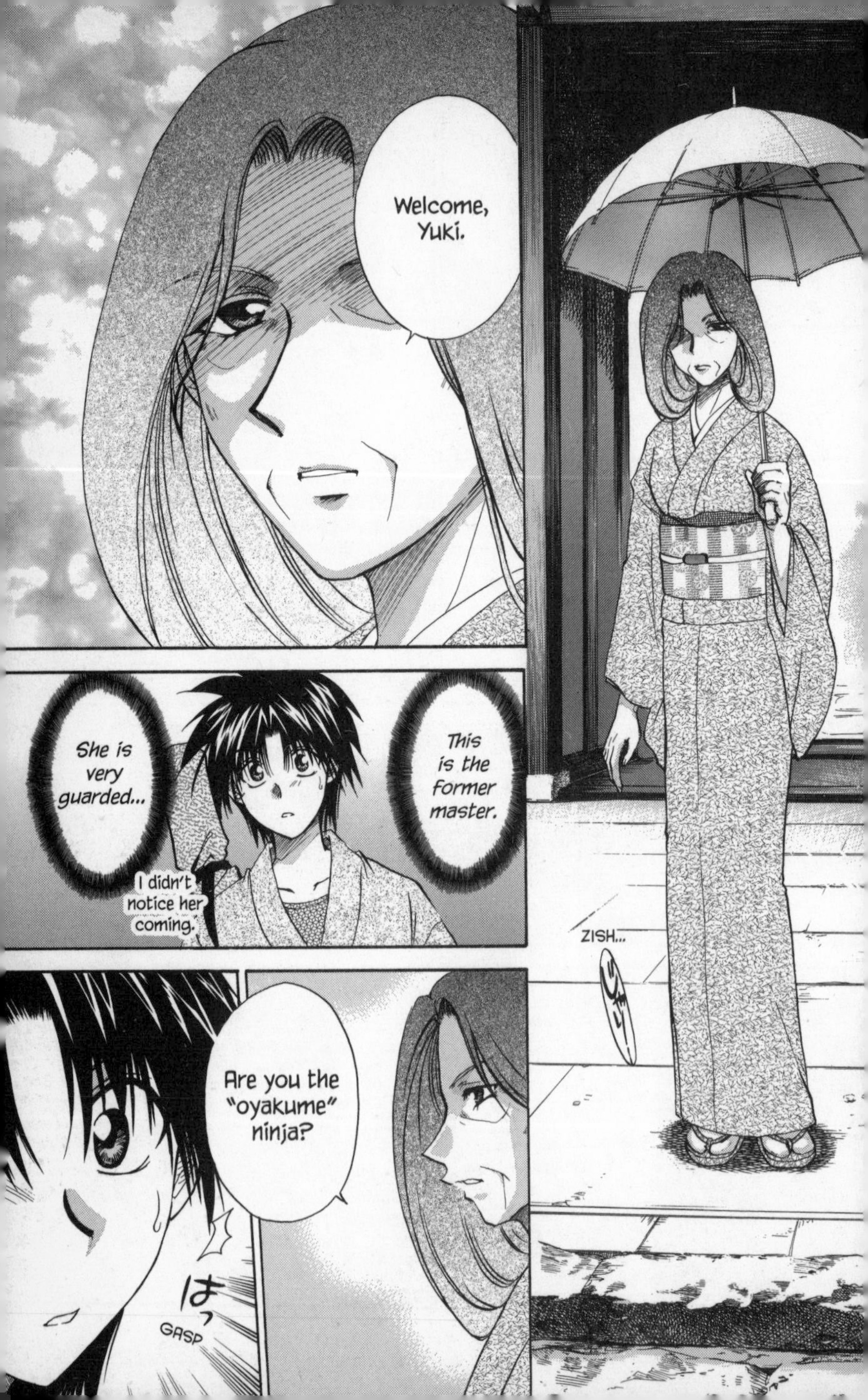
ZISH...
Welcome, Yuki.
This is the former master.
She is very guarded...
I didn't notice her coming.
Are you the "oyakume" ninja?
はっ
GASP

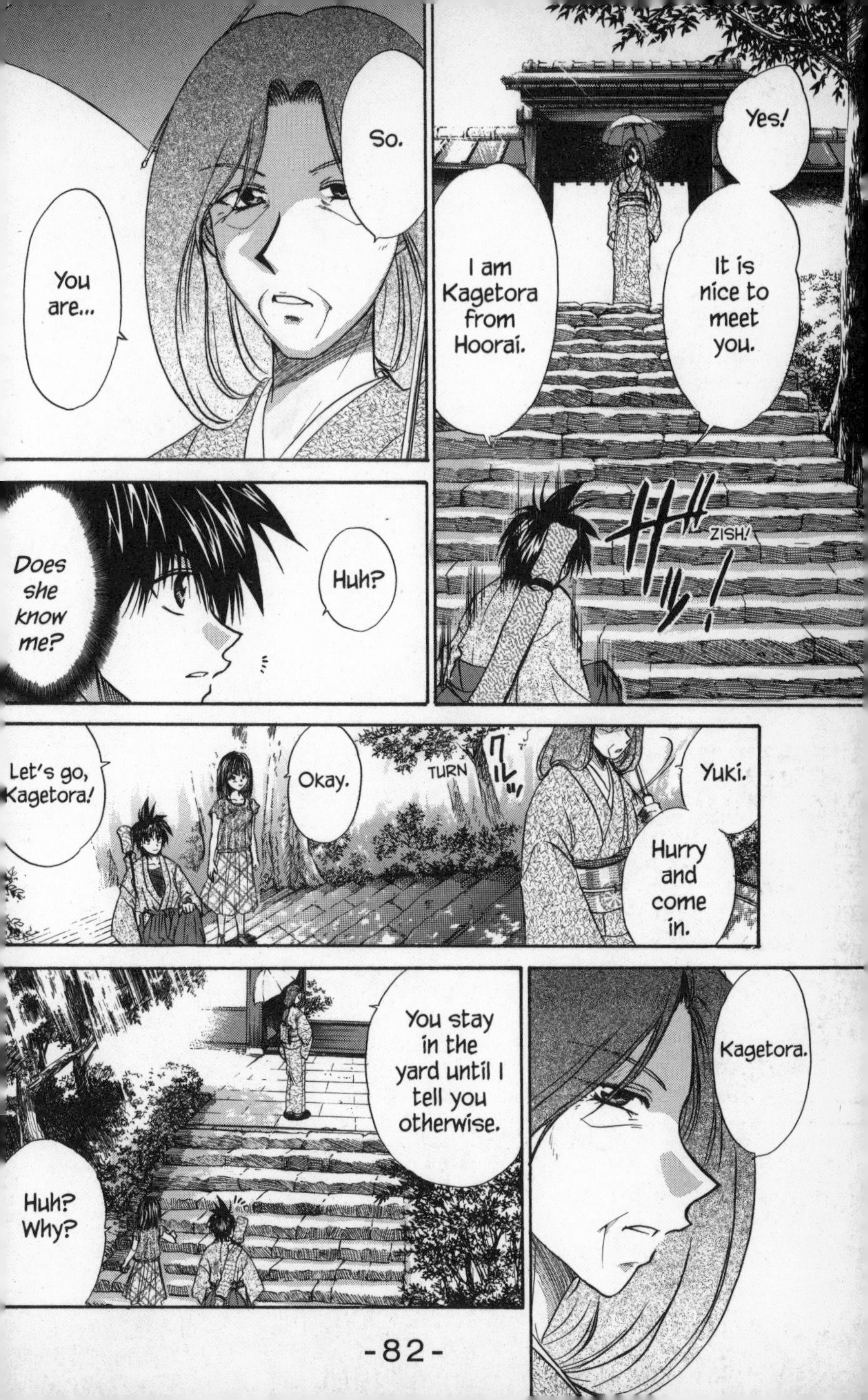

Yes!
It is nice to meet you.
I am Kagetora from Hoorai.
ZISH!
So.
You are...
Huh?
Does she know me?
Yuki.
Hurry and come in.
TURN
Okay.
Let's go, Kagetora!
Kagetora.
You stay in the yard until I tell you otherwise.
Huh? Why?

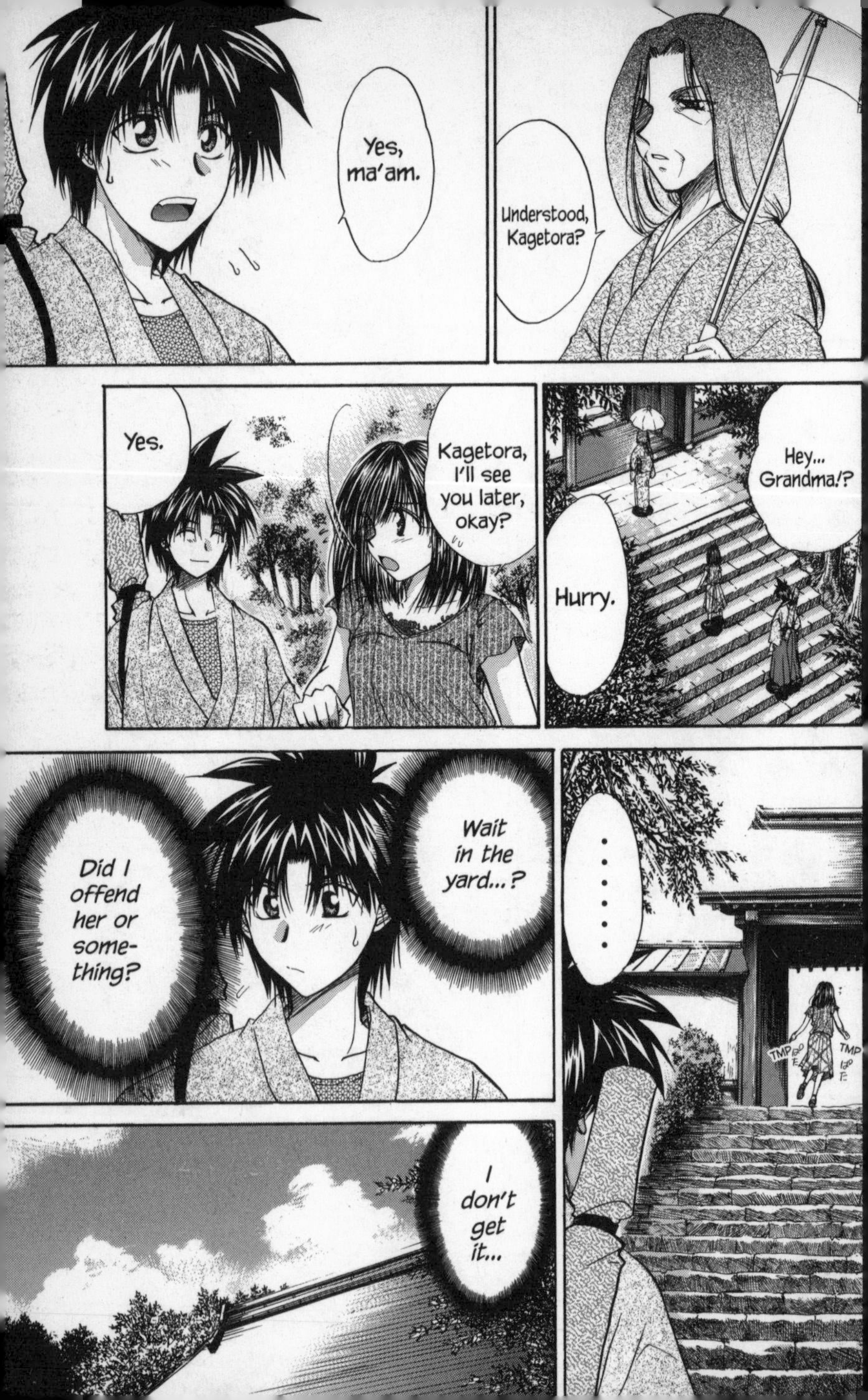
Understood, Kagetora?
Yes, ma'am.
Hey... Grandma!?
Hurry.
Kagetora, I'll see you later, okay?
Yes.
......
TMP
TMP
Wait in the yard...?
Did I offend her or something?
I don't get it...

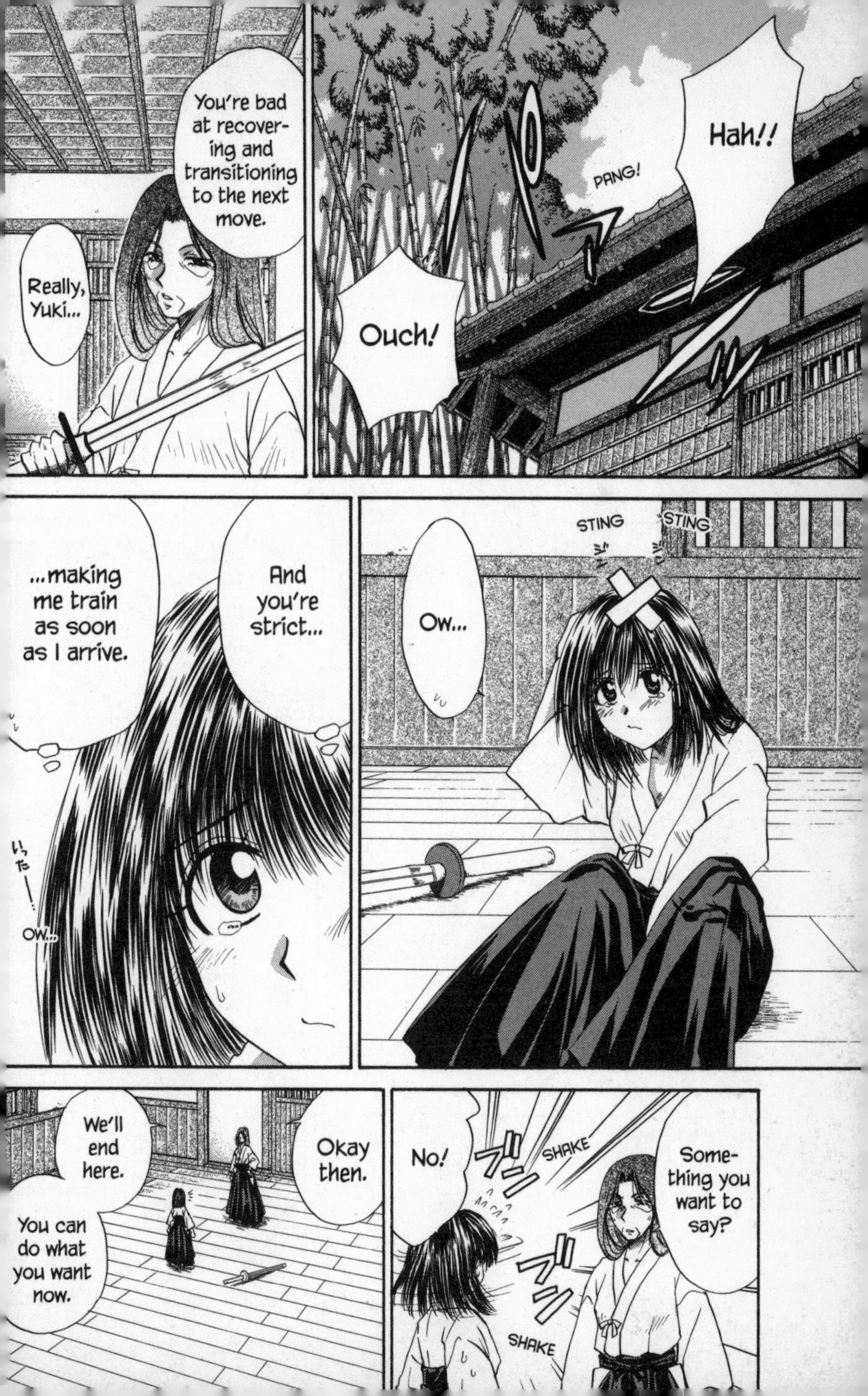
Hah!!
PANG!
Ouch!
You're bad at recovering and transitioning to the next move.
Really, Yuki...
STING
STING
Ow...
And you're strict...
...making me train as soon as I arrive.
Ow...
Something you want to say?
SHAKE
No!
SHAKE
Okay then.
We'll end here.
You can do what you want now.

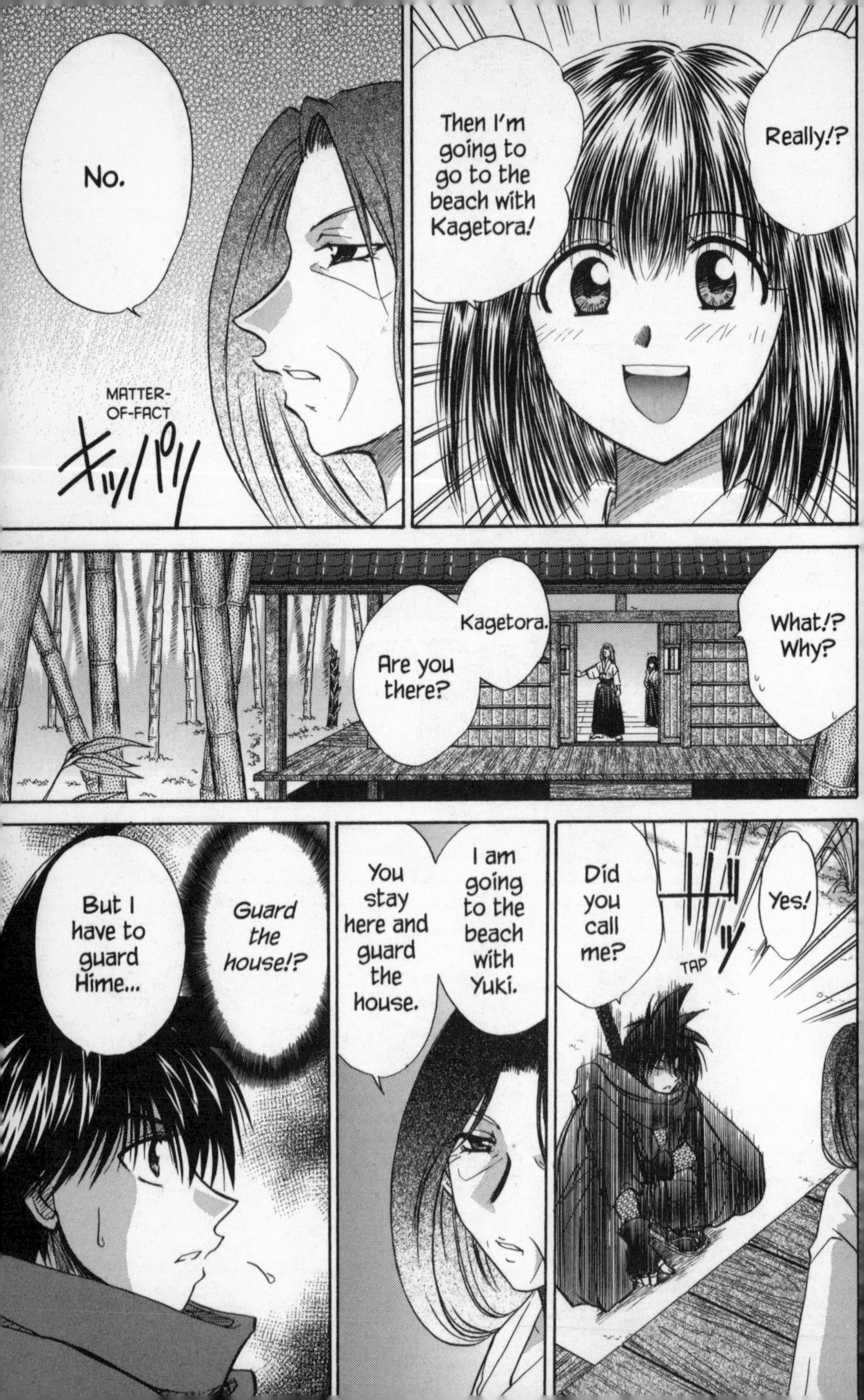
Really!?
Then I'm going to go to the beach with Kagetora!
No.
MATTER-OF-FACT
キッパリ
What!? Why?
Kagetora.
Are you there?
Yes!
Did you call me?
TAP
I am going to the beach with Yuki.
You stay here and guard the house.
Guard the house!?
But I have to guard Hime...

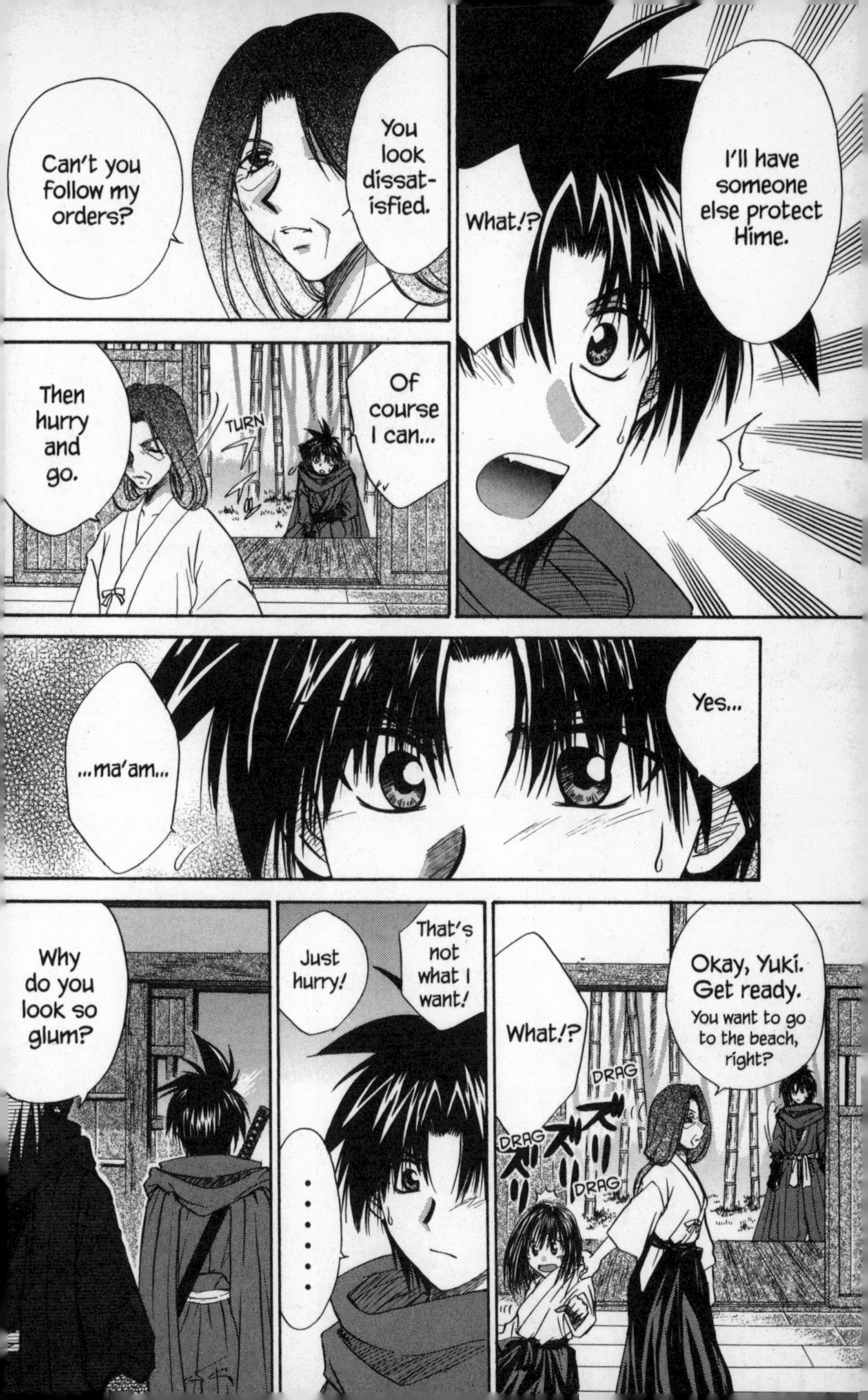
I'll have someone else protect Hime.
What!?
You look dissat-isfied.
Can't you follow my orders?
Of course I can...
TURN
Then hurry and go.
Yes...
...ma'am...
Okay, Yuki. Get ready. You want to go to the beach, right?
What!?
DRAG
DRAG
DRAG
That's not what I want!
Just hurry!
......
Why do you look so glum?

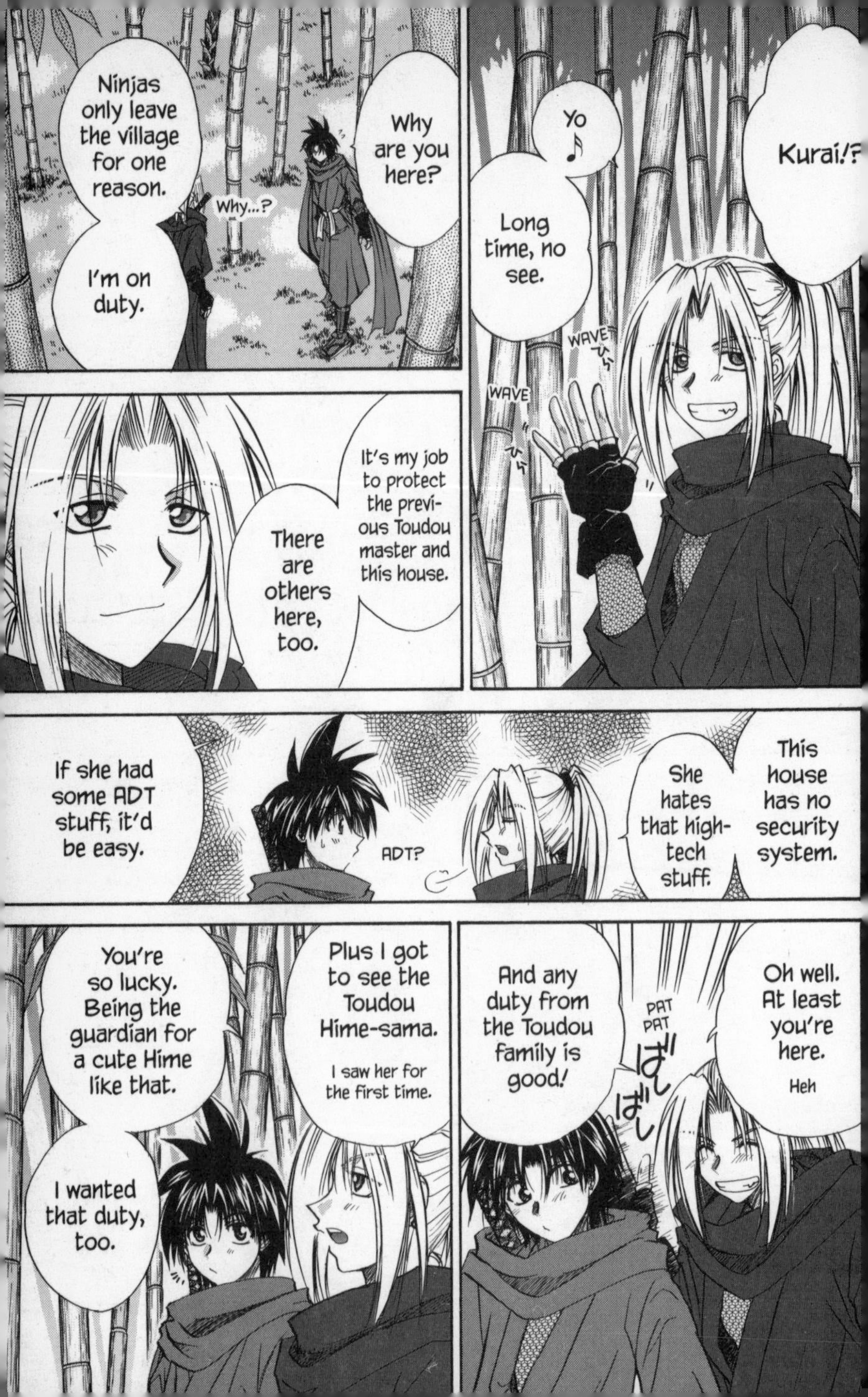
Kurai!?
Yo ♪
Long time, no see.
WAVE
WAVE
Why are you here?
Why...?
Ninjas only leave the village for one reason.
I'm on duty.
It's my job to protect the previous Toudou master and this house.
There are others here, too.
This house has no security system.
She hates that high-tech stuff.
ADT?
If she had some ADT stuff, it'd be easy.
Oh well. At least you're here.
Heh
PAT PAT
And any duty from the Toudou family is good!
Plus I got to see the Toudou Hime-sama.
I saw her for the first time.
You're so lucky. Being the guardian for a cute Hime like that.
I wanted that duty, too.

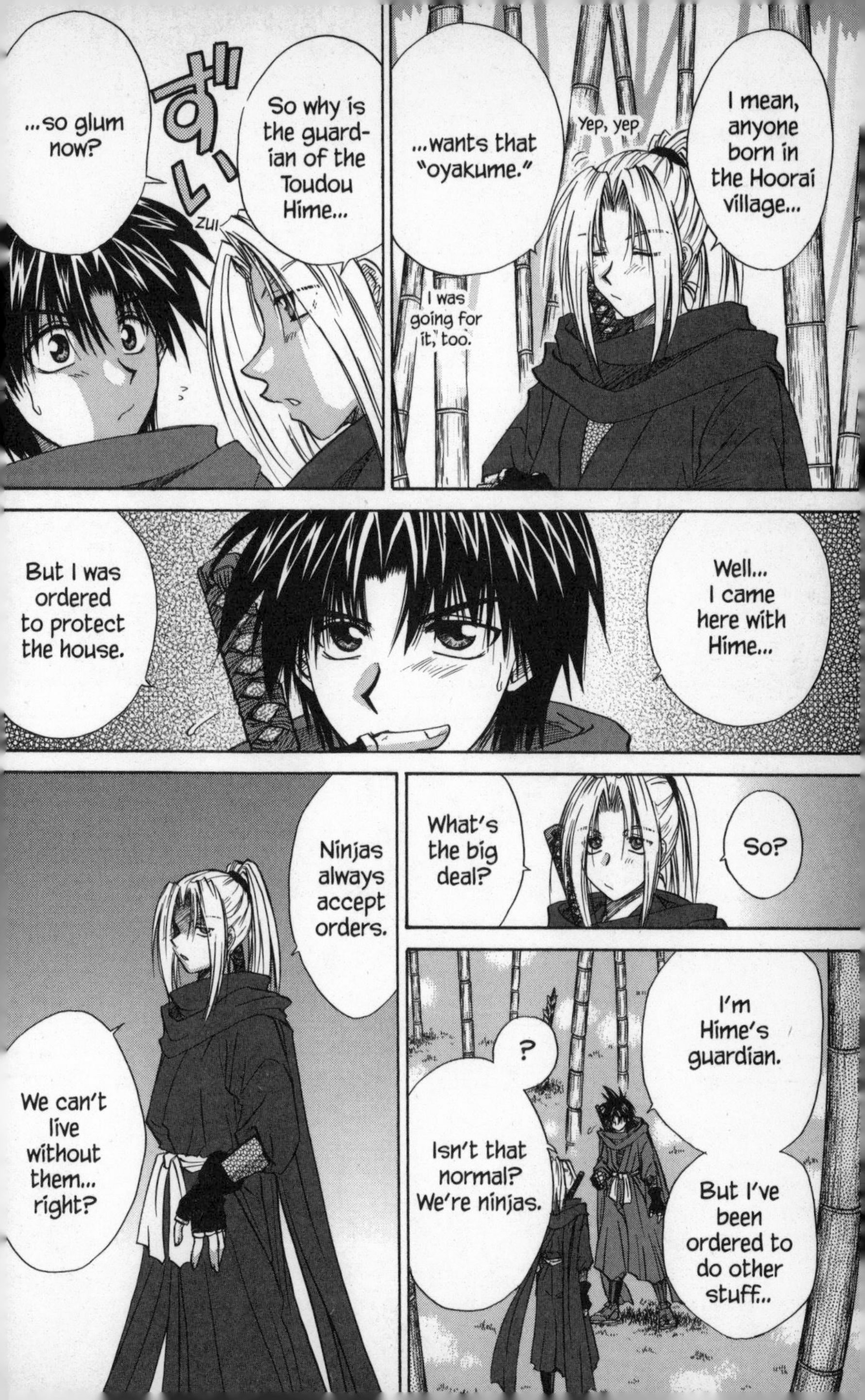
I mean, anyone born in the Hoorai village...
Yep, yep
...wants that "oyakume."
I was going for it, too.
So why is the guard-ian of the Toudou Hime...
ZUI
...so glum now?
Well... I came here with Hime...
But I was ordered to protect the house.
So?
What's the big deal?
I'm Hime's guardian.
But I've been ordered to do other stuff...
?
Isn't that normal? We're ninjas.
Ninjas always accept orders.
We can't live without them... right?

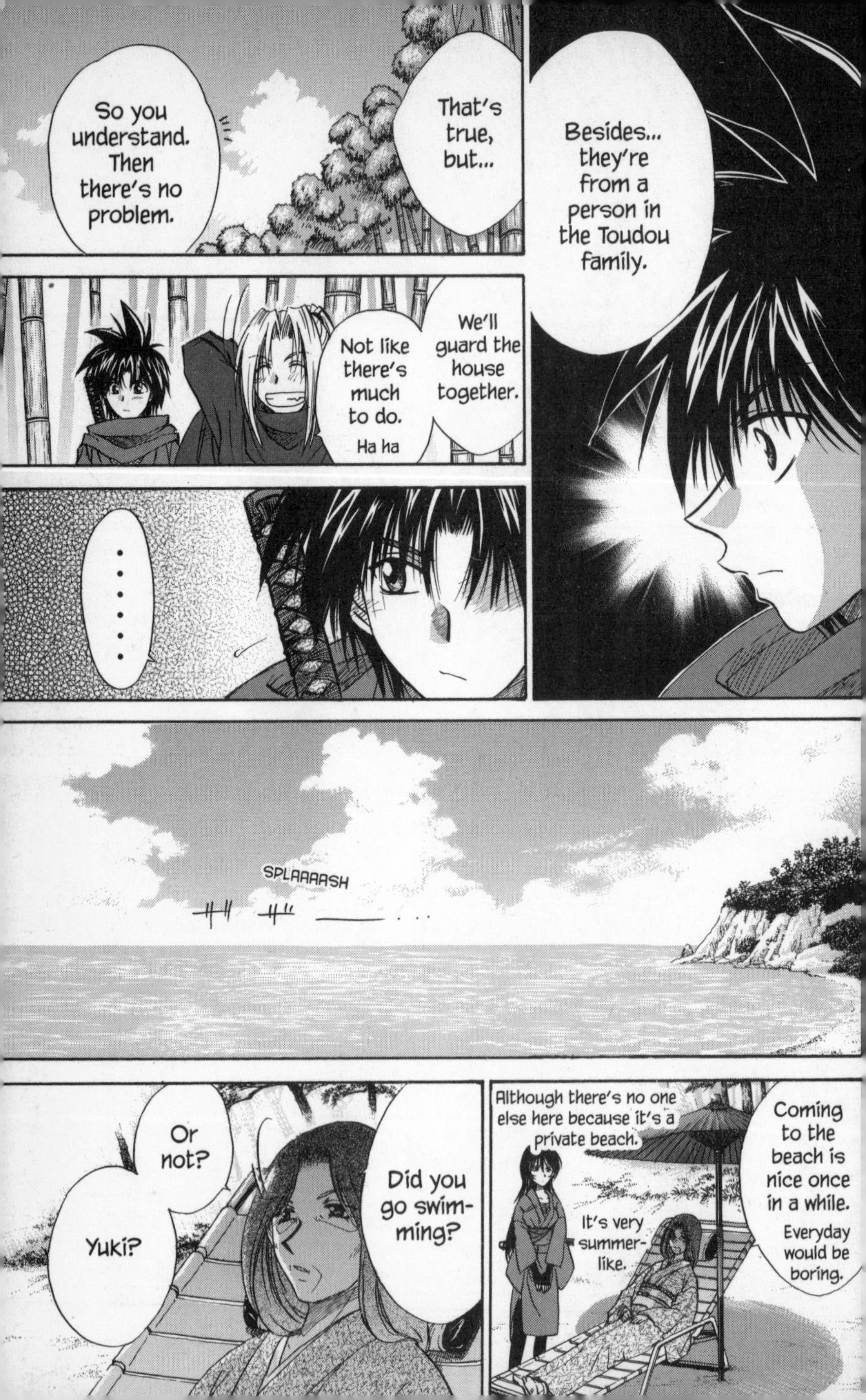
Besides... they're from a person in the Toudou family.
That's true, but...
So you understand. Then there's no problem.
We'll guard the house together.
Not like there's much to do.
Ha ha
......
SPLAAAASH
Coming to the beach is nice once in a while.
Everyday would be boring.
Although there's no one else here because it's a private beach.
It's very summer-like.
Did you go swimming?
Or not?
Yuki?

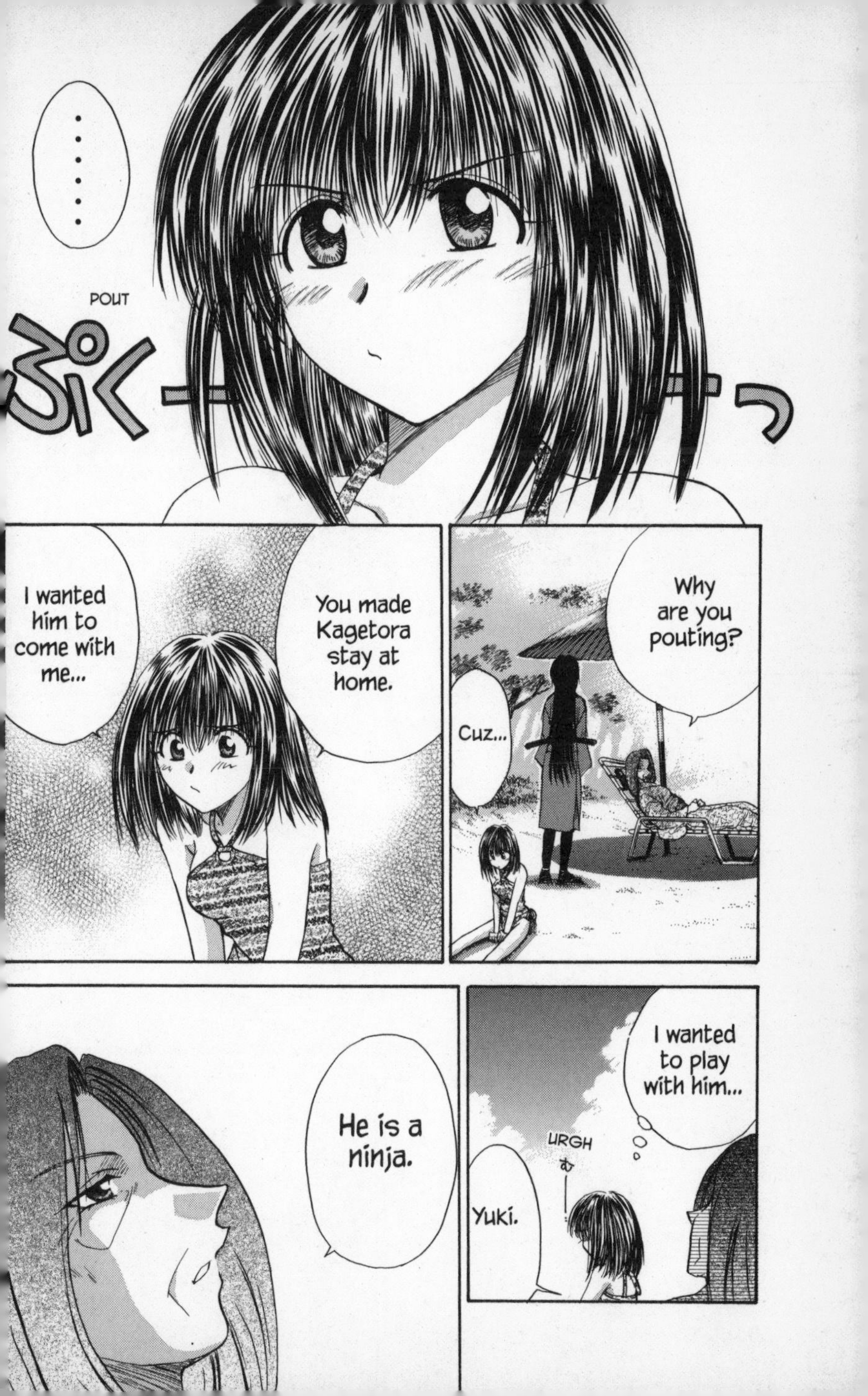
......
POUT
ぷくーーっ
Why are you pouting?
Cuz...
You made Kagetora stay at home.
I wanted him to come with me...
I wanted to play with him...
URGH
む
Yuki.
He is a ninja.

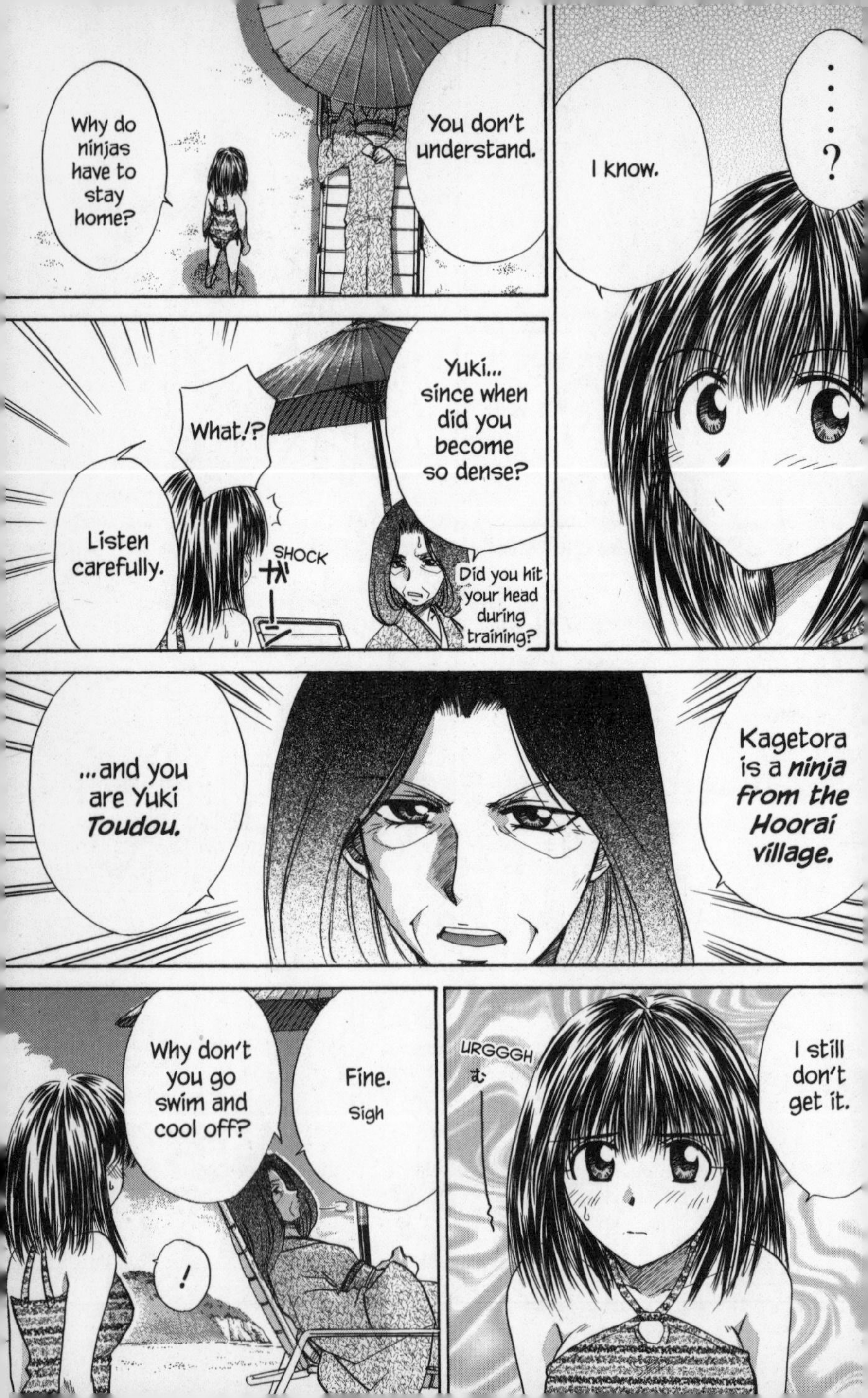
. . . ?
I know.
You don't understand.
Why do ninjas have to stay home?
Yuki... since when did you become so dense?
Did you hit your head during training?
SHOCK
What!?
Listen carefully.
Kagetora is a *ninja from the Hoorai village.*
...and you are Yuki *Toudou.*
I still don't get it.
URGGGH
Fine.
Sigh
Why don't you go swim and cool off?
!

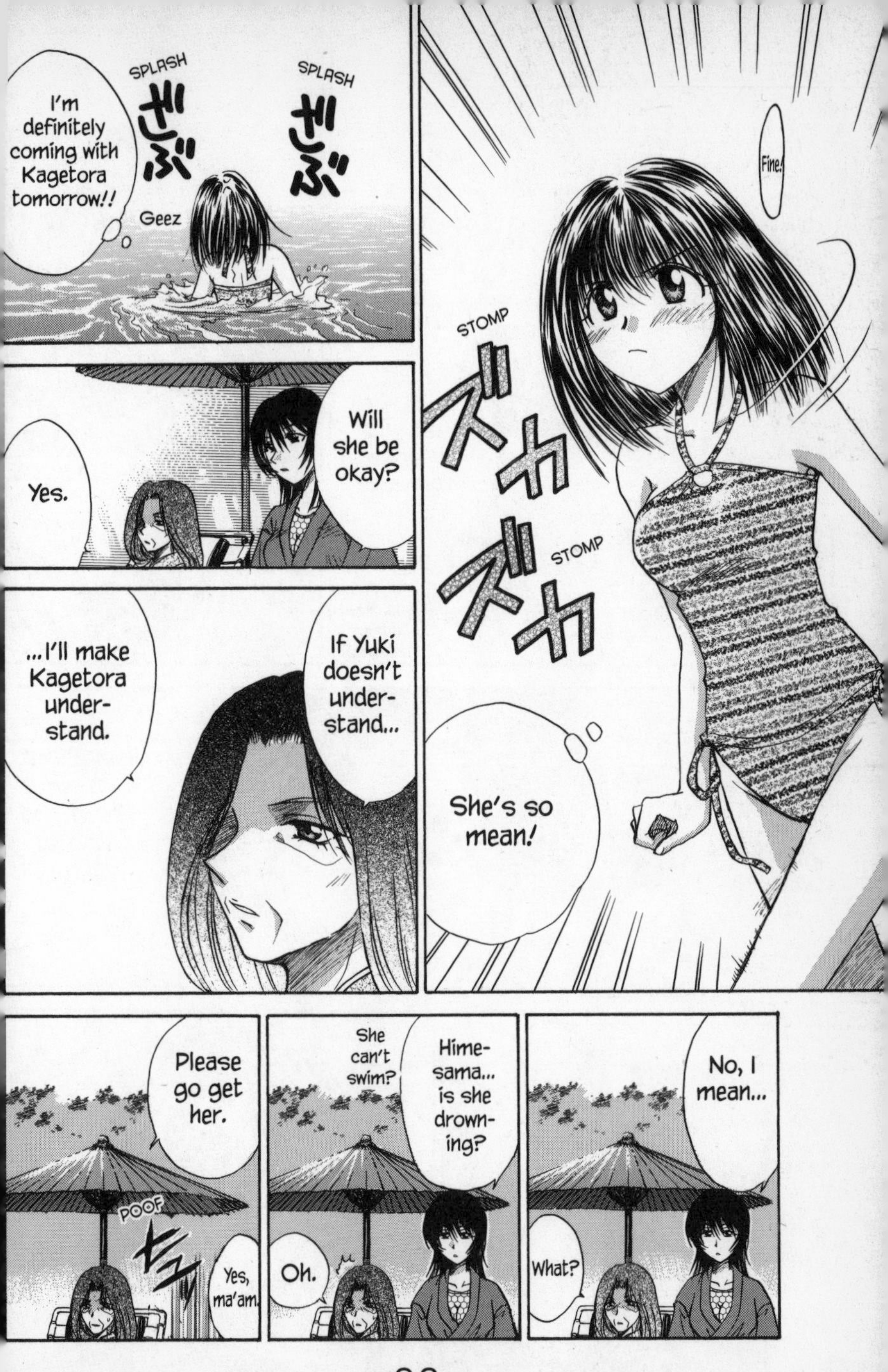
Fine!
STOMP
ズカ
STOMP
ズカ
She's so mean!
SPLASH
ざぶ
SPLASH
ざぶ
I'm definitely coming with Kagetora tomorrow!!
Geez
Will she be okay?
Yes.
If Yuki doesn't under-stand...
...I'll make Kagetora under-stand.
No, I mean...
What?
Hime-sama... is she drown-ing?
She can't swim?
Oh.
Please go get her.
POOF
Yes, ma'am.

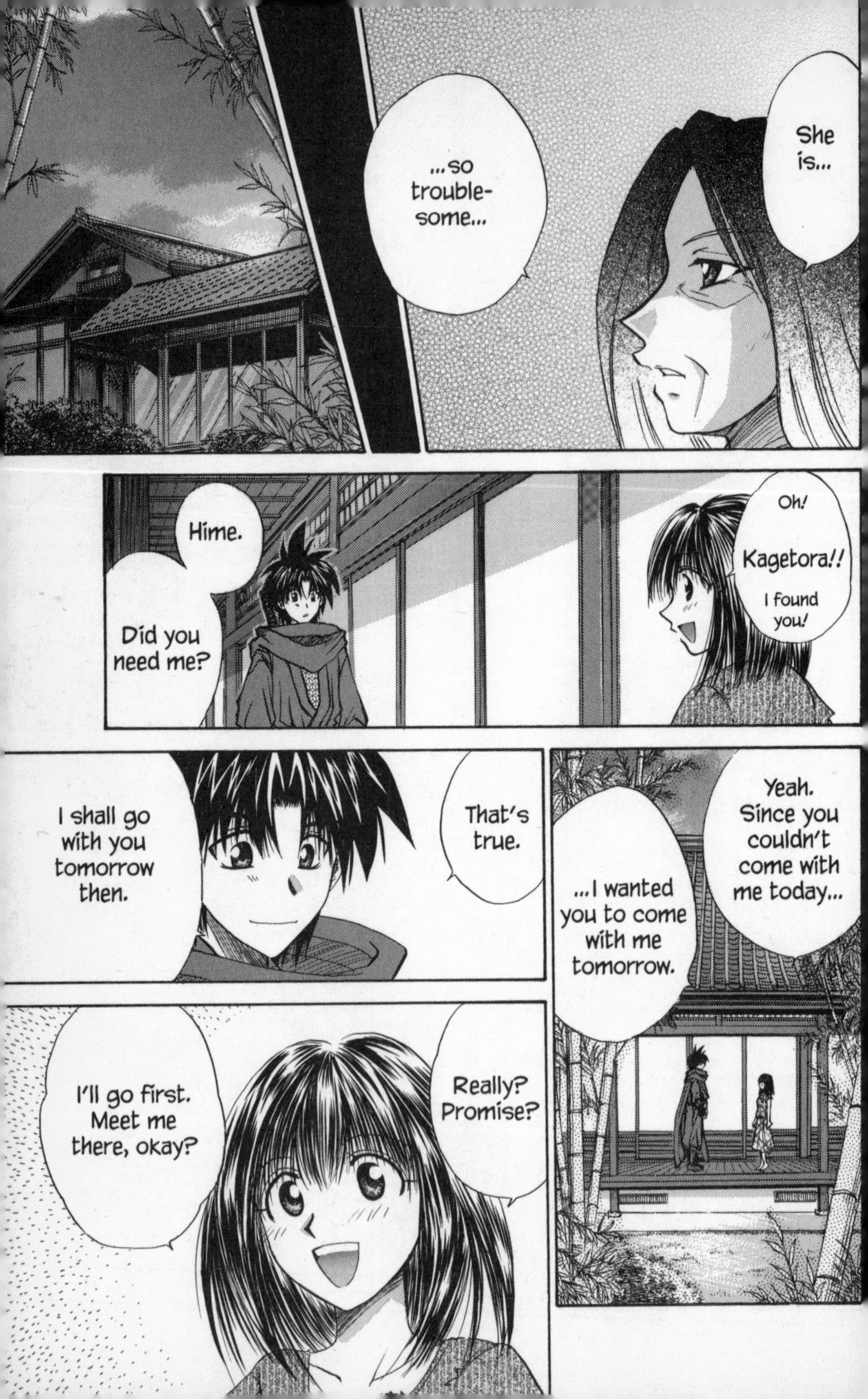
She is...
...so trouble-some...
Oh!
Kagetora!!
I found you!
Hime.
Did you need me?
Yeah. Since you couldn't come with me today...
...I wanted you to come with me tomorrow.
That's true.
I shall go with you tomorrow then.
Really? Promise?
I'll go first. Meet me there, okay?

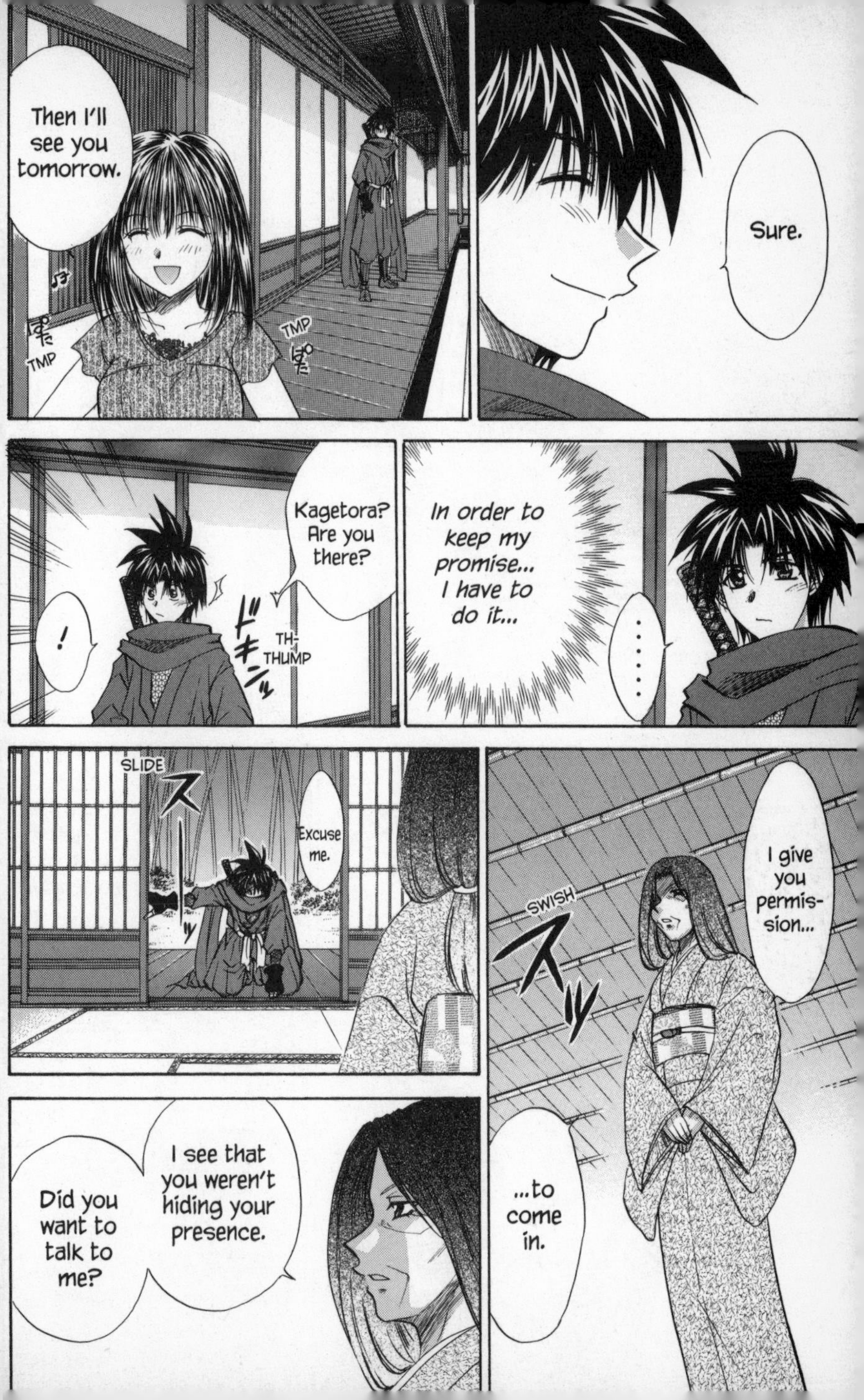
Then I'll see you tomorrow.
ぽた
TMP
TMP
ぽた
Sure.
Kagetora? Are you there?
!
ドキンッ
TH-THUMP
In order to keep my promise... I have to do it...
......
SLIDE
Excuse me.
I see that you weren't hiding your presence.
Did you want to talk to me?
SWISH
I give you permission...
...to come in.

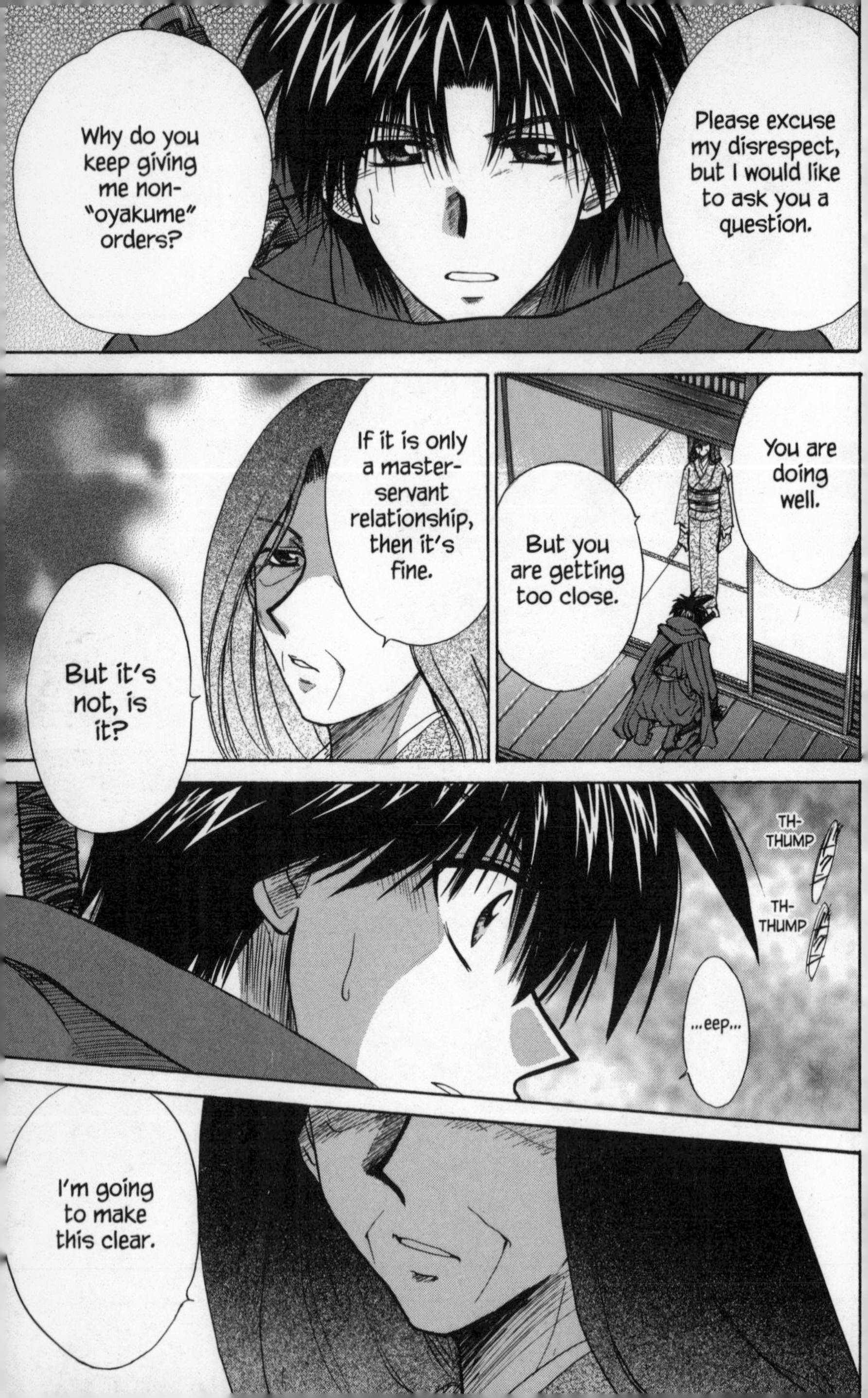
Please excuse my disrespect, but I would like to ask you a question.
Why do you keep giving me non-"oyakume" orders?
You are doing well.
But you are getting too close.
If it is only a master-servant relationship, then it's fine.
But it's not, is it?
TH-THUMP
TH-THUMP
...eep...
I'm going to make this clear.

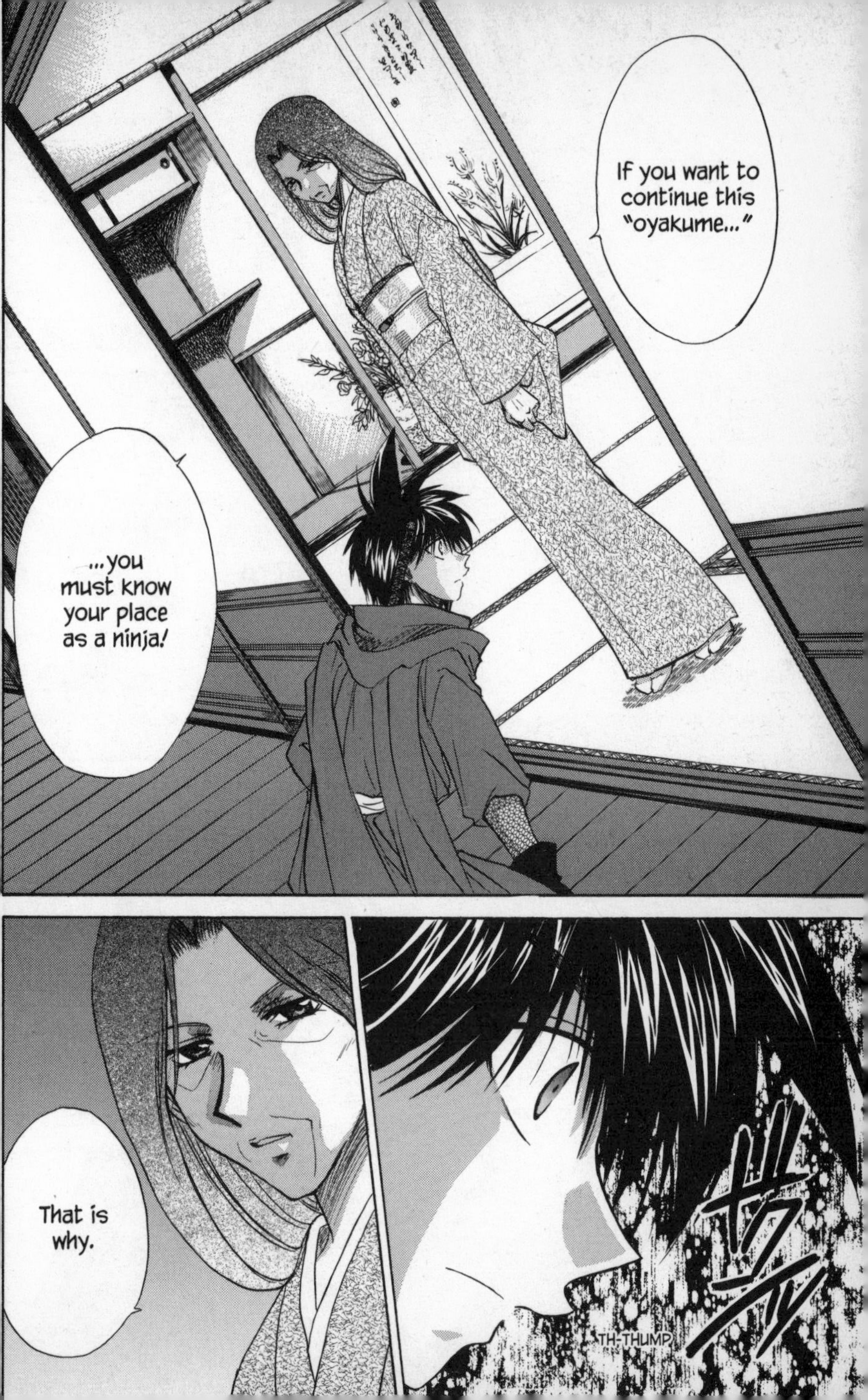
If you want to continue this "oyakume..."
...you must know your place as a ninja!
That is why.
TH-THUMP

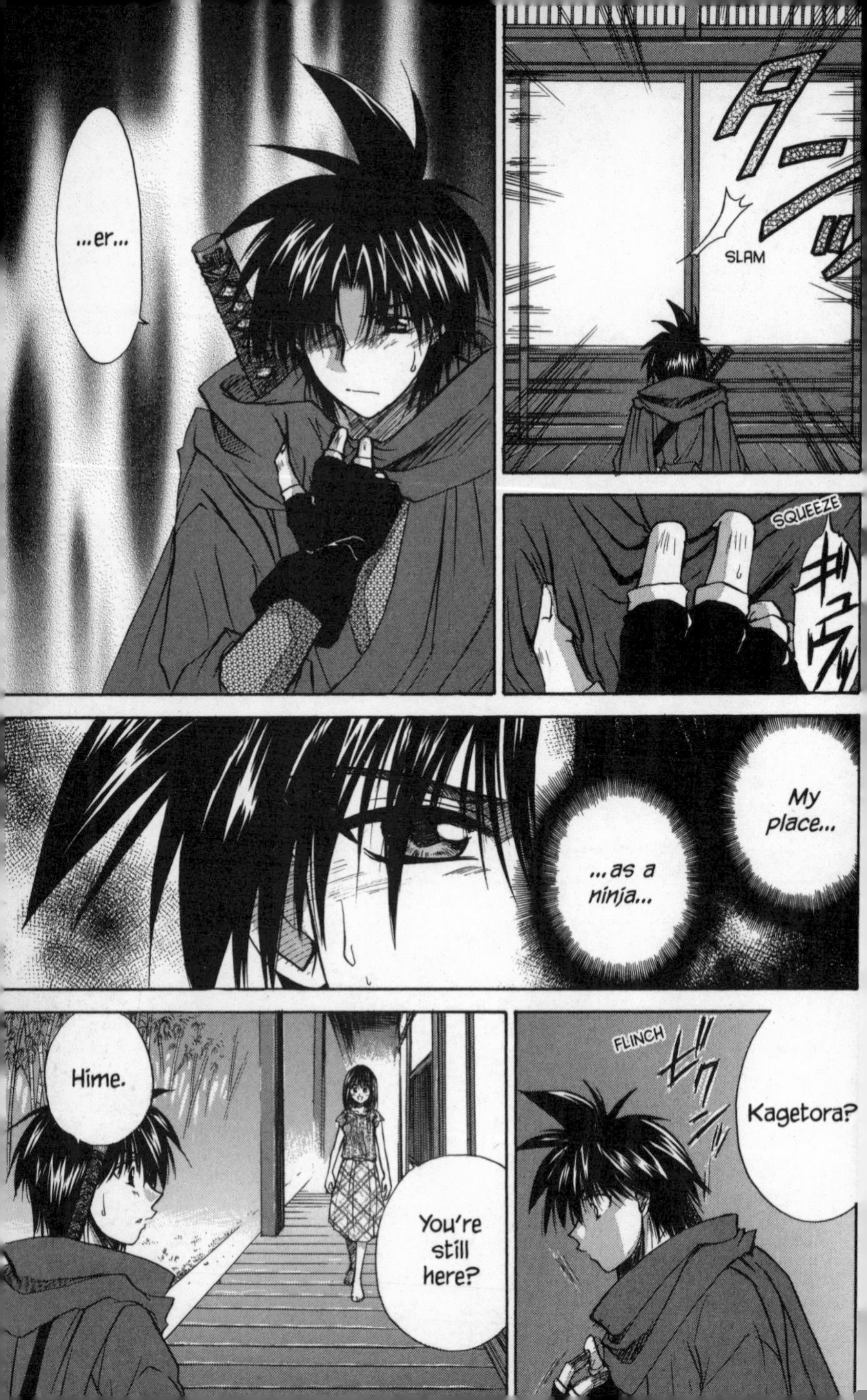
SLAM
SQUEEZE
...er...
My place...
...as a ninja...
FLINCH
Kagetora?
You're still here?
Hime.

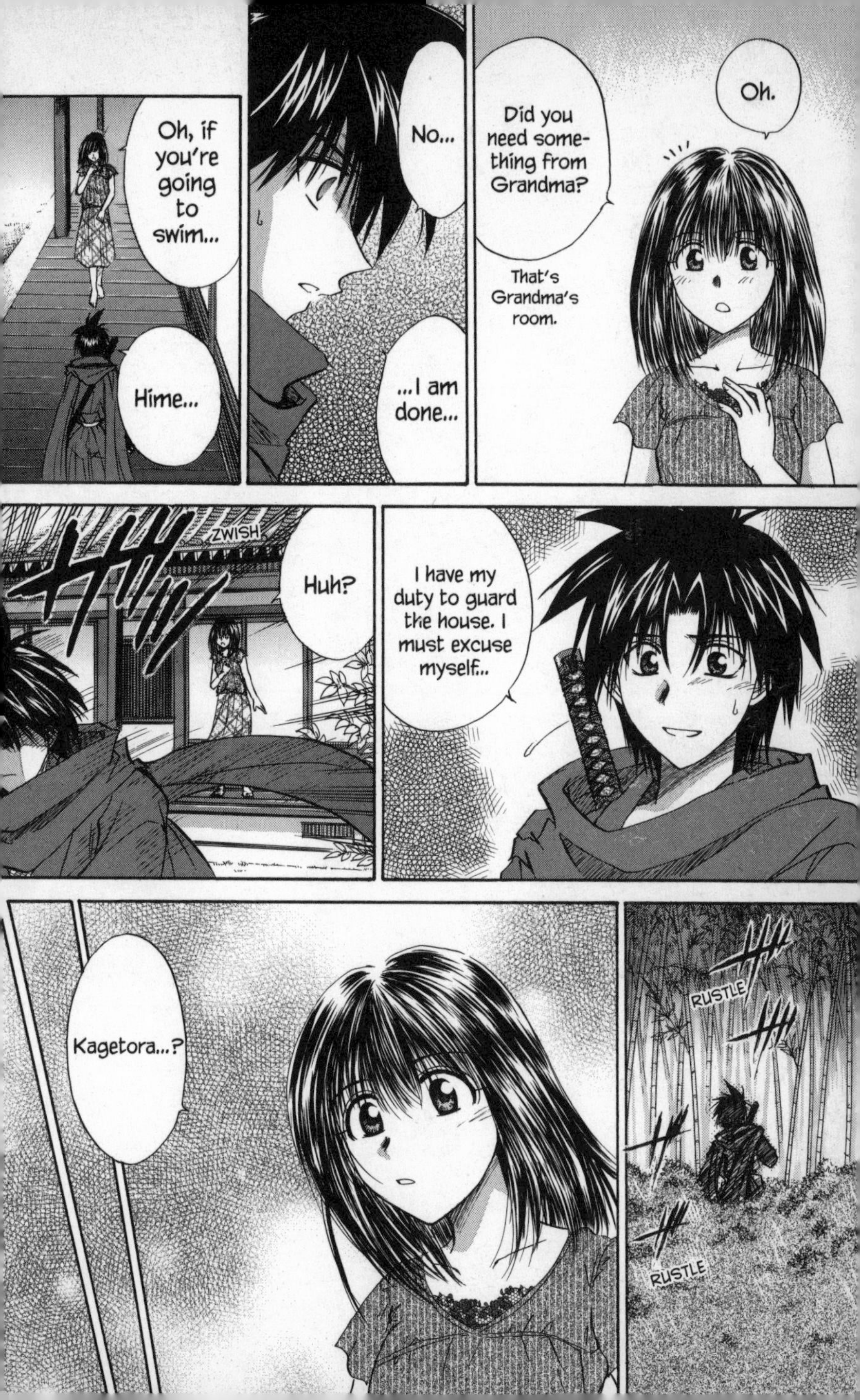
Oh.
Did you need some-thing from Grandma?
That's Grandma's room.
No...
...I am done...
Oh, if you're going to swim...
Hime...
I have my duty to guard the house. I must excuse myself...
Huh?
ZWISH
RUSTLE
RUSTLE
Kagetora...?

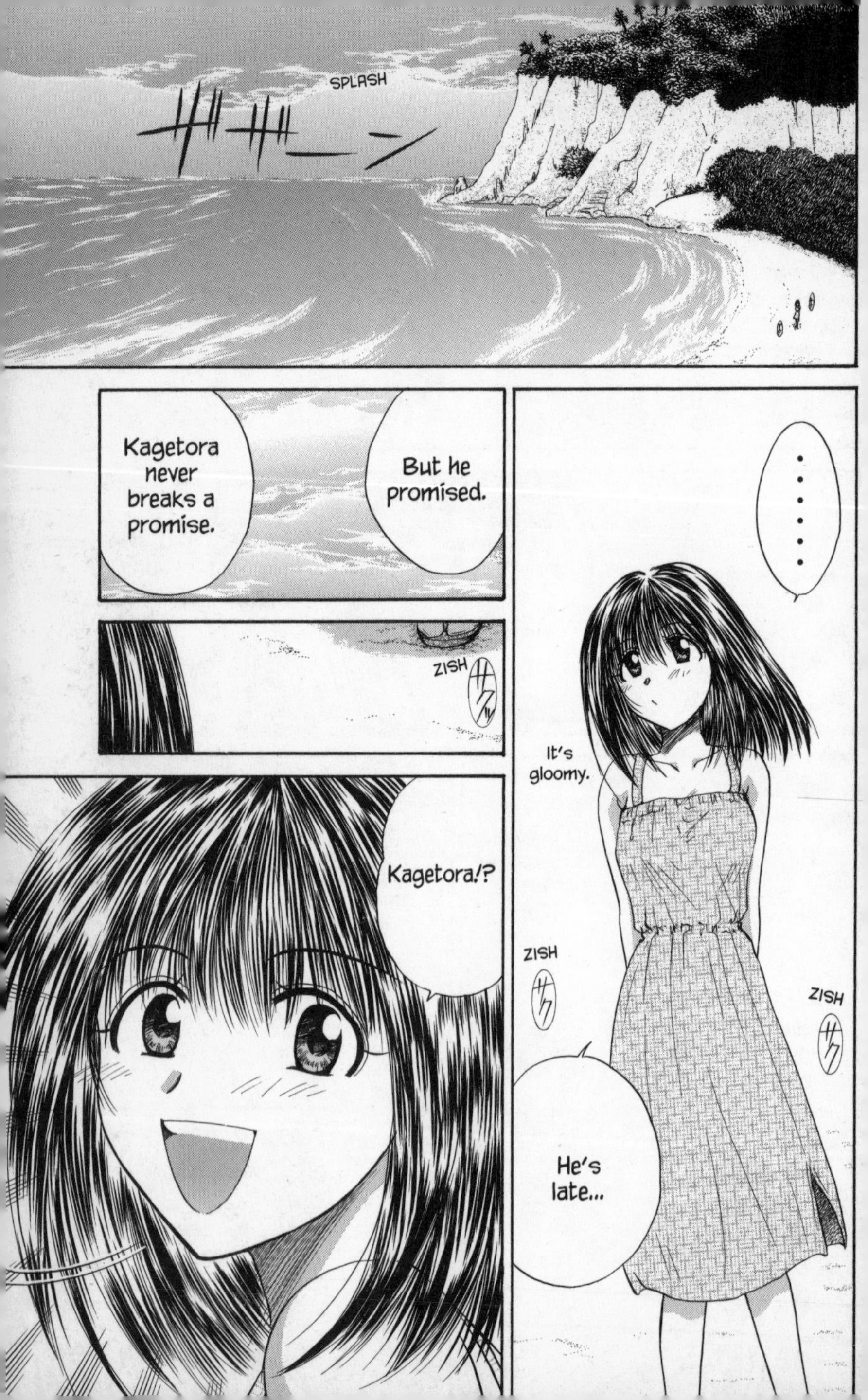
SPLASH
......
It's gloomy.
ZISH
ZISH
He's late...
But he promised.
Kagetora never breaks a promise.
ZISH
Kagetora!?

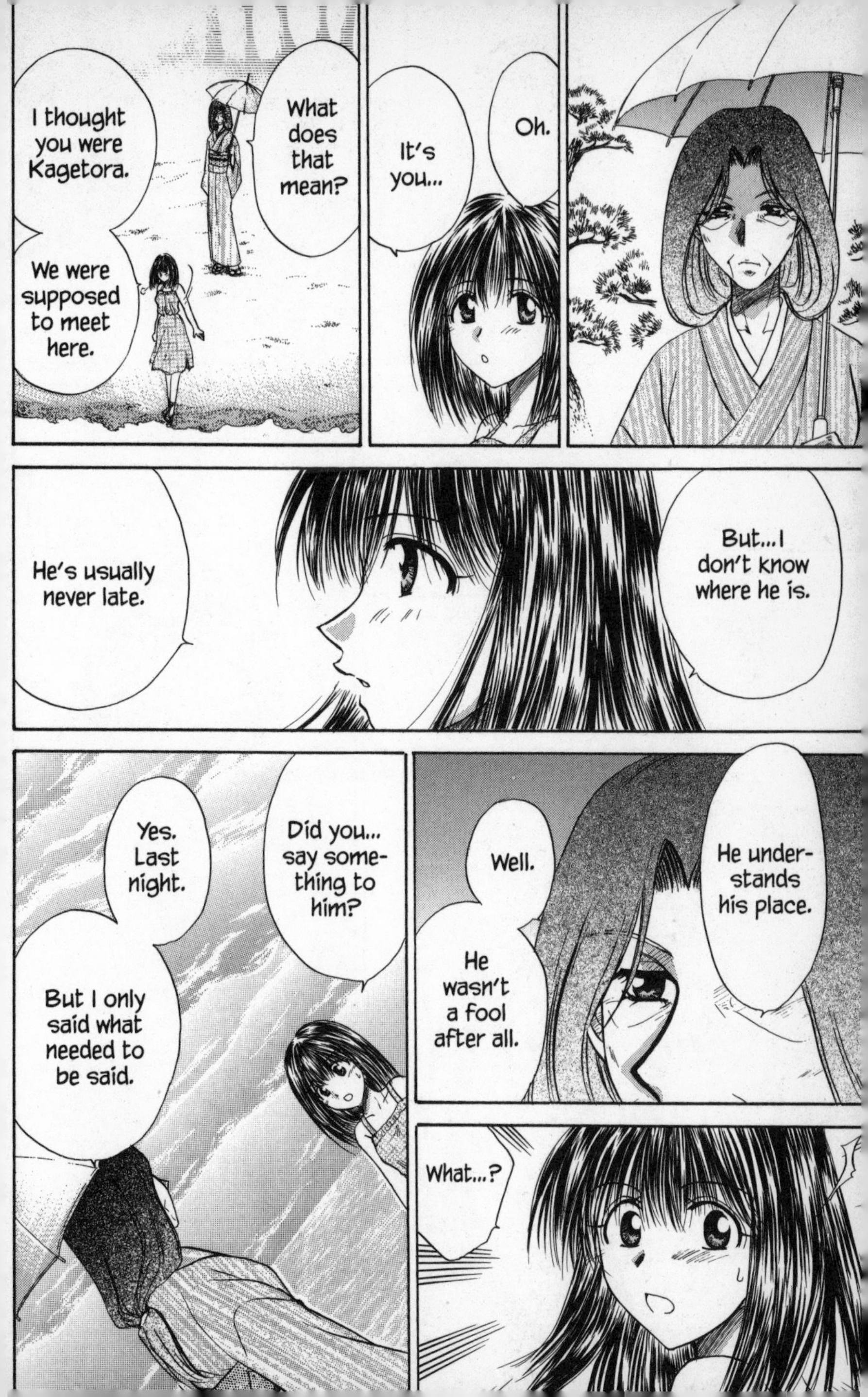

Oh.
It's you...
What does that mean?
I thought you were Kagetora.
We were supposed to meet here.
But...I don't know where he is.
He's usually never late.
He under-stands his place.
Well.
He wasn't a fool after all.
What...?
Did you... say some-thing to him?
Yes. Last night.
But I only said what needed to be said.

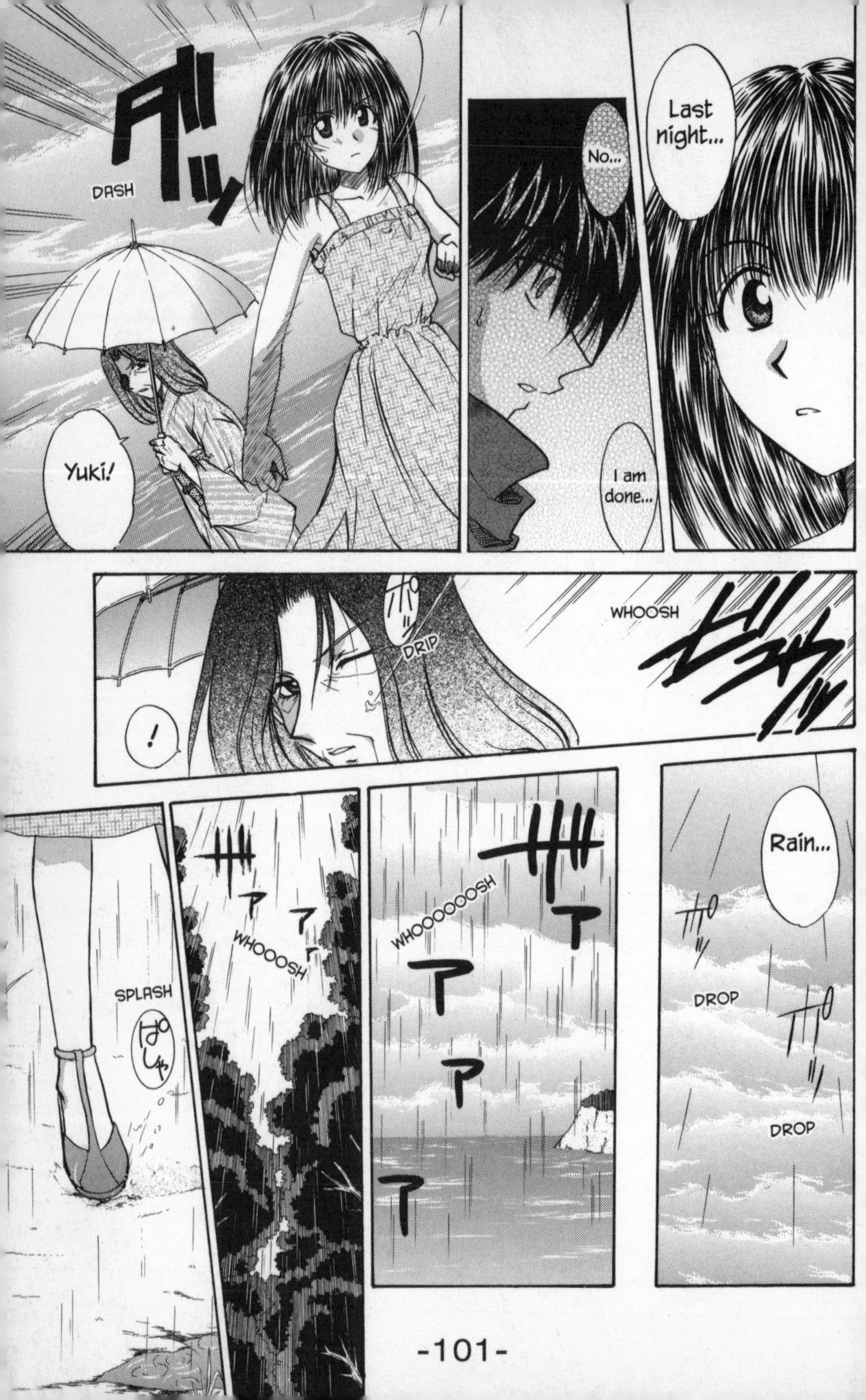

Last night...
No...
I am done...
DASH
Yuki!
WHOOSH
DRIP
!
Rain...
DROP
DROP
WHOOOOOOSH
WHOOOSH
SPLASH

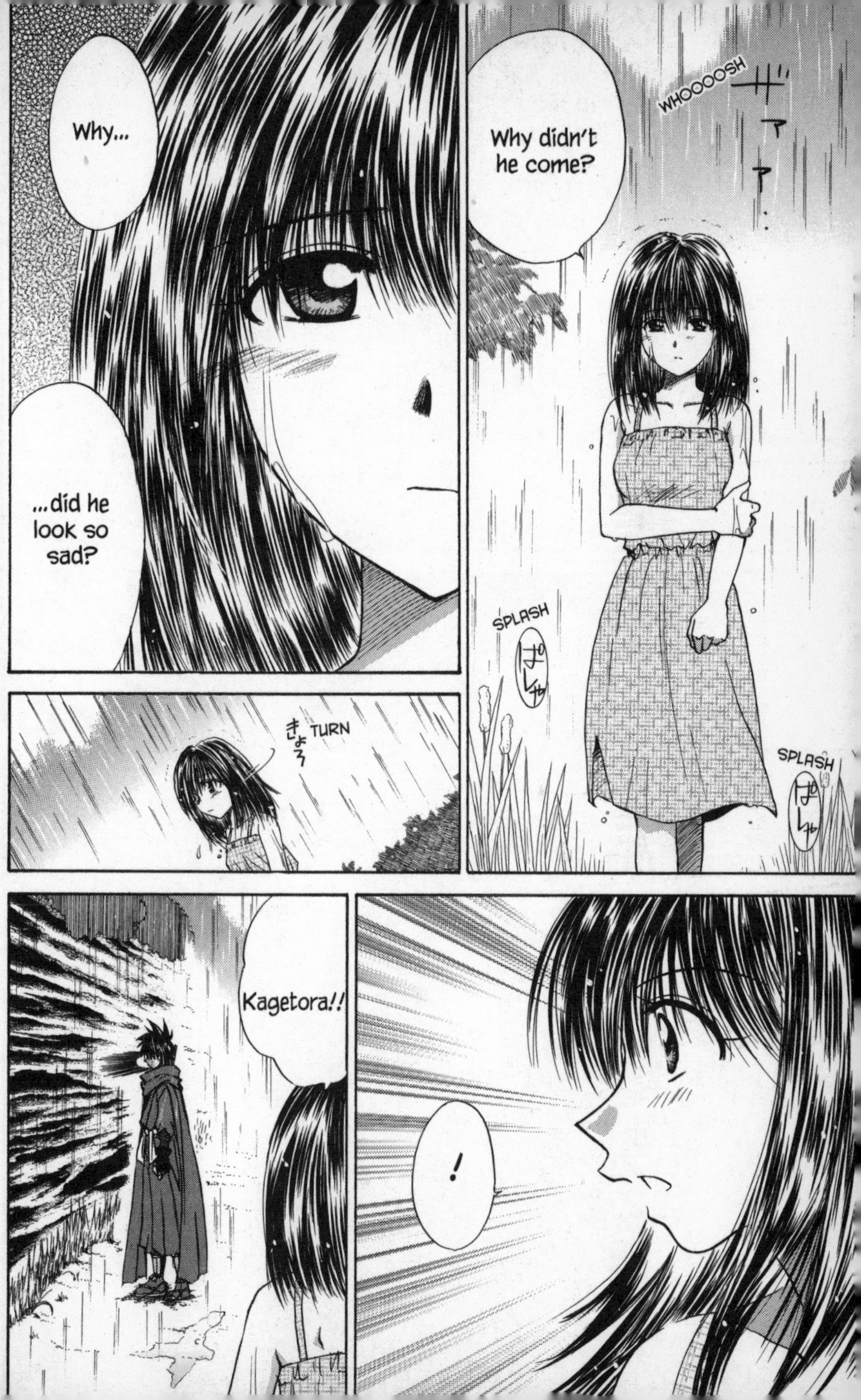
WHOOOOSH
ザァァ..
Why didn't he come?
SPLASH
ぱしゃ
SPLASH
ぱしゃ
Why...
...did he look so sad?
きょろ TURN
!
Kagetora!!

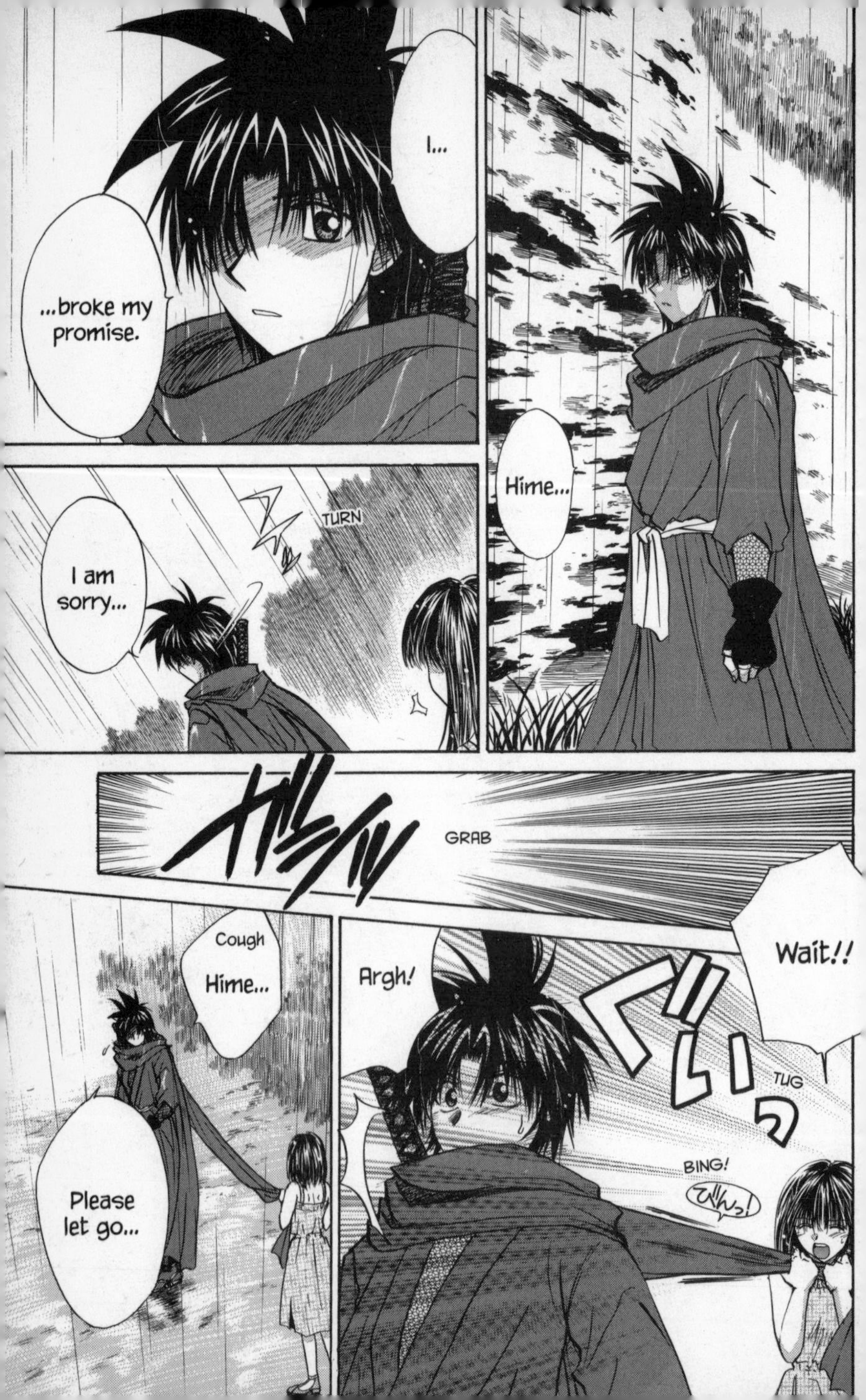
Hime...
I...
...broke my promise.
TURN
I am sorry...
GRAB
Wait!!
TUG
Argh!
BING!
Cough
Hime...
Please let go...

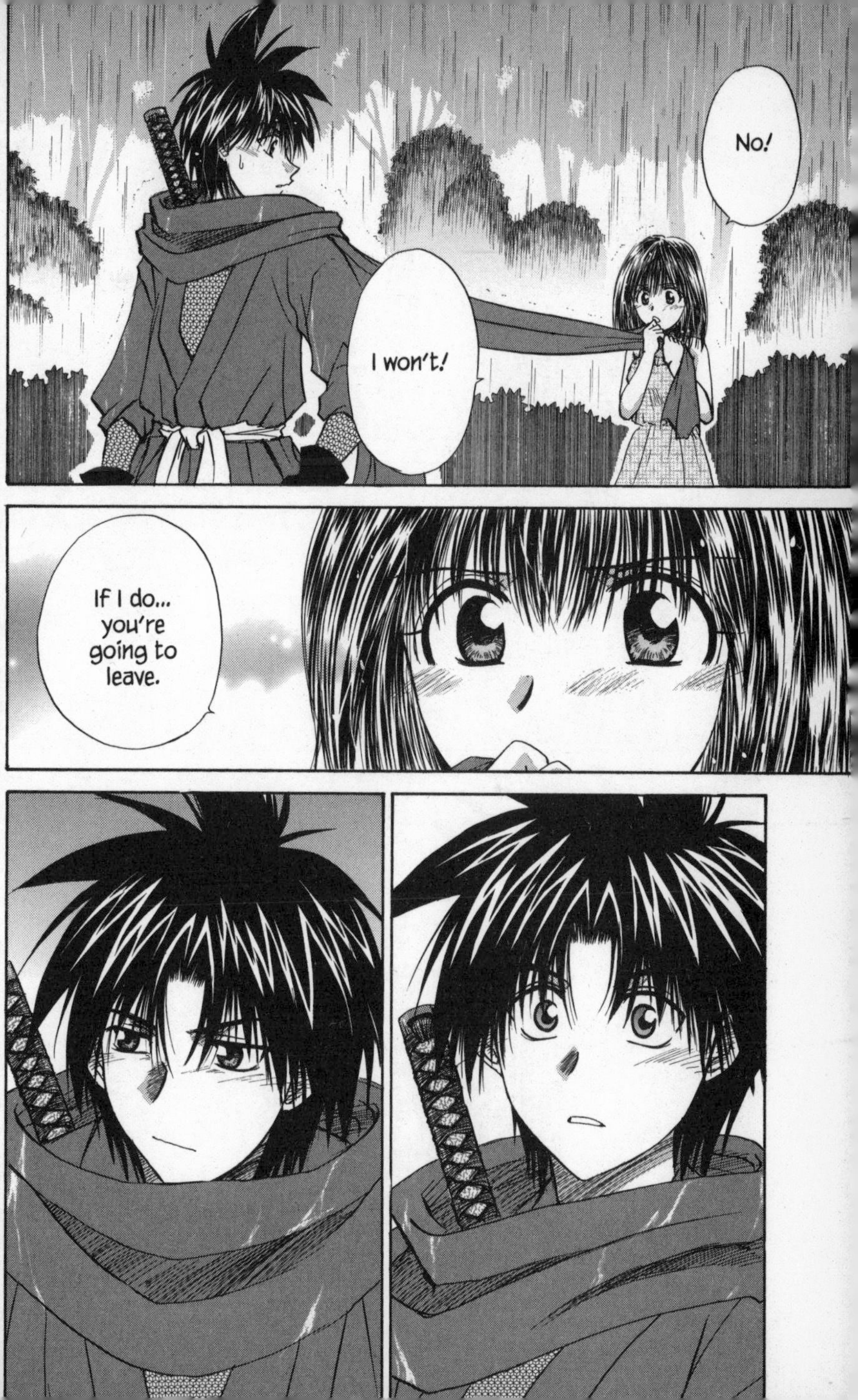
No!
I won't!
If I do... you're going to leave.

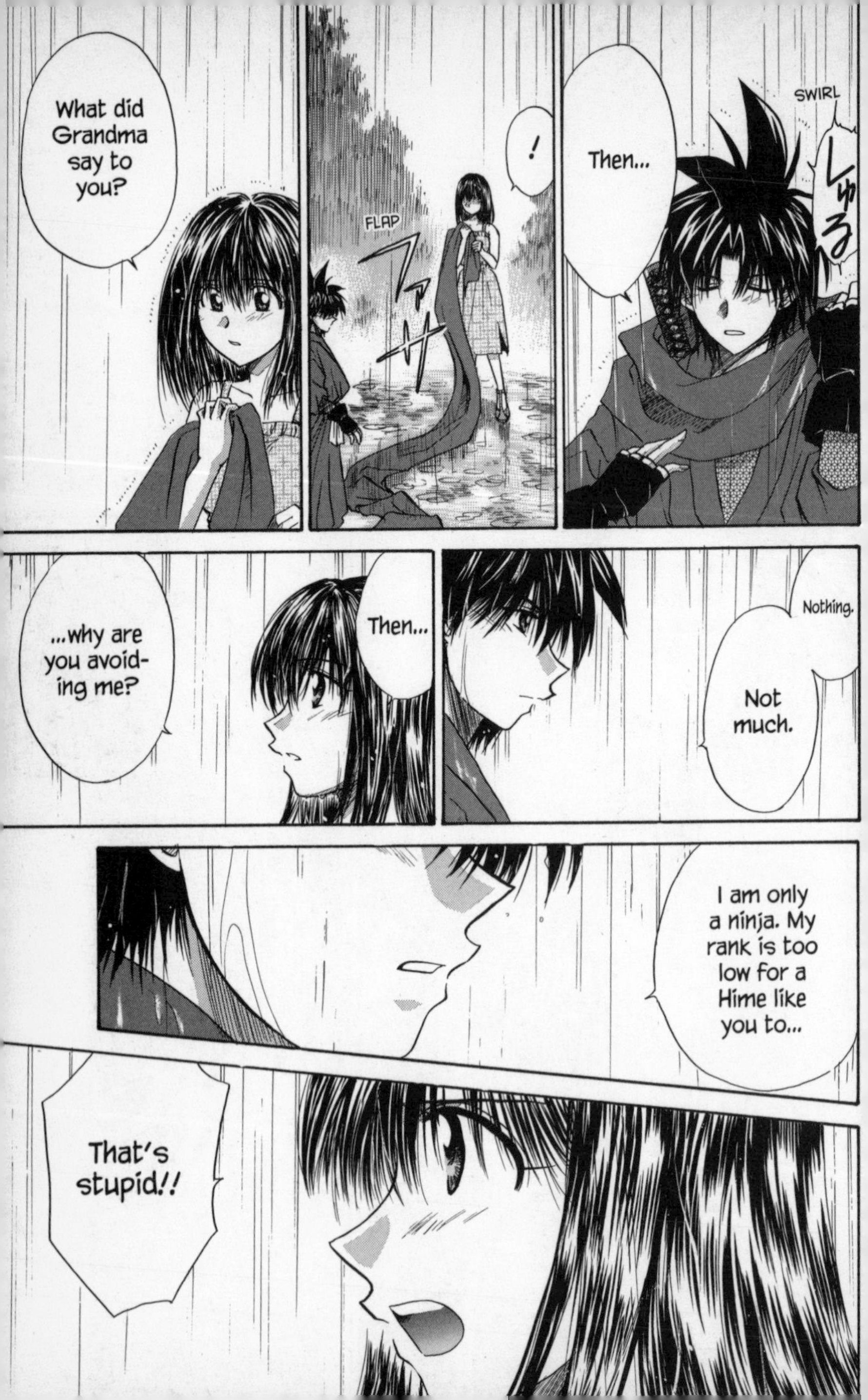
SWIRL
しゅる
Then...
!
FLAP
ファサ
What did Grandma say to you?
Nothing.
Not much.
Then...
...why are you avoiding me?
I am only a ninja. My rank is too low for a Hime like you to...
That's stupid!!

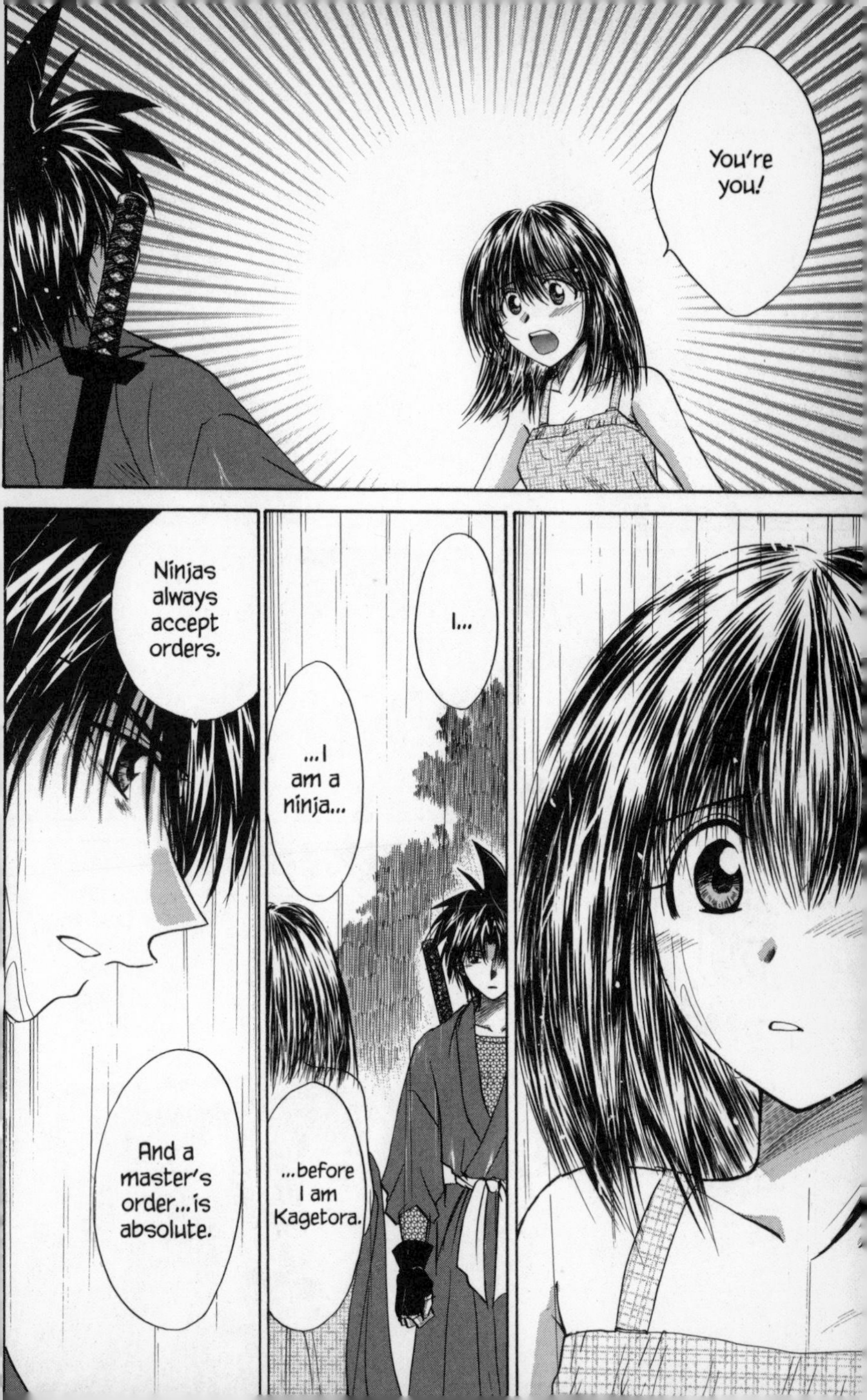
You're you!
I...
...I am a ninja...
...before I am Kagetora.
Ninjas always accept orders.
And a master's order...is absolute.

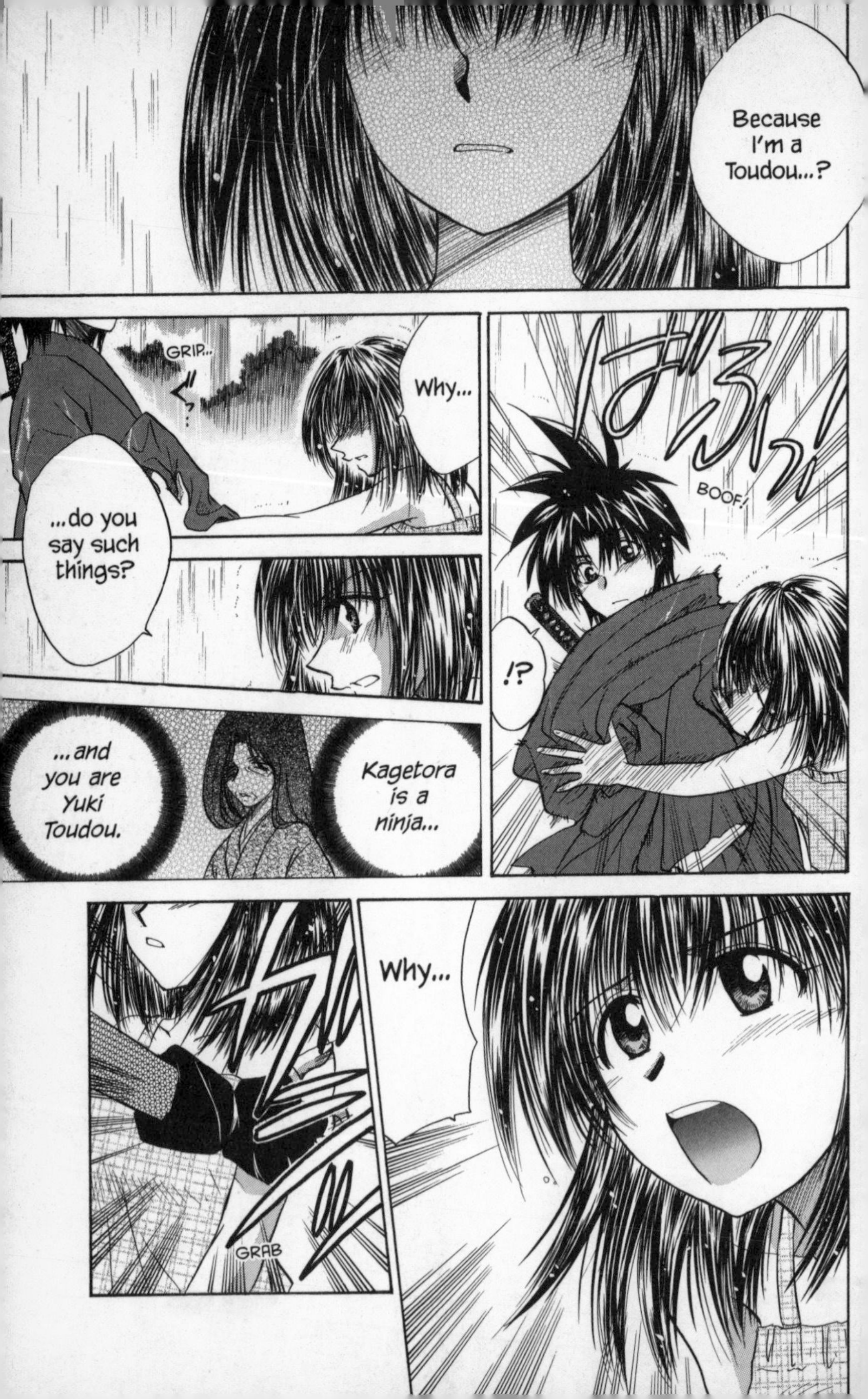
Because I'm a Toudou...?
BOOF!
!?
Why...
GRIP...
...do you say such things?
Kagetora is a ninja...
...and you are Yuki Toudou.
Why...
GRAB

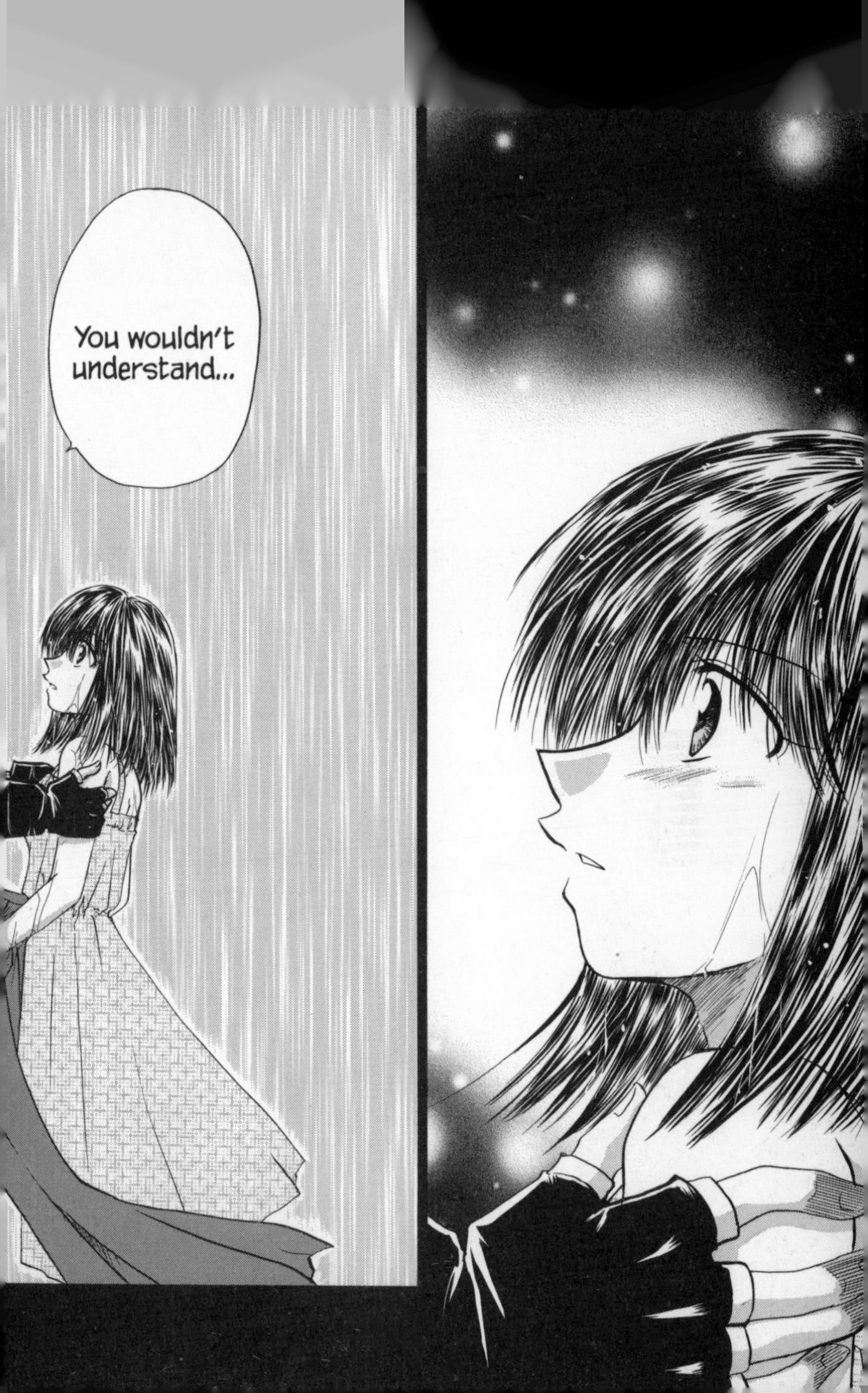
You wouldn't understand...

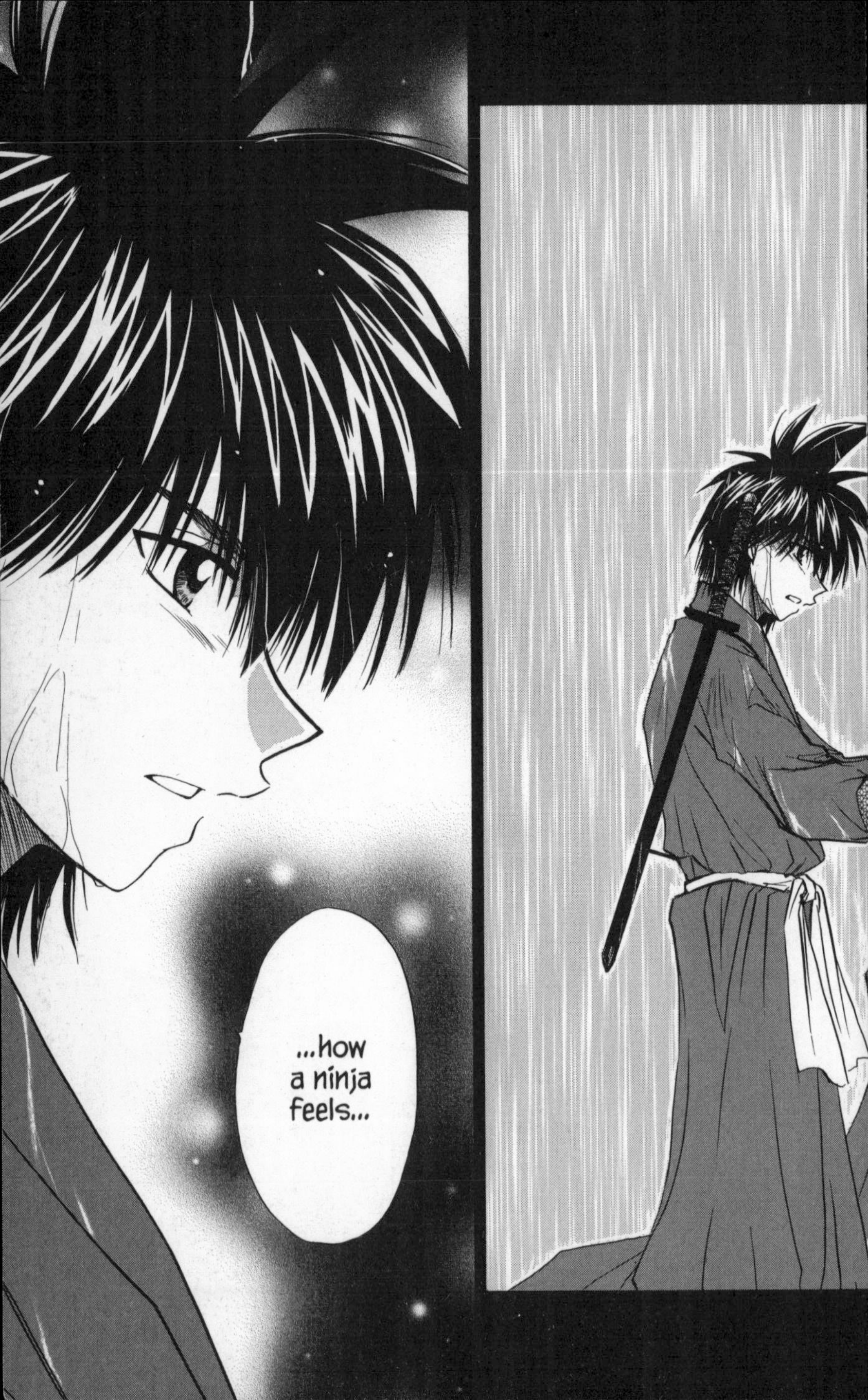
...how a ninja feels...

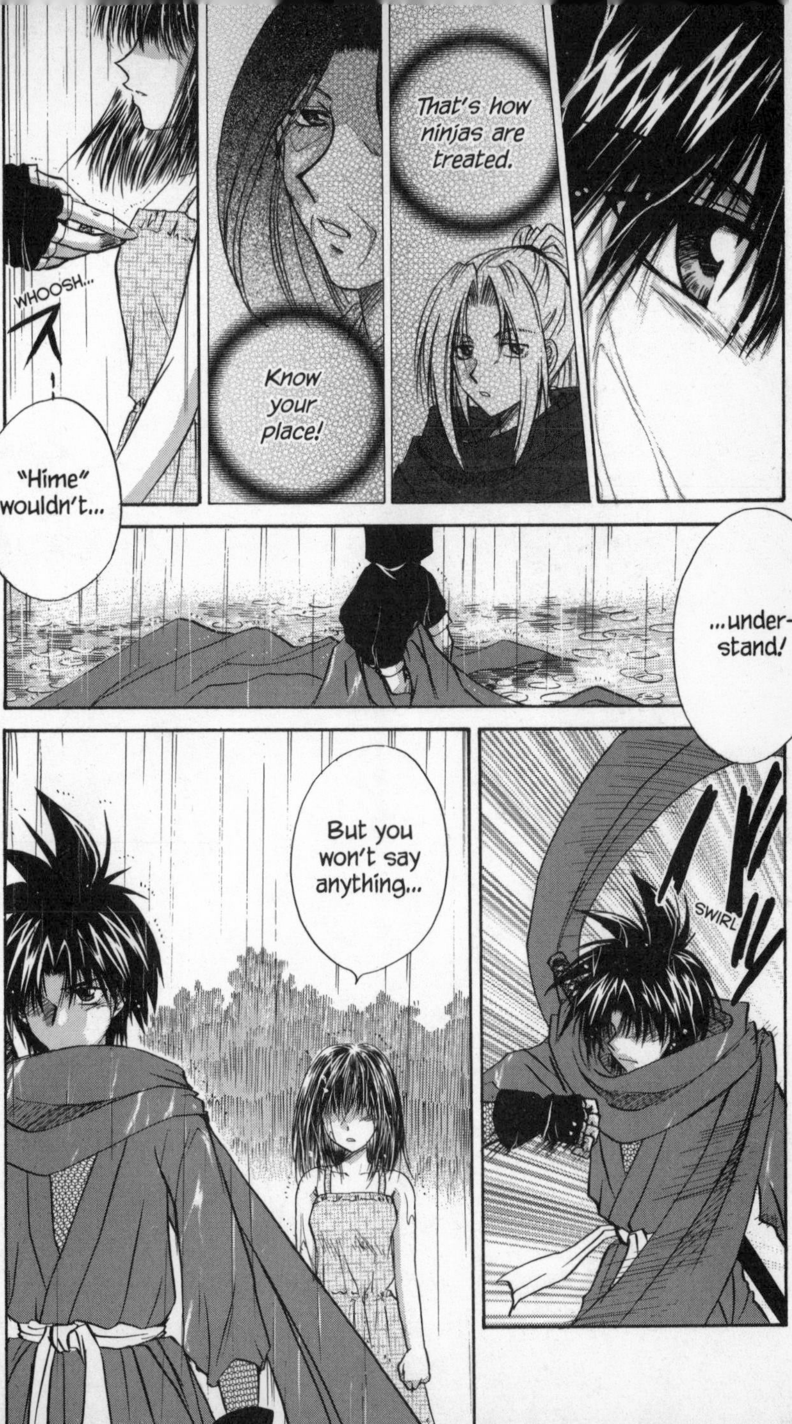
That's how ninjas are treated.
Know your place!
WHOOSH...
"Hime" wouldn't...
...under-stand!
SWIRL
But you won't say anything...

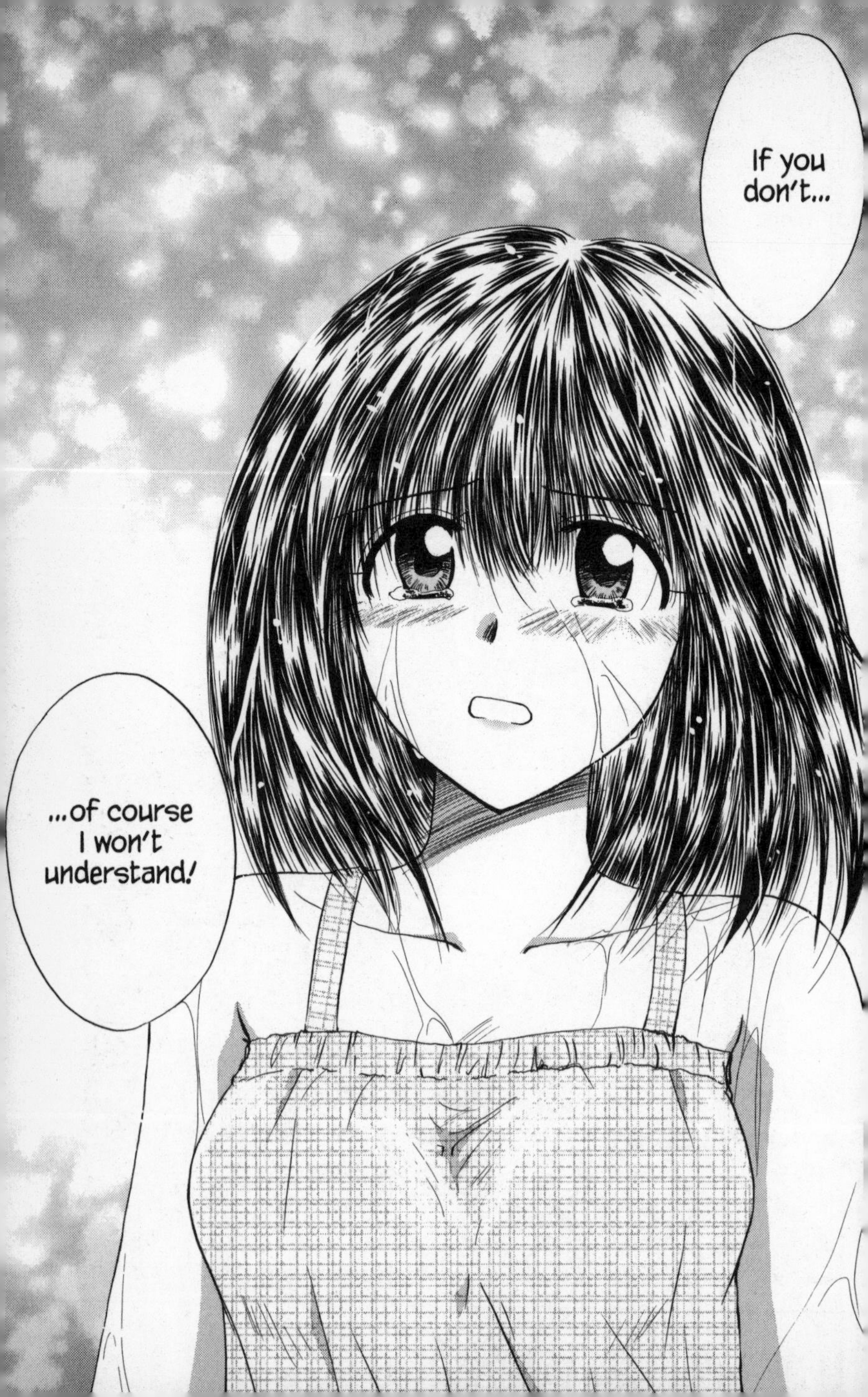
If you don't...
...of course I won't understand!

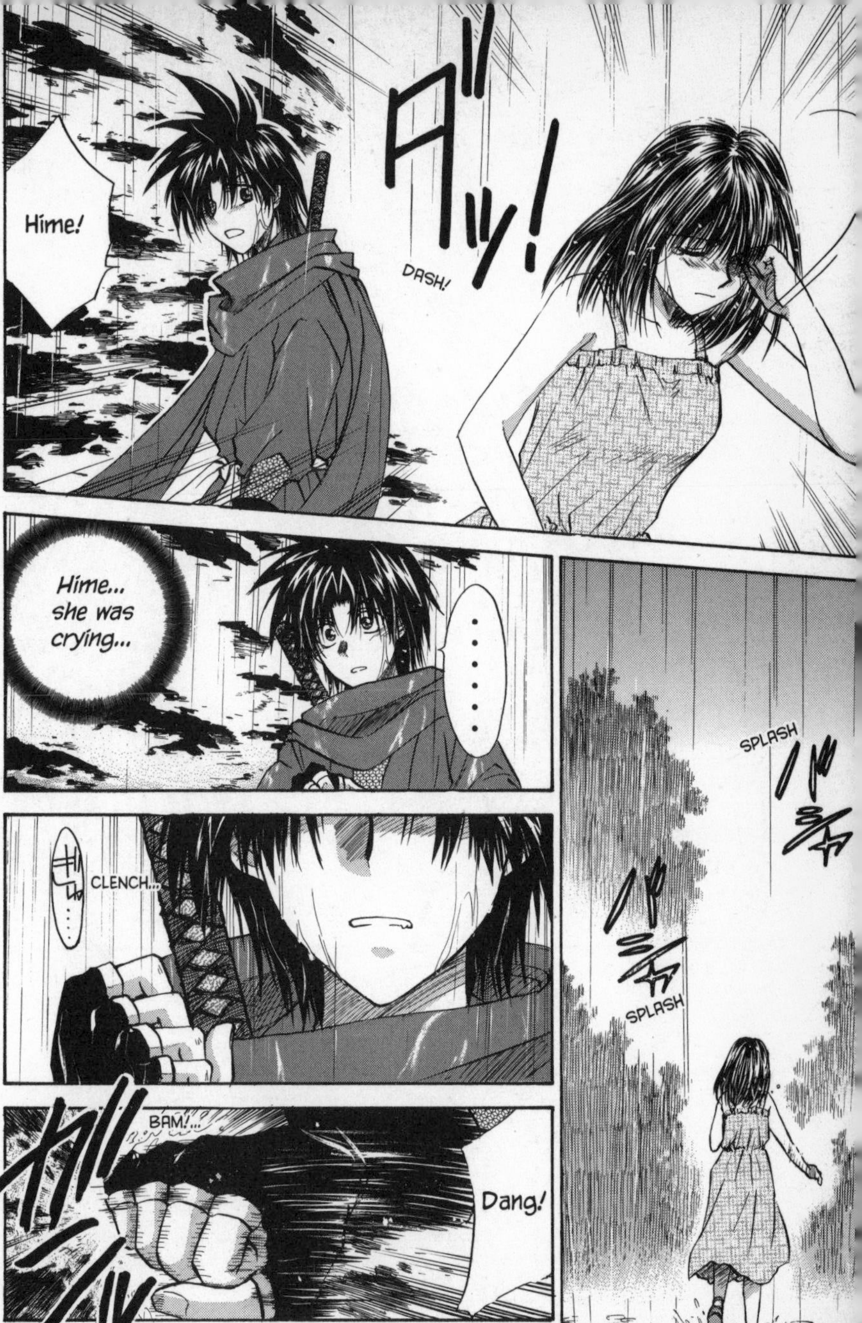
DASH!
Hime!
SPLASH
SPLASH
......
Hime... she was crying...
CLENCH...
Dang!
BAM!...

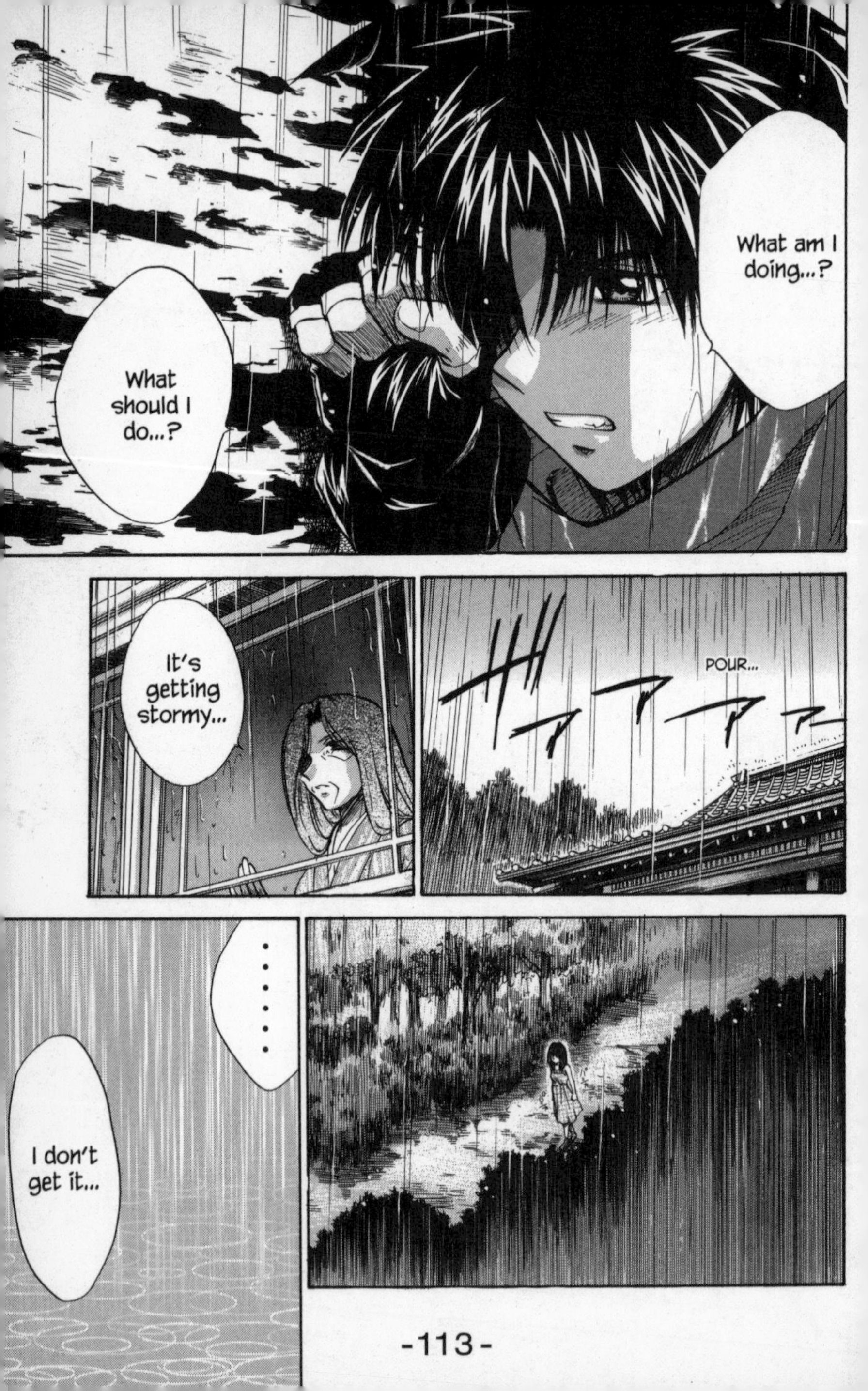
What am I doing...?
What should I do...?
POUR...
It's getting stormy...
......
I don't get it...

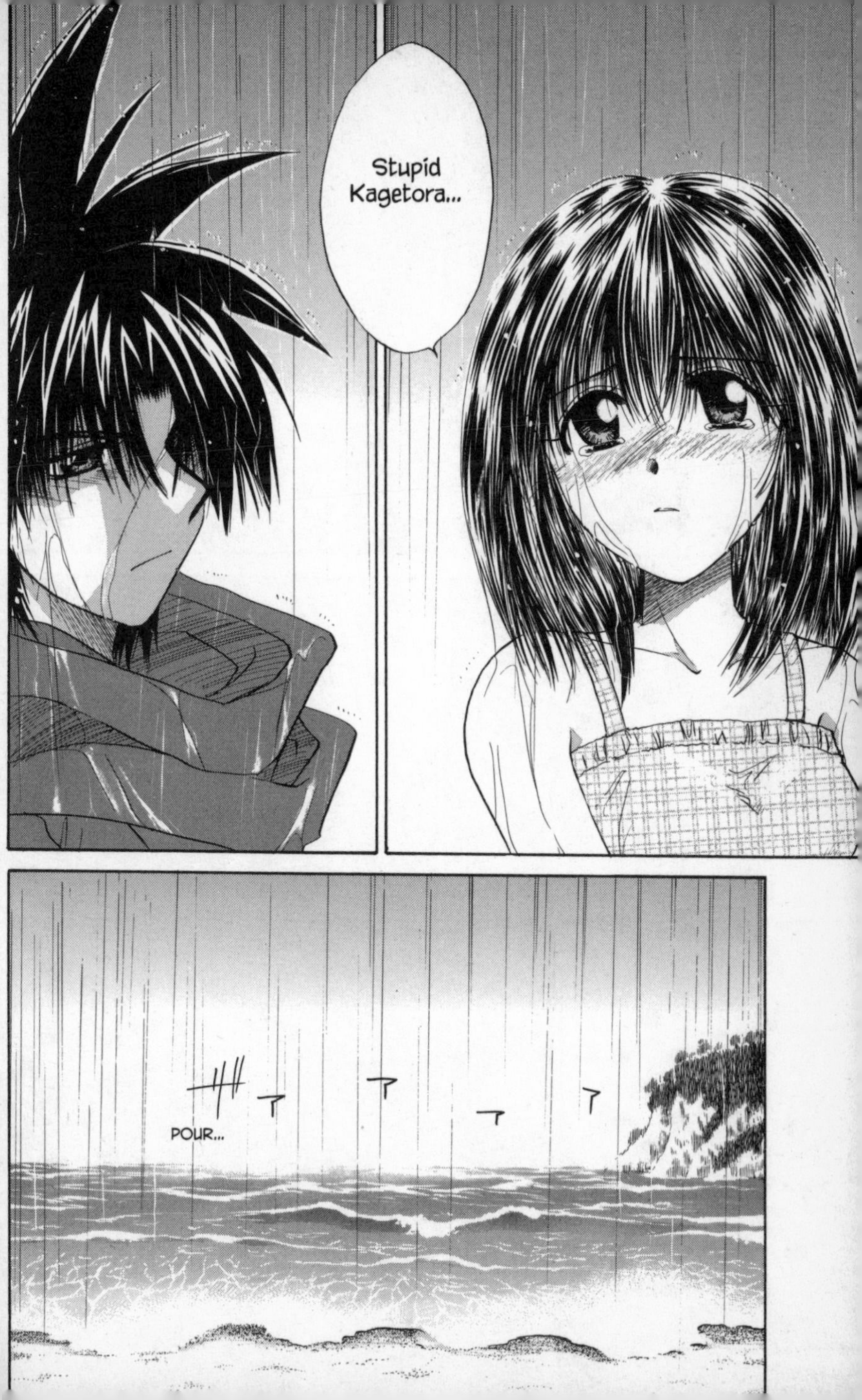
Stupid Kagetora...
POUR...

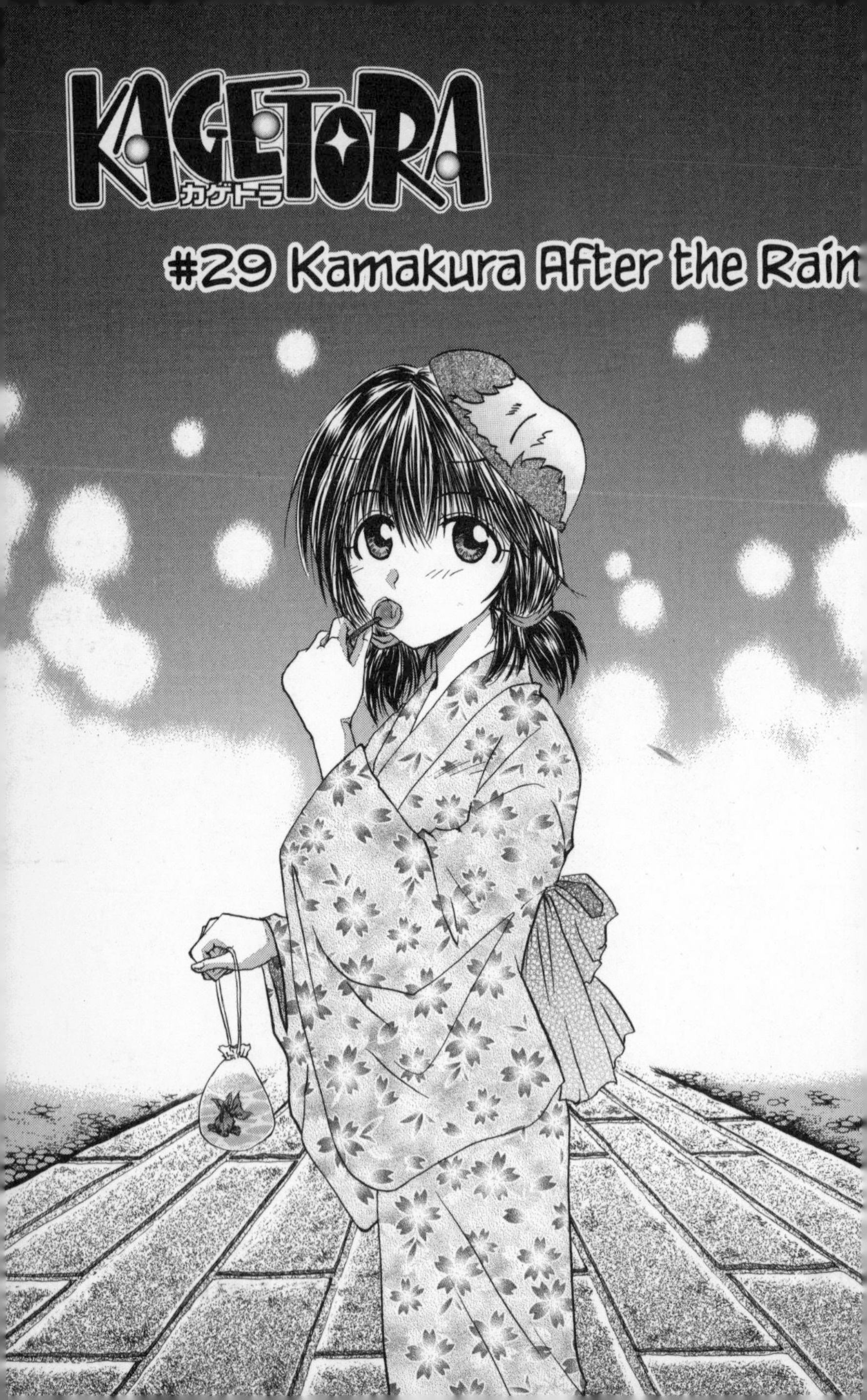
KAGETORA
カゲトラ
#29 Kamakura After the Rain

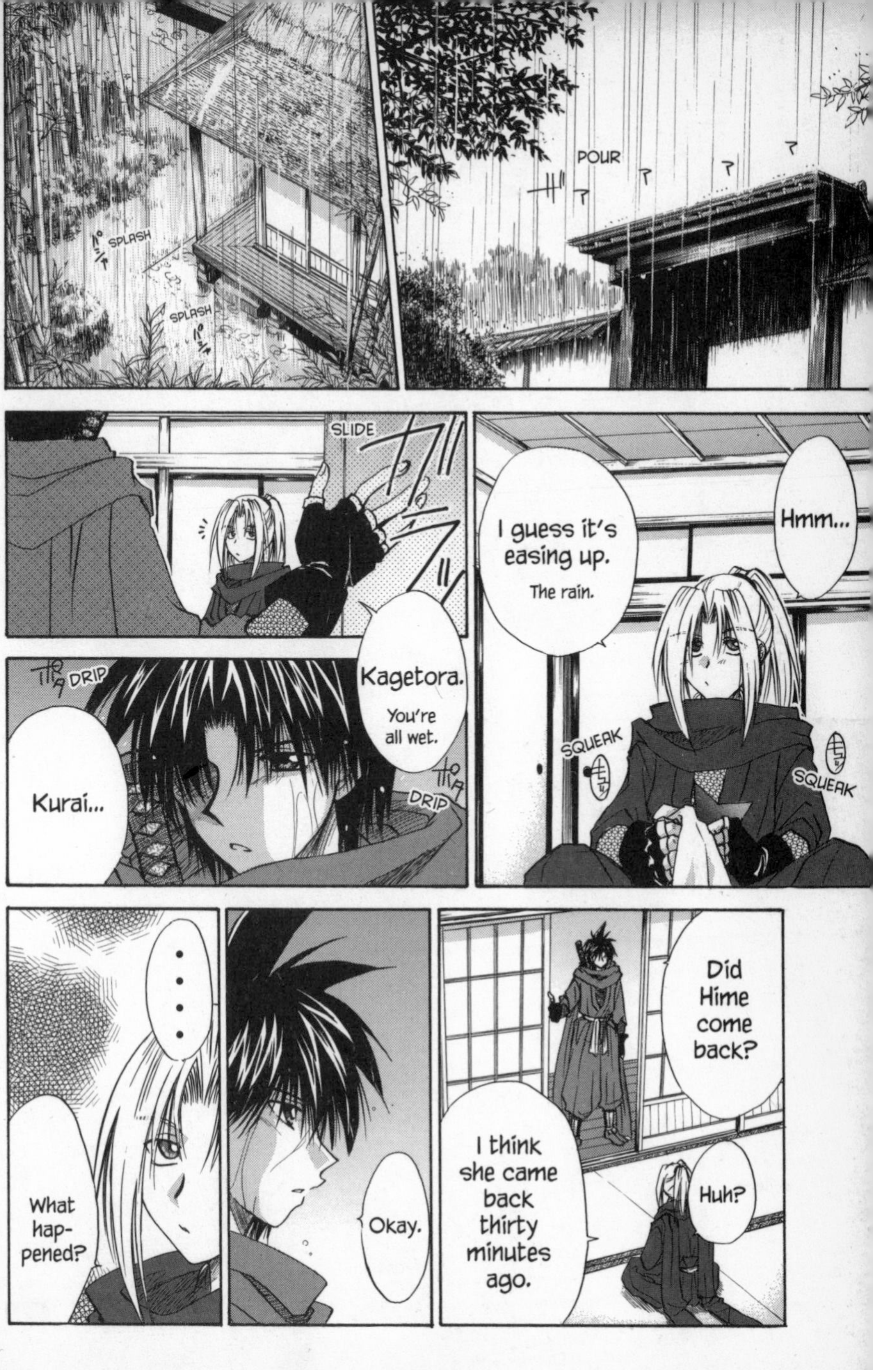
POUR
SPLASH
SPLASH
Hmm...
I guess it's easing up.
The rain.
SQUEAK
SQUEAK
SLIDE
Kagetora.
You're all wet.
DRIP
DRIP
Kurai...
Did Hime come back?
Huh?
I think she came back thirty minutes ago.
Okay.
...
What hap-pened?

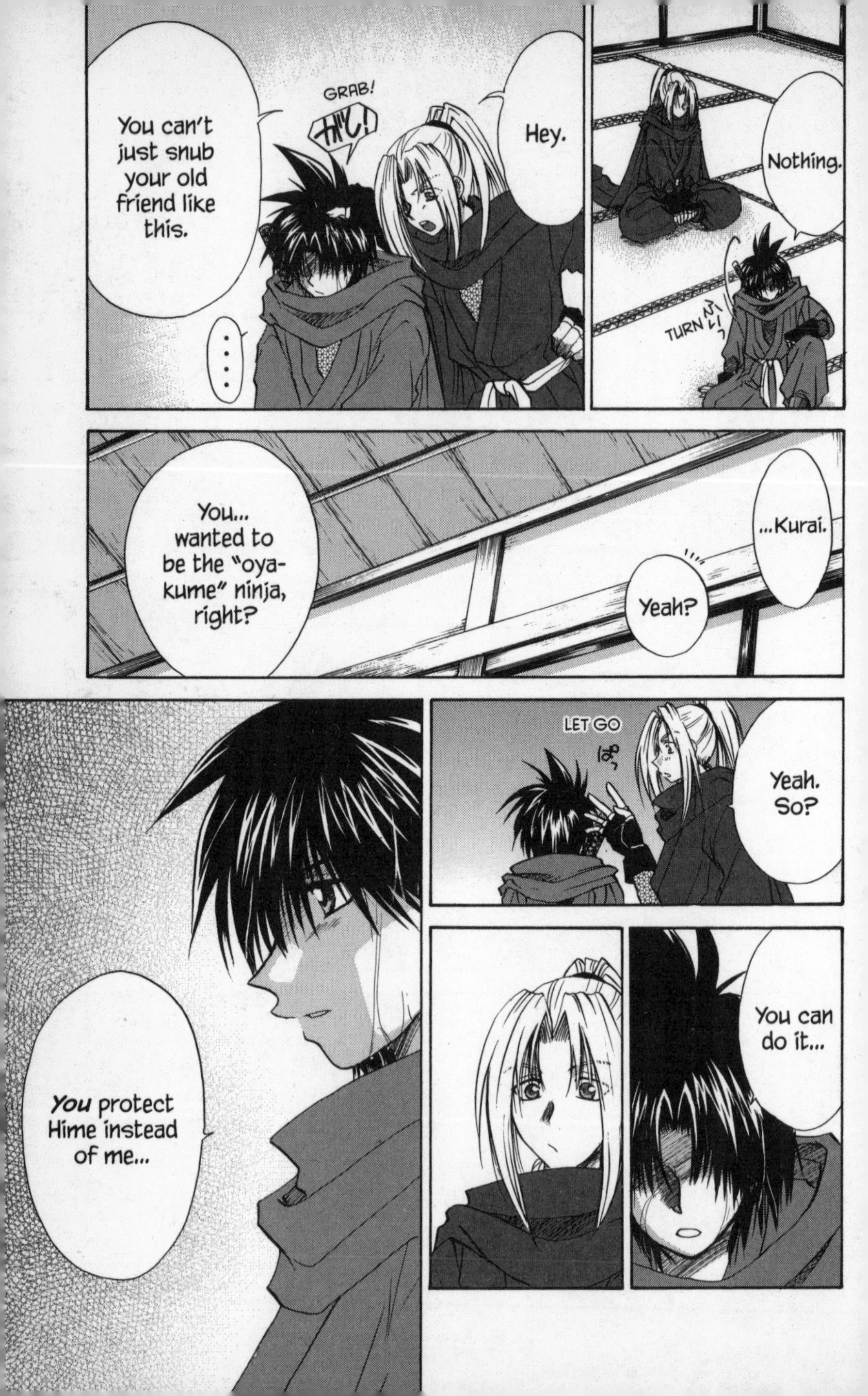

Nothing.
TURN
Hey.
GRAB!
You can't just snub your old friend like this.
.....
...Kurai.
Yeah?
You... wanted to be the "oya-kume" ninja, right?
Yeah. So?
LET GO
You can do it...
You protect Hime instead of me...

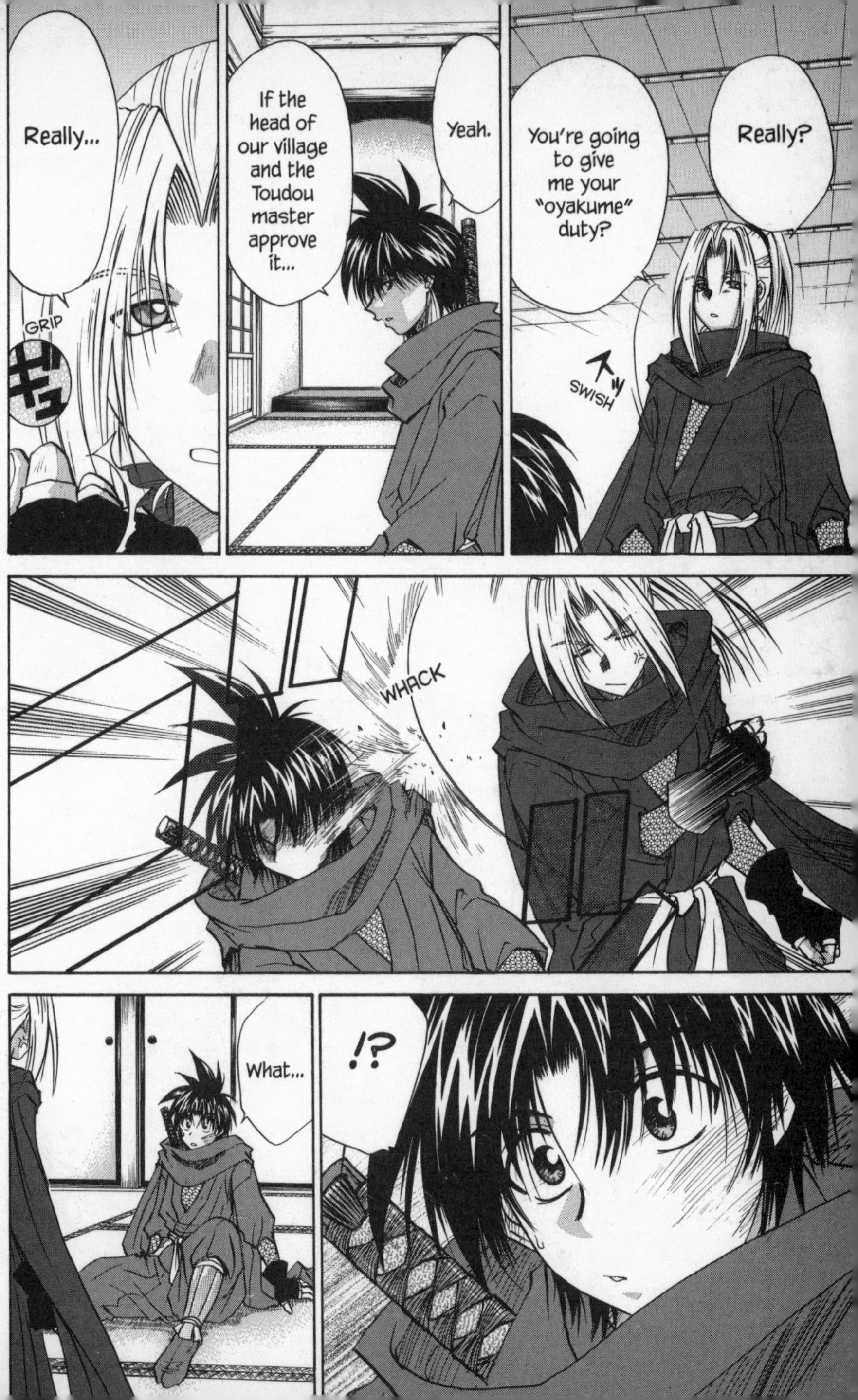
Really?
You're going to give me your "oyakume" duty?
SWISH
Yeah.
If the head of our village and the Toudou master approve it...
Really...
GRIP
WHACK
!?
What...

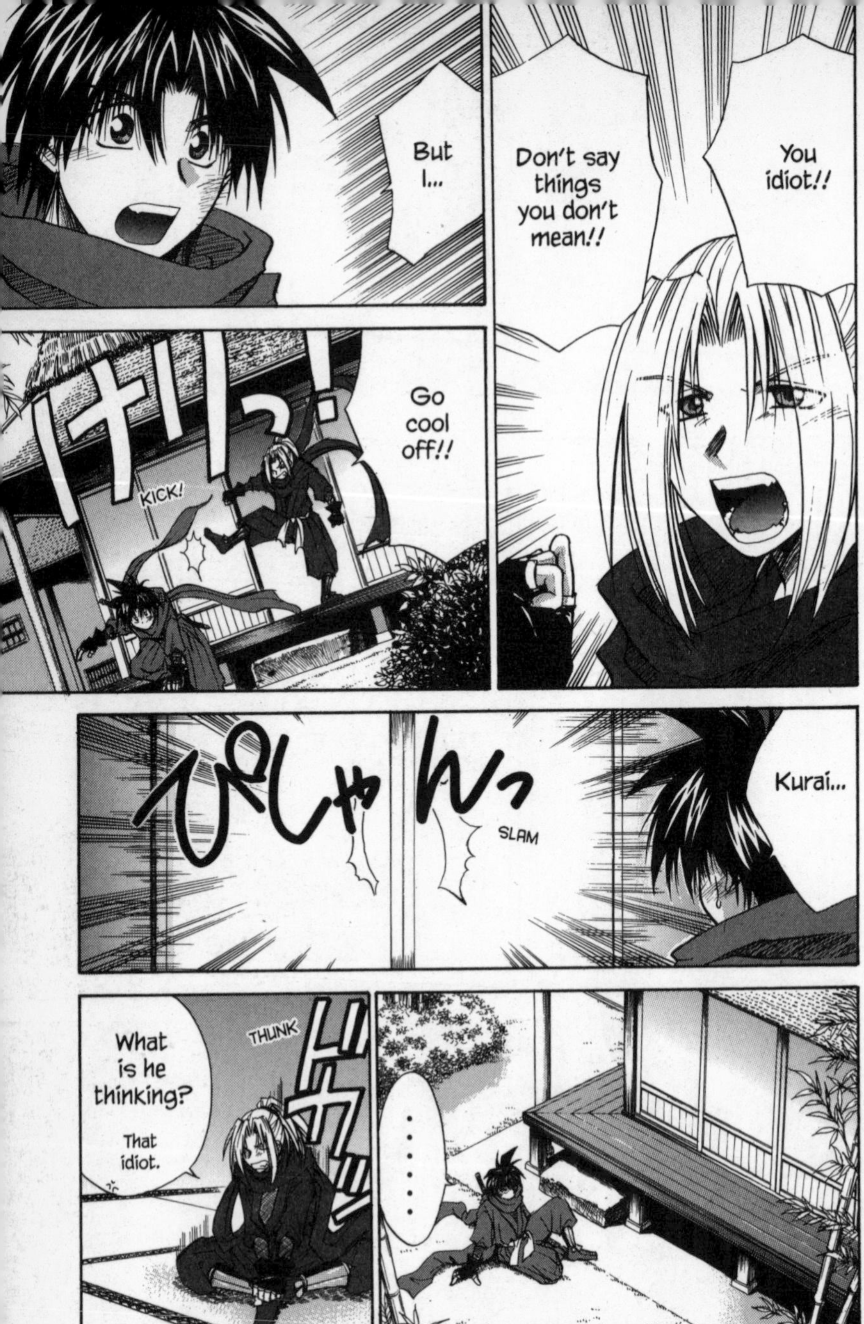

You idiot!!
Don't say things you don't mean!!
But I...
Go cool off!!
ケリっ!
KICK!
Kurai...
ぴしゃんっ
SLAM
......
What is he thinking?
That idiot.
ドカッ
THUNK

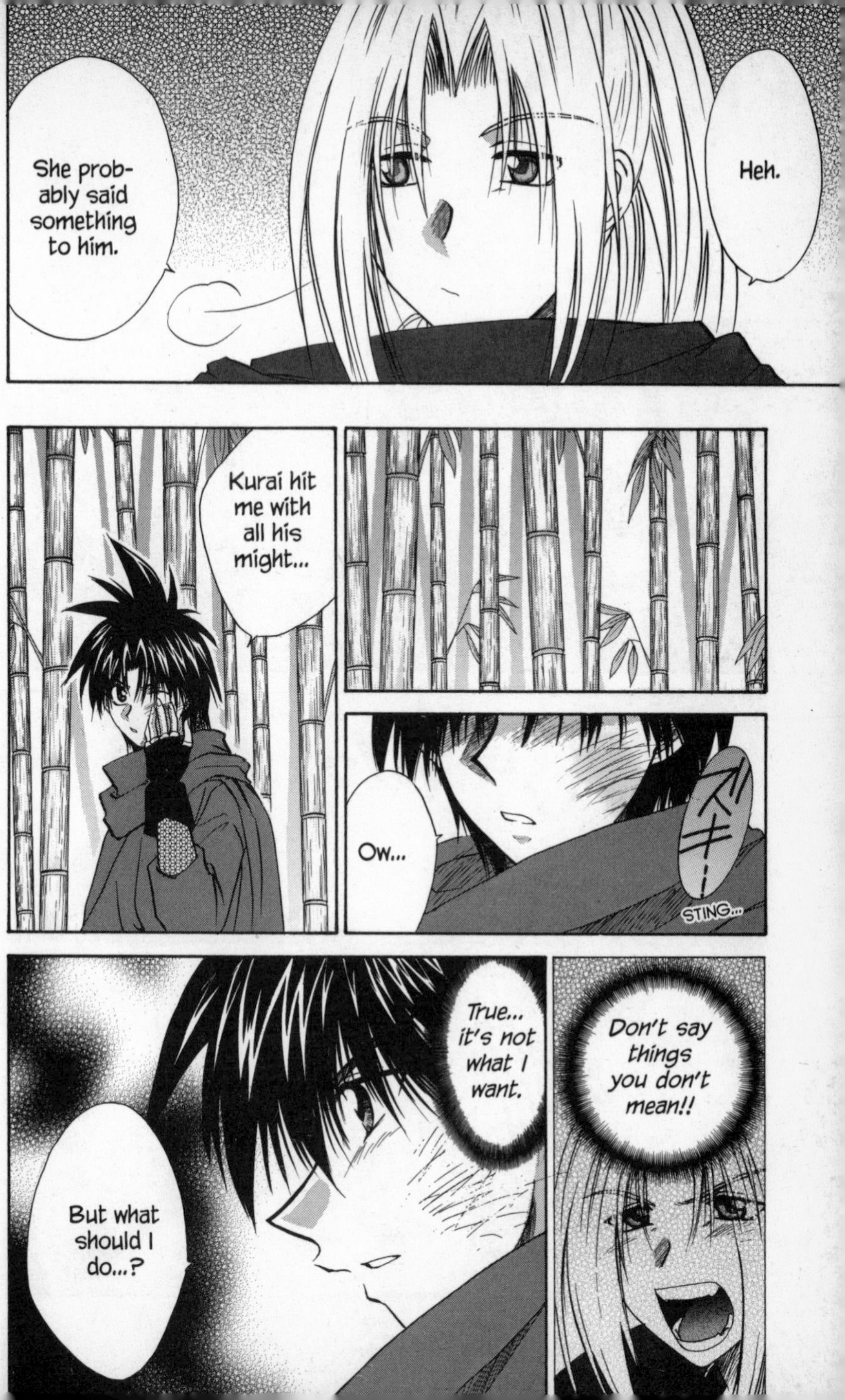
Heh.
She probably said something to him.
Ow...
STING...
Kurai hit me with all his might...
Don't say things you don't mean!!
True... it's not what I want.
But what should I do...?

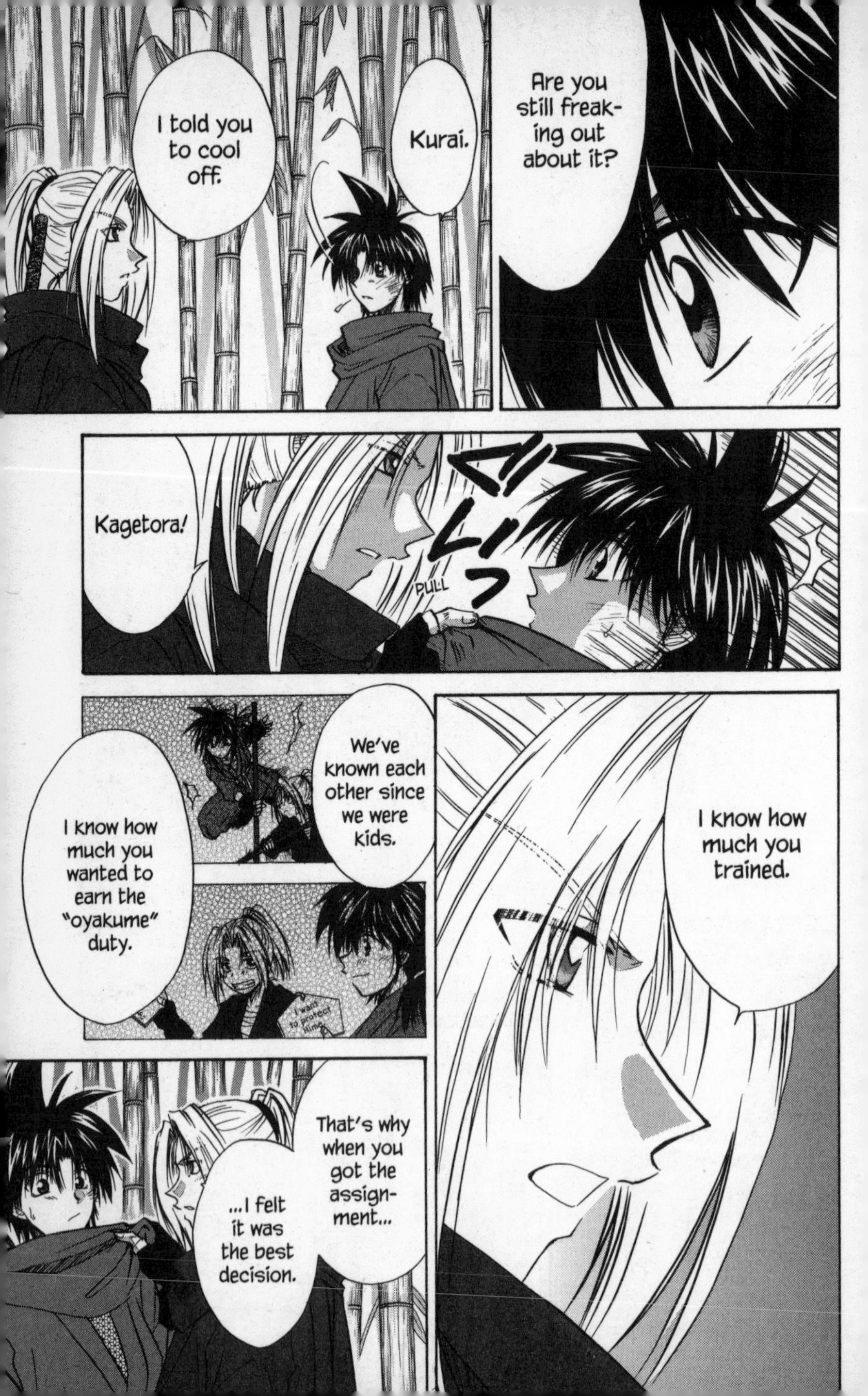
Are you still freak-ing out about it?
Kurai.
I told you to cool off.
PULL
Kagetora!
I know how much you trained.
We've known each other since we were kids.
I know how much you wanted to earn the "oyakume" duty.
I want to protect him.
That's why when you got the assign-ment...
...I felt it was the best decision.

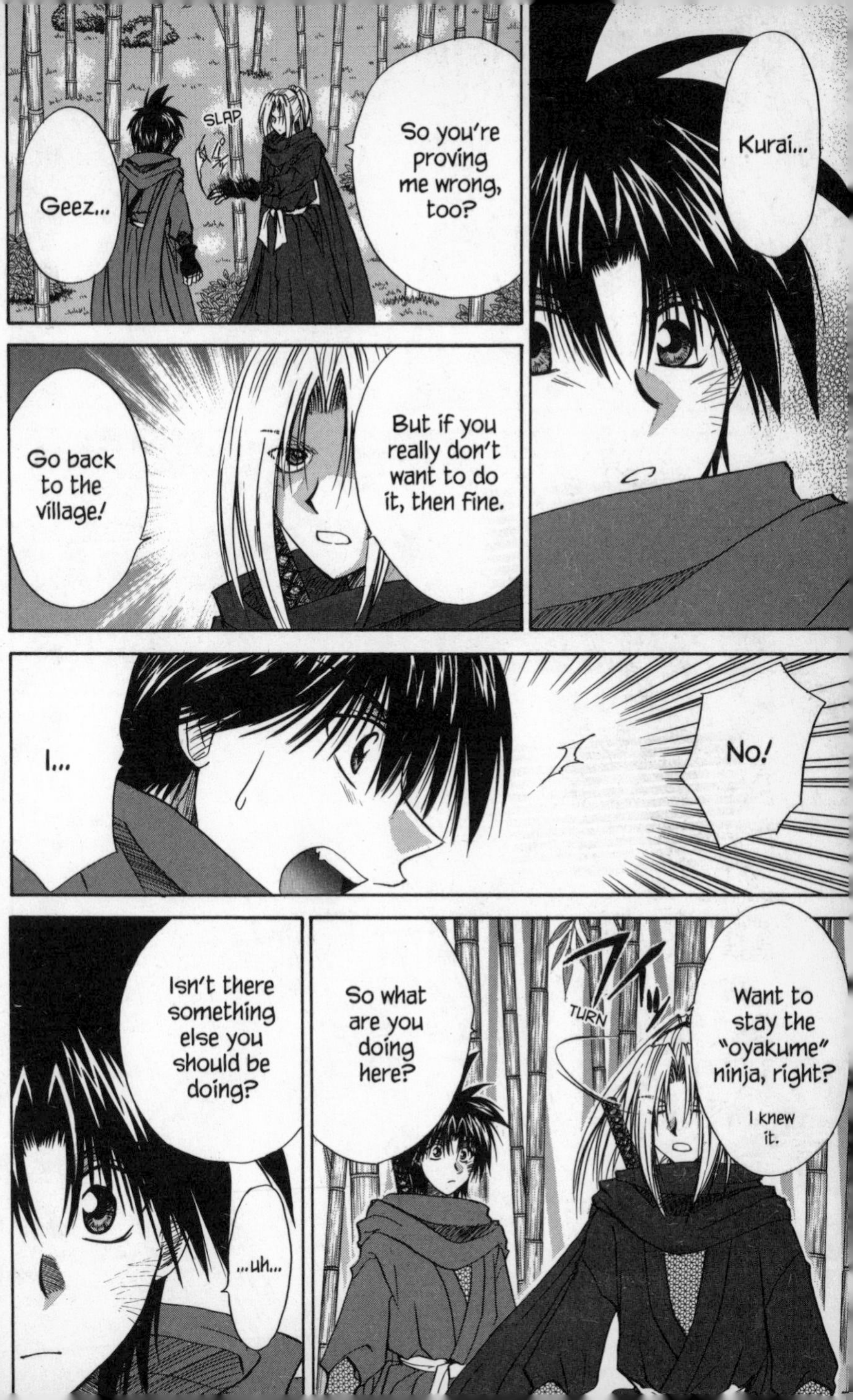
Kurai...
So you're proving me wrong, too?
SLAP
Geez...
But if you really don't want to do it, then fine.
Go back to the village!
No!
I...
Want to stay the "oyakume" ninja, right?
I knew it.
TURN
So what are you doing here?
Isn't there something else you should be doing?
...uh...

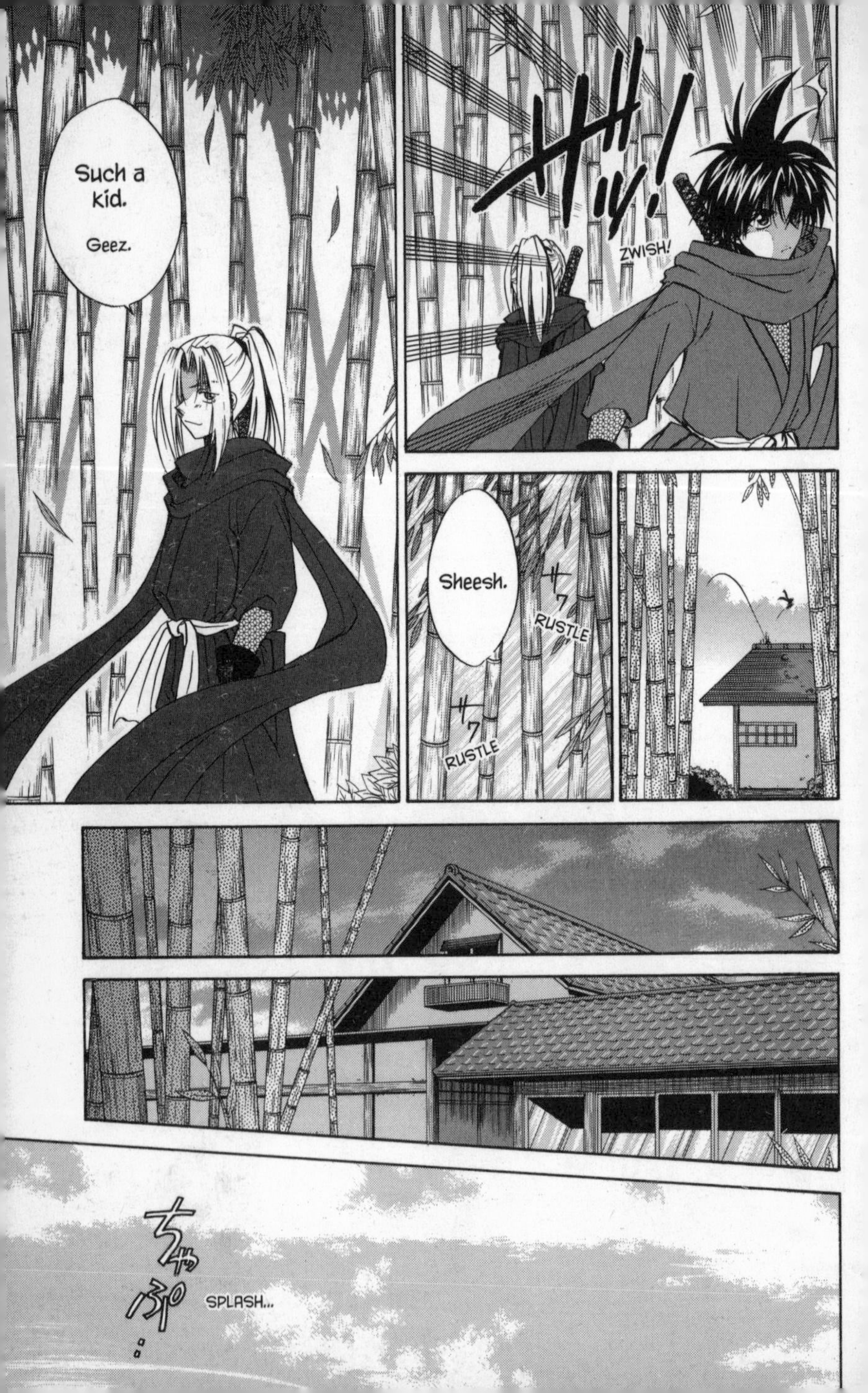
ZWISH!
Sheesh.
RUSTLE
RUSTLE
Such a kid.
Geez.
SPLASH...

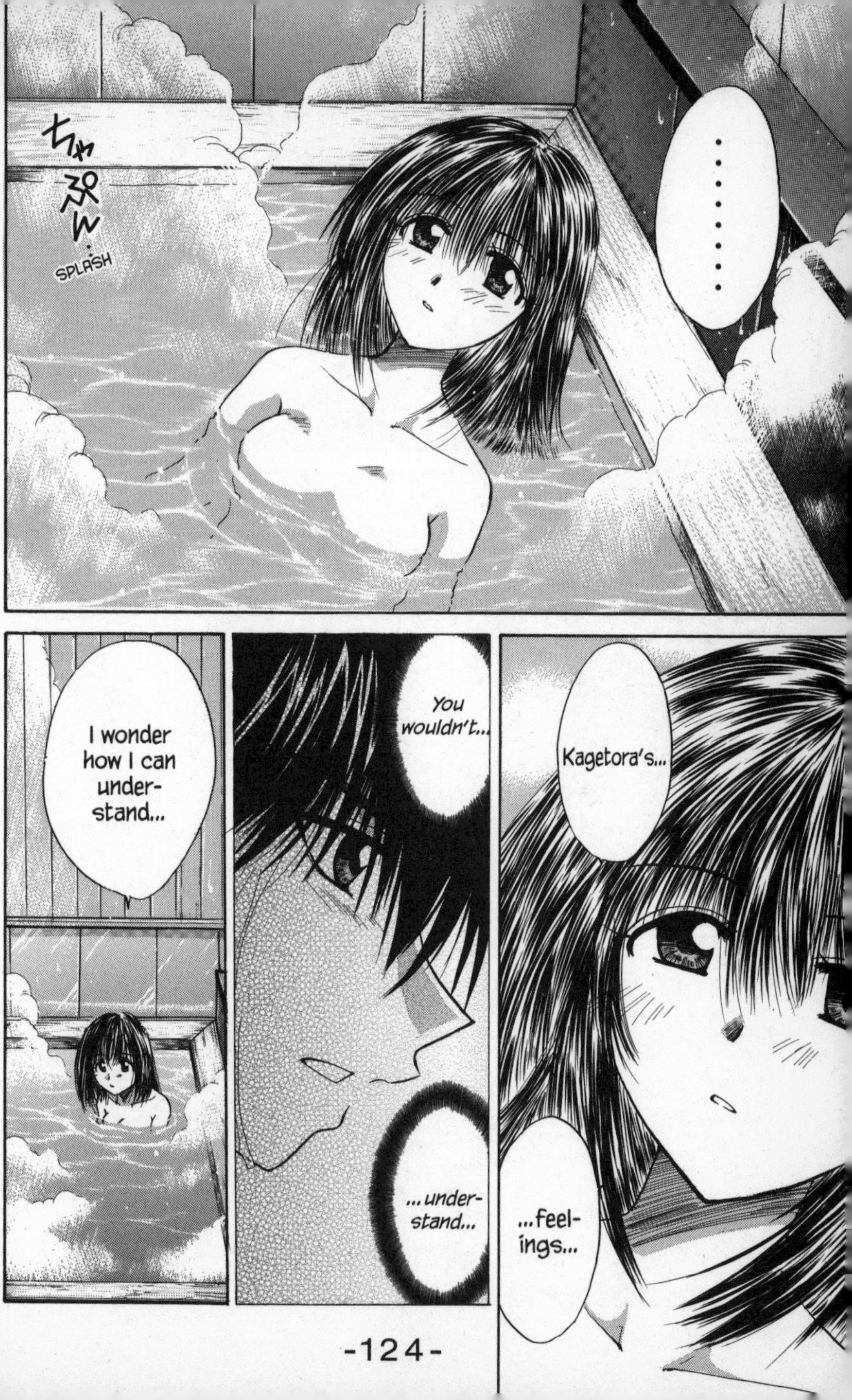
......
ちゃぷん
SPLASH
Kagetora's...
...feel-ings...
You wouldn't...
...under-stand...
I wonder how I can under-stand...

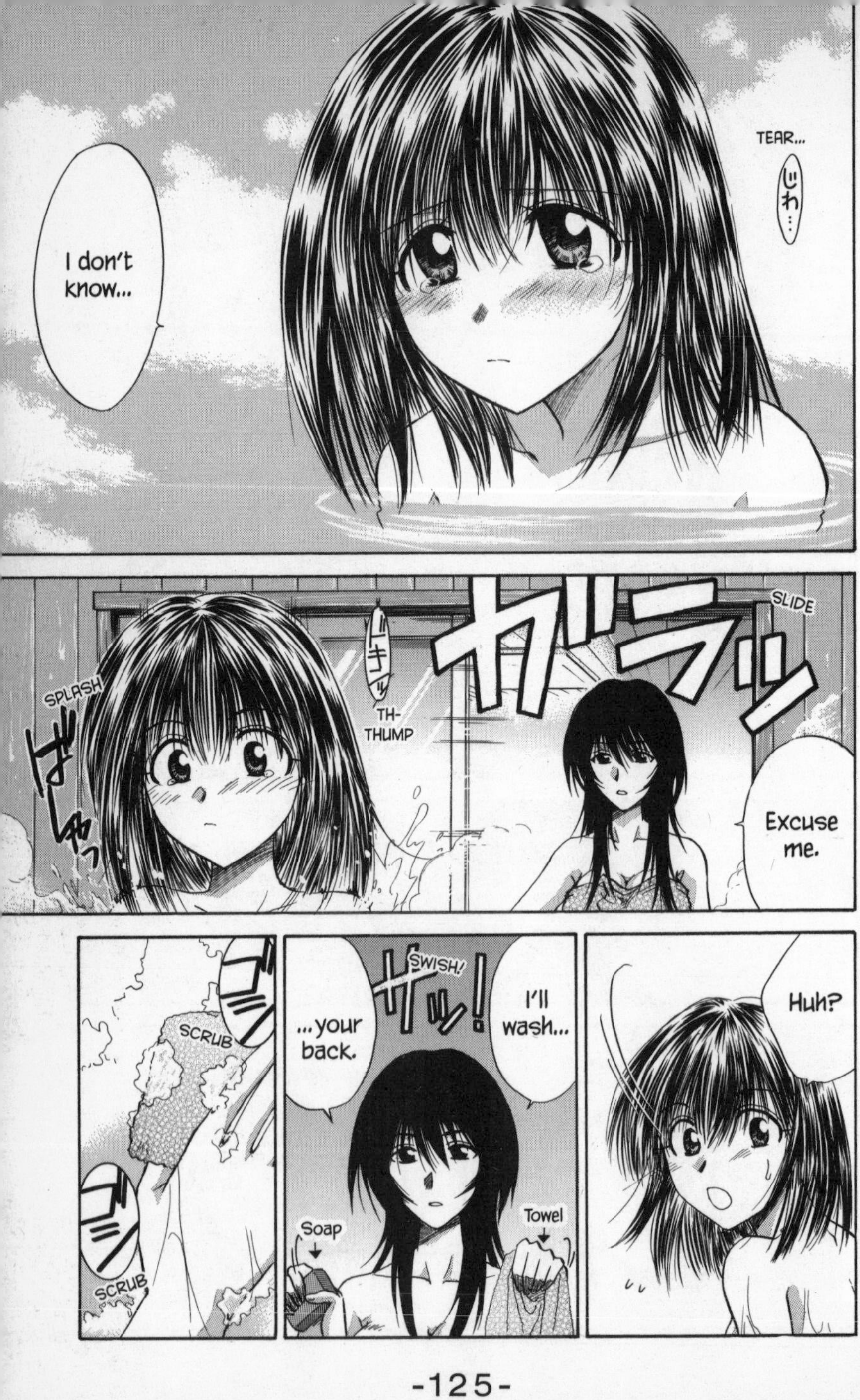
TEAR...
じわ…
I don't know...
Excuse me.
SLIDE
ガラッ
TH-THUMP
ドキッ
SPLASH
ばしゃっ
Huh?
I'll wash...
SWISH!
サッ!
...your back.
Towel
Soap
SCRUB
SCRUB

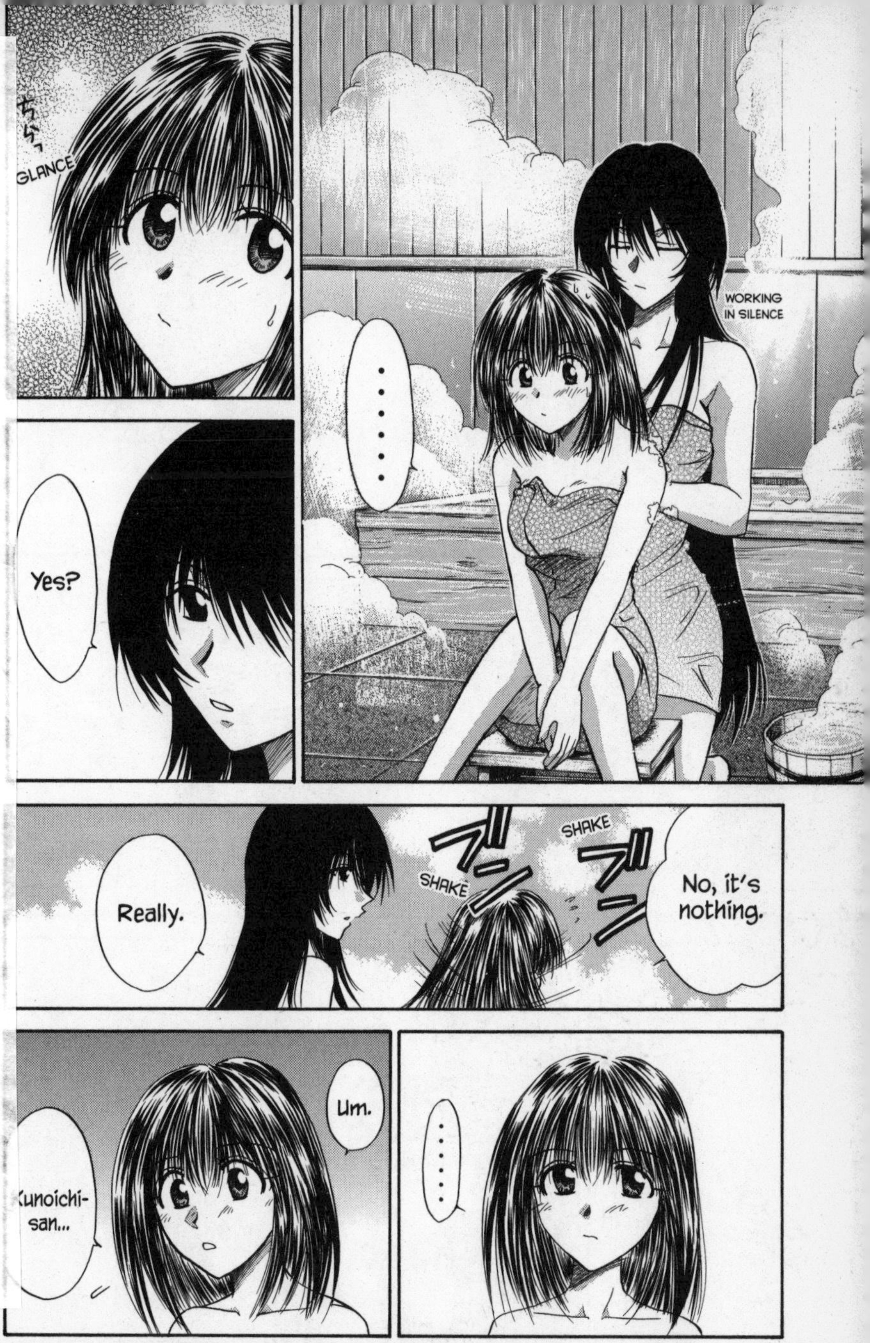
WORKING IN SILENCE
......
ちらっ
GLANCE
Yes?
SHAKE
SHAKE
No, it's nothing.
Really.
......
Um.
Kunoichi-san...

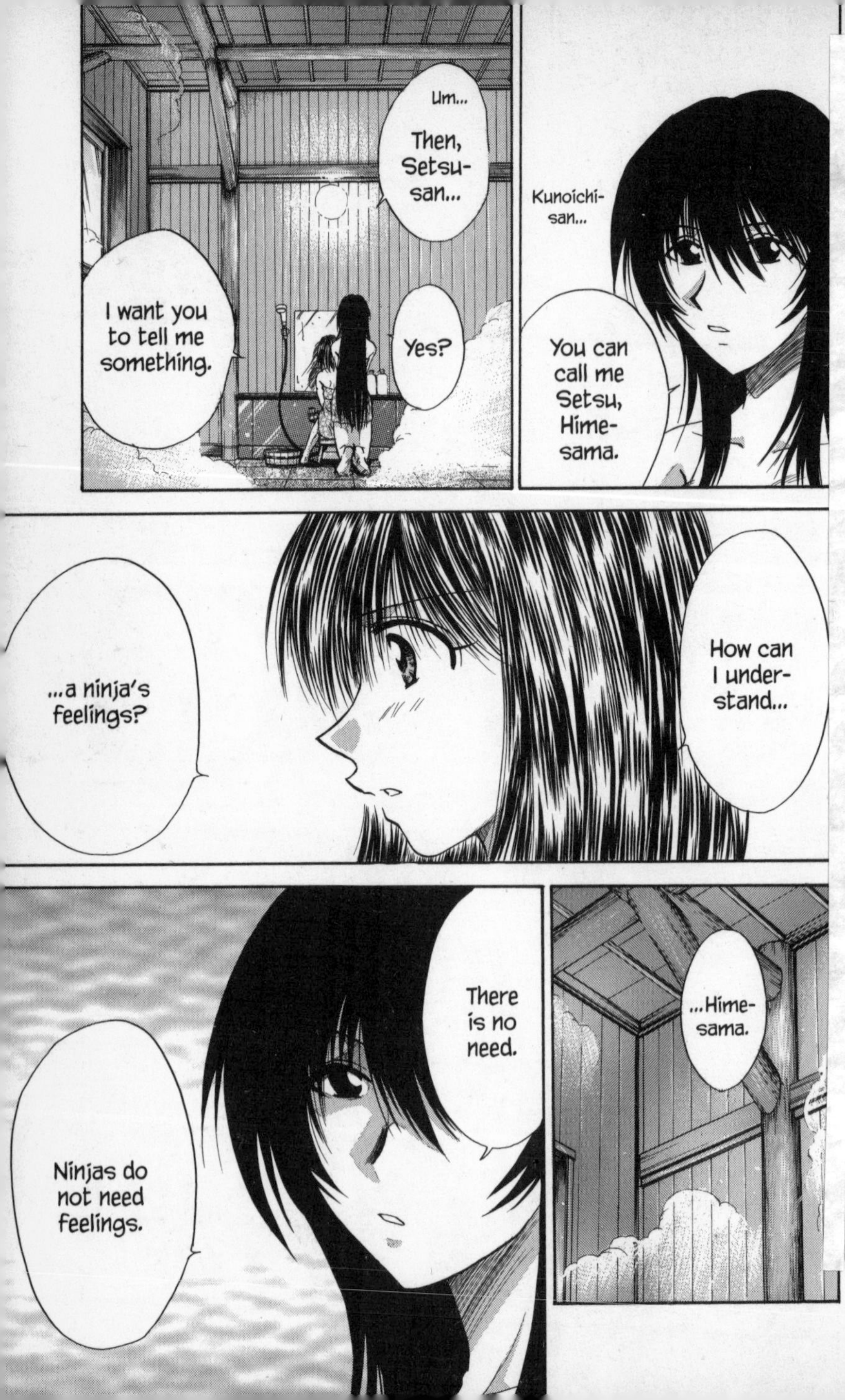
Kunoichi-san...
You can call me Setsu, Hime-sama.
Um...
Then, Setsu-san...
Yes?
I want you to tell me something.
How can I understand...
...a ninja's feelings?
...Hime-sama.
There is no need.
Ninjas do not need feelings.

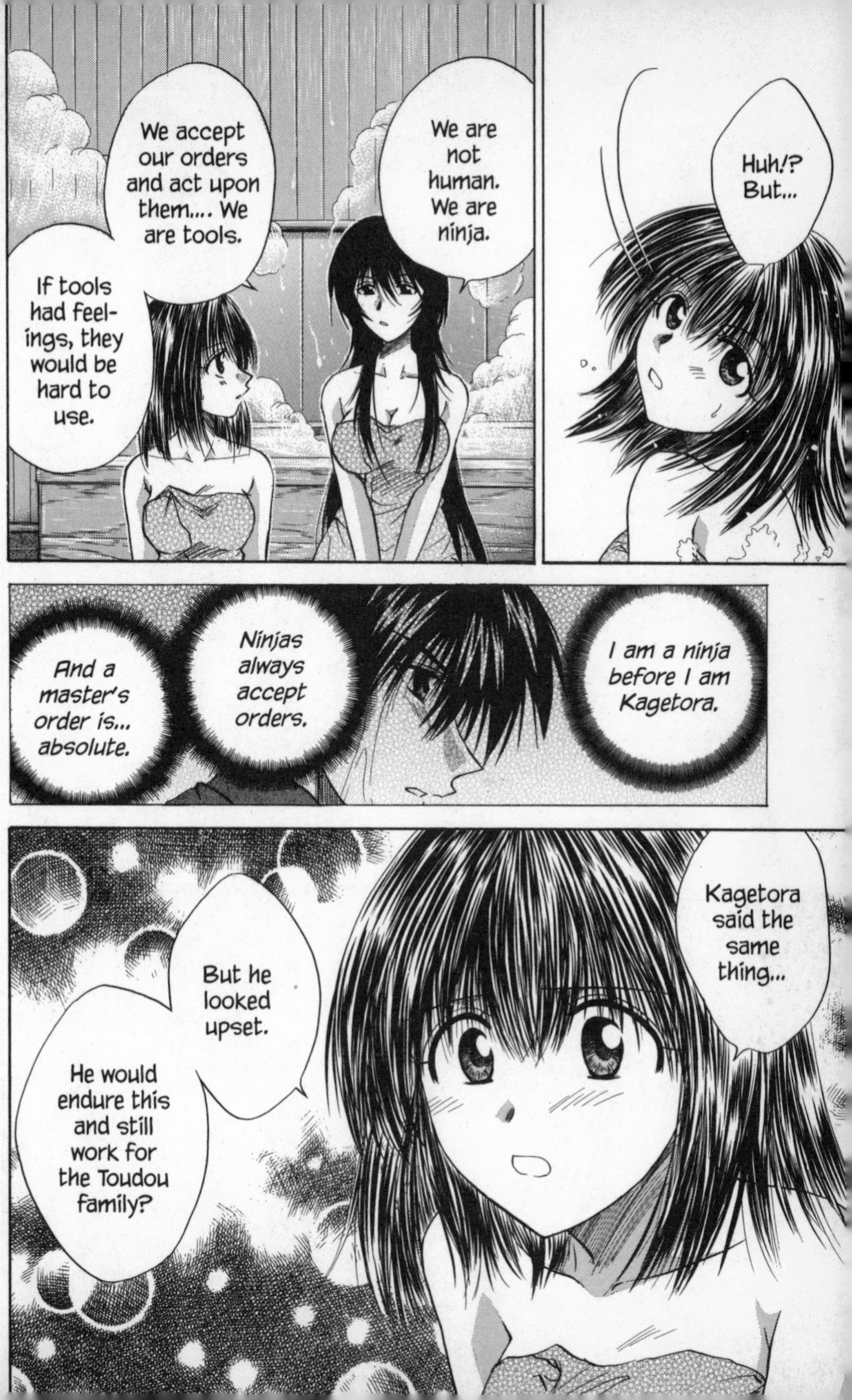
Huh!? But...
We are not human. We are ninja.
We accept our orders and act upon them.... We are tools.
If tools had feel-ings, they would be hard to use.
I am a ninja before I am Kagetora.
Ninjas always accept orders.
And a master's order is... absolute.
Kagetora said the same thing...
But he looked upset.
He would endure this and still work for the Toudou family?

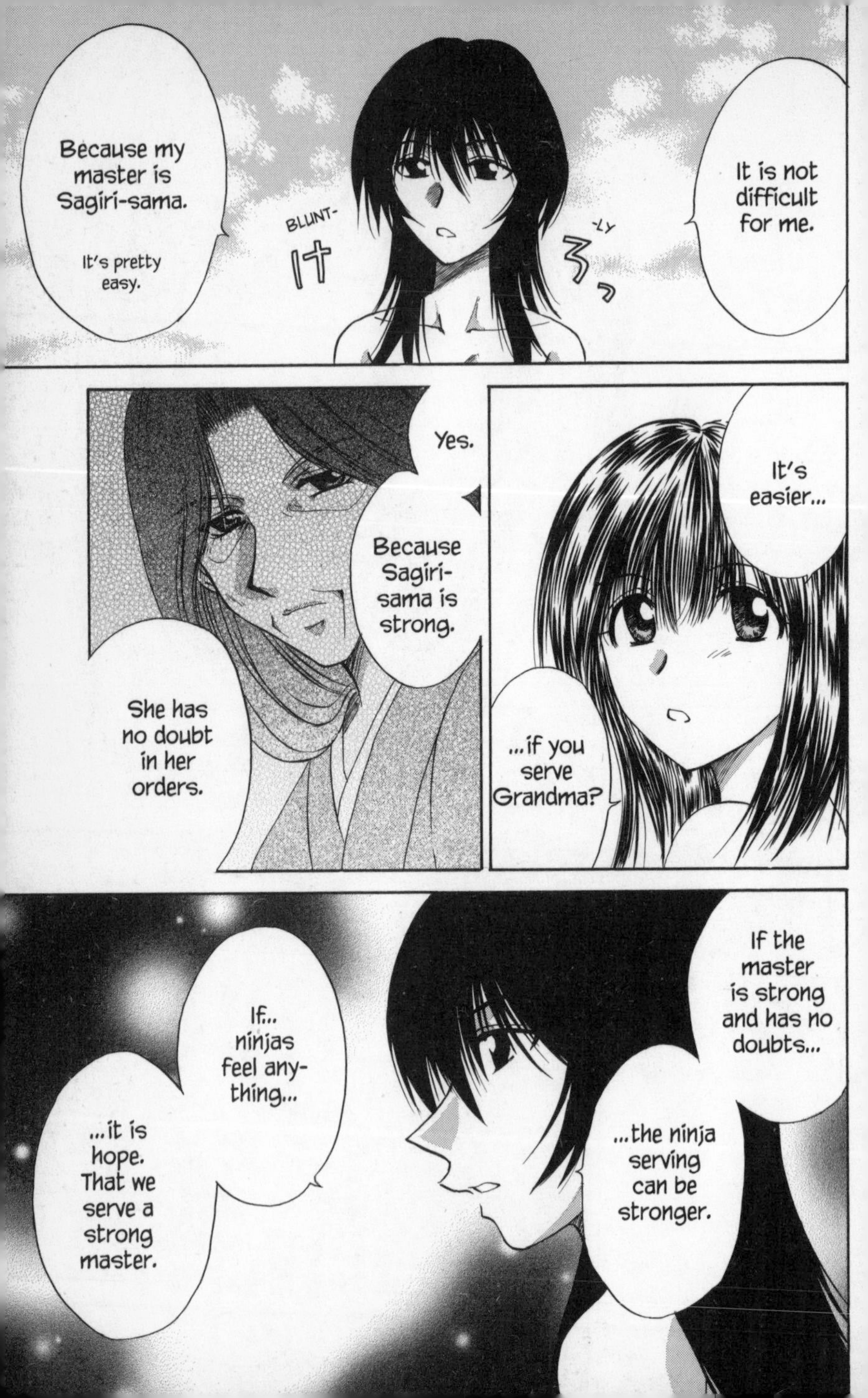
It is not difficult for me.
BLUNT- -LY
Because my master is Sagiri-sama.
It's pretty easy.
It's easier...
...if you serve Grandma?
Yes.
Because Sagiri-sama is strong.
She has no doubt in her orders.
If the master is strong and has no doubts...
...the ninja serving can be stronger.
If... ninjas feel any-thing...
...it is hope. That we serve a strong master.

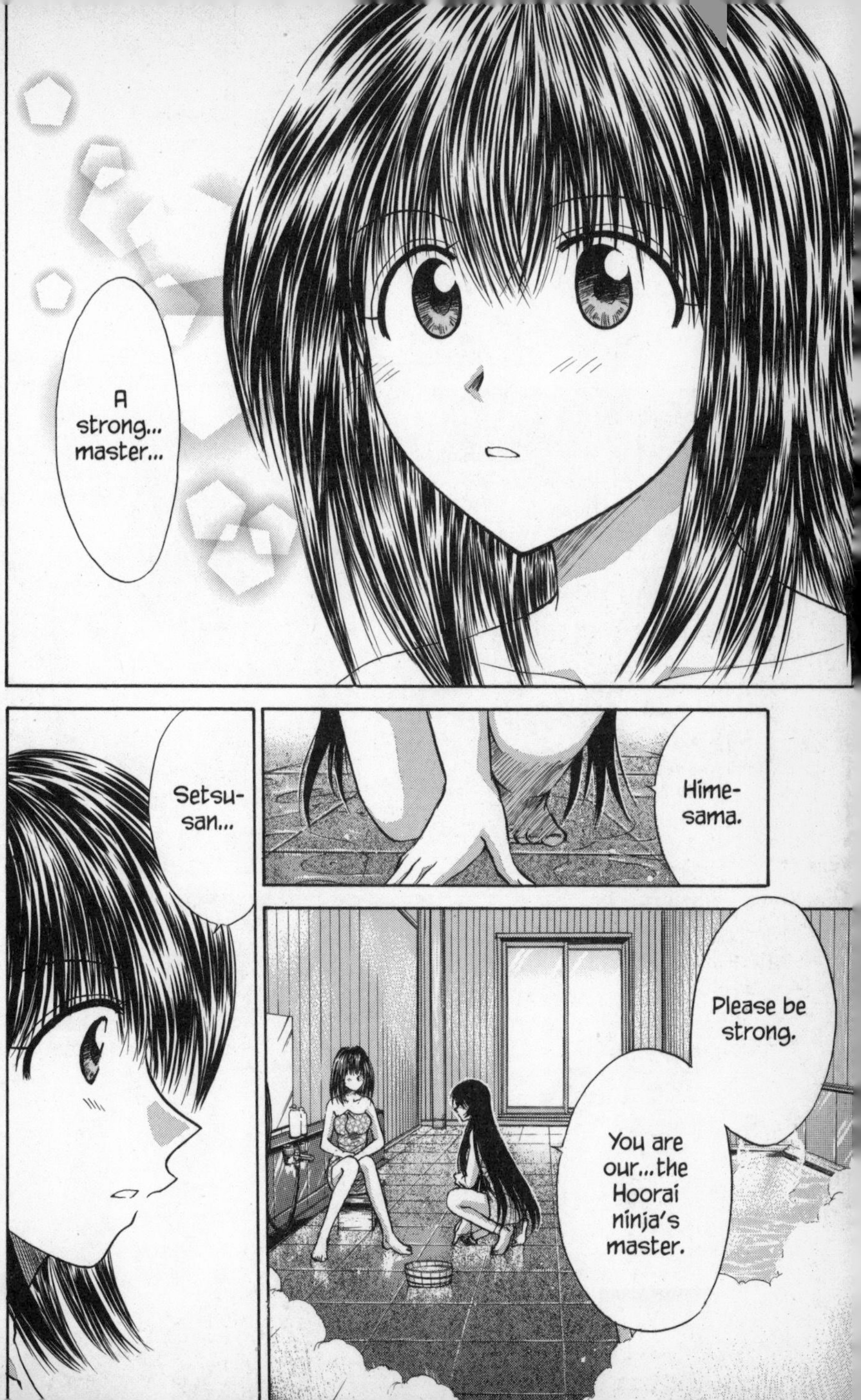
A strong... master...
Hime-sama.
Setsu-san...
Please be strong.
You are our...the Hoorai ninja's master.

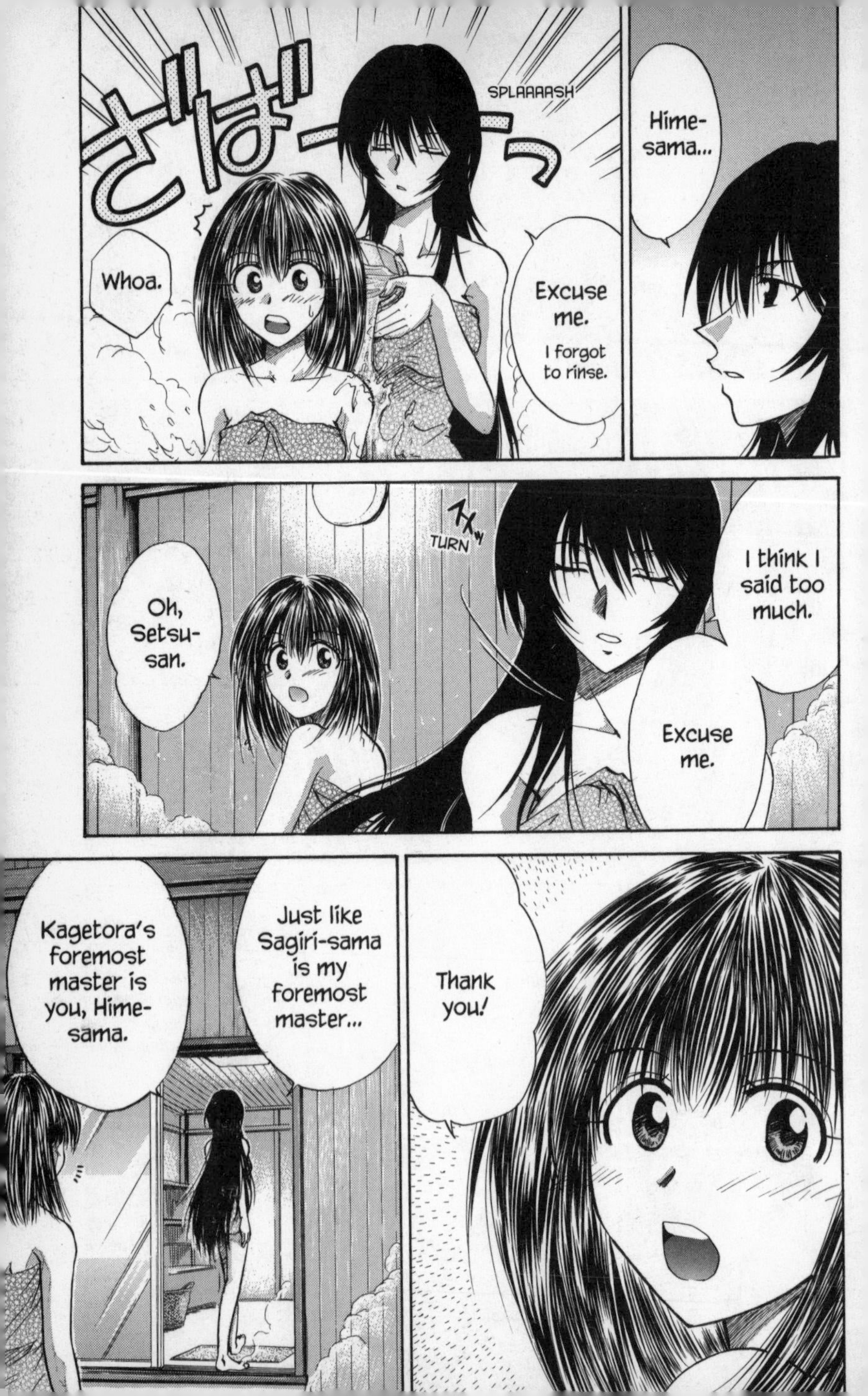
Hime-sama...
SPLAAAASH
さばーっ
Excuse me.
I forgot to rinse.
Whoa.
I think I said too much.
Excuse me.
TURN
Oh, Setsu-san.
Thank you!
Just like Sagiri-sama is my foremost master...
Kagetora's foremost master is you, Hime-sama.

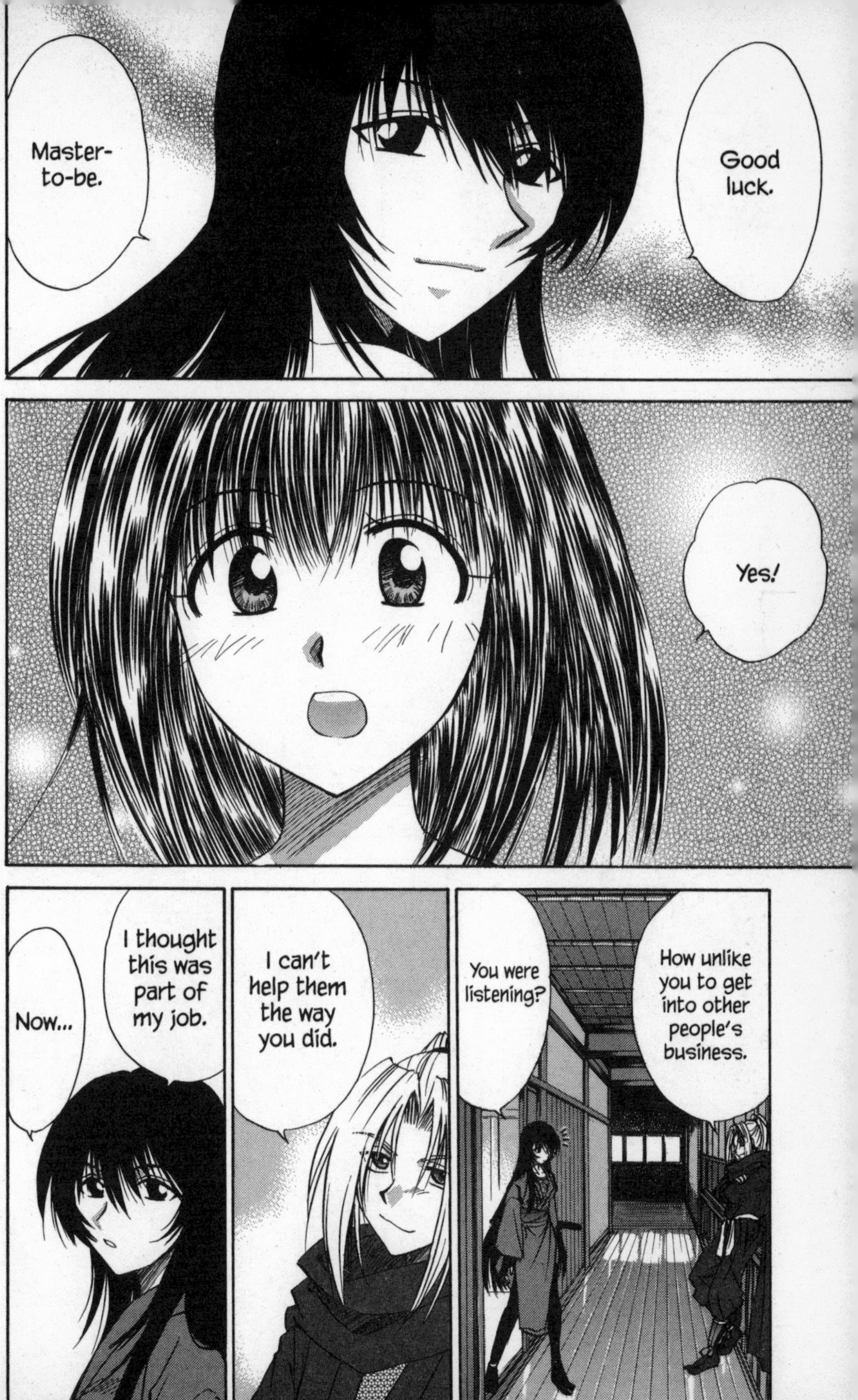
Good luck.
Master-to-be.
Yes!
How unlike you to get into other people's business.
You were listening?
I can't help them the way you did.
I thought this was part of my job.
Now...

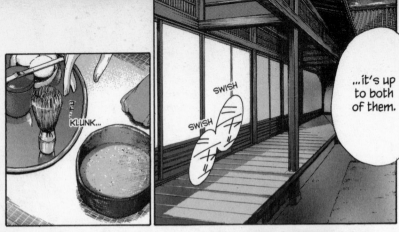

...it's up to both of them.

KLUNK...

SWISH

SWISH

SIP...

Yuki, please try to be quieter.

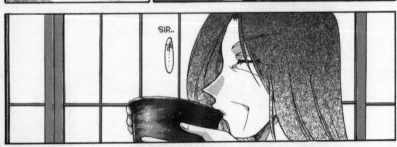

What is it?

SLIDE

Grandma!

URGH

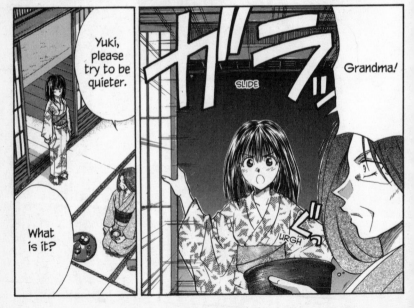

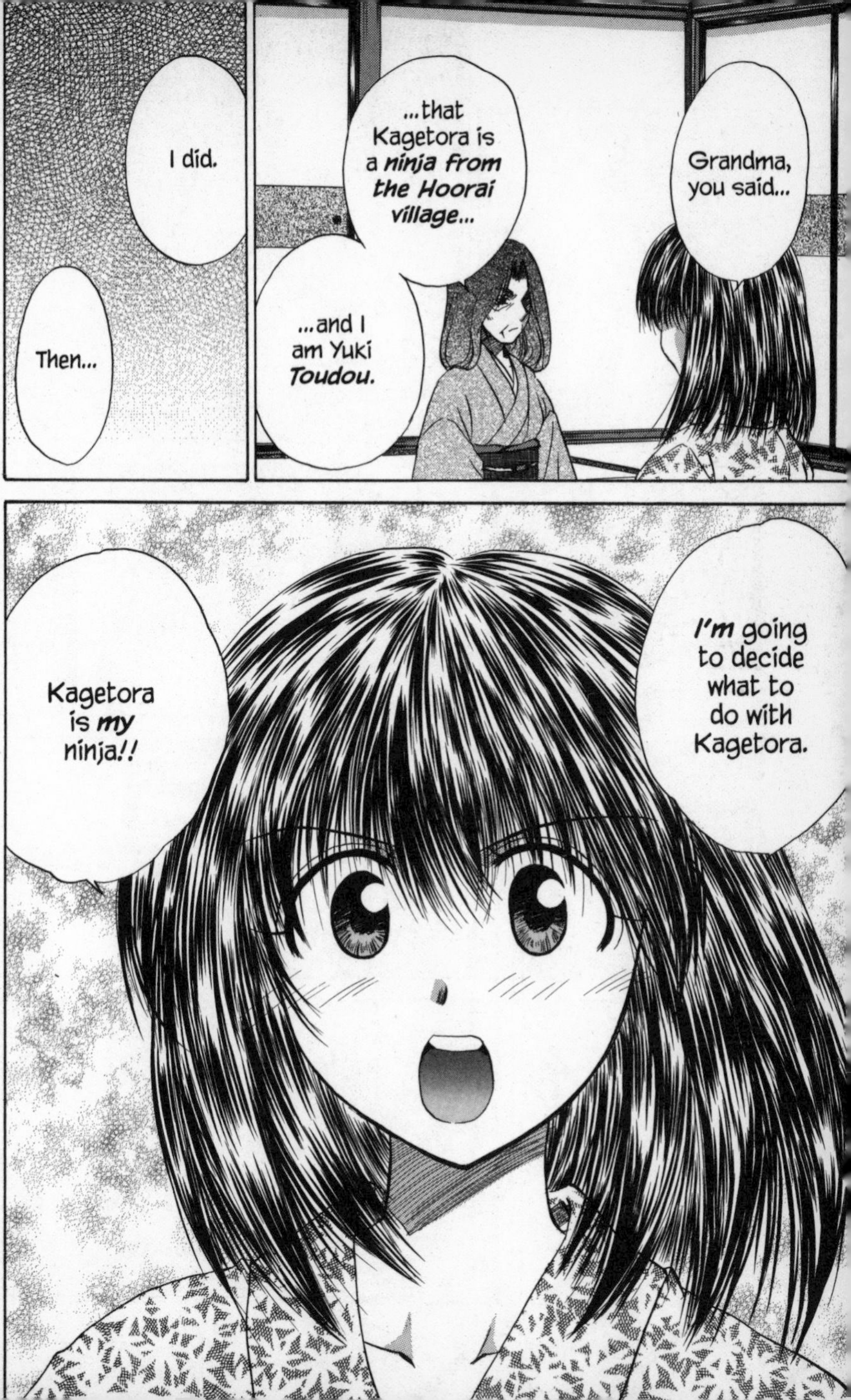
Grandma, you said...
...that Kagetora is a *ninja from the Hoorai village*...
...and I am Yuki *Toudou*.
I did.
Then...
I'm going to decide what to do with Kagetora.
Kagetora is *my* ninja!!

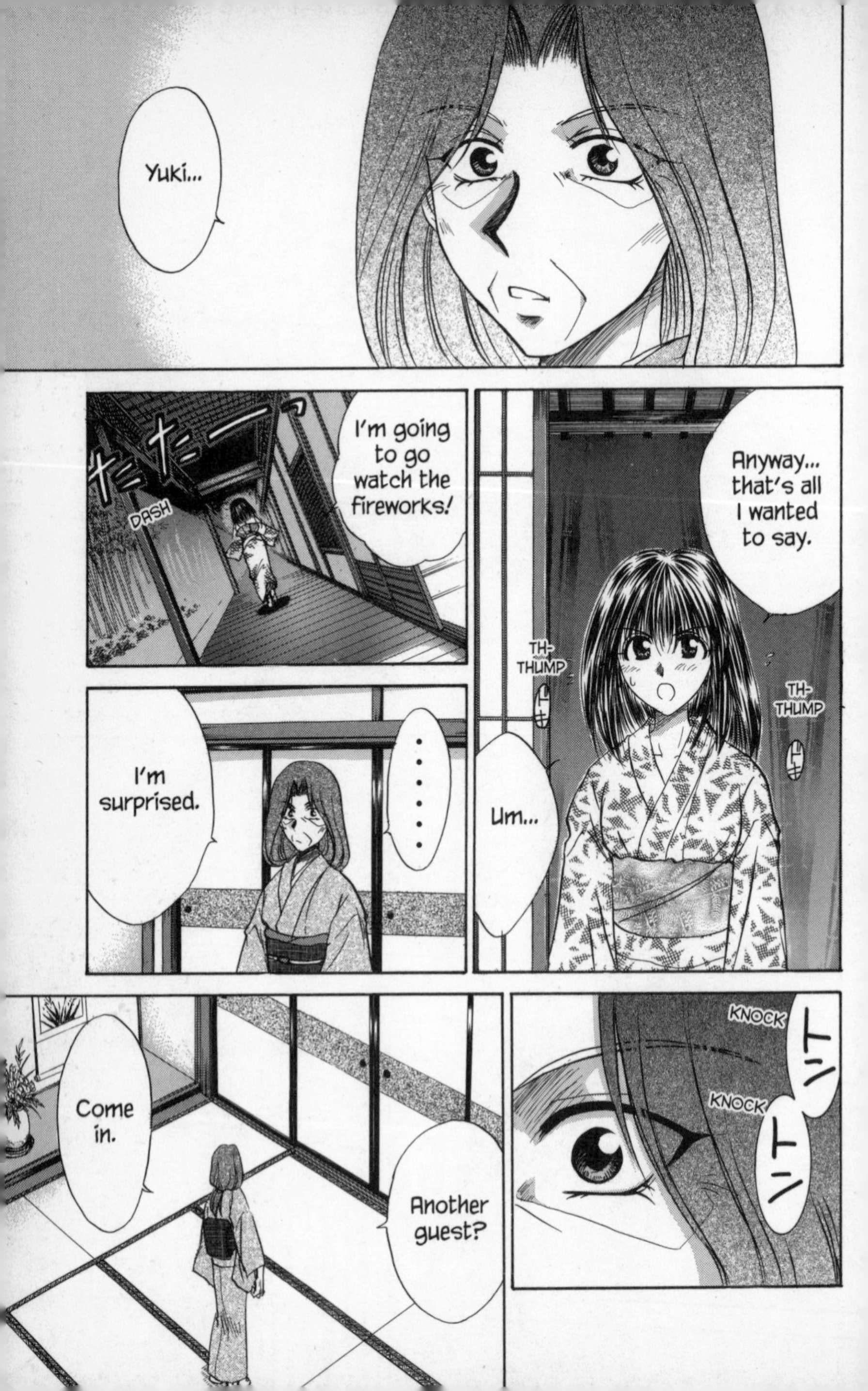
Yuki...
Anyway... that's all I wanted to say.
TH-THUMP
TH-THUMP
Um...
I'm going to go watch the fireworks!
DASH
......
I'm surprised.
KNOCK
トン
KNOCK
トン
Another guest?
Come in.

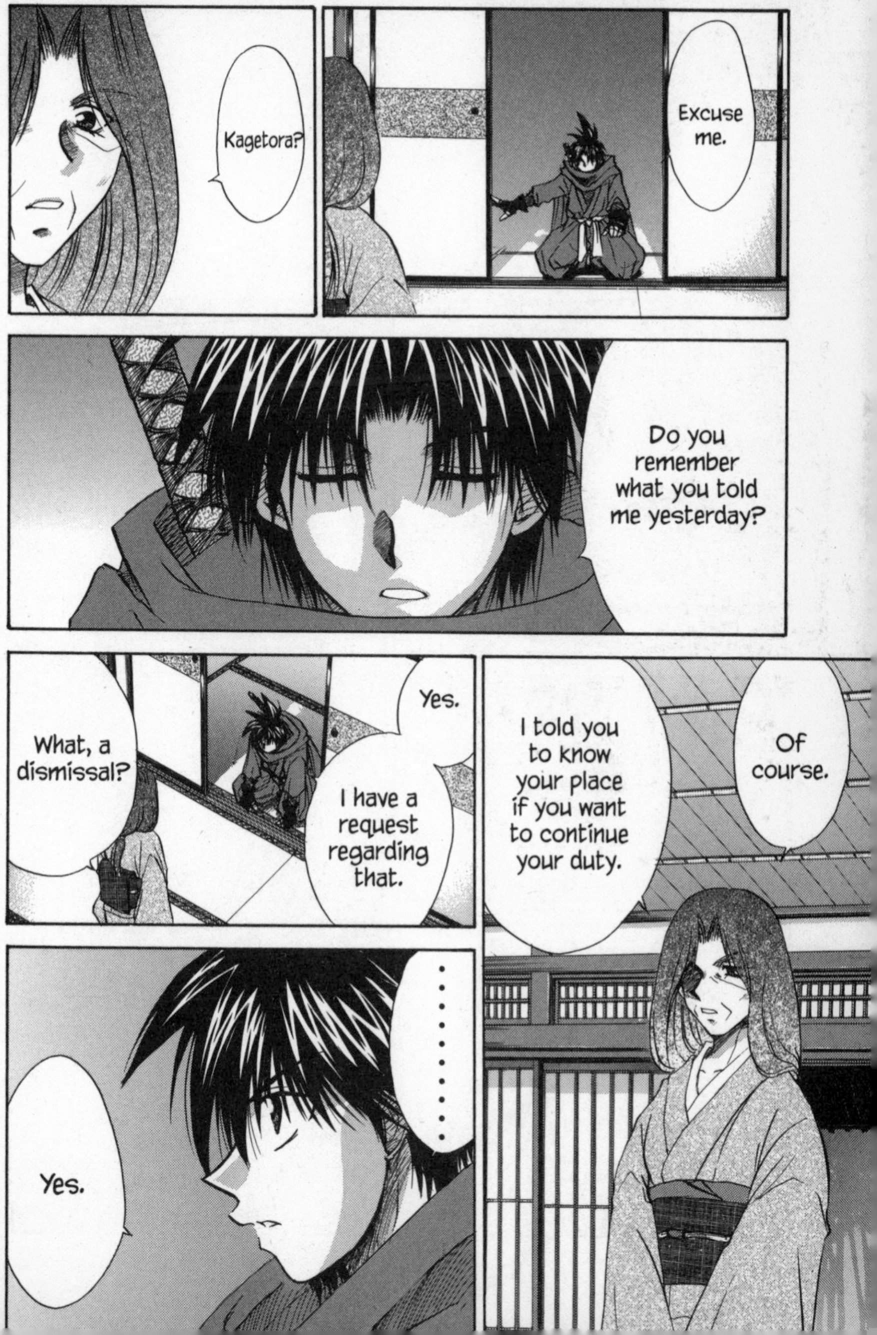
Excuse me.
Kagetora?
Do you remember what you told me yesterday?
Of course.
I told you to know your place if you want to continue your duty.
Yes.
I have a request regarding that.
What, a dismissal?
......
Yes.

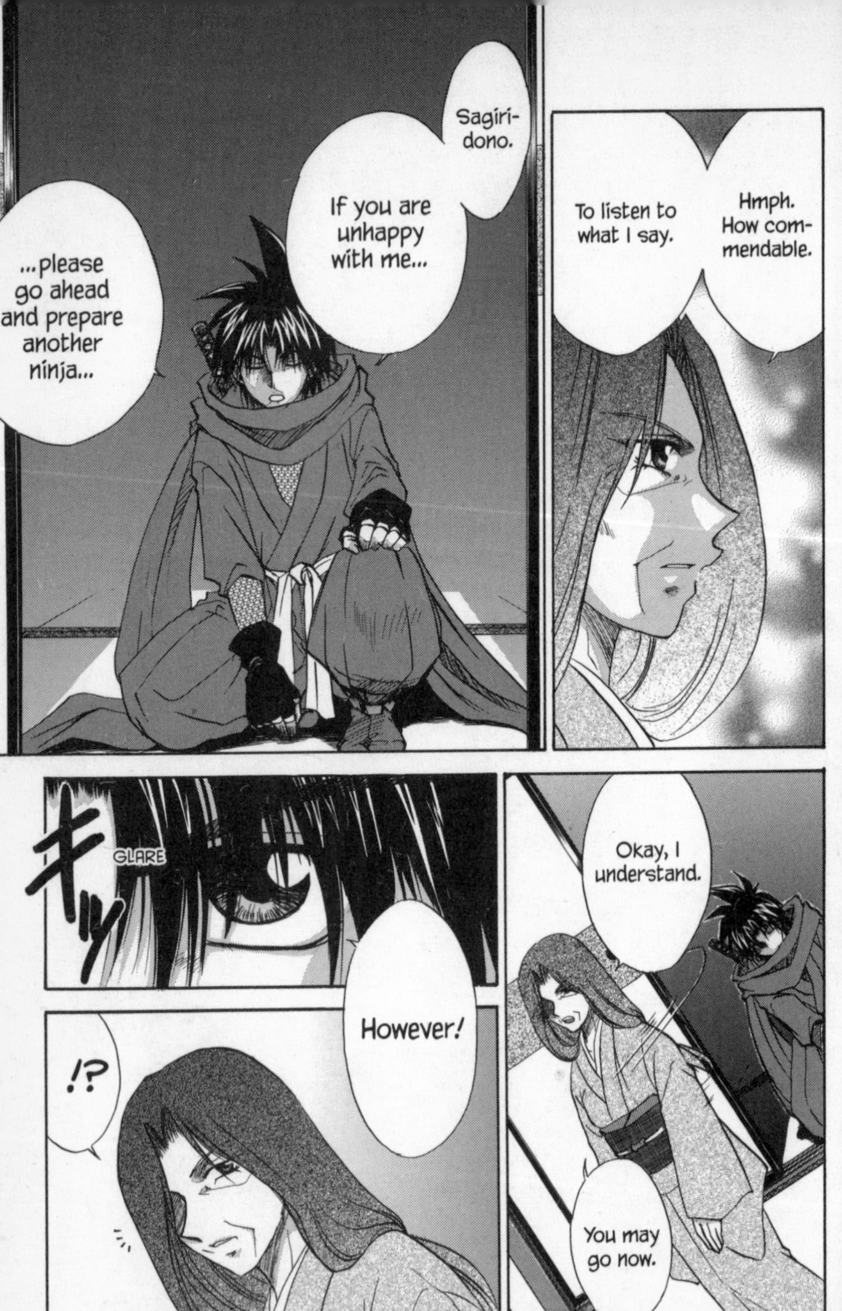
Hmph. How commendable.
To listen to what I say.
Sagiri-dono.
If you are unhappy with me...
...please go ahead and prepare another ninja...
Okay, I understand.
You may go now.
キッ
GLARE
However!
!?
...

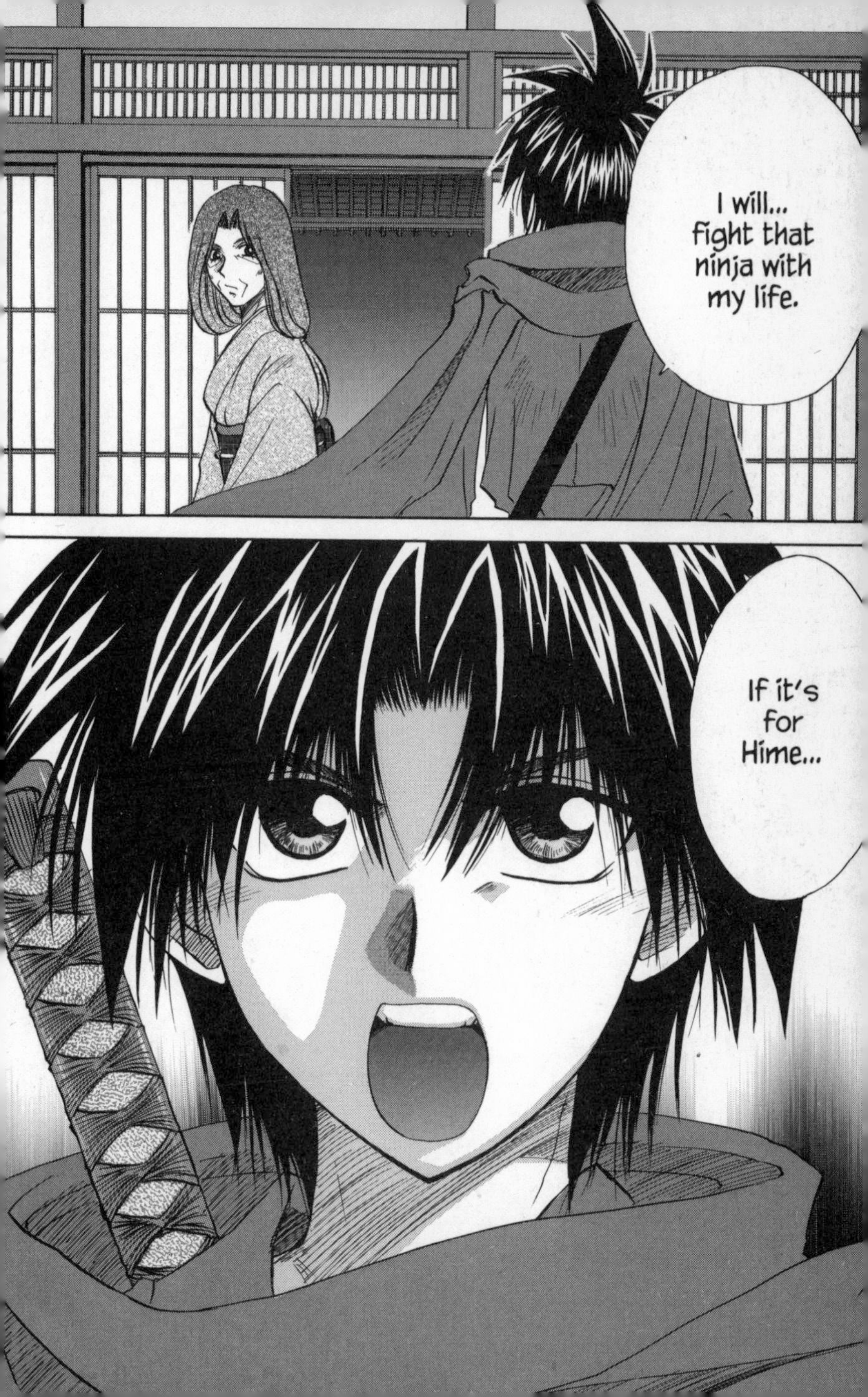
I will... fight that ninja with my life.
If it's for Hime...

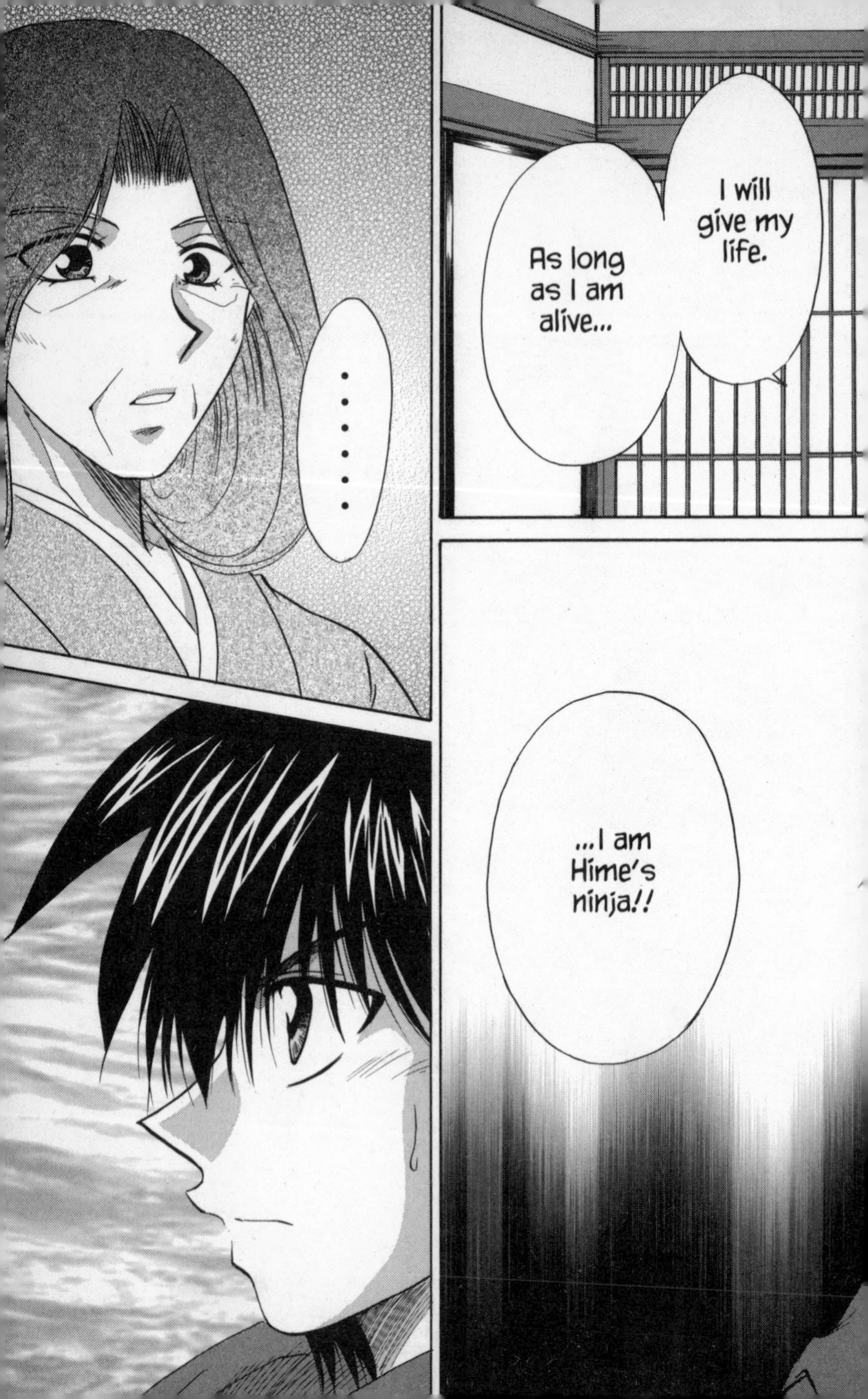
I will give my life.
As long as I am alive...
......
...I am Hime's ninja!!

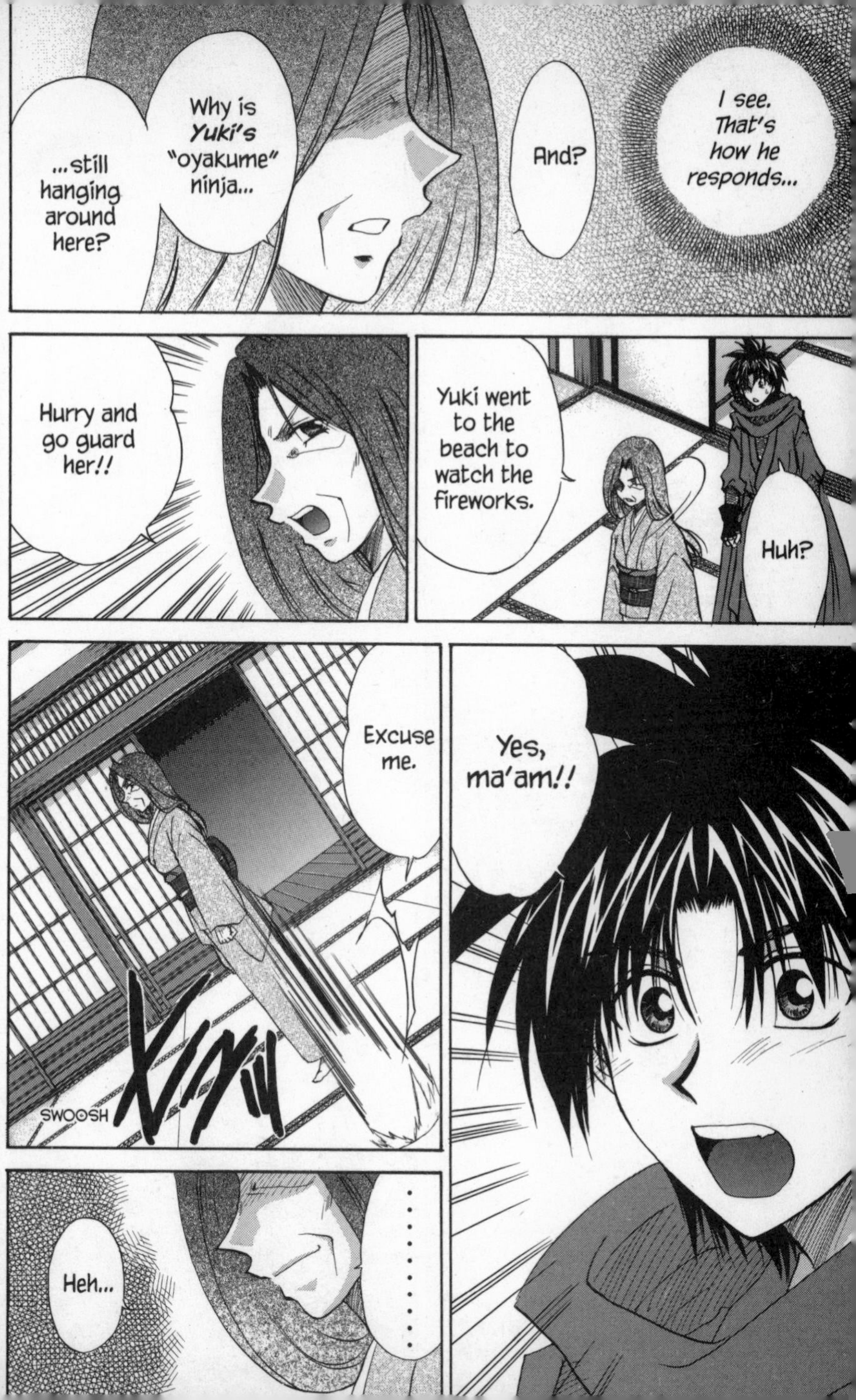
I see. That's how he responds...
And?
Why is Yuki's "oyakume" ninja...
...still hanging around here?
Huh?
Yuki went to the beach to watch the fireworks.
Hurry and go guard her!!
Yes, ma'am!!
Excuse me.
SWOOSH
......
Heh...

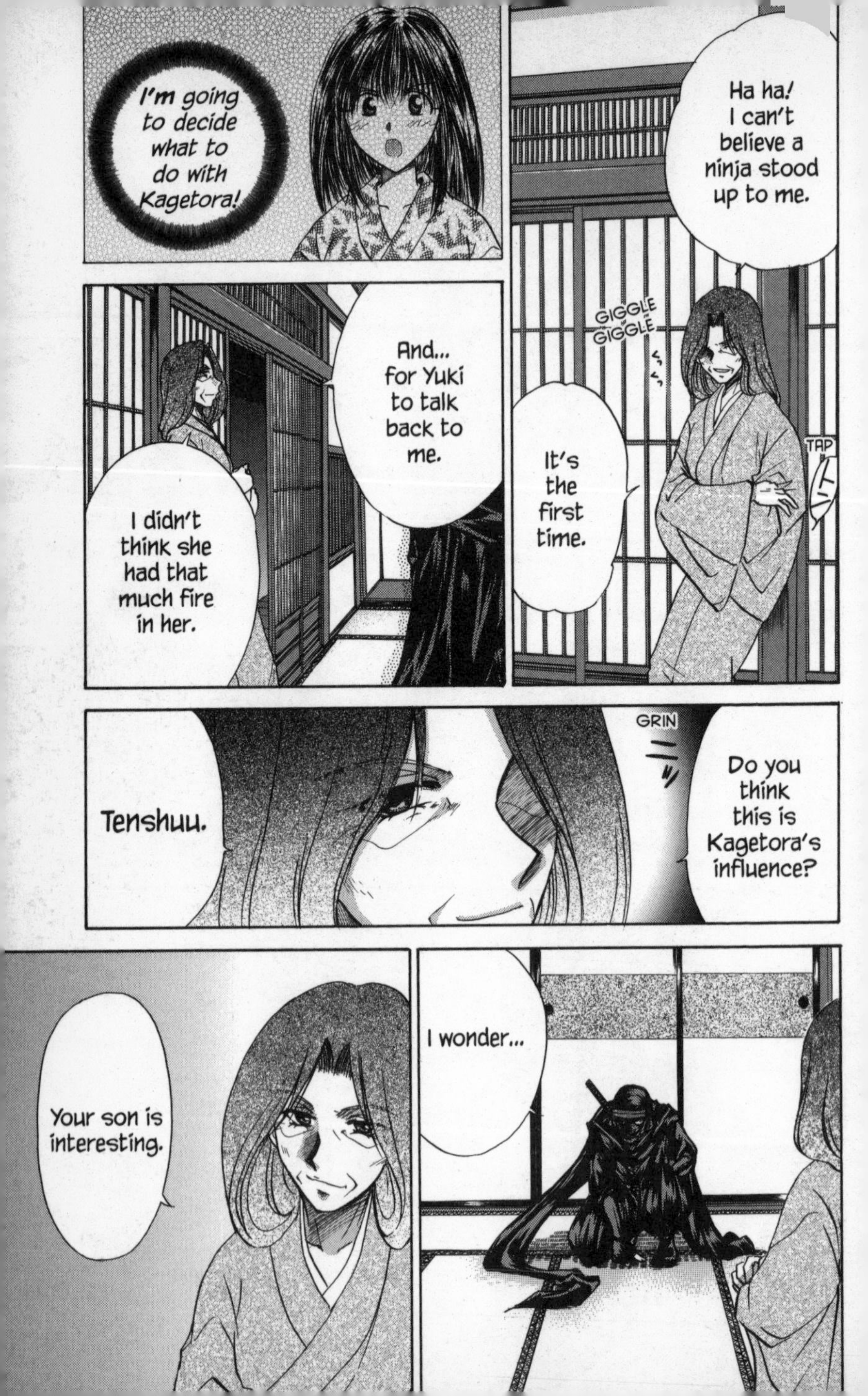
Ha ha! I can't believe a ninja stood up to me.
GIGGLE GIGGLE
TAP
It's the first time.
I'm going to decide what to do with Kagetora!
And... for Yuki to talk back to me.
I didn't think she had that much fire in her.
GRIN
Do you think this is Kagetora's influence?
Tenshuu.
I wonder...
Your son is interesting.

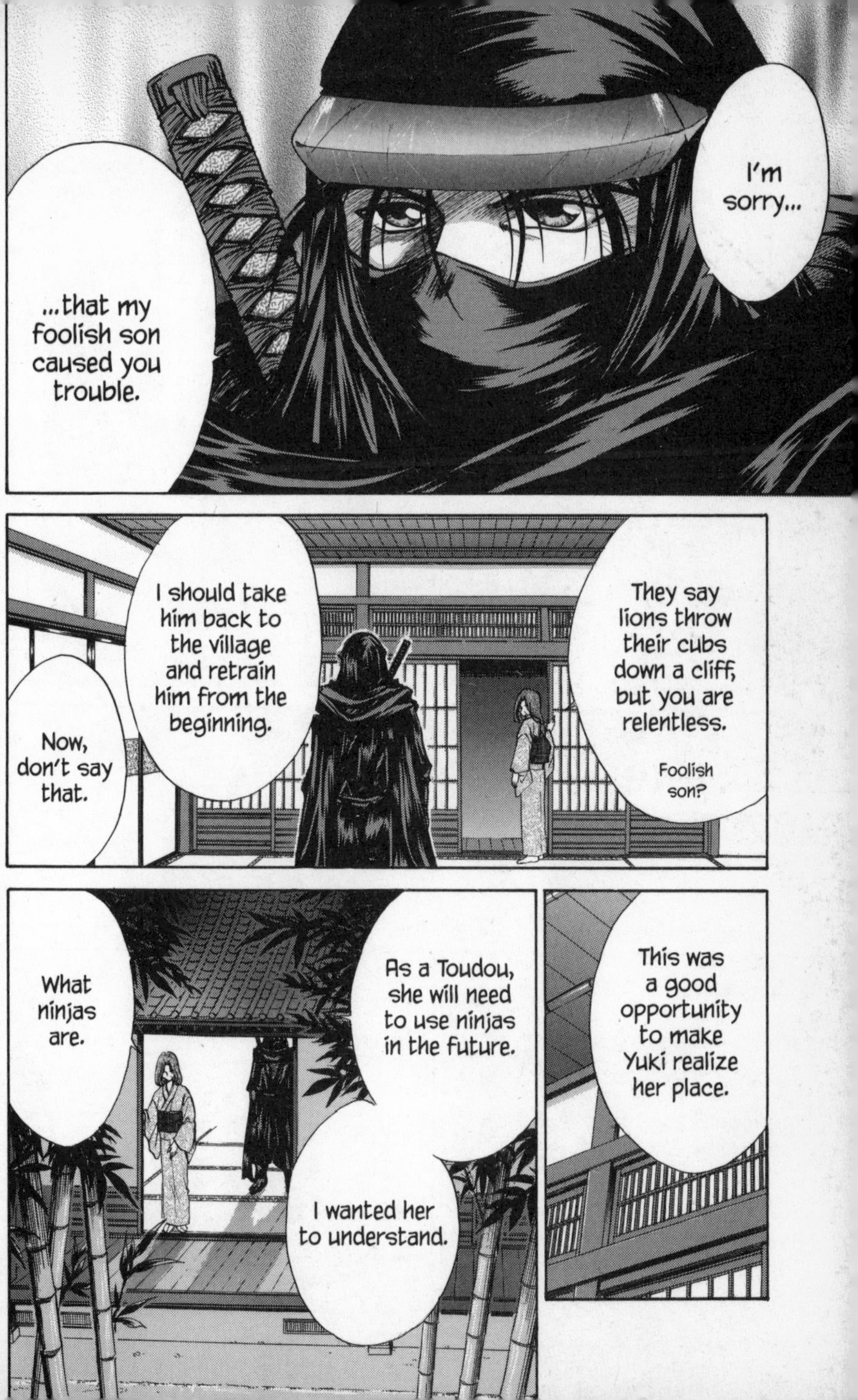
I'm sorry...
...that my foolish son caused you trouble.
They say lions throw their cubs down a cliff, but you are relentless.
Foolish son?
I should take him back to the village and retrain him from the beginning.
Now, don't say that.
This was a good opportunity to make Yuki realize her place.
As a Toudou, she will need to use ninjas in the future.
I wanted her to understand.
What ninjas are.

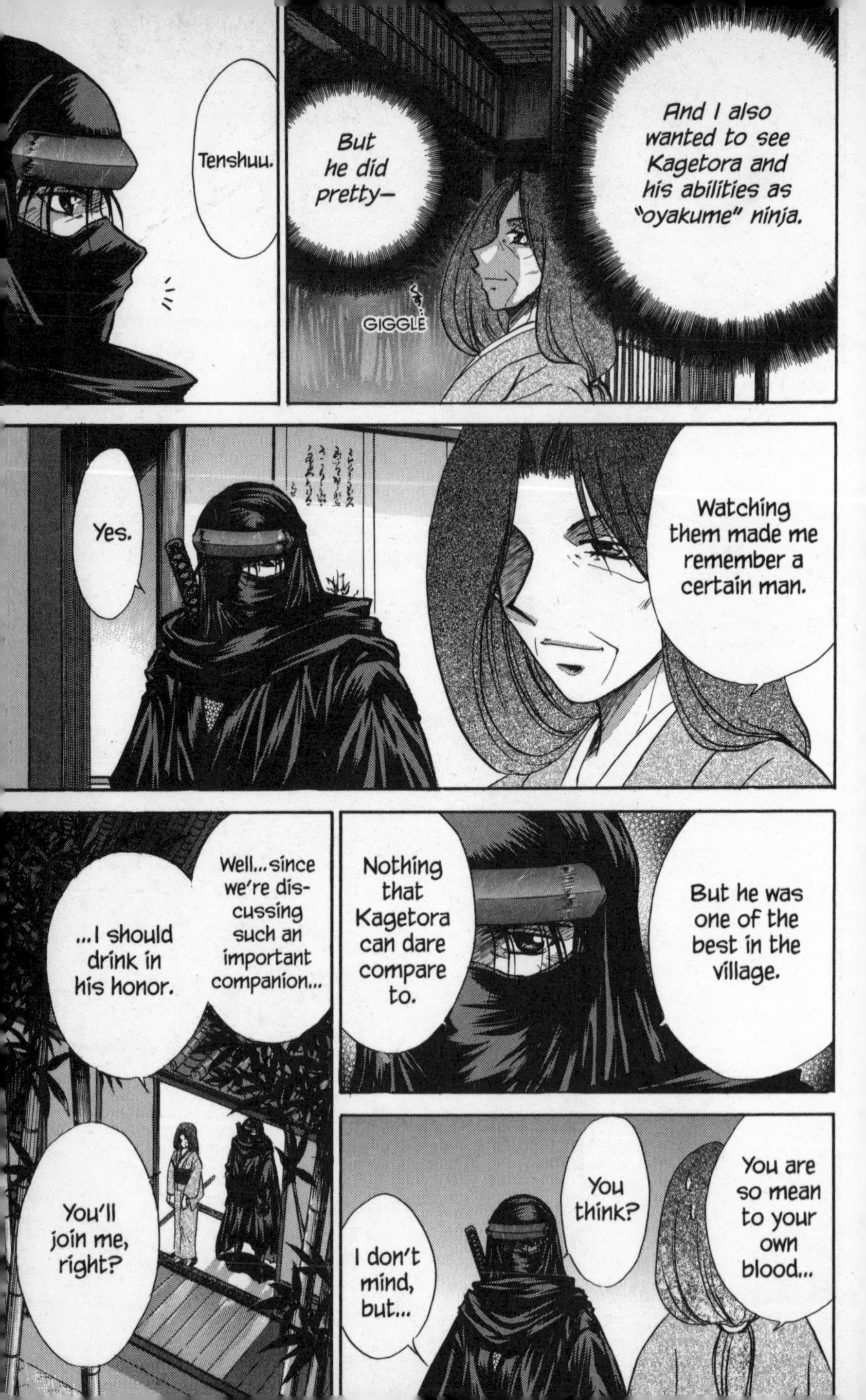
And I also wanted to see Kagetora and his abilities as "oyakume" ninja.
But he did pretty—
GIGGLE
Tenshuu.
Watching them made me remember a certain man.
Yes.
But he was one of the best in the village.
Nothing that Kagetora can dare compare to.
You are so mean to your own blood...
You think?
I don't mind, but...
Well...since we're dis- cussing such an important companion...
...I should drink in his honor.
You'll join me, right?

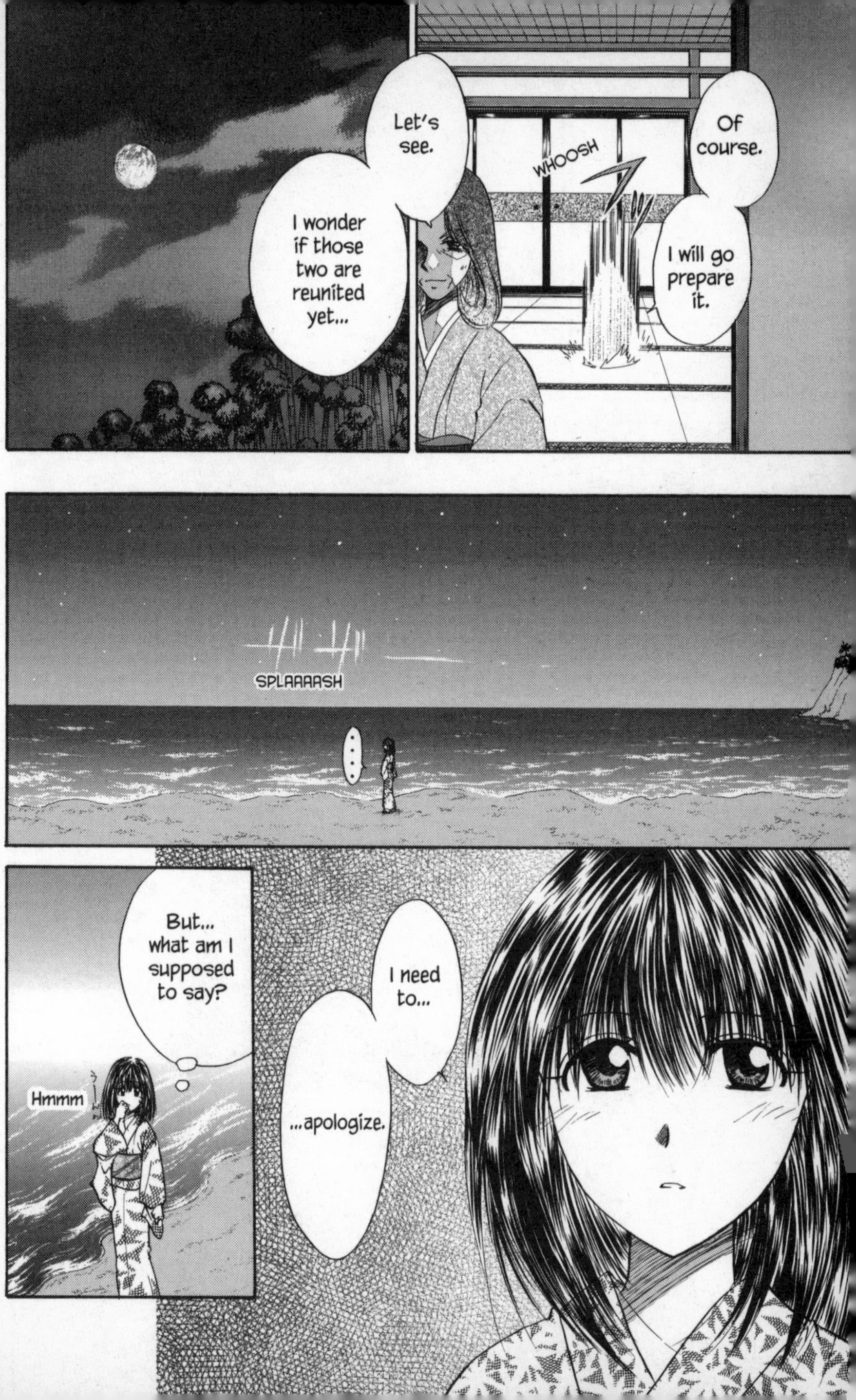
Of course.
I will go prepare it.
WHOOSH
Let's see.
I wonder if those two are reunited yet...
SPLAAAASH
...
I need to...
...apologize.
But... what am I supposed to say?
Hmmm

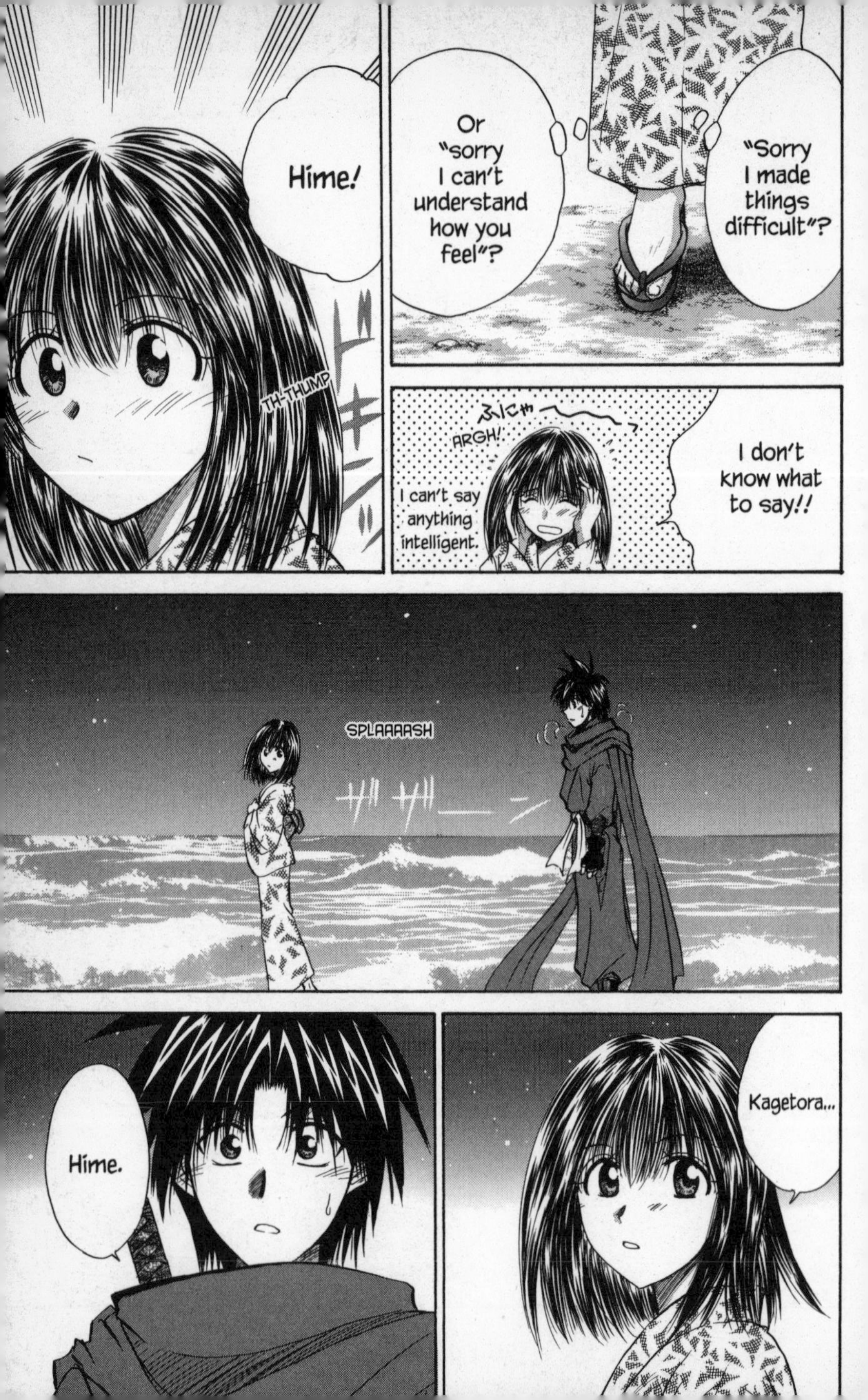
"Sorry I made things difficult"?
Or "sorry I can't understand how you feel"?
I don't know what to say!!
ふにゃ
ARGH!
I can't say anything intelligent.
Hime!
TH-THUMP
SPLAAAASH
Kagetora...
Hime.

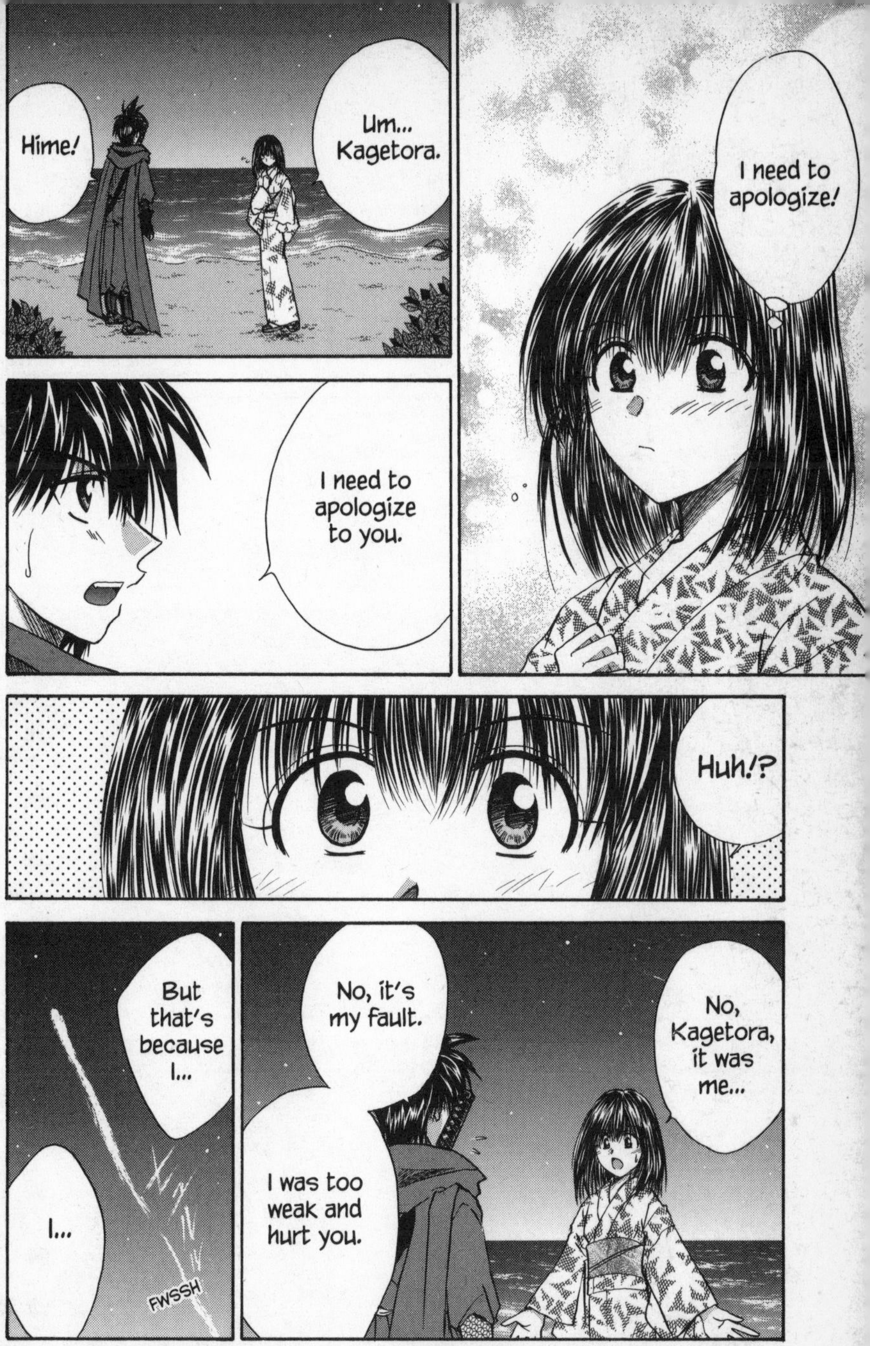
I need to apologize!
Um... Kagetora.
Hime!
I need to apologize to you.
Huh!?
No, Kagetora, it was me...
No, it's my fault.
I was too weak and hurt you.
But that's because I...
I...
FWSSH

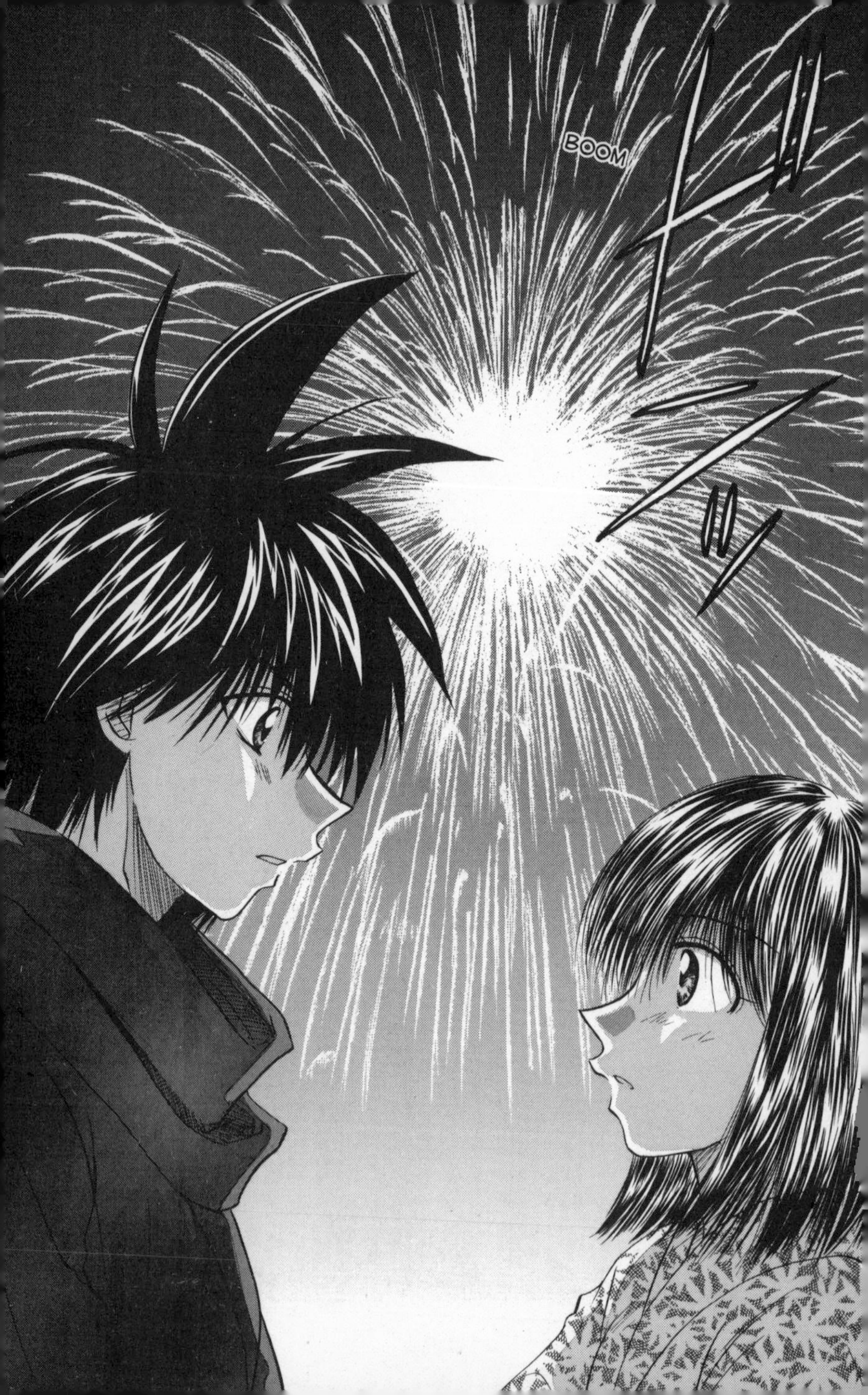
BOOM

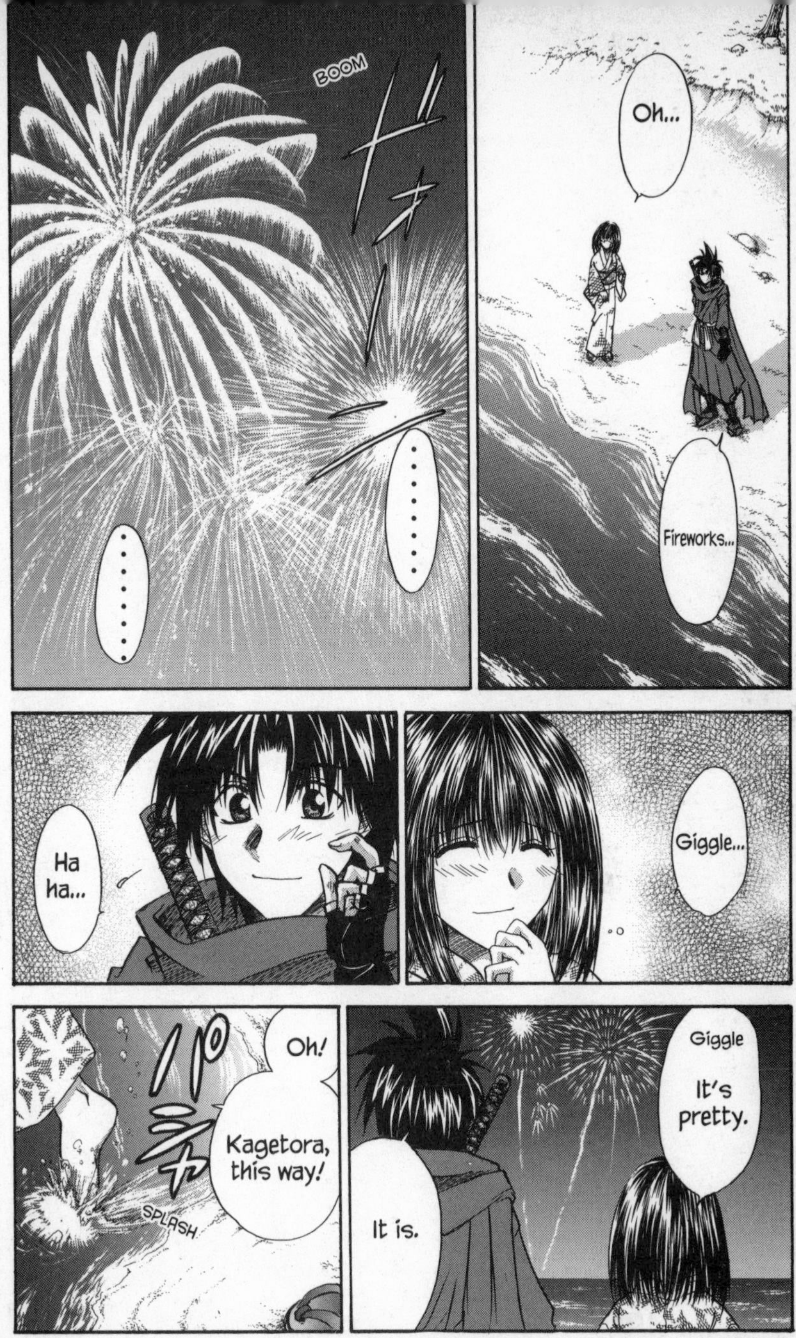
Oh...
Fireworks...
BOOM
....
....
Giggle...
Ha ha...
Giggle
It's pretty.
It is.
Oh!
Kagetora, this way!
SPLASH

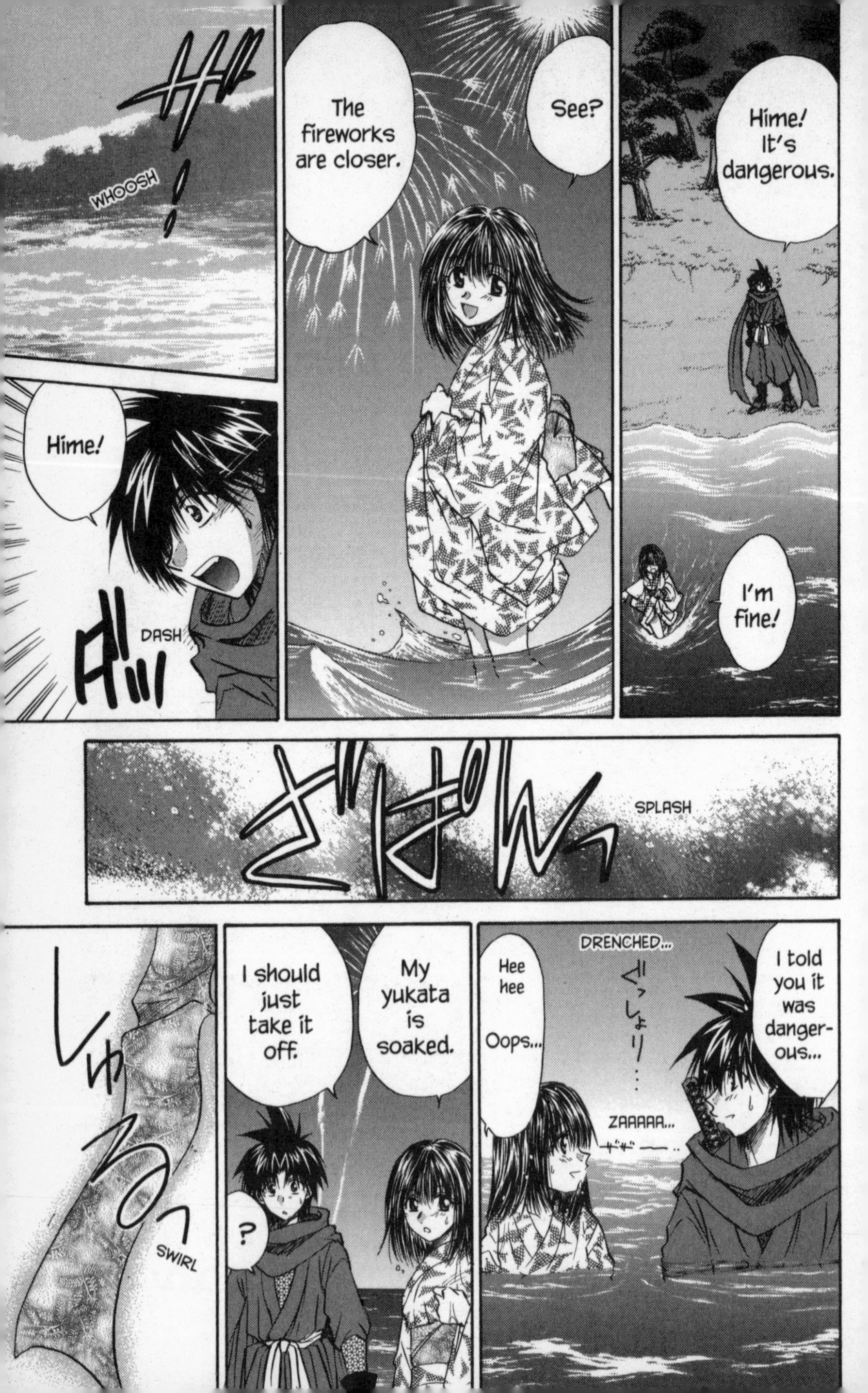
Hime! It's dangerous.
I'm fine!
See?
The fireworks are closer.
WHOOSH
Hime!
DASH
SPLASH
I told you it was dangerous...
DRENCHED...
ぐっしょり…
Hee hee
Oops...
ZAAAAA...
My yukata is soaked.
I should just take it off.
?
SWIRL

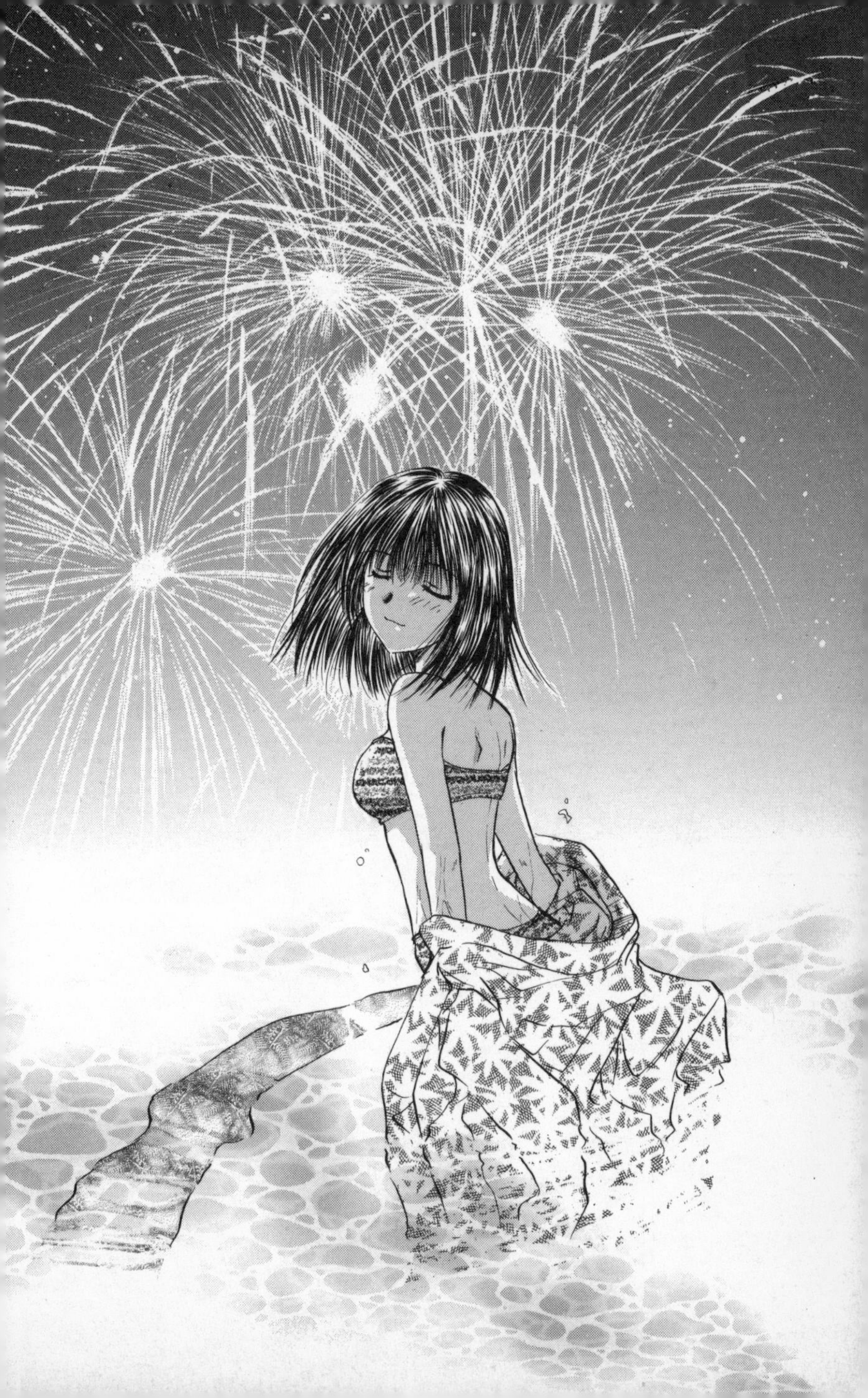

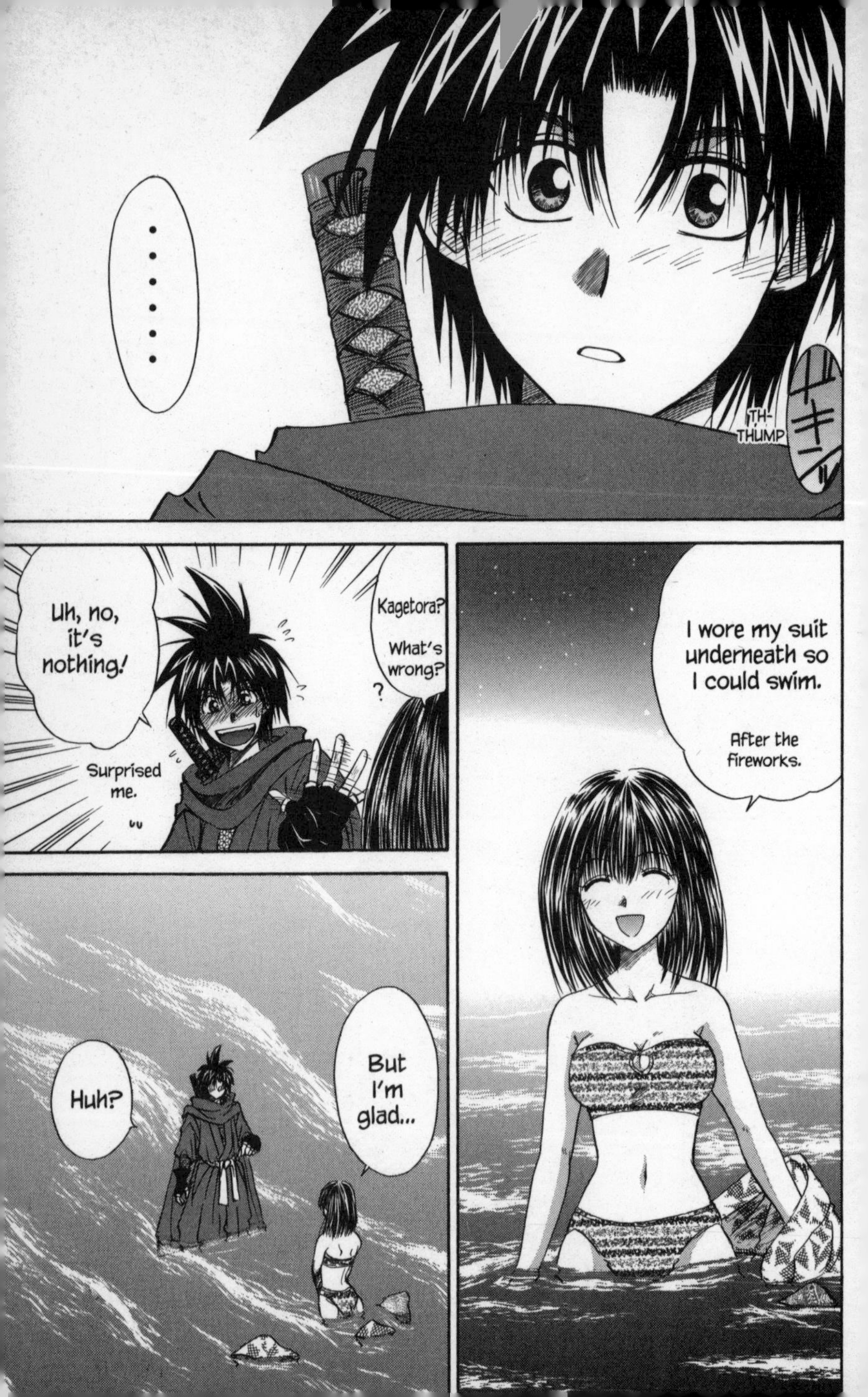
......
TH-THUMP
I wore my suit underneath so I could swim.
After the fireworks.
Kagetora? What's wrong?
?
Uh, no, it's nothing!
Surprised me.
But I'm glad...
Huh?

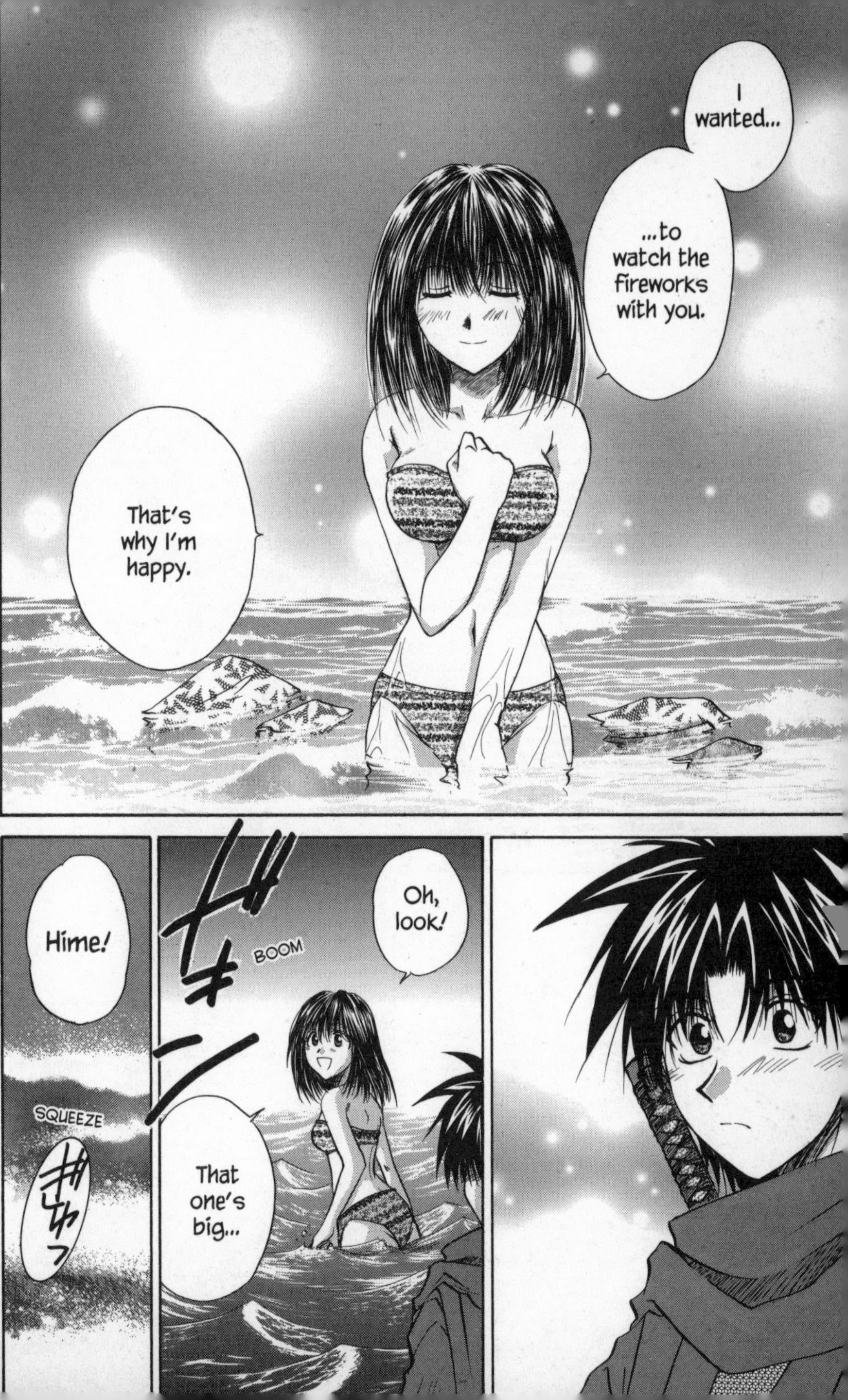
I wanted...
...to watch the fireworks with you.
That's why I'm happy.
Oh, look!
BOOM
That one's big...
Hime!
SQUEEZE

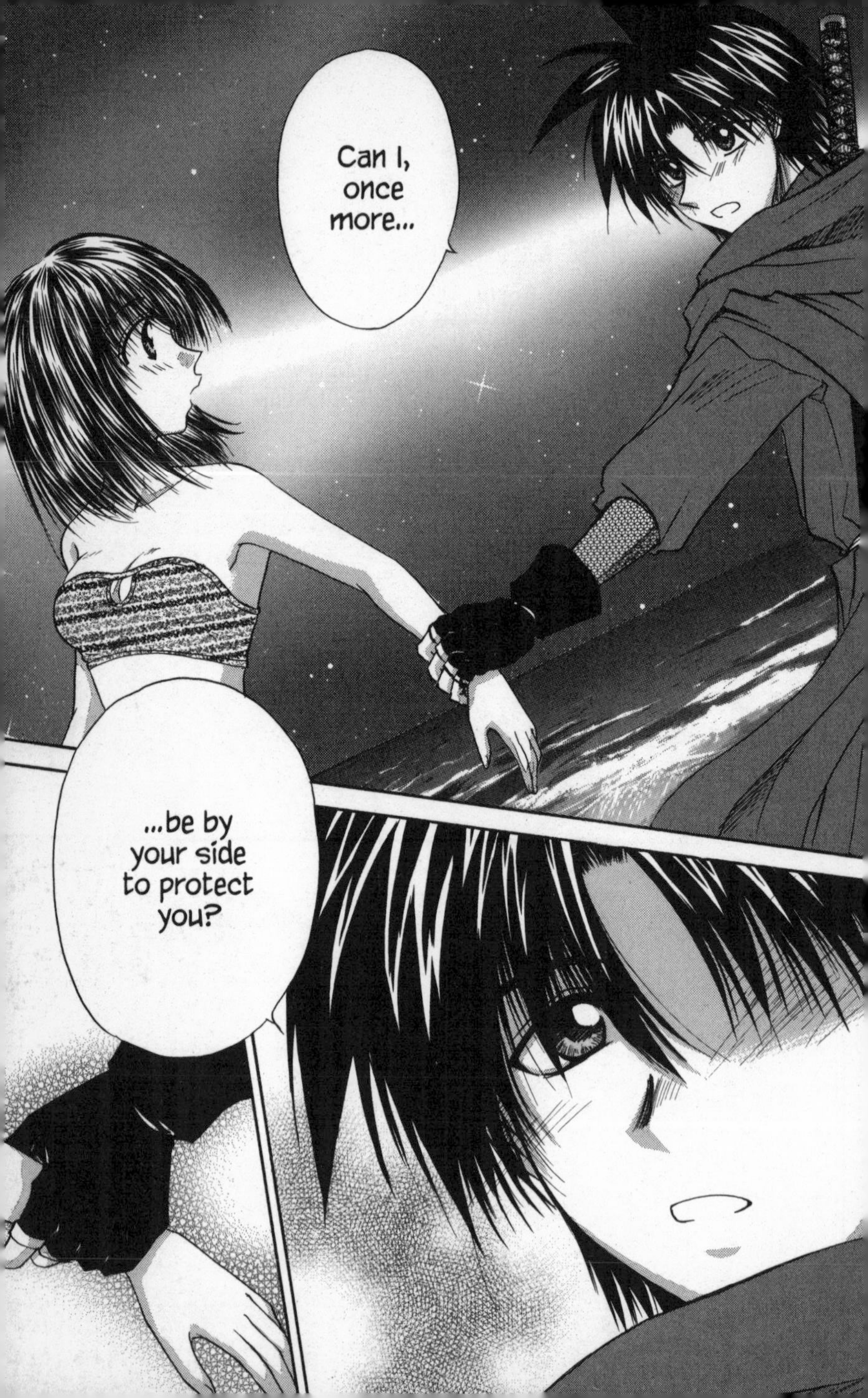
Can I, once more...
...be by your side to protect you?

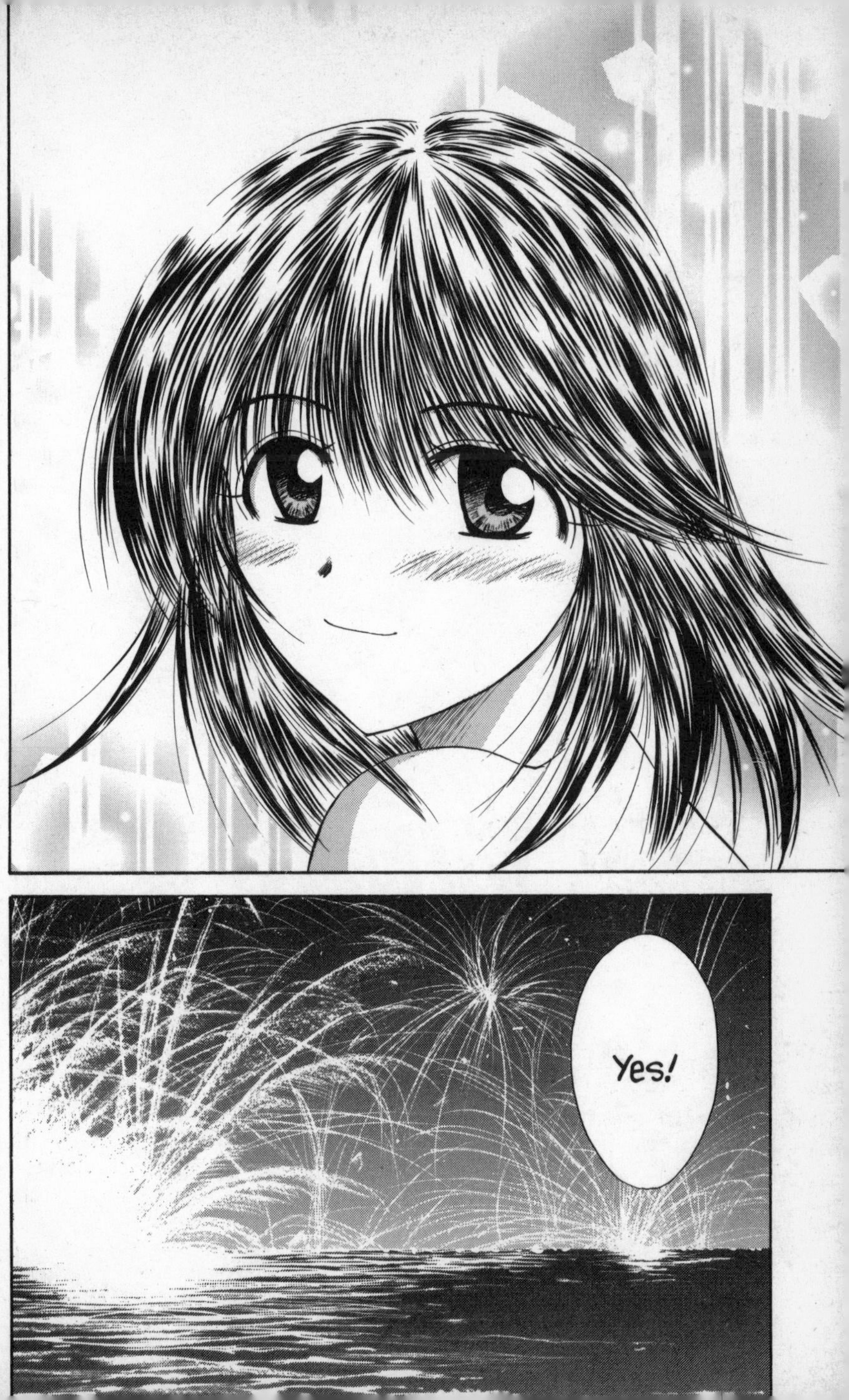
Yes!

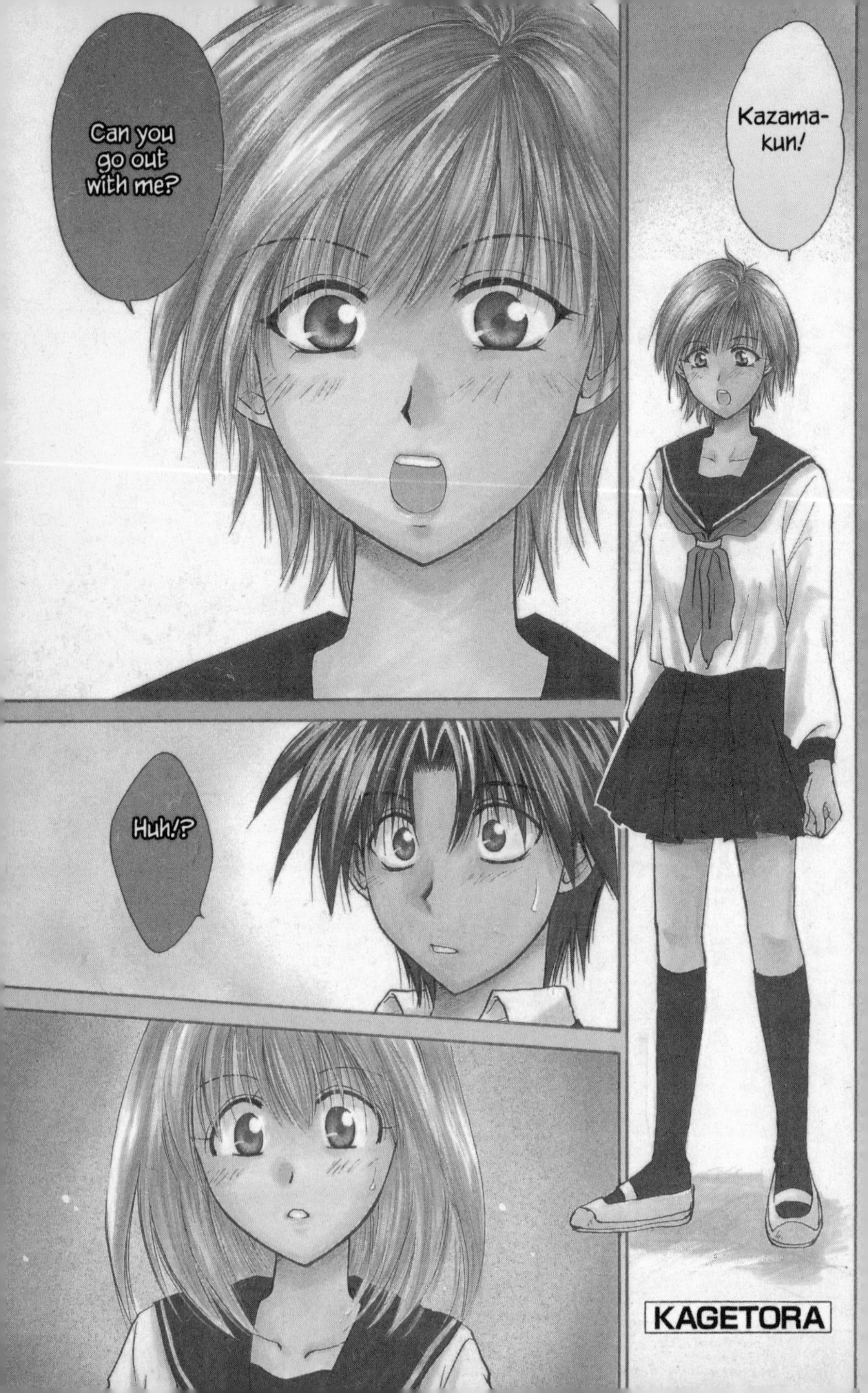
Kazama-kun!
Can you go out with me?
Huh!?

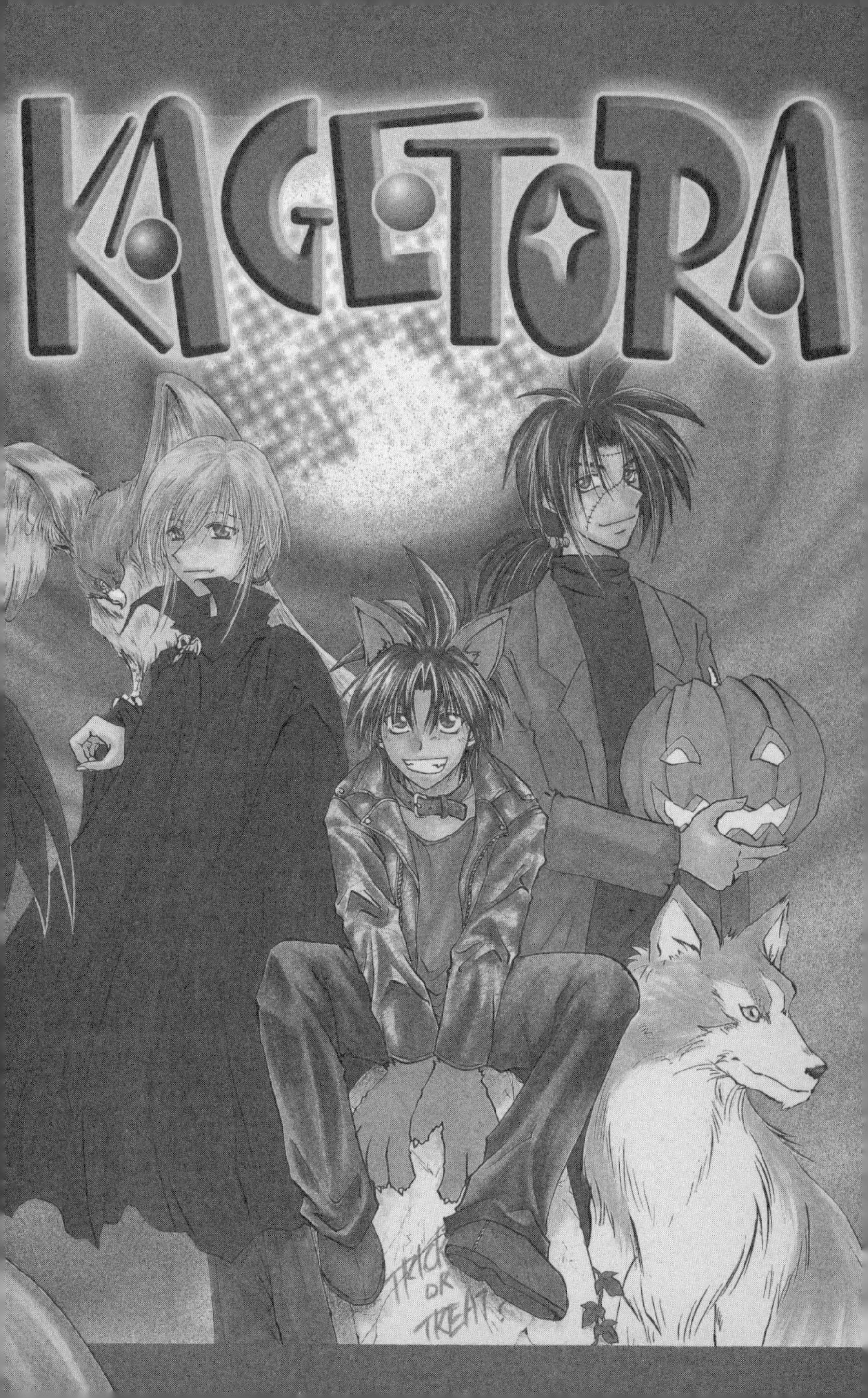
KAGETORA
TRICK OR TREAT

#30 Prelude to a Love Triangle

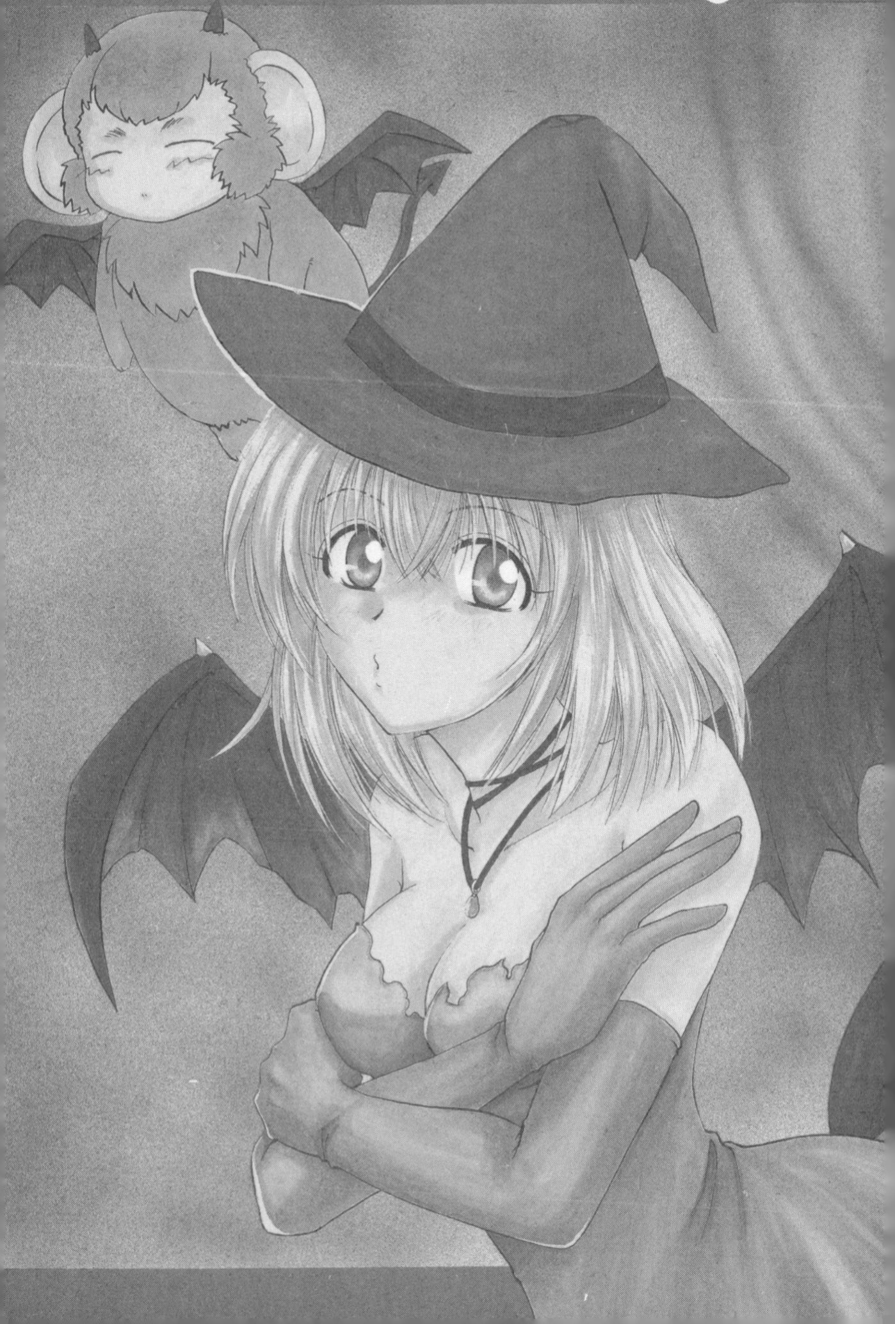

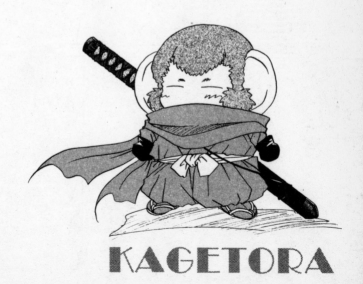

KAGETORA

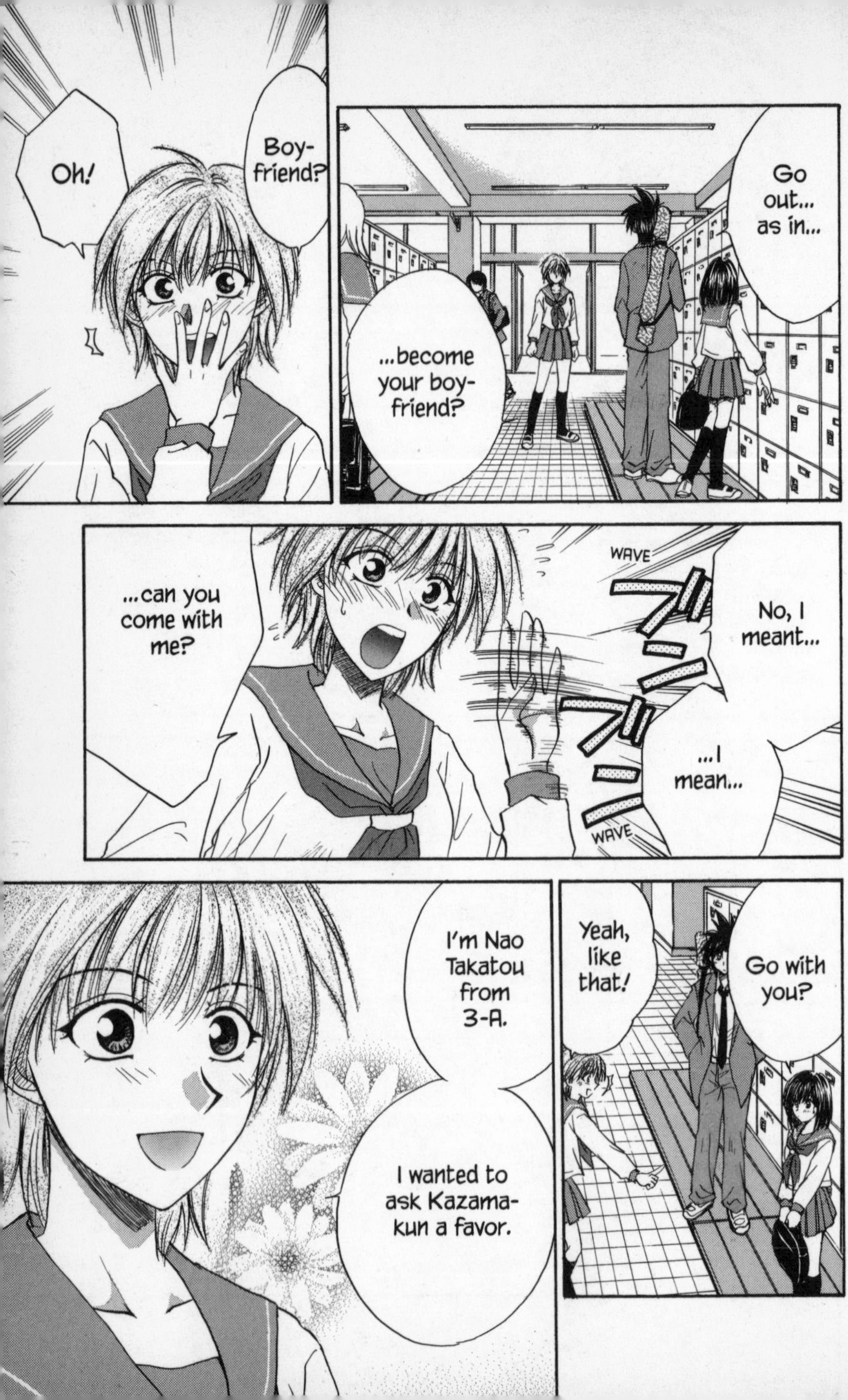

Go out... as in...
...become your boy-friend?
Boy-friend?
Oh!
WAVE
No, I meant...
...I mean...
WAVE
...can you come with me?
Go with you?
Yeah, like that!
I'm Nao Takatou from 3-A.
I wanted to ask Kazama-kun a favor.

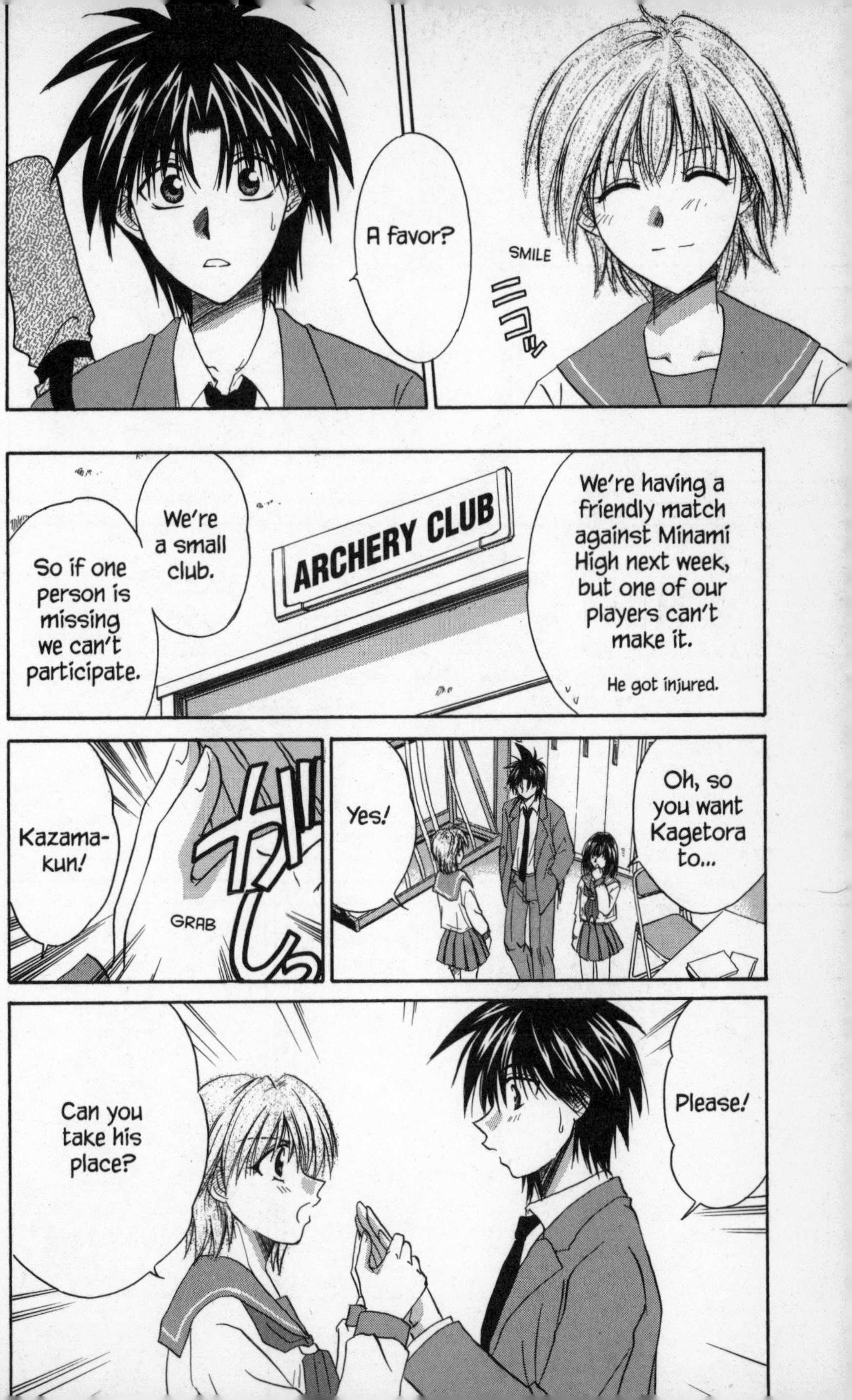
SMILE
A favor?
We're having a friendly match against Minami High next week, but one of our players can't make it.
He got injured.
We're a small club.
ARCHERY CLUB
So if one person is missing we can't participate.
Oh, so you want Kagetora to...
Yes!
Kazama-kun!
GRAB
Please!
Can you take his place?

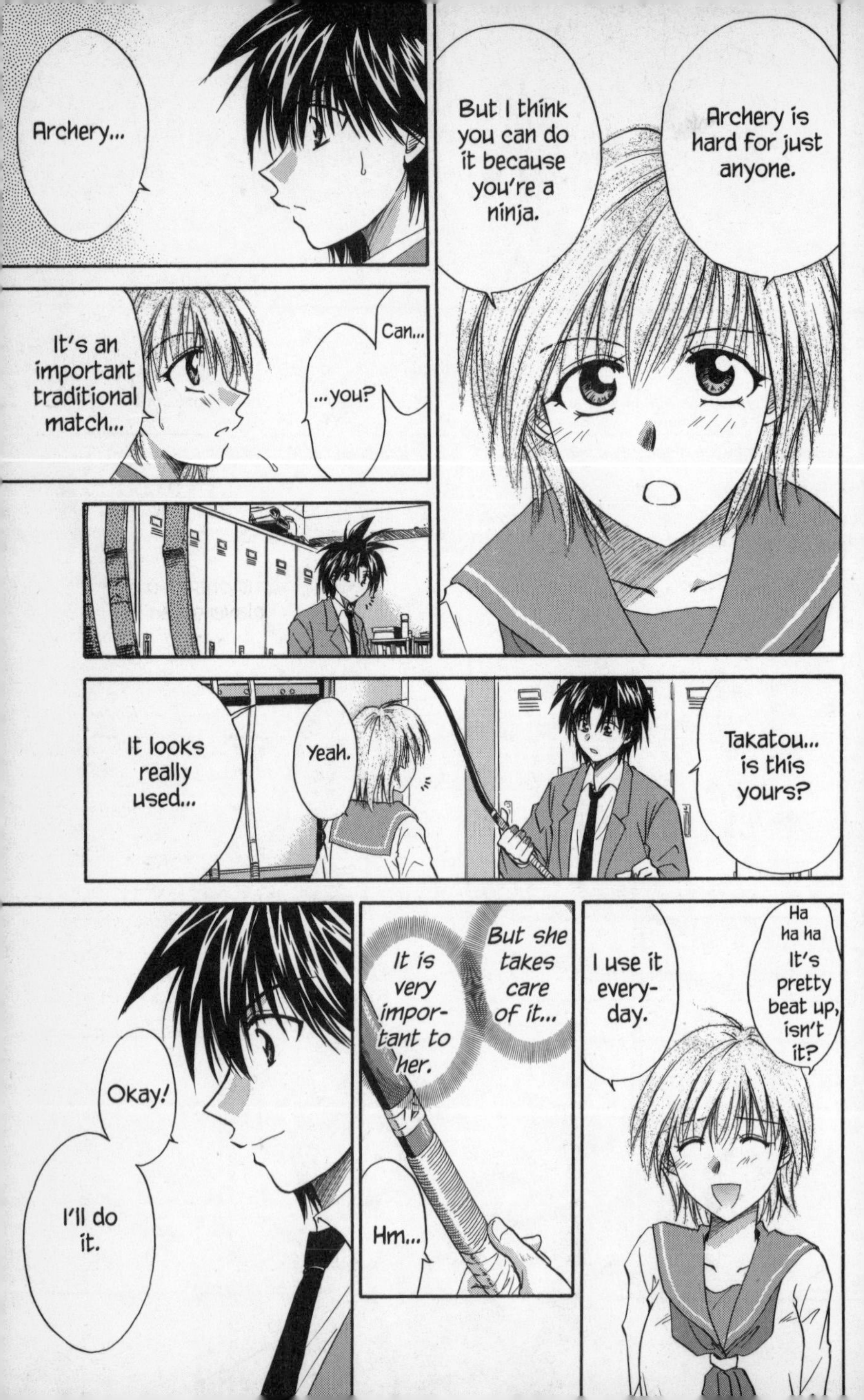
Archery is hard for just anyone.
But I think you can do it because you're a ninja.
Archery...
Can...
...you?
It's an important traditional match...
Takatou... is this yours?
Yeah.
It looks really used...
Ha ha ha
It's pretty beat up, isn't it?
I use it every-day.
But she takes care of it...
It is very impor-tant to her.
Hm...
Okay!
I'll do it.

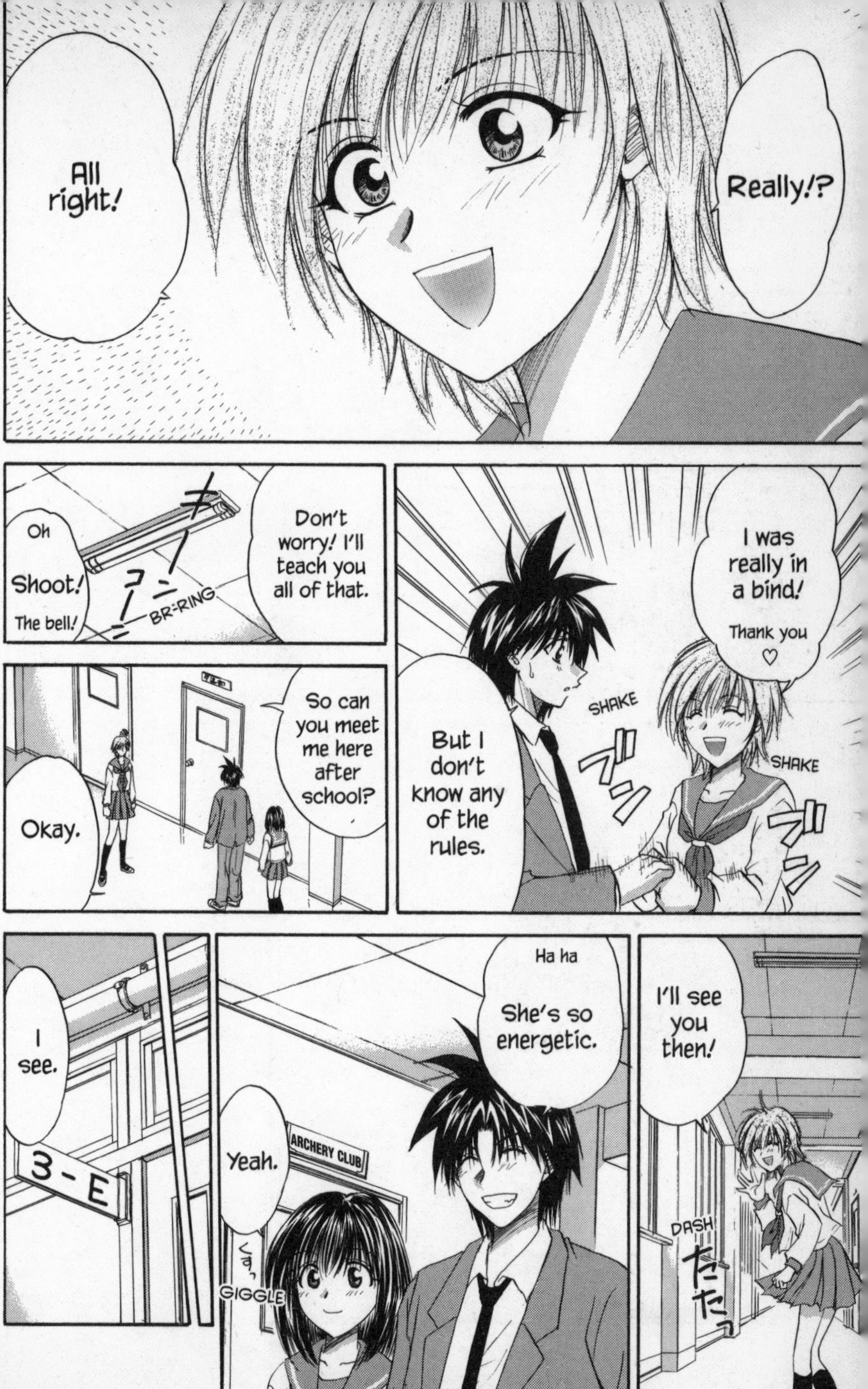
Really!?
All right!
I was really in a bind!
Thank you ♡
SHAKE
SHAKE
But I don't know any of the rules.
Don't worry! I'll teach you all of that.
BR-RING
Oh
Shoot!
The bell!
So can you meet me here after school?
Okay.
I'll see you then!
DASH
Ha ha
She's so energetic.
Yeah.
ARCHERY CLUB
GIGGLE
I see.
3 - E

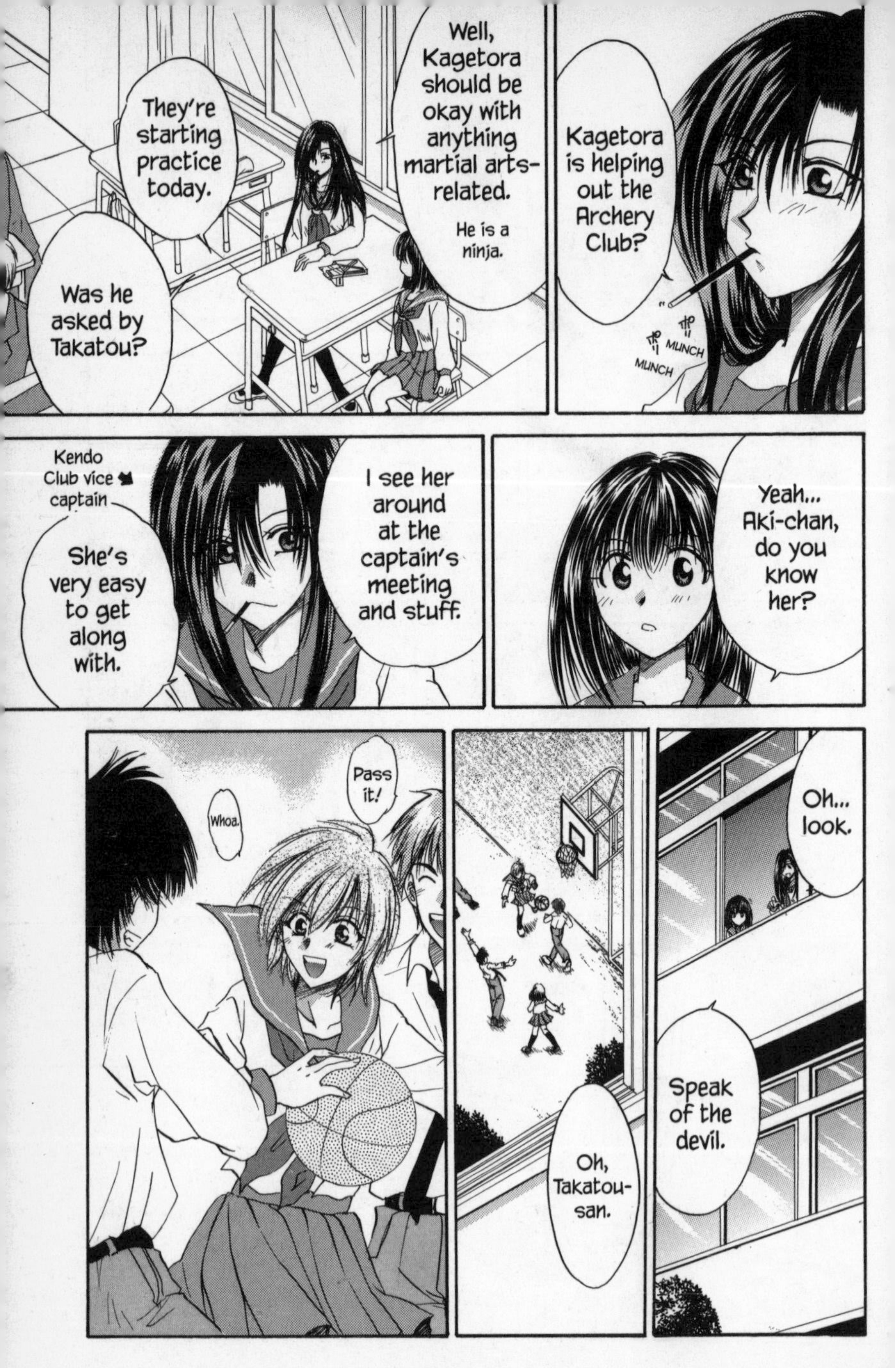
Kagetora is helping out the Archery Club?
MUNCH
MUNCH
Well, Kagetora should be okay with anything martial arts-related.
He is a ninja.
They're starting practice today.
Was he asked by Takatou?
Yeah... Aki-chan, do you know her?
I see her around at the captain's meeting and stuff.
Kendo Club vice captain
She's very easy to get along with.
Oh... look.
Speak of the devil.
Oh, Takatou-san.
Pass it!
Whoa.

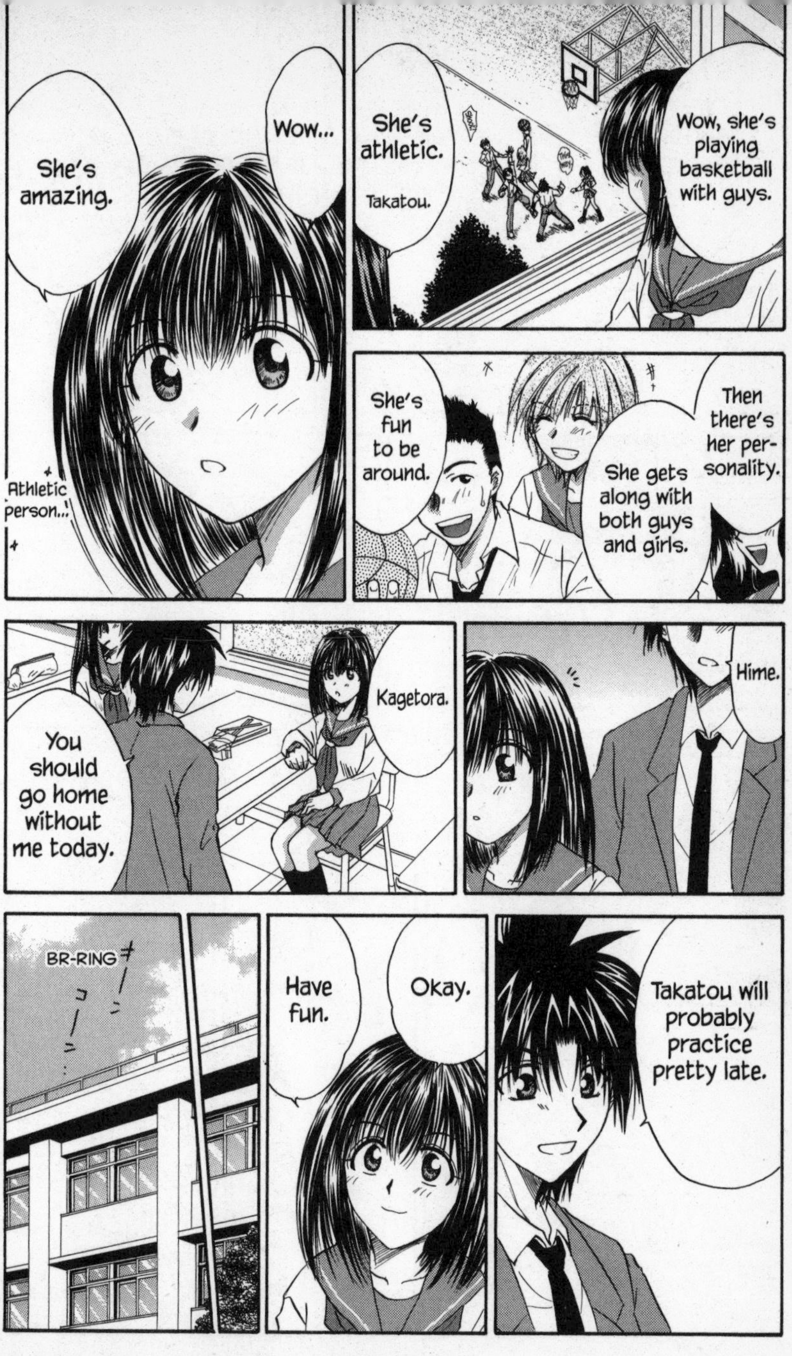
Wow, she's playing basketball with guys.
She's athletic.
Takatou.
Then there's her personality.
She gets along with both guys and girls.
She's fun to be around.
Wow...
She's amazing.
Athletic person...!
Hime.
Kagetora.
You should go home without me today.
Takatou will probably practice pretty late.
Okay.
Have fun.
BR-RING

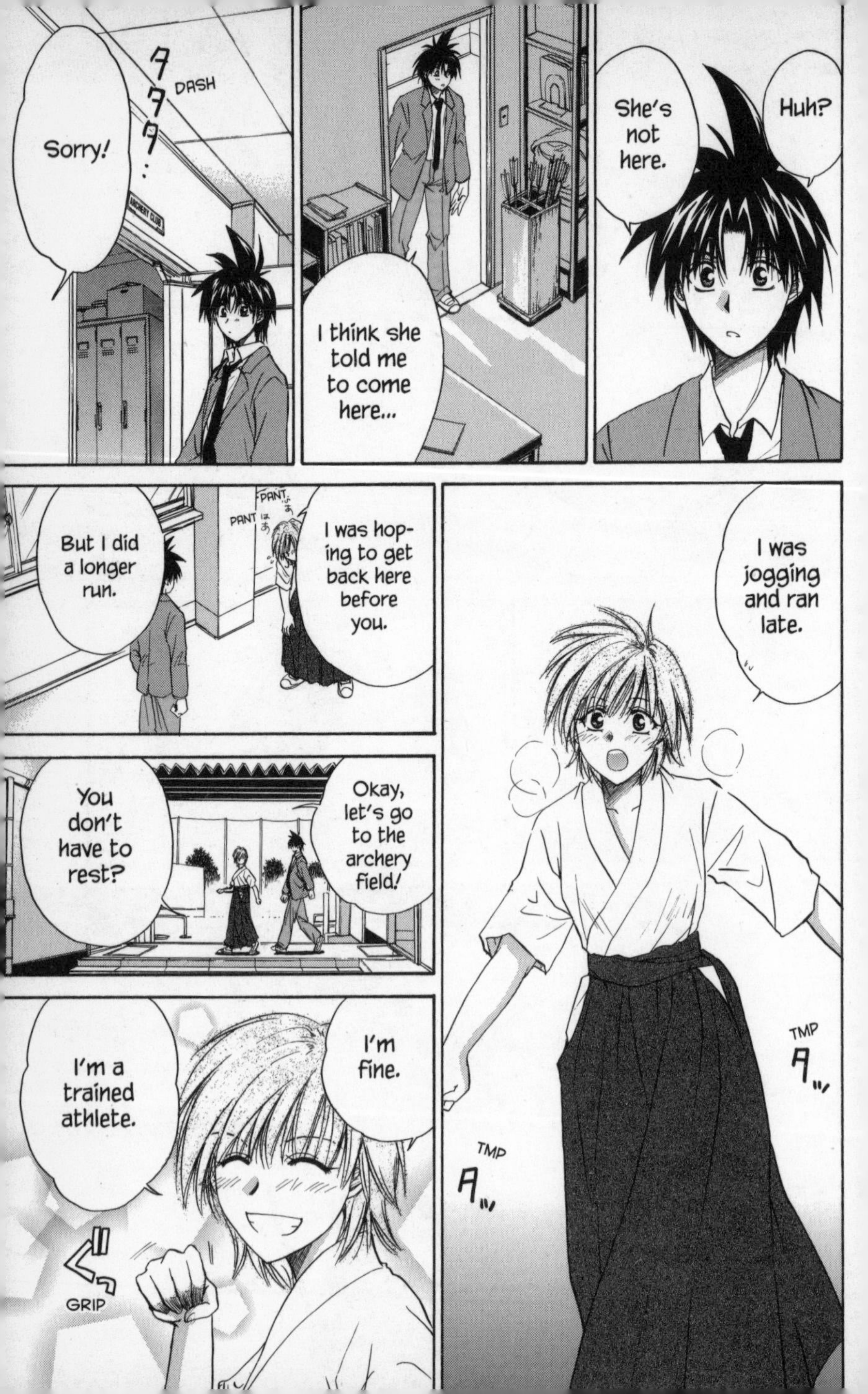
Huh?
She's not here.
I think she told me to come here...
DASH
ARCHERY CLUB
Sorry!
I was jogging and ran late.
TMP
TMP
PANT PANT
I was hop-ing to get back here before you.
But I did a longer run.
Okay, let's go to the archery field!
You don't have to rest?
I'm fine.
I'm a trained athlete.
GRIP

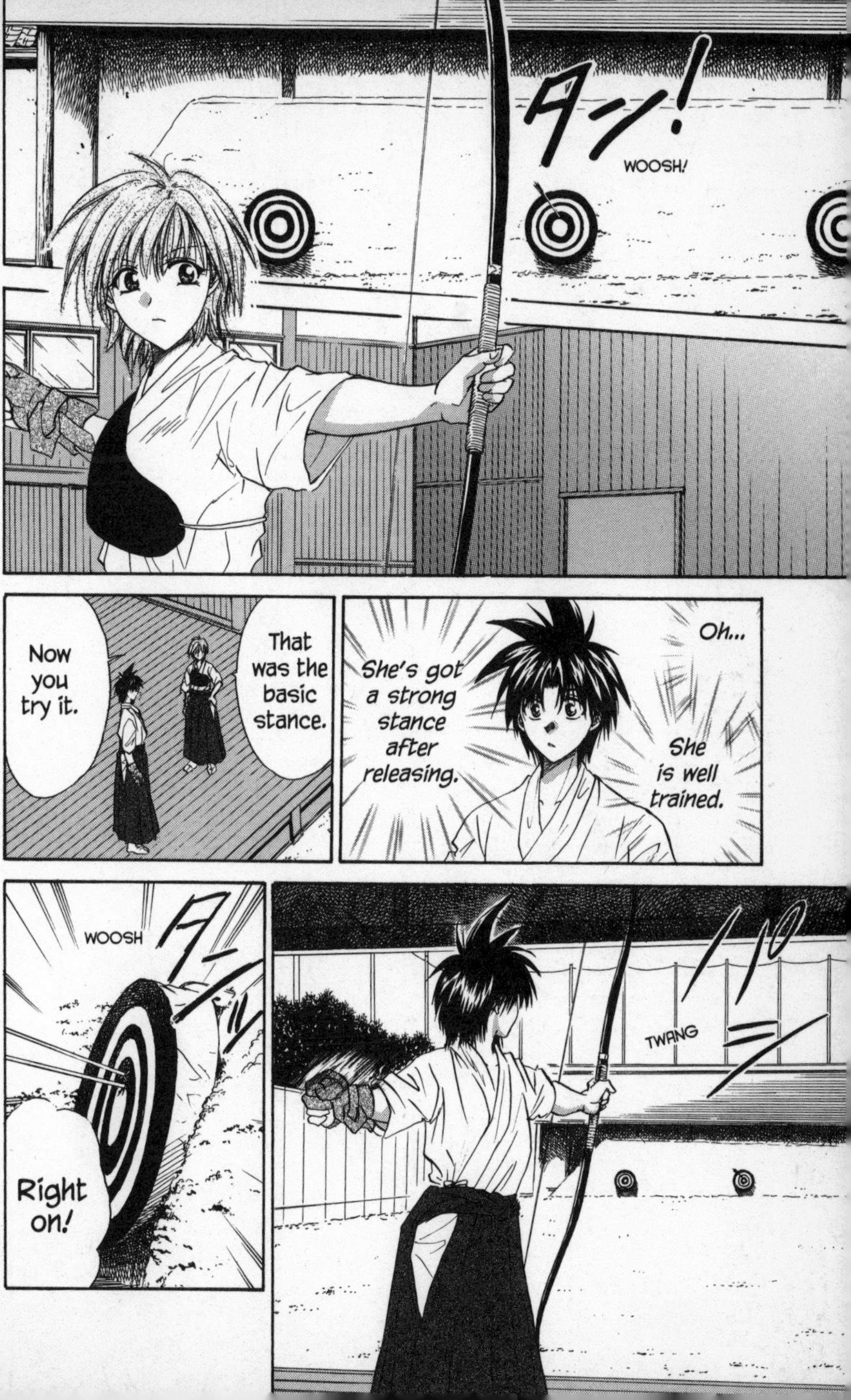

タン!
WOOSH!
Oh...
She's got a strong stance after releasing.
She is well trained.
That was the basic stance.
Now you try it.
TWANG
WOOSH
Right on!

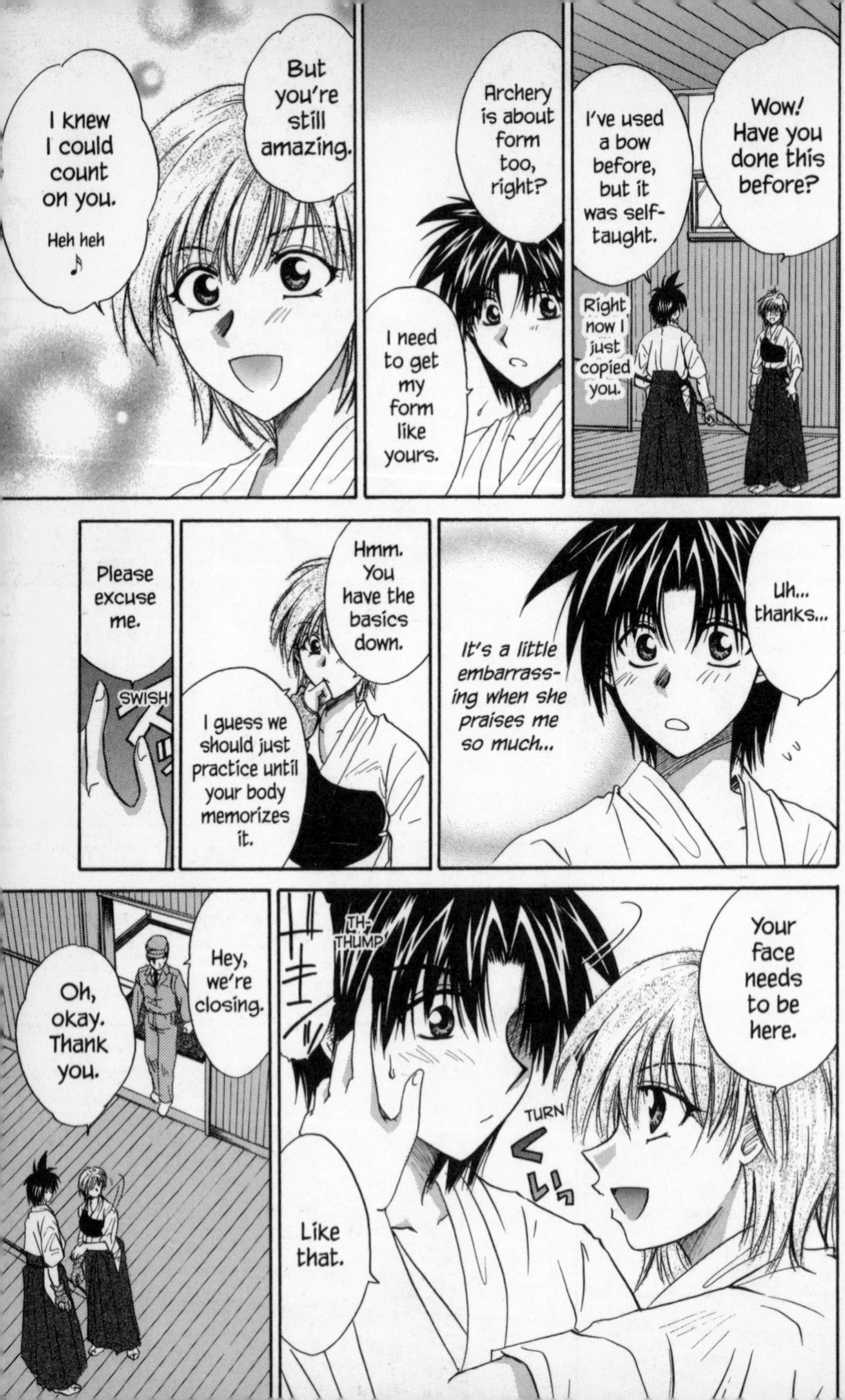
Wow! Have you done this before?
I've used a bow before, but it was self-taught.
Right now I just copied you.
Archery is about form too, right?
I need to get my form like yours.
But you're still amazing.
I knew I could count on you.
Heh heh ♪
Uh... thanks...
It's a little embarrassing when she praises me so much...
Hmm. You have the basics down.
I guess we should just practice until your body memorizes it.
Please excuse me.
SWISH
Your face needs to be here.
TH-THUMP
TURN
Like that.
Hey, we're closing.
Oh, okay. Thank you.

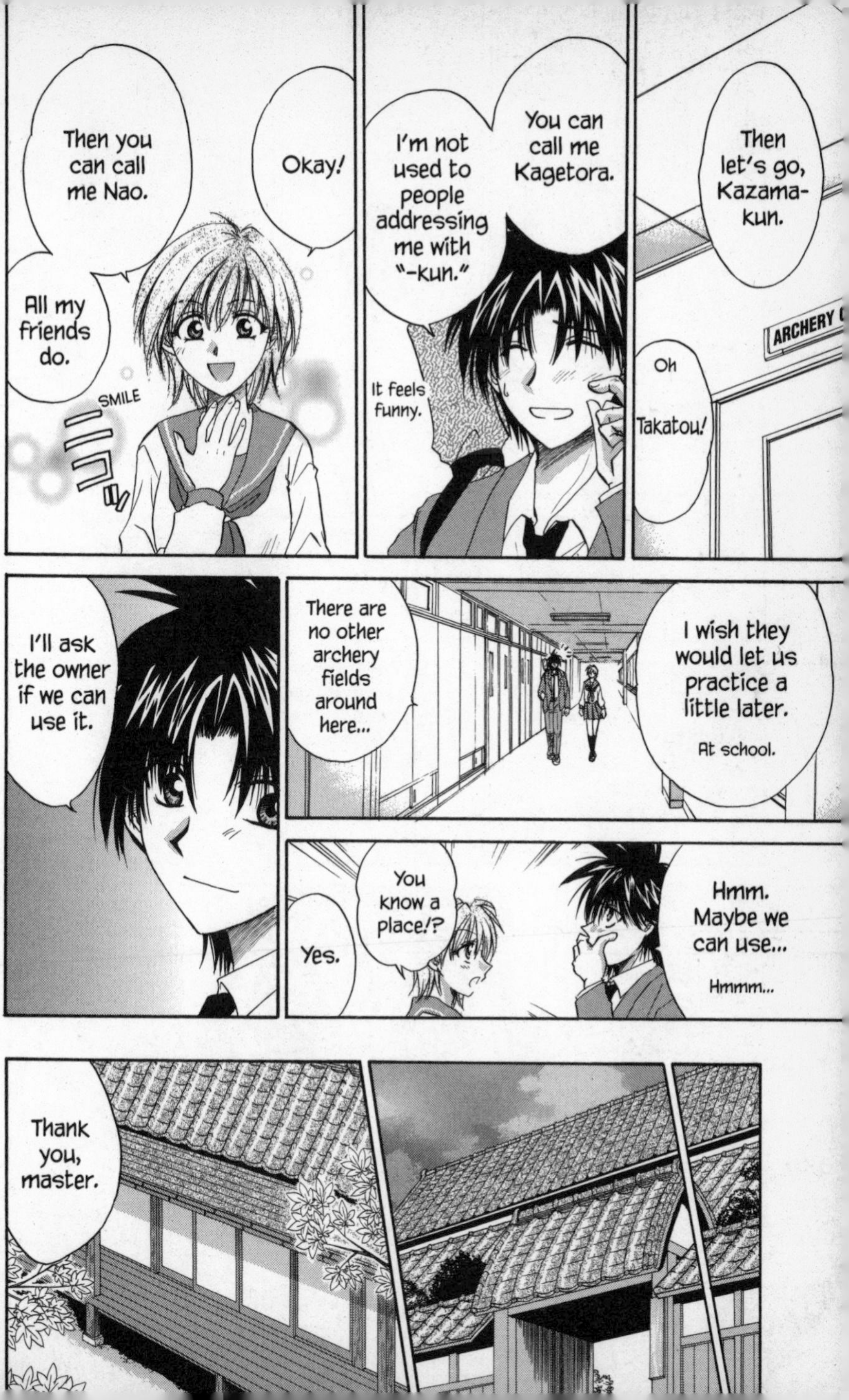
Then let's go, Kazama-kun.
ARCHERY
Oh Takatou!
You can call me Kagetora.
I'm not used to people addressing me with "-kun."
It feels funny.
Okay!
Then you can call me Nao.
All my friends do.
SMILE
I wish they would let us practice a little later.
At school.
There are no other archery fields around here...
Hmm. Maybe we can use...
Hmmm...
You know a place!?
Yes.
I'll ask the owner if we can use it.
Thank you, master.

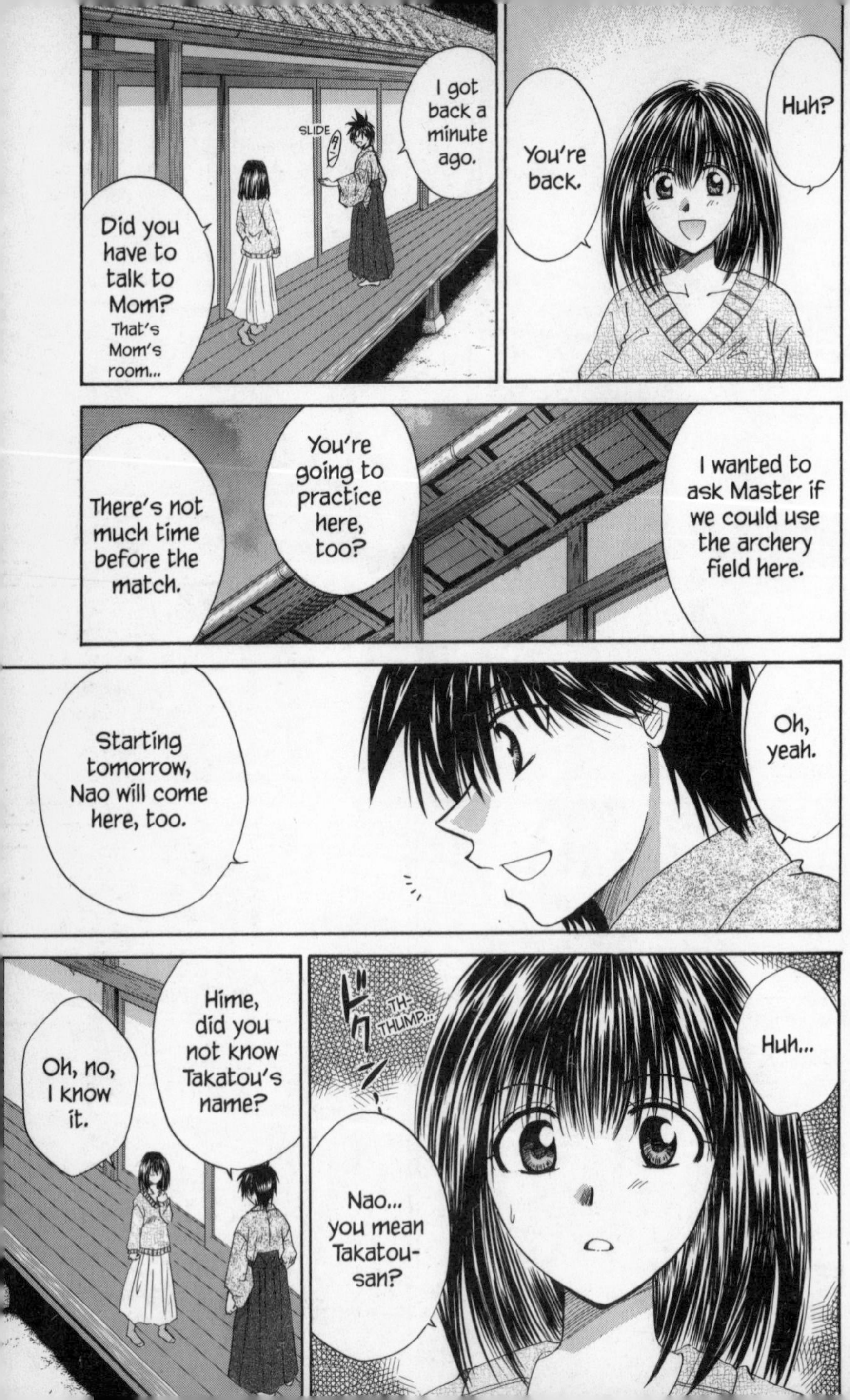
Huh?
You're back.
I got back a minute ago.
SLIDE
Did you have to talk to Mom? That's Mom's room...
I wanted to ask Master if we could use the archery field here.
You're going to practice here, too?
There's not much time before the match.
Oh, yeah.
Starting tomorrow, Nao will come here, too.
Huh...
TH-THUMP...
Nao... you mean Takatou-san?
Hime, did you not know Takatou's name?
Oh, no, I know it.

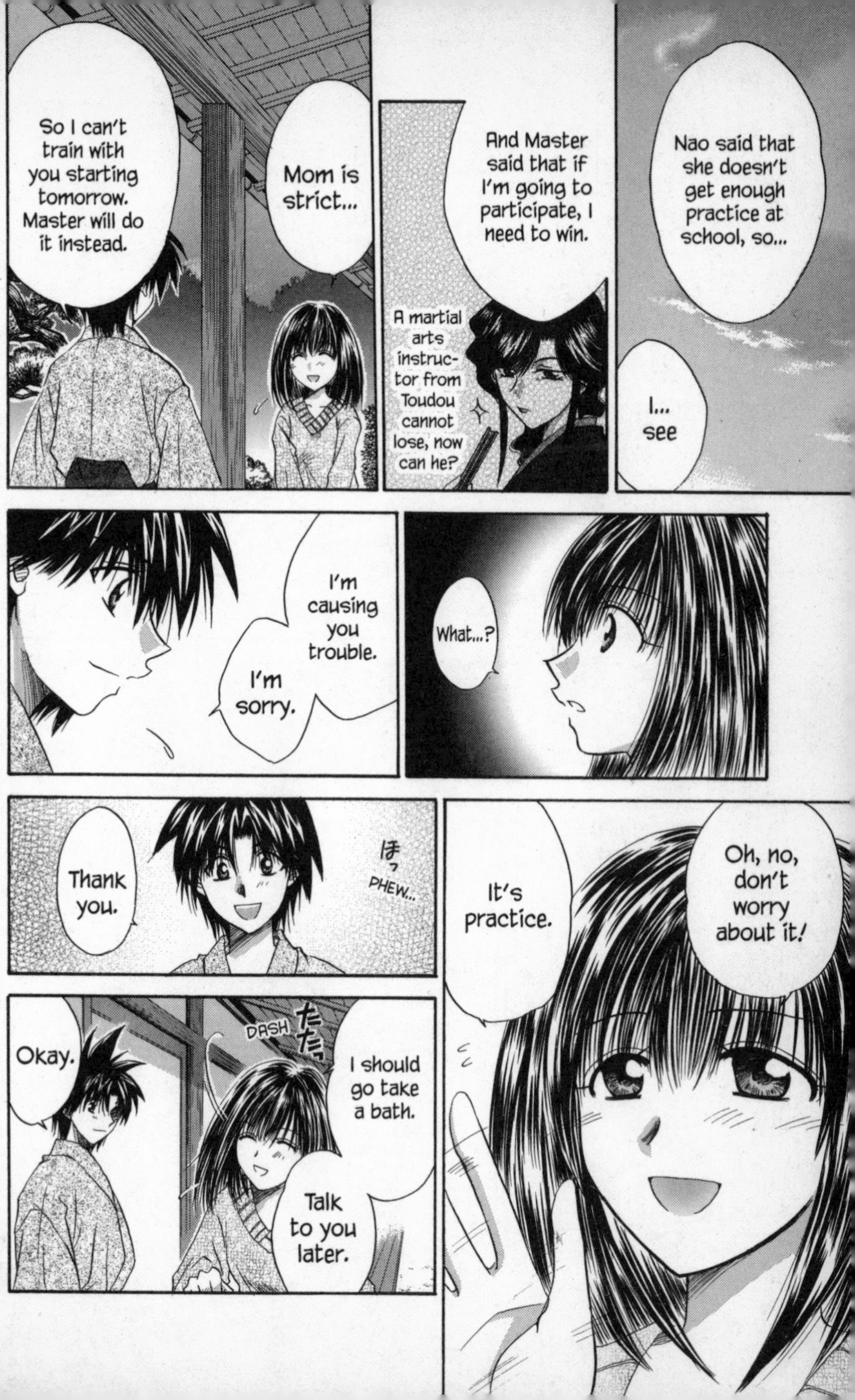
Nao said that she doesn't get enough practice at school, so...
I... see
And Master said that if I'm going to participate, I need to win.
A martial arts instructor from Toudou cannot lose, now can he?
Mom is strict...
So I can't train with you starting tomorrow. Master will do it instead.
What...?
I'm causing you trouble.
I'm sorry.
Oh, no, don't worry about it!
It's practice.
ほっ
PHEW...
Thank you.
たたっ
DASH
I should go take a bath.
Talk to you later.
Okay.

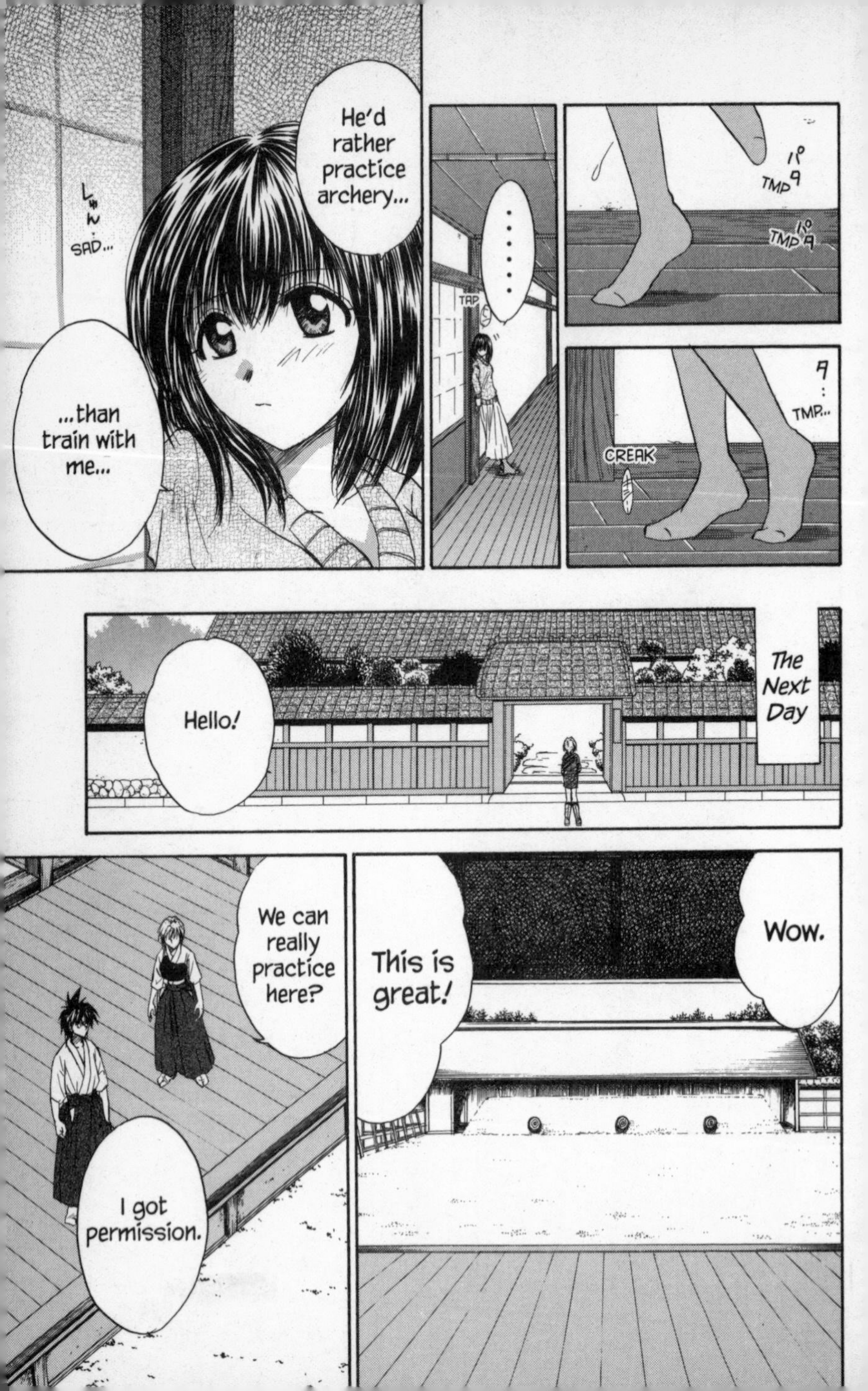
TMP
TMP
TMP...
CREAK
......
TAP
He'd rather practice archery...
SAD...
...than train with me...
The Next Day
Hello!
Wow.
This is great!
We can really practice here?
I got permission.

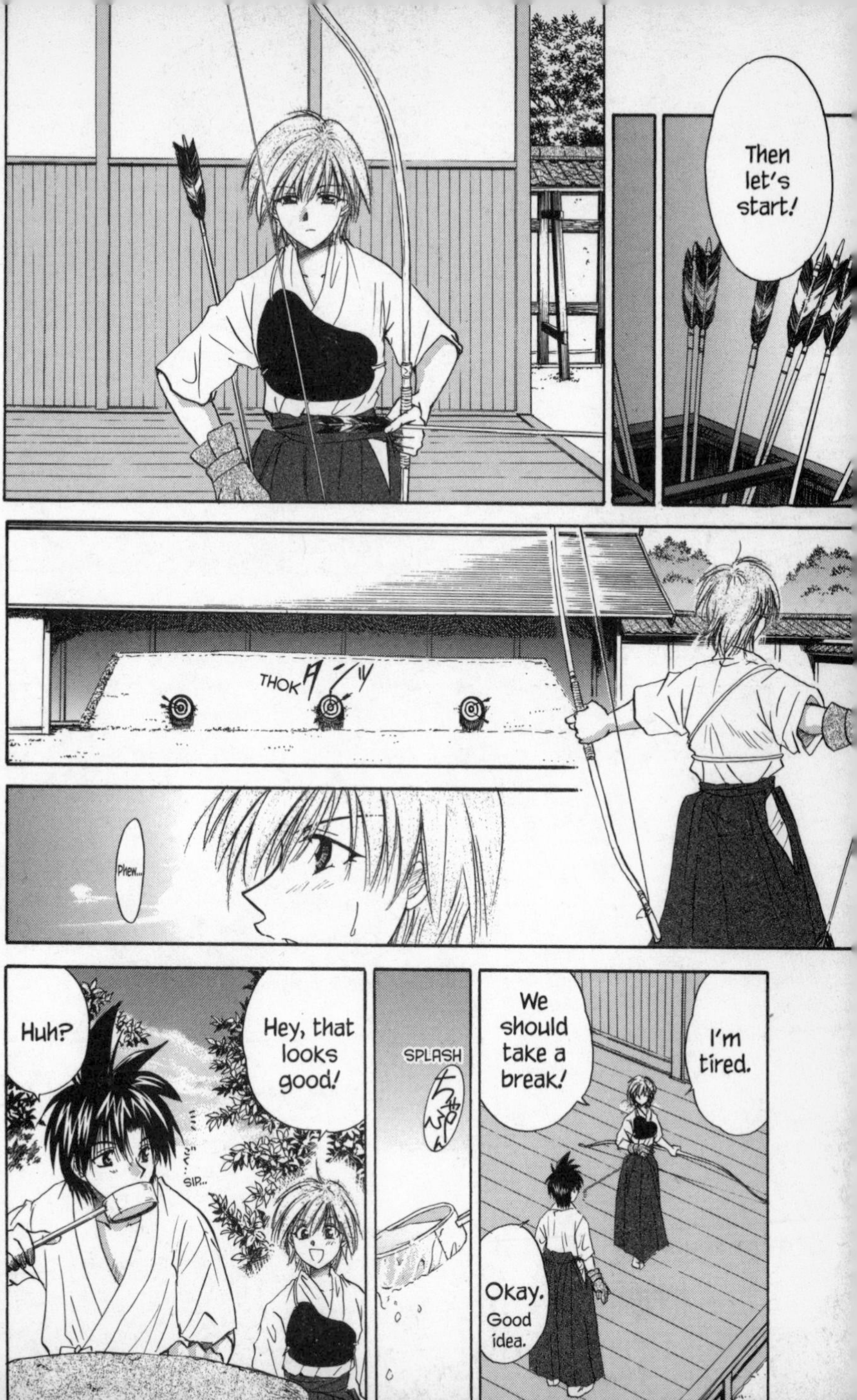
Then let's start!
THOK
タンッ
Phew...
I'm tired.
We should take a break!
Okay. Good idea.
SPLASH
ちゃぷん
Hey, that looks good!
SIP...
Huh?

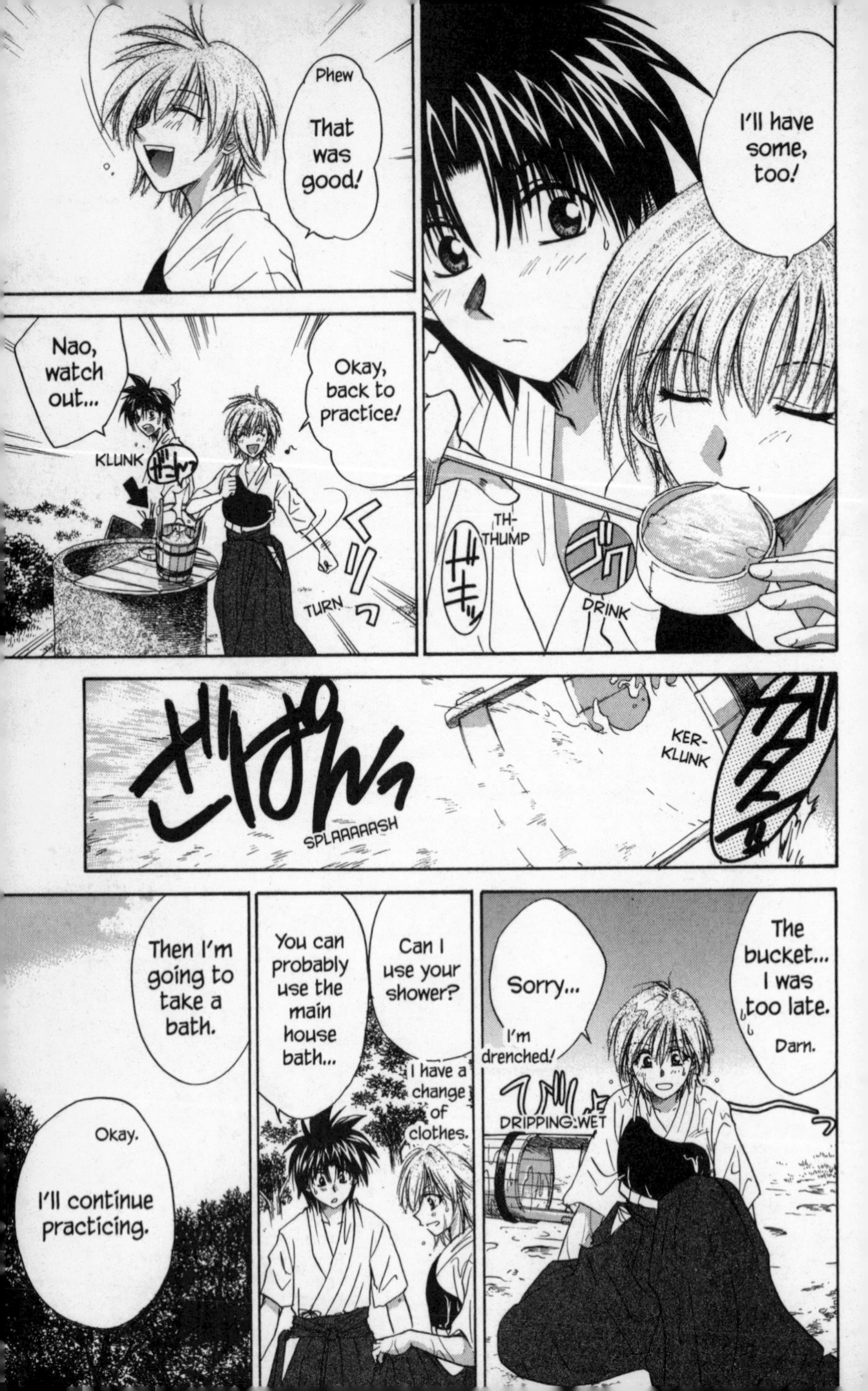
I'll have some, too!
TH-THUMP
DRINK
Phew
That was good!
Okay, back to practice!
Nao, watch out...
KLUNK
TURN
KER-KLUNK
SPLAAAAASH
The bucket... I was too late.
Darn.
Sorry...
I'm drenched!
DRIPPING WET
Can I use your shower?
You can probably use the main house bath...
I have a change of clothes.
Then I'm going to take a bath.
Okay.
I'll continue practicing.

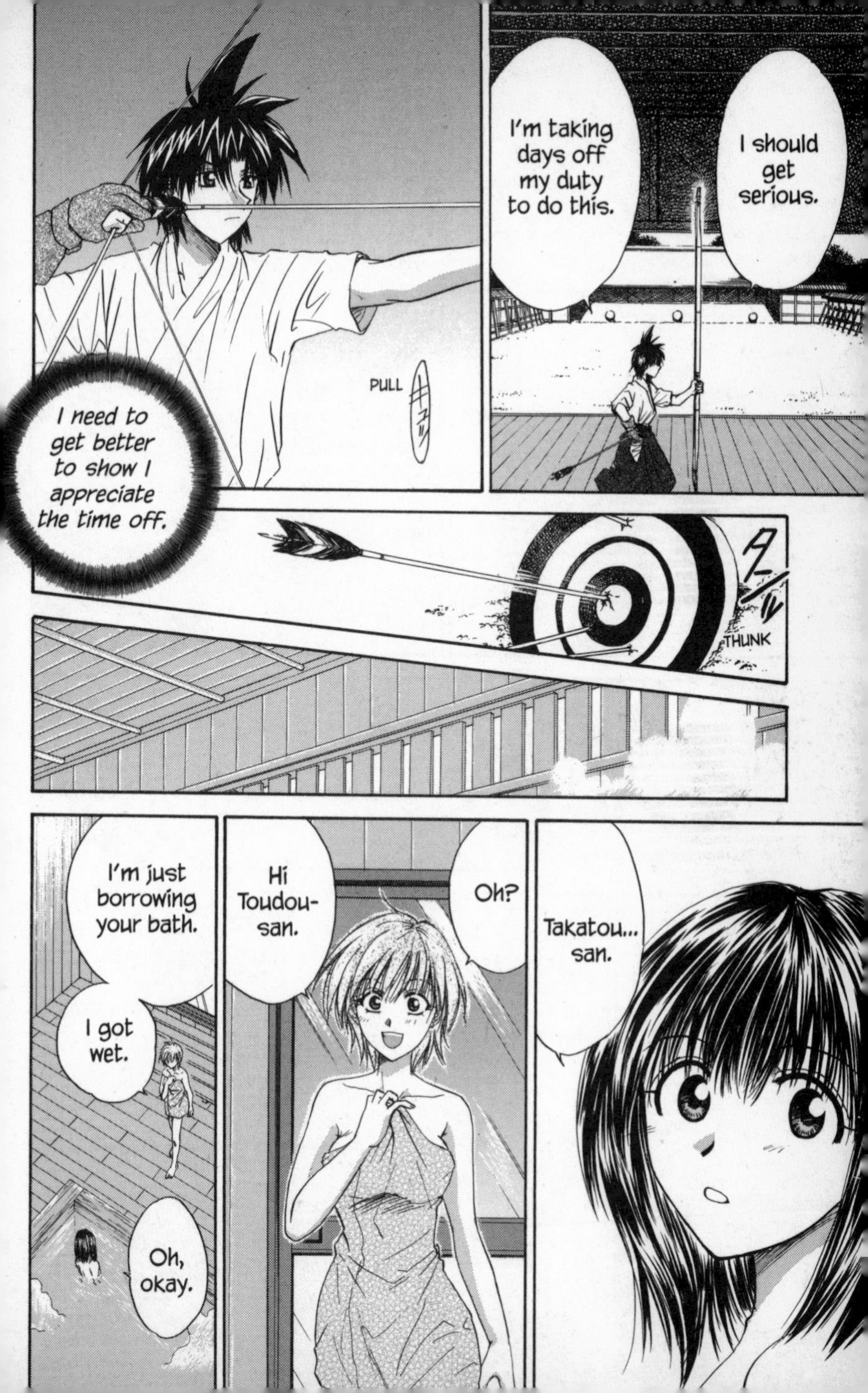
I should get serious.
I'm taking days off my duty to do this.
PULL
I need to get better to show I appreciate the time off.
THUNK
Takatou... san.
Oh?
Hi Toudou-san.
I'm just borrowing your bath.
I got wet.
Oh, okay.

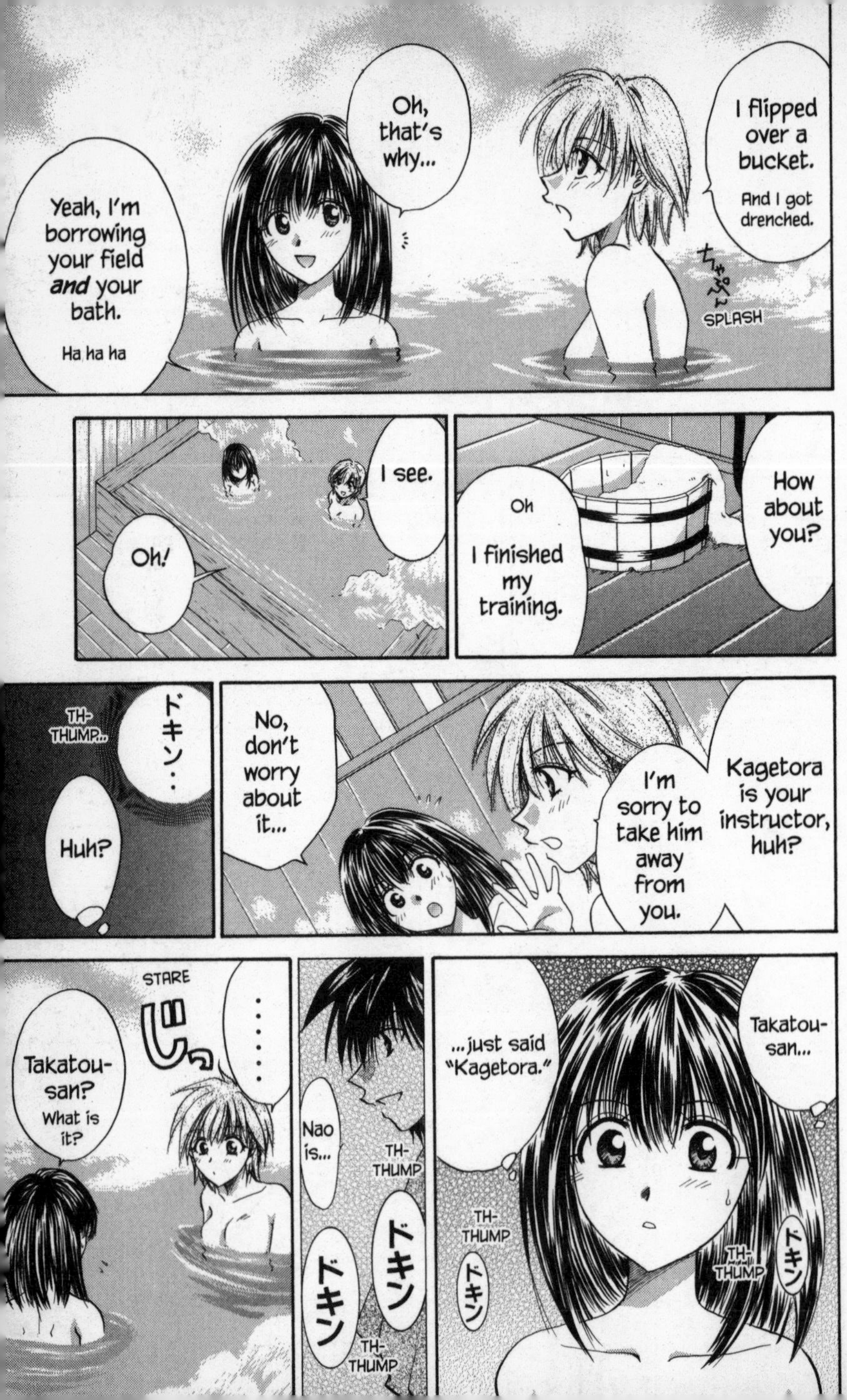
I flipped over a bucket.
And I got drenched.
SPLASH
Oh, that's why...
Yeah, I'm borrowing your field *and* your bath.
Ha ha ha
How about you?
Oh
I finished my training.
I see.
Oh!
Kagetora is your instructor, huh?
I'm sorry to take him away from you.
No, don't worry about it...
ドキン・・
TH-THUMP...
Huh?
Takatou-san...
...just said "Kagetora."
ドキン
TH-THUMP
Nao is...
TH-THUMP
ドキン
TH-THUMP
ドキン
TH-THUMP
ドキン
TH-THUMP
......
STARE
じっ
Takatou-san? What is it?

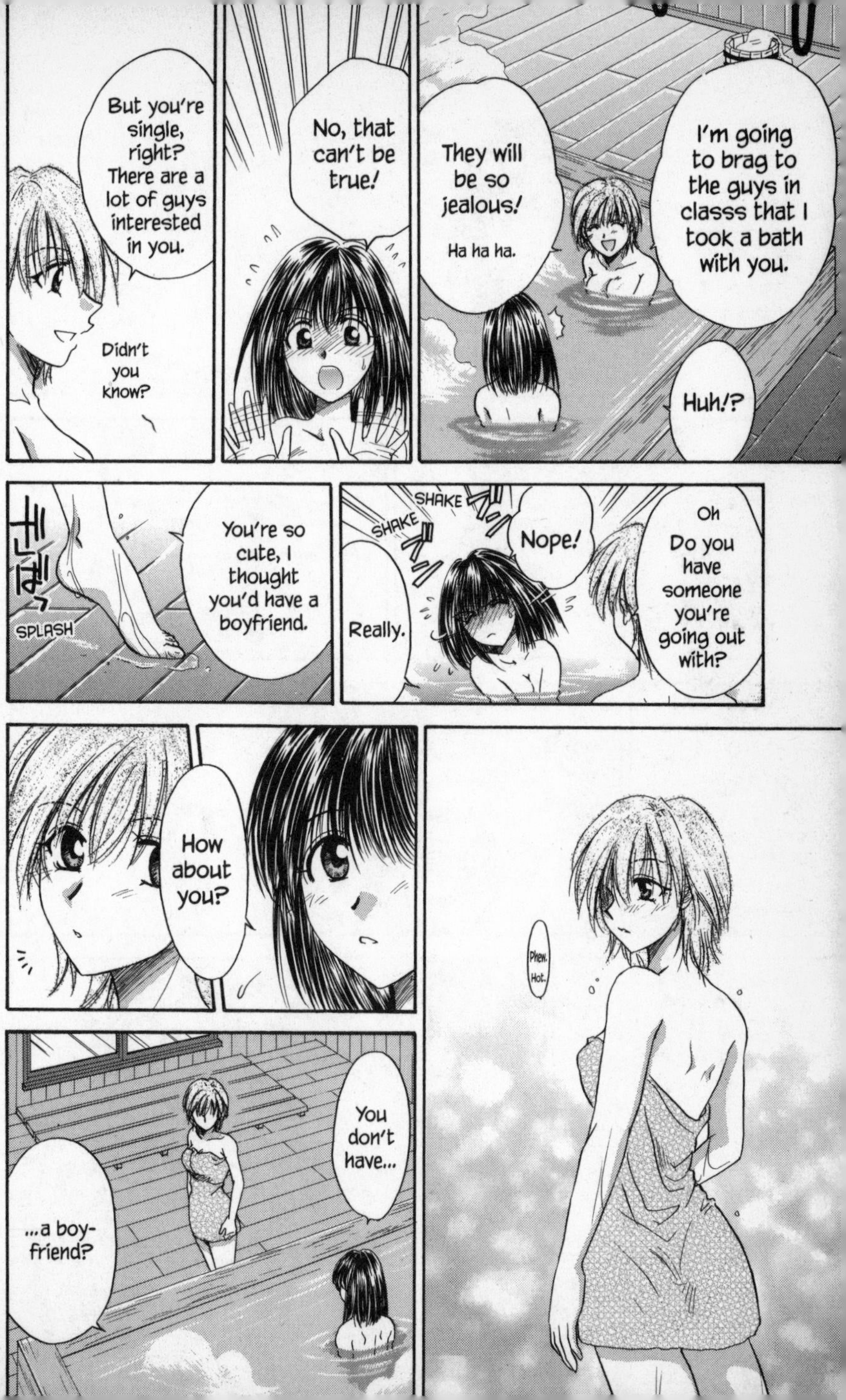
I'm going to brag to the guys in classs that I took a bath with you.
Huh!?
They will be so jealous!
Ha ha ha.
No, that can't be true!
But you're single, right? There are a lot of guys interested in you.
Didn't you know?
Oh
Do you have someone you're going out with?
SHAKE
SHAKE
Nope!
Really.
You're so cute, I thought you'd have a boyfriend.
SPLASH
Phew. Hot.
How about you?
You don't have...
...a boy-friend?

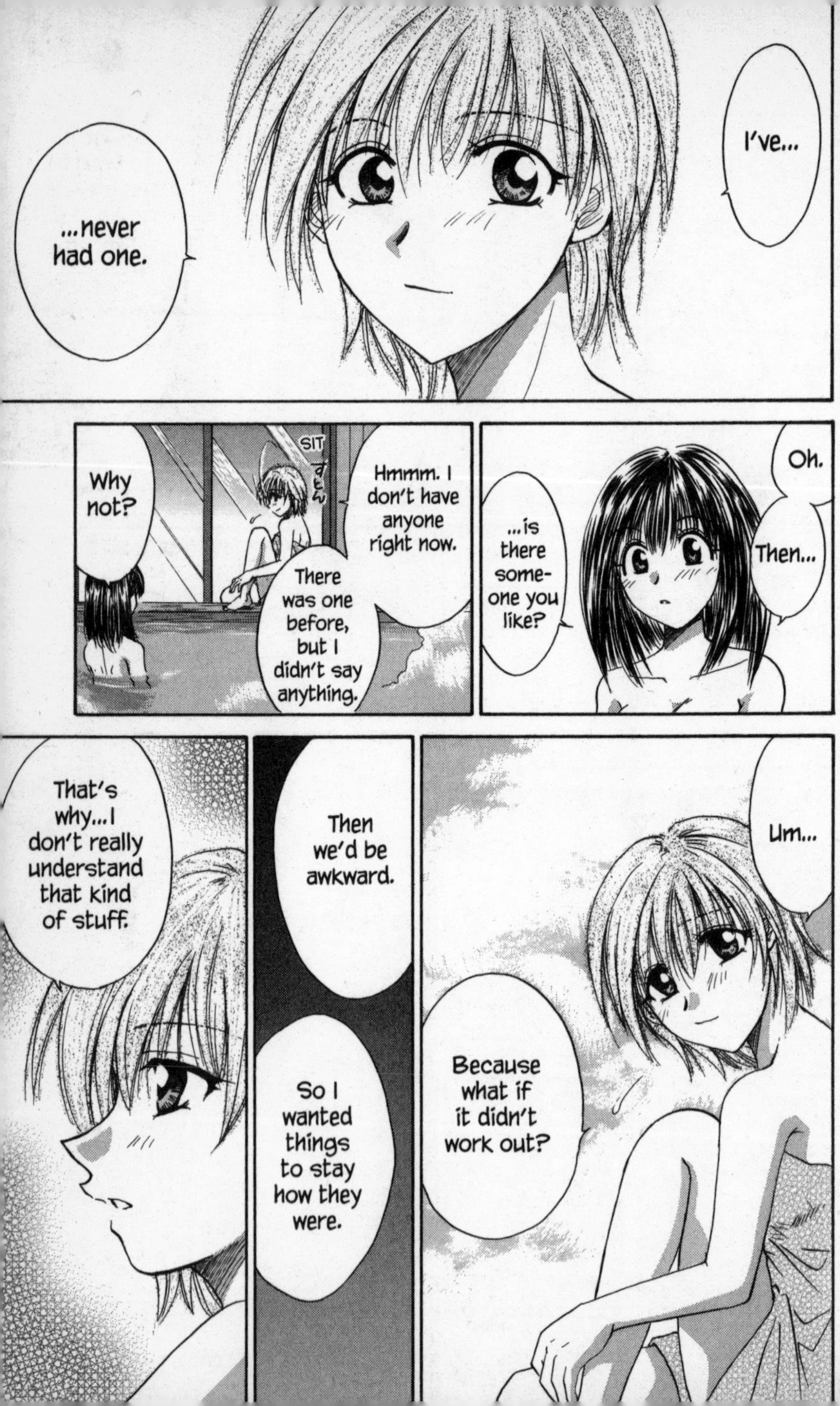
I've...
...never had one.
Oh.
Then...
...is there someone you like?
SIT
すとん
Hmmm. I don't have anyone right now.
There was one before, but I didn't say anything.
Why not?
Um...
Because what if it didn't work out?
Then we'd be awkward.
So I wanted things to stay how they were.
That's why...I don't really understand that kind of stuff.

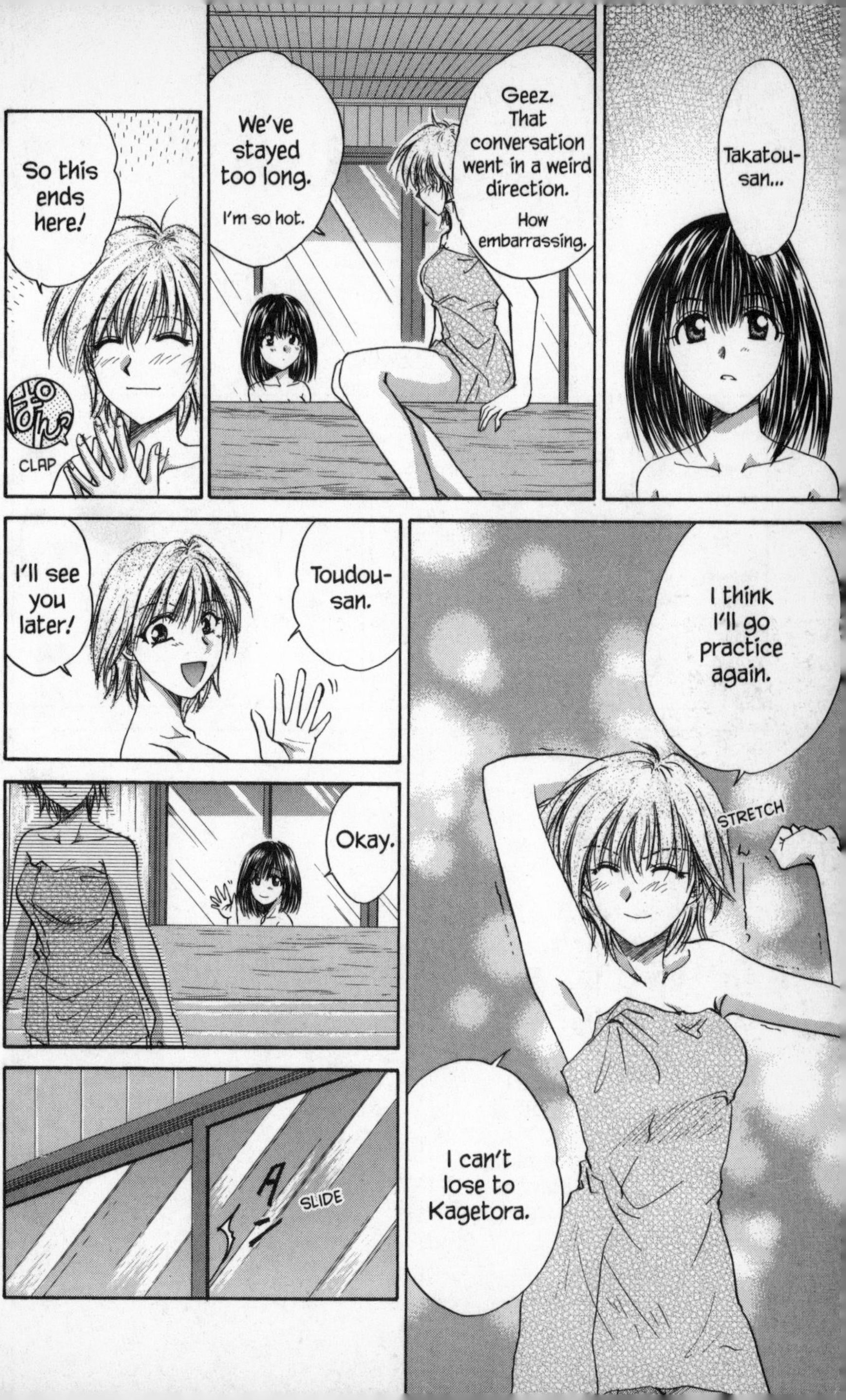
Takatou-san...
Geez. That conversation went in a weird direction.
How embarrassing.
We've stayed too long.
I'm so hot.
So this ends here!
ぱん
CLAP
I think I'll go practice again.
STRETCH
I can't lose to Kagetora.
Toudou-san.
I'll see you later!
Okay.
SLIDE

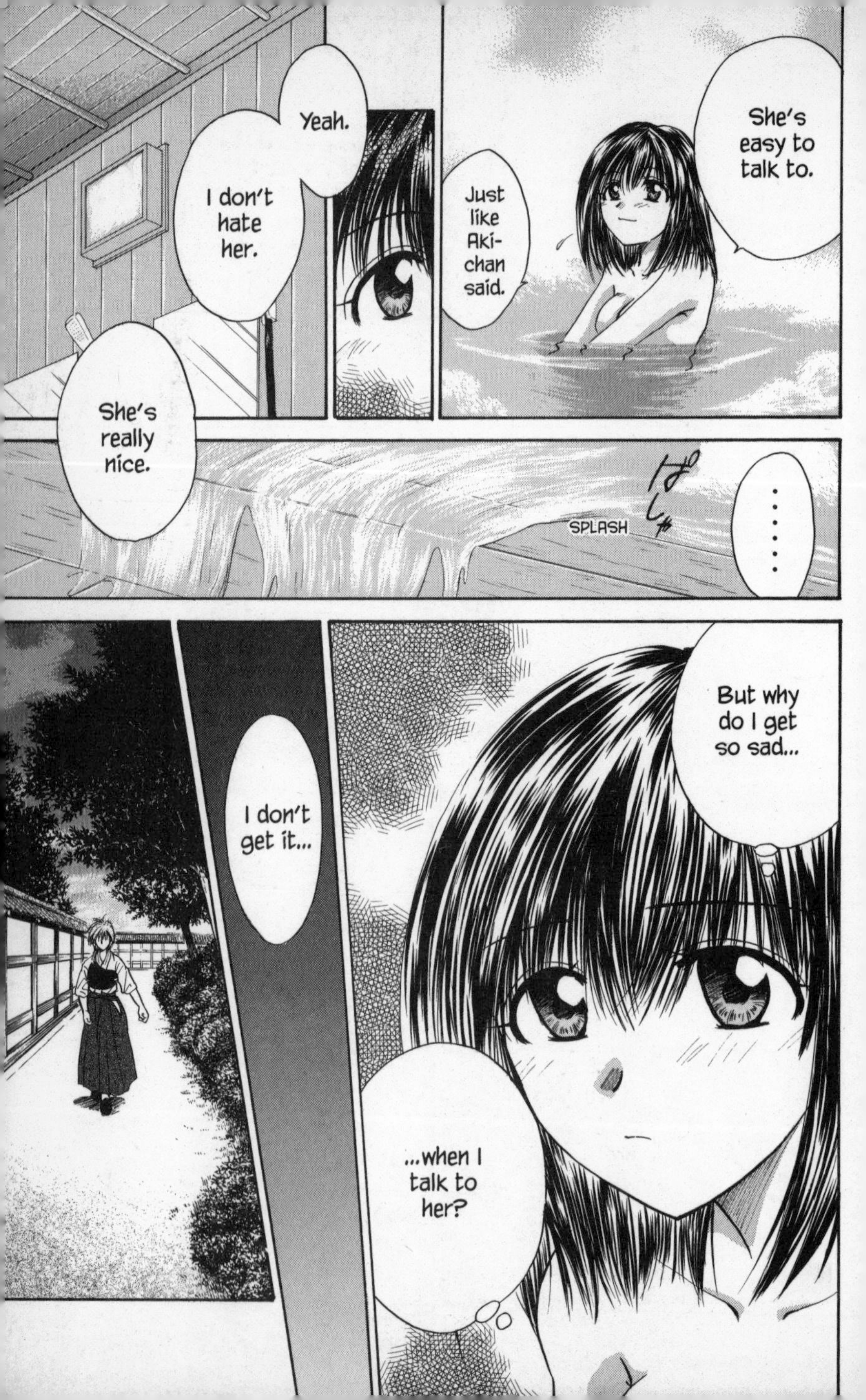
She's easy to talk to.
Just like Aki-chan said.
Yeah.
I don't hate her.
She's really nice.
......
ぱしゃ
SPLASH
But why do I get so sad...
...when I talk to her?
I don't get it...

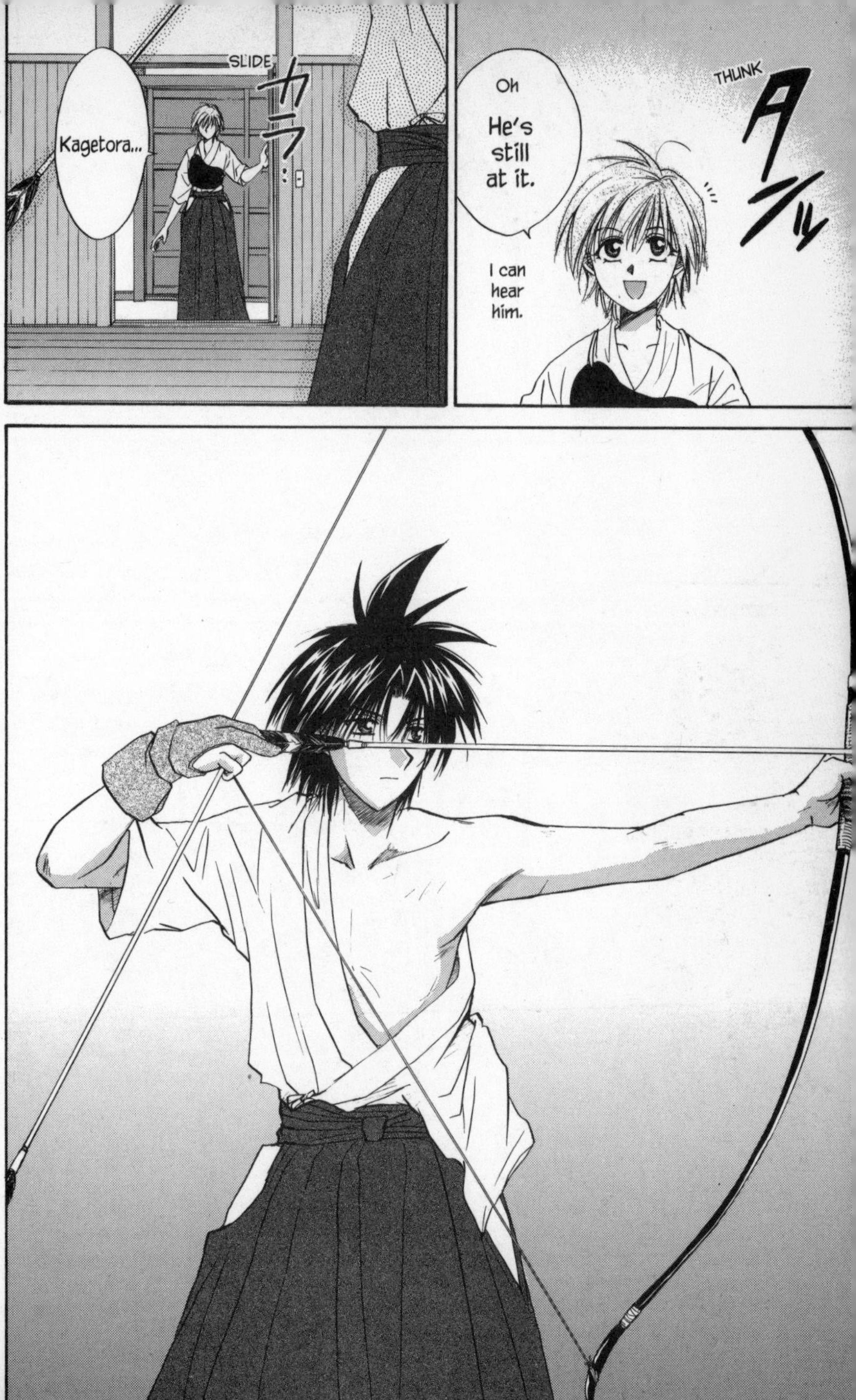
THUNK
タンッ
Oh
He's still at it.
I can hear him.
SLIDE
カラ…
Kagetora...

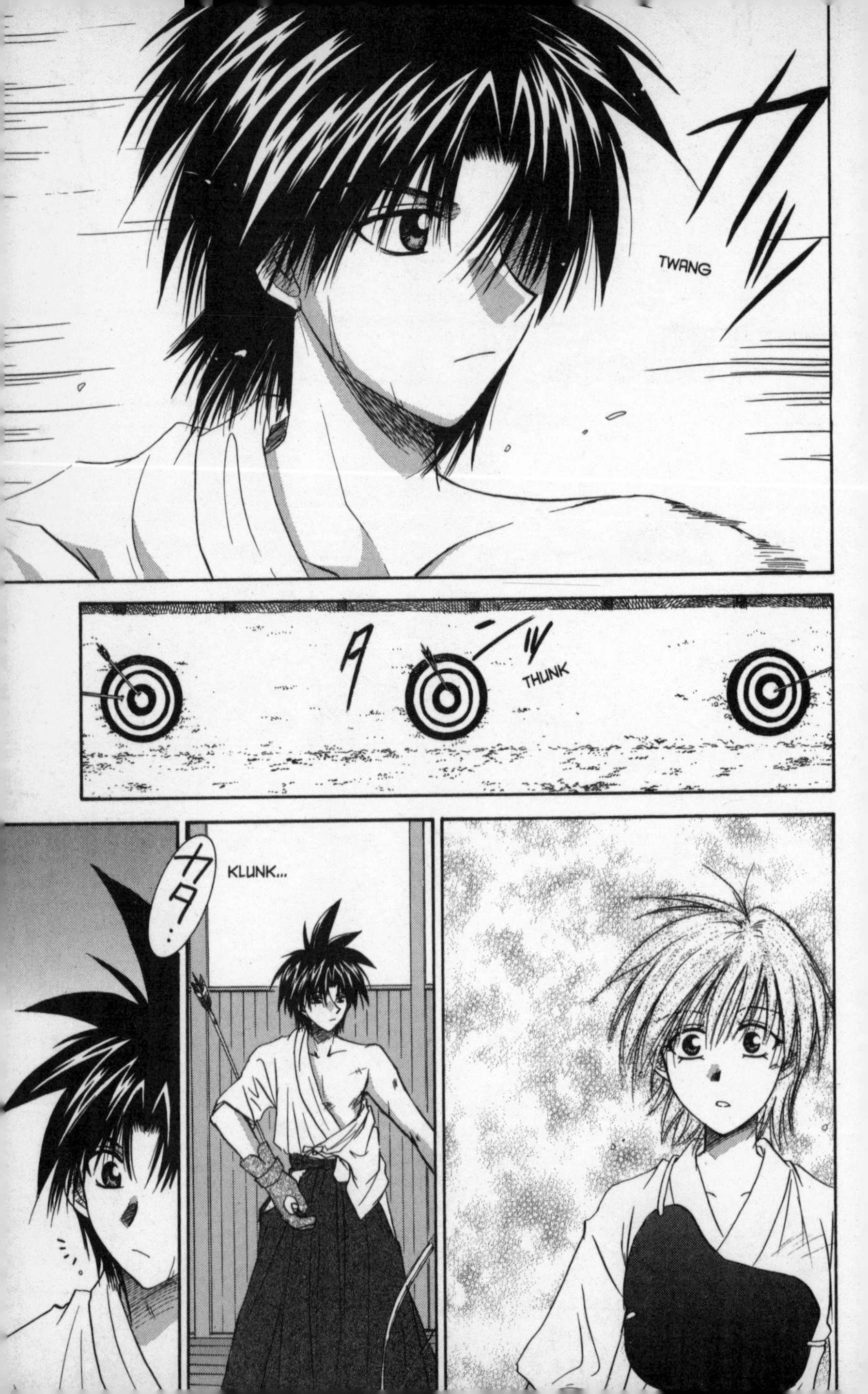

カッ
TWANG
タ－ン
THUNK
カタ…
KLUNK...

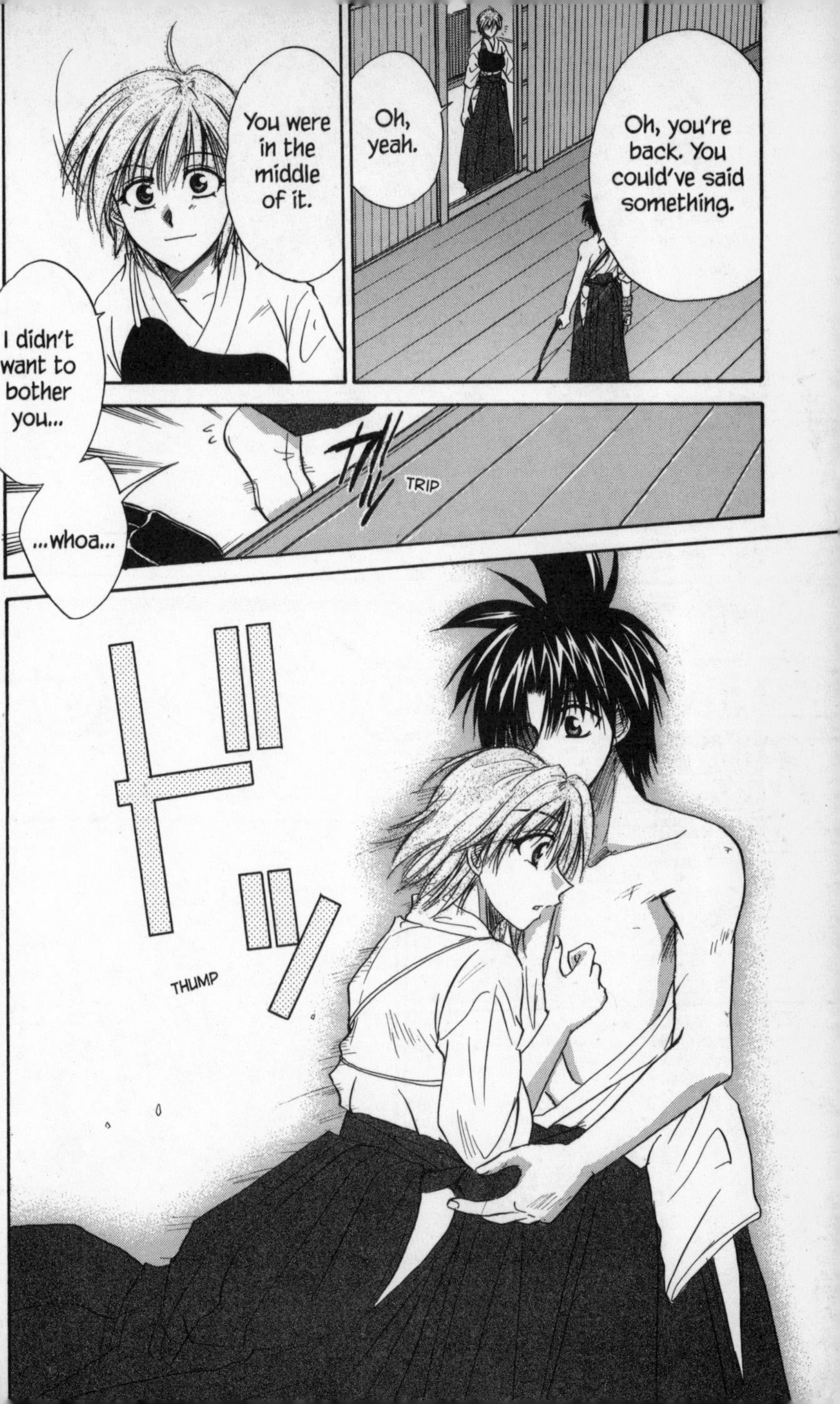

Oh, you're back. You could've said something.
Oh, yeah.
You were in the middle of it.
I didn't want to bother you...
TRIP
...whoa...
THUMP

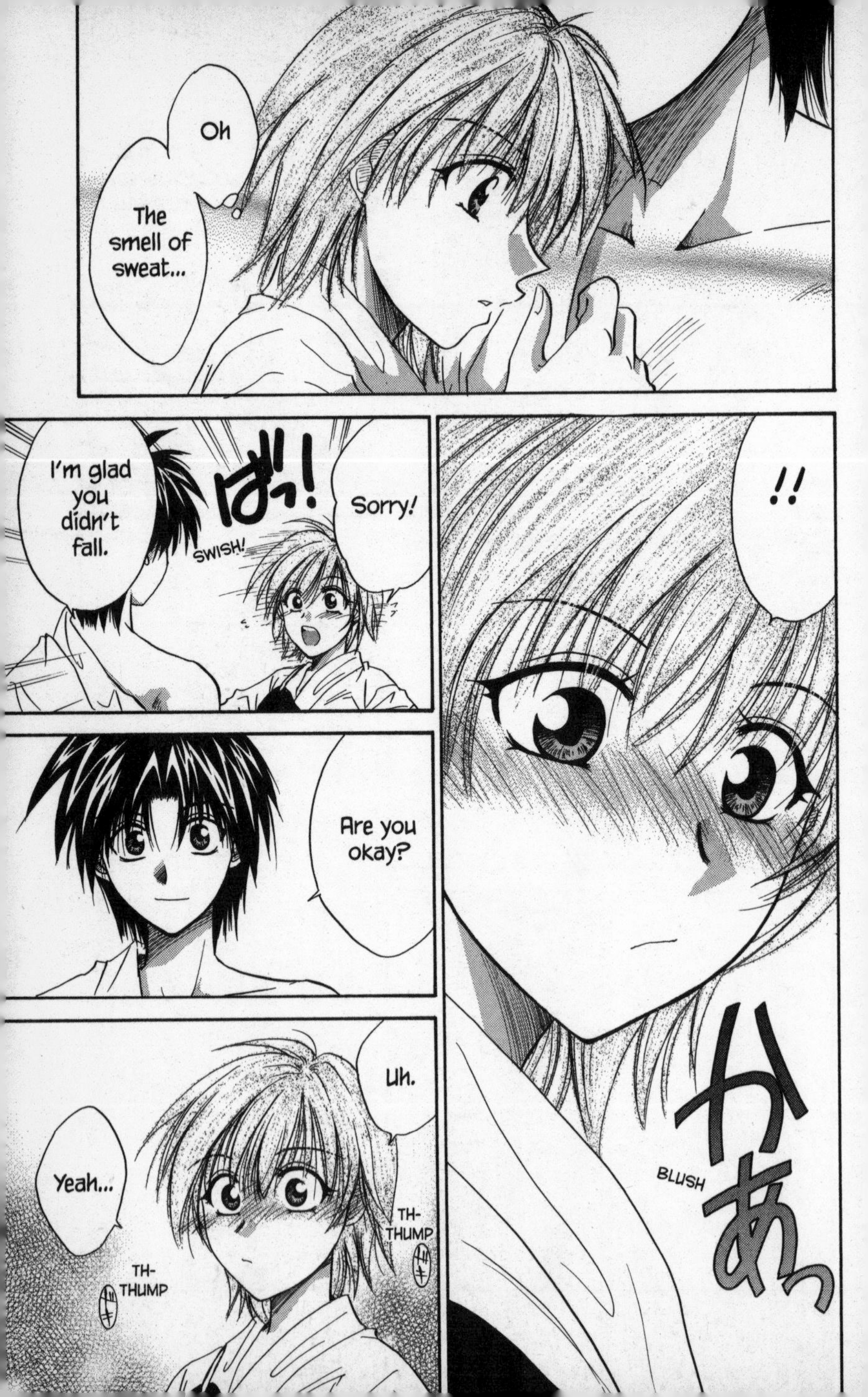
Oh
The smell of sweat...
!!
かあっ
BLUSH
Sorry!
ばっ!
SWISH!
I'm glad you didn't fall.
Are you okay?
Uh.
ドキ
TH-THUMP
Yeah...
ドキ
TH-THUMP

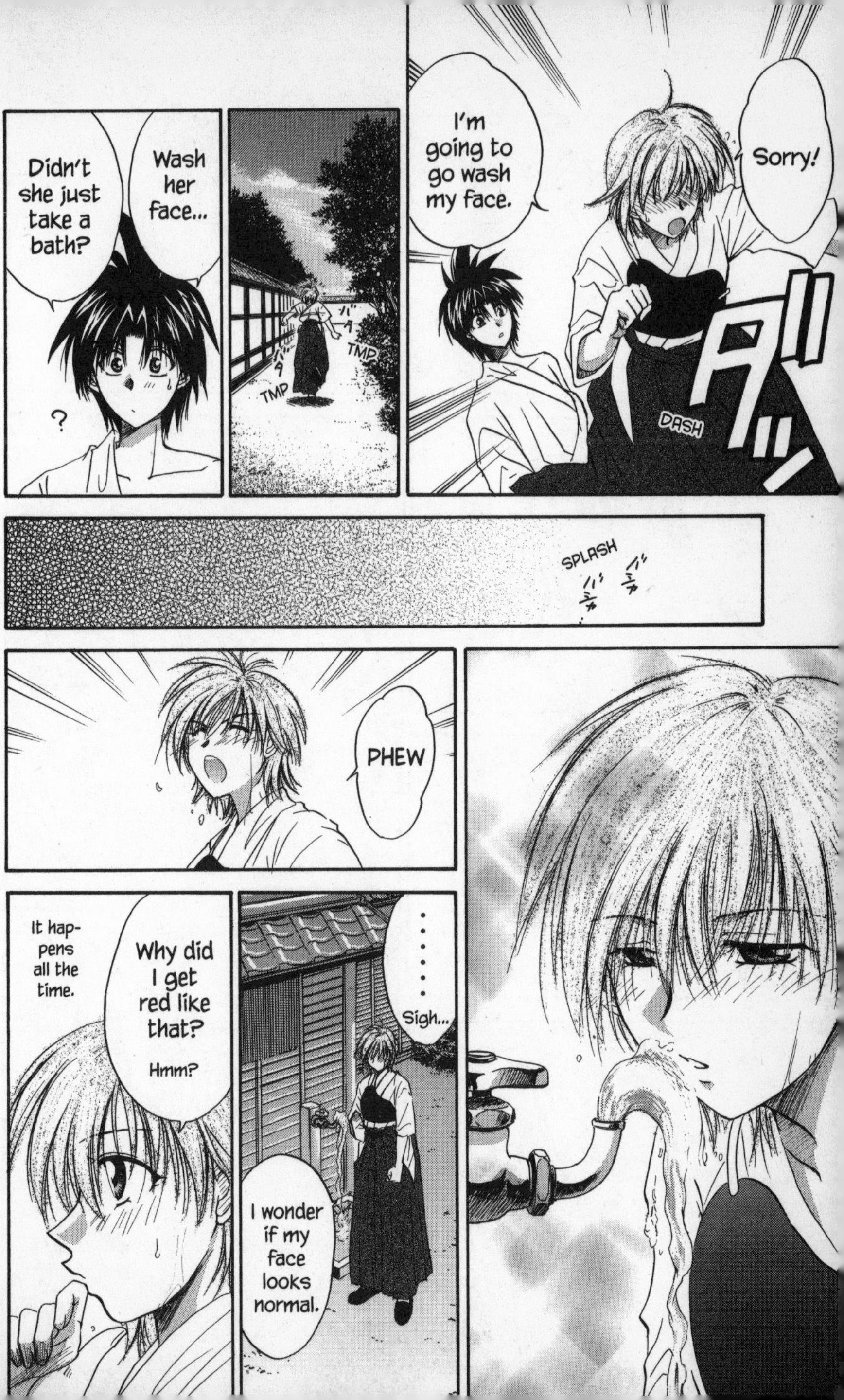
Sorry!
I'm going to go wash my face.
DASH
TMP
TMP
Wash her face...
Didn't she just take a bath?
?
SPLASH
PHEW
......
Sigh...
I wonder if my face looks normal.
Why did I get red like that?
Hmm?
It happens all the time.

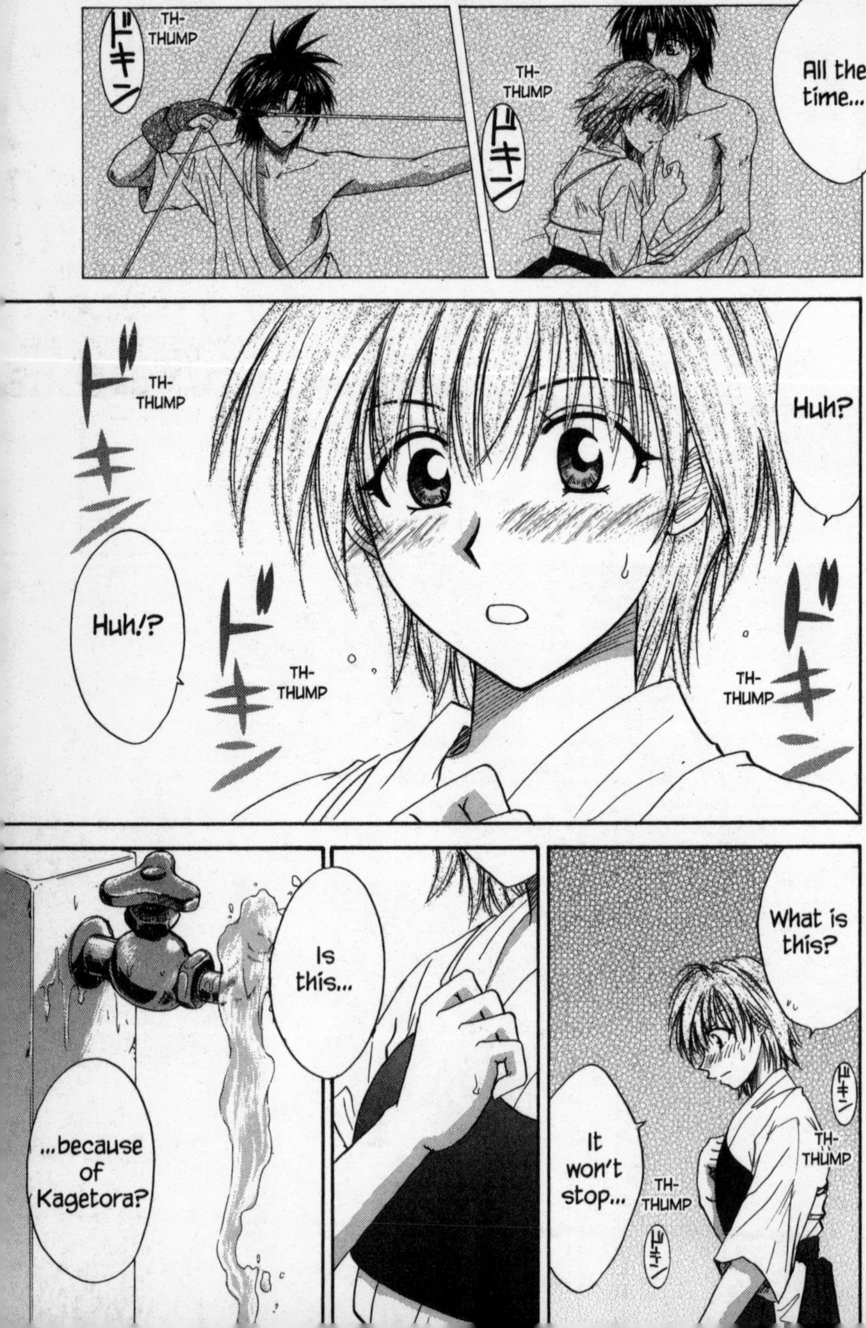
All the time...
TH-THUMP
ドキン
TH-THUMP
ドキン
Huh?
TH-THUMP
ドキン
TH-THUMP
ドキン
Huh!?
TH-THUMP
ドキン
What is this?
TH-THUMP
It won't stop...
TH-THUMP
Is this...
...because of Kagetora?

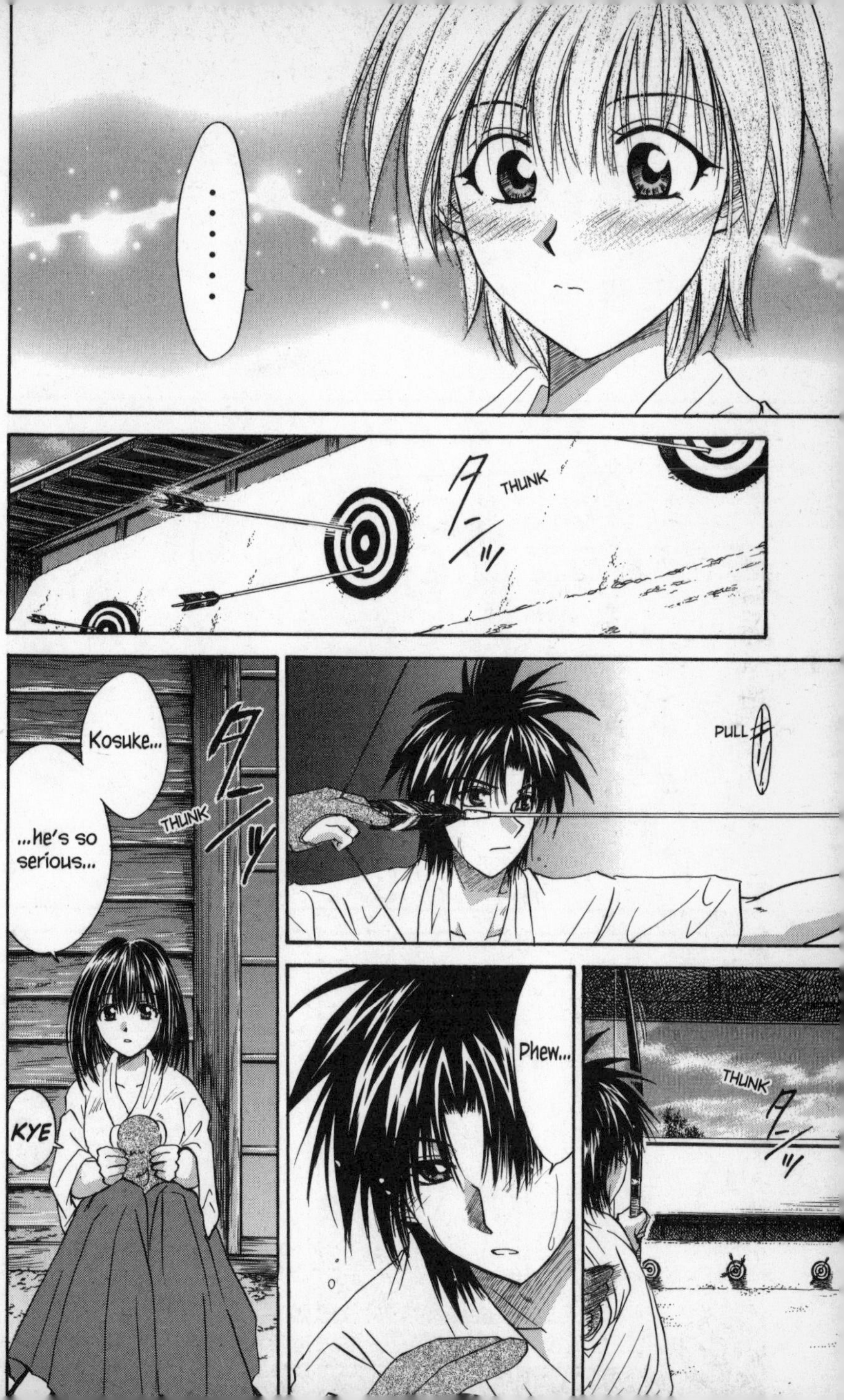
......
THUNK
PULL
Kosuke...
...he's so serious...
THUNK
KYE
Phew...
THUNK

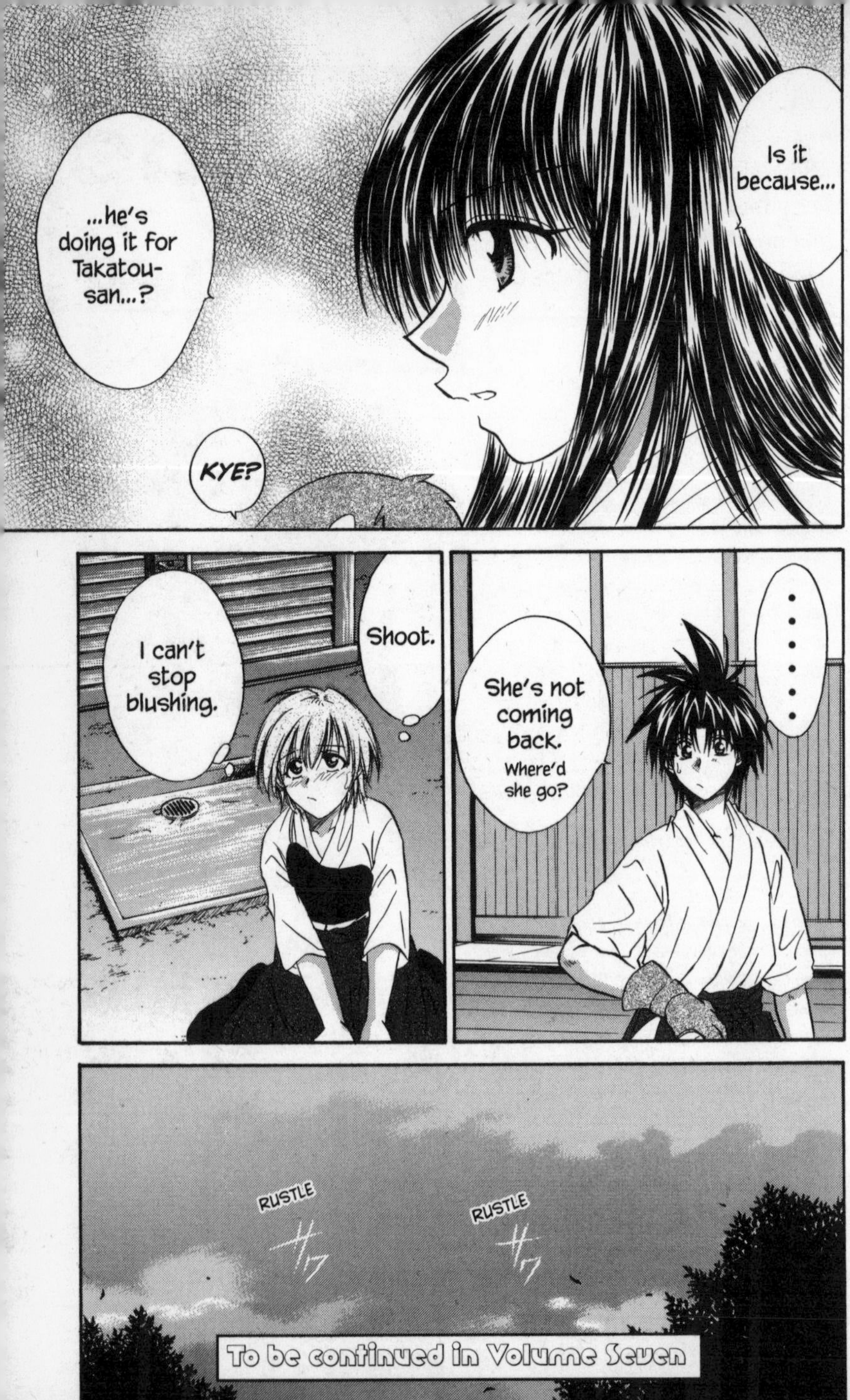
Is it because...
...he's doing it for Takatou-san...?
KYE?
......
She's not coming back. Where'd she go?
Shoot.
I can't stop blushing.
RUSTLE
RUSTLE
To be continued in Volume Seven

Bonus Page

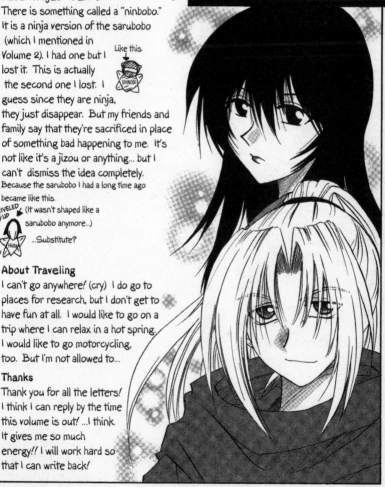

Hello. This is Segami. Wow, it's Volume Six. Six! The year goes by so fast lately. I guess it means that my life is full. So that's a good thing. This time there's bonus manga, so please enjoy it. ♪

About Ninjas - Part 6

There is something called a "ninbobo." It is a ninja version of the sarubobo (which I mentioned in Volume 2). I had one but I lost it. This is actually the second one I lost. I guess since they are ninja, they just disappear. But my friends and family say that they're sacrificed in place of something bad happening to me. It's not like it's a jizou or anything... but I can't dismiss the idea completely.

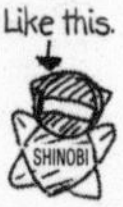

Like this.
SHINOBI

Because the sarubobo I had a long time ago became like this.

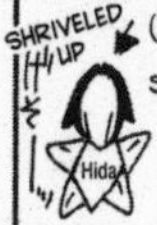

SHRIVELED UP
Hida

(It wasn't shaped like a sarubobo anymore...)

...Substitute?

About Traveling

I can't go anywhere! (cry) I do go to places for research, but I don't get to have fun at all. I would like to go on a trip where I can relax in a hot spring. I would like to go motorcycling, too. But I'm not allowed to...

Thanks

Thank you for all the letters! I think I can reply by the time this volume is out! ...I think. It gives me so much energy!! I will work hard so that I can write back!

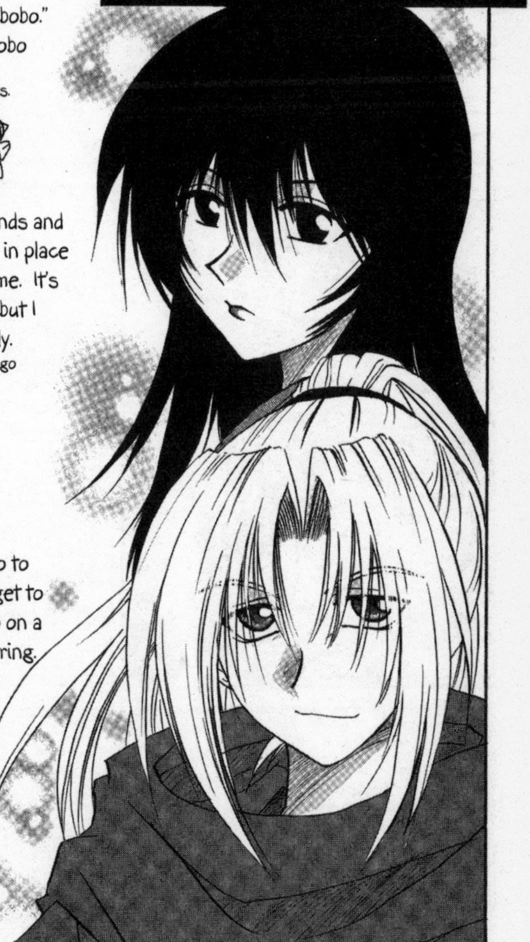

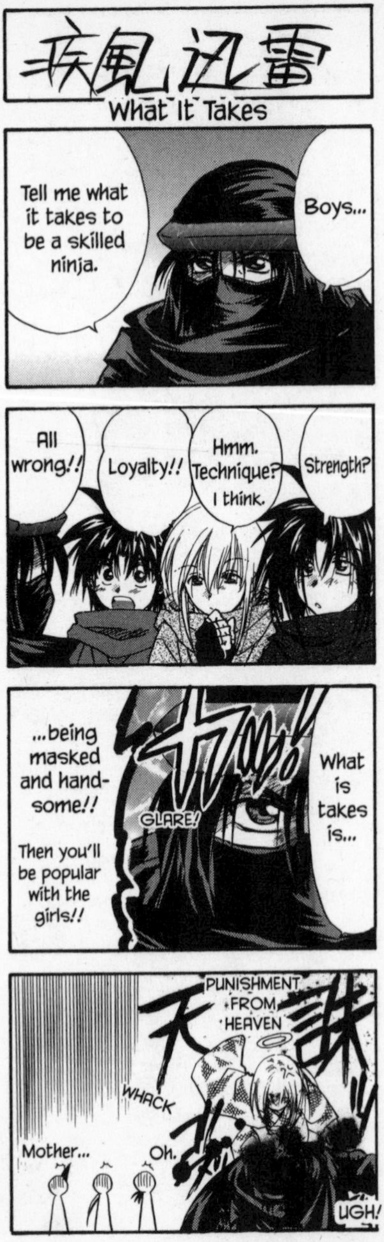
疾風迅雷
What It Takes
Boys...
Tell me what it takes to be a skilled ninja.
Strength?
Hmm. Technique? I think.
Loyalty!!
All wrong!!
What is takes is...
GLARE!
...being masked and hand-some!!
Then you'll be popular with the girls!!
PUNISHMENT FROM HEAVEN
WHACK
UGH!
Oh.
Mother...

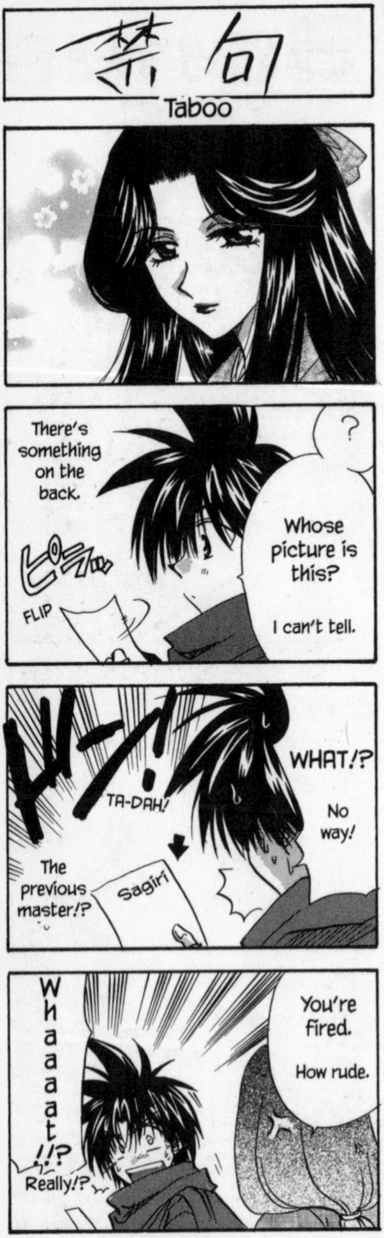
禁句
Taboo
?
Whose picture is this?
I can't tell.
There's something on the back.
FLIP
WHAT!?
No way!
TA-DAH!
Sagiri
The previous master!?
You're fired.
How rude.
Whaaaaat!!?
Really!?

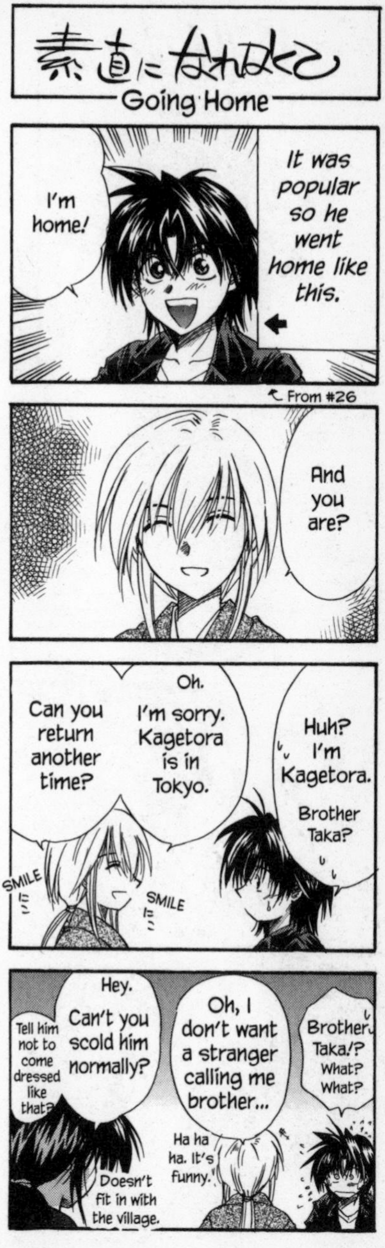
素直になれなくて
Going Home
It was popular so he went home like this.
I'm home!
From #26
And you are?
Huh? I'm Kagetora.
Brother Taka?
Oh. I'm sorry. Kagetora is in Tokyo.
Can you return another time?
SMILE
SMILE
Brother Taka!? What? What?
Oh, I don't want a stranger calling me brother...
Hey. Can't you scold him normally?
Tell him not to come dressed like that?
Ha ha ha. It's funny.
Doesn't fit in with the village.

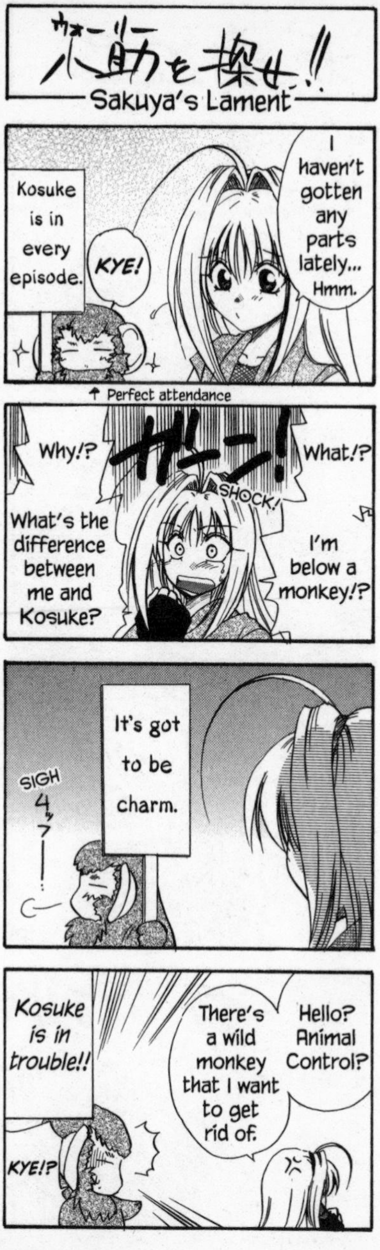
ウォーリー
小助を探せ!!
Sakuya's Lament
I haven't gotten any parts lately... Hmm.
KYE!
Kosuke is in every episode.
Perfect attendance
What!?
I'm below a monkey!?
SHOCK!
Why!?
What's the difference between me and Kosuke?
It's got to be charm.
SIGH
Hello? Animal Control?
There's a wild monkey that I want to get rid of.
Kosuke is in trouble!!
KYE!?

One-Panel Bonus

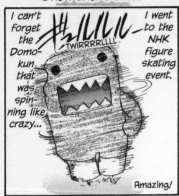

I can't forget the Domo-kun that was spinning like crazy...

TWIRRRRLLL

I went to the NHK figure skating event.

Amazing!

Of course the skaters were very good, too. By the way, if that Domo-kun falls, he can't get up on his own...

Special Thanks !!

Assistants:	Tanaka-kun, Oshima-chan
Help:	Takaeda, Keisui-sama
Editor:	Mr. Morita
Comics Editor:	Houjou-san

And all of the readers.

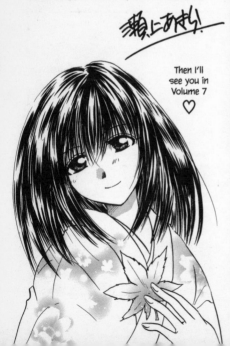

Then I'll see you in Volume 7 ♡

Roller Coaster Ride

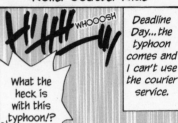

WHOOOSH

What the heck is with this typhoon!?

Deadline Day... the typhoon comes and I can't use the courier service.

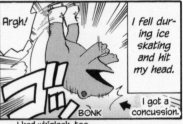

Argh!

BONK

I fell during ice skating and hit my head.

I got a concussion.

I had whiplash, too.

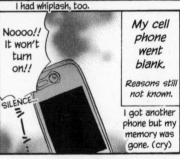

Nooooo!! It won't turn on!!

SILENCE...

My cell phone went blank.

Reasons still not known.

I got another phone but my memory was gone. (cry)

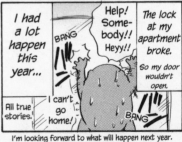

I had a lot happen this year...

All true stories.

BANG

Help! Somebody!! Heyy!!

I can't go home!

BANG

The lock at my apartment broke.

So my door wouldn't open.

I'm looking forward to what will happen next year.

About the Author

Segami's first manga was published by Shogakukan in 1996. He went on to do a few other small projects, including two short stories entitled "Kagetora" in 2001 and 2002. The character proved to be popular with fans, so Segami began his first ongoing series, Kagetora, with Kodansha in 2003. The series continues to run today.

Translation Notes

Japanese is a tricky language for most Westerners, and translation is often more art than science. For your edification and reading pleasure, here are notes on some of the places where we could have gone in a different direction in our translation of the work, or where a Japanese cultural reference is used.

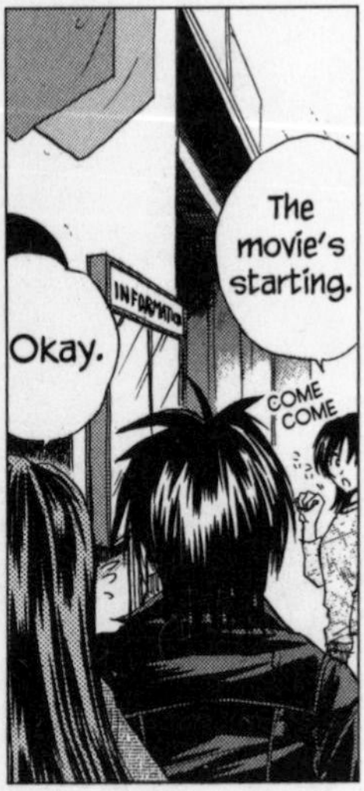
The movie's starting.
Okay.
COME COME

Beckoning gesture, Page 16

In Japan, the gesture of beckoning is performed by waving a hand downward, as opposed to the western way of waving a hand upward.

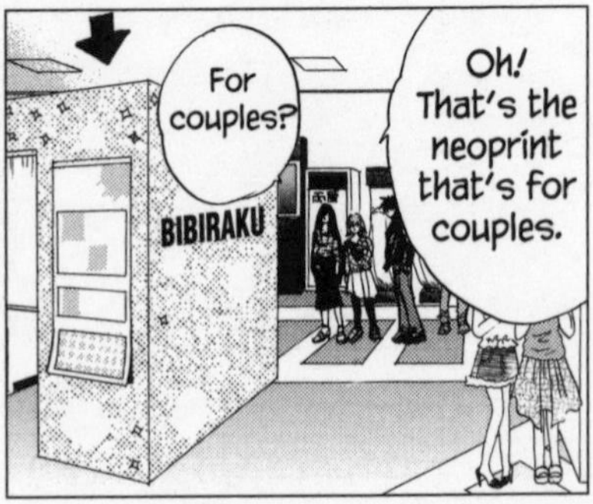
Oh! That's the neoprint that's for couples.
For couples?
BIBIRAKU

***Bibiraku*/Neoprint, Page 20**

Bibiraku is the system's name. All the neoprint machines now have a name that sounds something like this.

Cicadas, Page 41

These are sounds made by cicadas. Almost anywhere you go in Japan, you will hear the annoying sounds of cicadas in the summer. This is a very common sound effect to let readers know it's summertime.

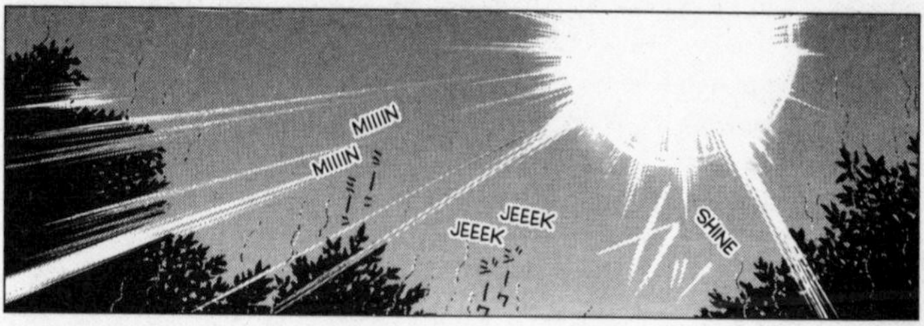
SHINE
JEEEK
JEEEK
MIIIIN
MIIIIN

Clear Your Mind . . . Page 42

Kosuke's sign says "Clear your mind and you will find even fire cool." This is a Japanese proverb.

***Aiki Jujitstu*, Page 55**

Aiki Jujitsu is a Japanese martial art, in which artists use the attacker's force and redirect it against them.

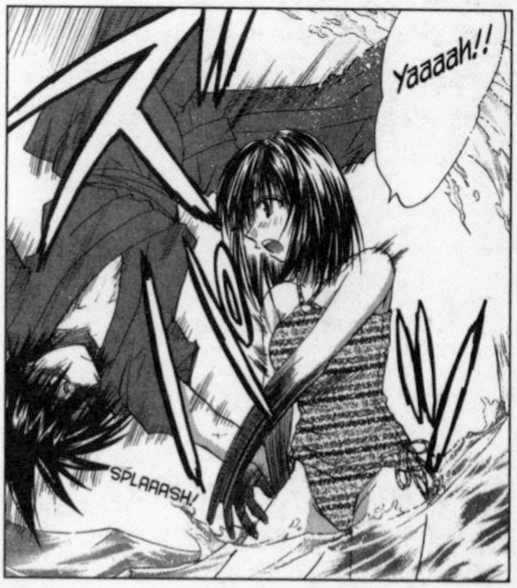
Yaaaah!!
SPLAAASH!

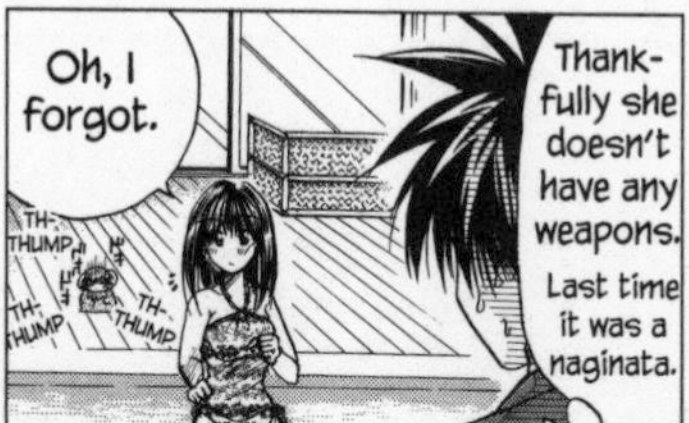
Thankfully she doesn't have any weapons.
Last time it was a naginata.
Oh, I forgot.
TH-THUMP
TH-THUMP
TH-THUMP

***Naginata*, Page 58**

A *naginata* is a long-handled sword. It looks like a spear with a short sword at the tip of it. In modern Japan, it is usually a martial art for women.

Kamakura, Page 75
Kamakura is a city located in Kanagawa prefecture, which is southwest of Tokyo. It is a popular tourist spot because of all the temples and shrines, as well as the beach.

***Oyakume*, Page 81**
Oyakume translates as "a duty." Its use in this book is more formal, suggesting a specific and honored duty.

***Kunoichi*, Page 126**
A *kunoichi* refers to a female ninja. Historically, *kunoichi* were trained in deception and seduction, but in modern terminology, a *kunoichi* is simply a female ninja, trained in ninjutsu like their male counterparts.

Lions, Page 142
This is from a proverb "Lions throw their cubs down a cliff to test their strength." Lions do so because they want their cubs to be strong and independent. It speaks of parents who are strict with their children.

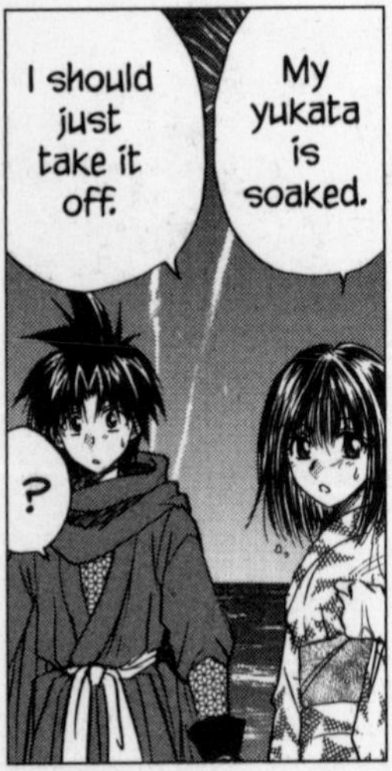
My yukata is soaked.
I should just take it off.
?

***Yukata*, Page 149**
Yukatas are kimonos worn mainly in the summer. They are made of lighter fabric than kimonos, and have fewer garments underneath. The word *yukata* comes from the words "bath" and "clothing." In old Japan, people wore clothing to take a bath, and something simpler and lighter than a *yukata* was worn. Eventually people came to wear it loosely after a bath, and in modern Japan people wear it at hot springs in Japanese hotels, festivals, or just simply around the house during the summer.

Jizou, Page 188

Jizou are Buddhist statues that protect the people, mainly children. What Segami is talking about here is the *migawari jizou*, which translates to "substitute *jizou*." The idea is that the *jizou* will take on your illness or suffering to cure you.

NHK and Domo-kun, Page 191

NHK is Nihon Housou Kyoku, which is the Japan Broadcasting Station. The government runs them. Domo-kun is a brown, fuzzy, boxlike character and is NHK's mascot.

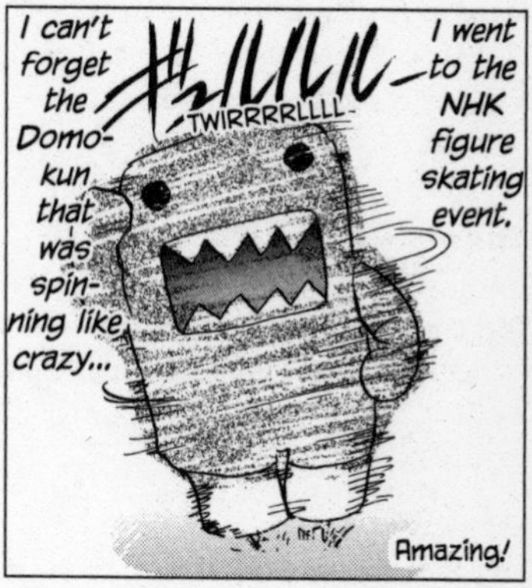
I went to the NHK figure skating event.
-TWIRRRRLLLL-
I can't forget the Domo-kun that was spinning like crazy...
Amazing!

Preview of Volume 7

We're pleased to present you a preview from Volume 7. This volume will be available on September 25, 2007.

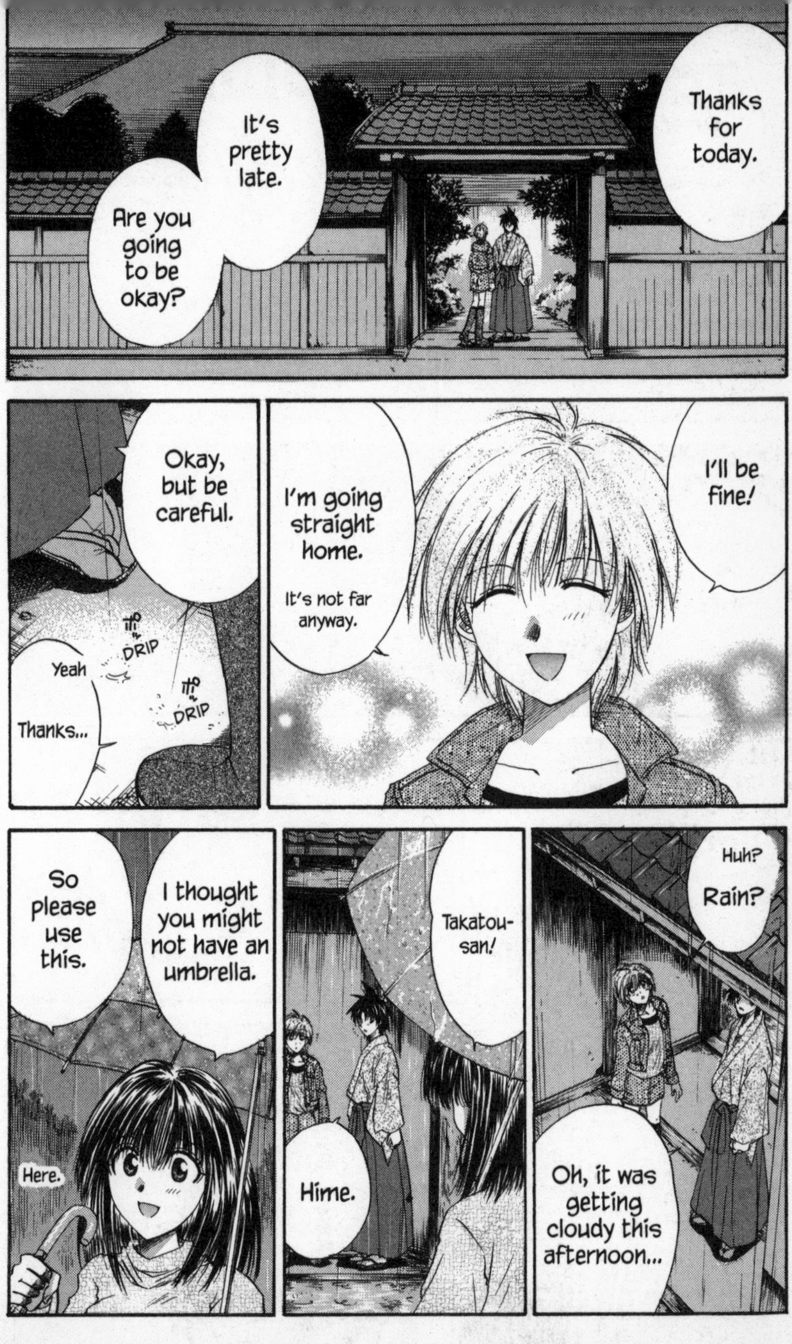
Thanks for today.
It's pretty late.
Are you going to be okay?
I'll be fine!
I'm going straight home.
It's not far anyway.
Okay, but be careful.
DRIP
DRIP
Yeah
Thanks...
Huh?
Rain?
Oh, it was getting cloudy this afternoon...
Takatou-san!
Hime.
I thought you might not have an umbrella.
So please use this.
Here.

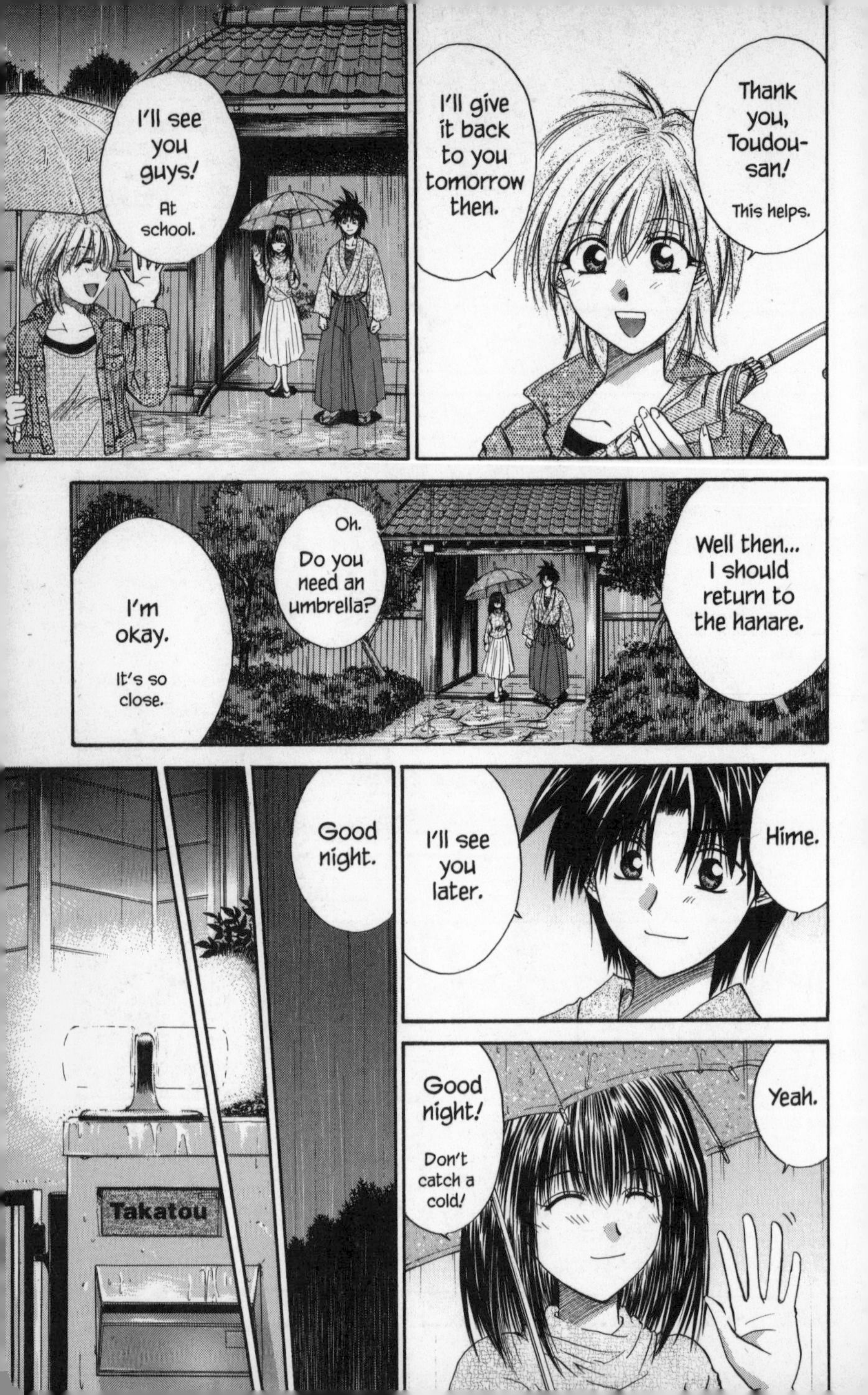
Thank you, Toudou-san!
This helps.
I'll give it back to you tomorrow then.
I'll see you guys!
At school.
Well then... I should return to the hanare.
Oh.
Do you need an umbrella?
I'm okay.
It's so close.
Hime.
I'll see you later.
Yeah.
Good night!
Don't catch a cold!
Good night.
Takatou

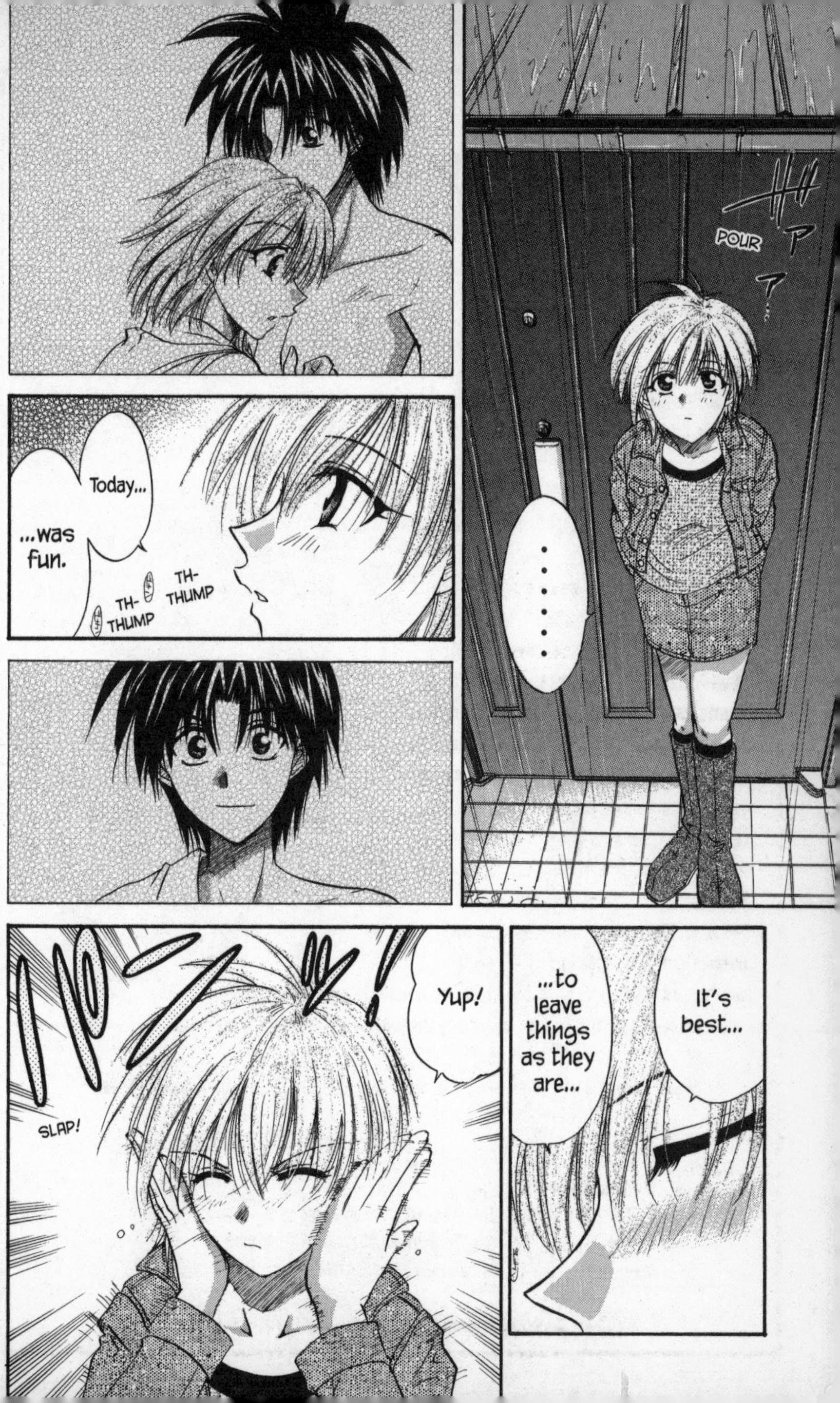
POUR
......
Today...
...was fun.
TH-THUMP
TH-THUMP
It's best...
...to leave things as they are...
Yup!
SLAP!

AIR GEAR

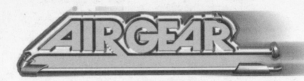

BY OH!GREAT

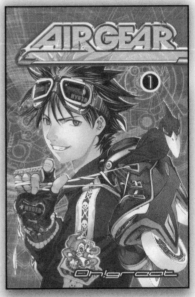

Itsuki Minami needs no introduction—everybody's heard of the "Babyface" of the Eastside. He's the strongest kid at Higashi Junior High School, easy on the eyes but dangerously tough when he needs to be. Plus, Itsuki lives with the mysterious and sexy Noyamano sisters. Life's never dull, but it becomes downright dangerous when Itsuki leads his school to victory over vindictive Westside punks with gangster connections. Now he stands to lose his school, his friends, and everything he cares about. But in his darkest hour, the Noyamano girls give him an amazing gift, one that just might help him save his school: a pair of Air Trecks. These high-tech skates are more than just supercool. They'll enable Itsuki to execute the wildest, most aggressive moves ever seen—and introduce him to a thrilling and terrifying new world.

AIRGEAR
1
Oh!great

Ages: 16 +

Special extras in each volume! Read them all!

DEL REY

VISIT WWW.DELREYMANGA.COM TO:
- Read sample pages
- View release date calendars for upcoming volumes
- Sign up for Del Rey's free manga e-newsletter
- Find out the latest about new Del Rey Manga series

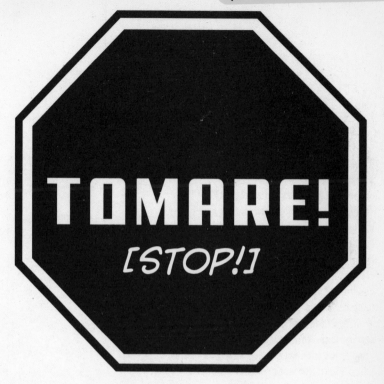

TOMARE!

[STOP!]

You are going the wrong way!

Manga is a completely different
type of reading experience.

To start at the *beginning*, go to the *end*!

That's right! Authentic manga is read the traditional Japanese
way—from right to left. Exactly the *opposite* of how American
books are read. It's easy to follow: Just go to the other end of
the book, and read each page—and each panel—from right side
to left side, starting at the top right. Now you're experiencing
manga as it was meant to be.